Ole Bull

Ole Bull

NORWAY'S ROMANTIC MUSICIAN
AND COSMOPOLITAN PATRIOT

*Einar Haugen
and
Camilla Cai*

The University of Wisconsin Press

The University of Wisconsin Press
114 North Murray Street
Madison, Wisconsin 53715

3 Henrietta Street
London WC2E 8LU, England

Printed in the United States of America

Library of Congress Cataloging-in-Publication Data
Haugen, Einar Ingvald, 1906–
Ole Bull : Norway's romantic musician and cosmopolitan patriot /
Einar Haugen and Camilla Cai.
384 p.   cm.
Includes bibliographical references and index.
ISBN 0-299-13250-1
1. Bull, Ole, 1810–1880.   2. Violinists—Norway—Biography.
I. Cai, Camilla.   II. Title.
ML418.B9H38   1992
787.2'092—dc20
[B]   91-50989

In Memory of

Ola Linge (1885–1973)

Bull Biographer, Composer, Music Dealer

I had a very pleasant little party-kin last night at Cambridge at Longfellow's, where there was a mad-cap fiddler Ole Bull, who played most wonderfully on his instrument, and charmed me still more by his oddities and character. Quite a character for a book.

—William Makepeace Thackeray, 1852
(from James Grant Wilson,
Thackeray in the United States, 1904)

Det maatte vera ein Mann at skriva ei Bok om, det, og ei slik kjem vel ogso. (That would be a man to write a book about, and such a book will no doubt come.)

—Aasmund Olavsson Vinje
(*Dølen*, 25 December 1859)

Contents

Contents

Illustrations

Illustrations

Music Examples

xv

Music Examples

Preface

THE NAME Ole Bull has been known to me since childhood. The first Norwegian city I saw was his birthplace, Bergen, when I traveled on the Norwegian-America Line to my parents' birthplace in Norway. This was in the fateful year of 1914, when World War I was about to break out, the war which led to our return to the United States in 1916. When I was fortunate enough in 1931 to become a successor (after Julius E. Olson) to the professorship of Rasmus B. Anderson at the University of Wisconsin, I felt as if I were in an apostolic succession. Anderson was still living in Madison, and he shared with me memories of his experiences as a protégé of Bull's. He could even show me a letter from Ole Bull's hand. One of my first sightseeing trips on visiting Norway again in 1935 was to Lysøen, where Bull spent his last summers.

But I would not have ventured on a biography of the great musician without securing the enthusiastic promise of support from my daughter Camilla Cai, Associate Professor of Musicology at Kenyon College. Her contribution is evident throughout this book. Her special knowledge of nineteenth-century European music has been invaluable. She is the author of chapters 18 to 22 and the List of Works.

My decision to try my hand at a new biography of Ole Bull can be seen as evidence of my continuing interest in the lives of Norwegian-American figures. Previously I have written about Ole Edvart Rölvaag (1983) and Waldemar Theodore Ager (1989), and my wife, Eva Lund Haugen, and I edited the American letters of Bjørnson, *Land of the Free* (1978). I see Ole Bull as probably the most famous Norwegian-American, who without becoming an American citizen did abjure Norwegian allegiance and flitted back and forth between two continents. He has been described as at once an ardent Norwegian patriot and a well-traveled cosmopolite, who was as much at home in Paris, Bologna, Vienna, and Berlin as in Washington and New York, or for that matter in pioneer communities in Pennsylvania and Wisconsin. His playing entranced audiences from Alexandria, Egypt, to San Francisco, California.

Besides being the world's most celebrated violin virtuoso of his time, he was also a self-promoter, a true child of the generation of P. T. Barnum. His mastery of the violin earned him the title of a "northern Paganini," and there were critics who called him a charlatan because of what seemed like magic tricks in his playing. Critics were not always kind to him, but he was idolized by his European and American public. To the Norwegian people he was a hero who had helped to inspire self-confidence in a long-slighted and neglected nation.

While there were abundant traces of Bull's life in Madison, Wisconsin, there were more in Cambridge, Massachusetts, at Harvard, where I completed my years of teaching. Here was Elmwood, the home Bull made with his second wife. Here was Craigie House, where he could call on his friend Longfellow. Here would stand the statue of Leif Ericson that was essentially a memorial to Ole Bull. Here were also the many monuments erected by Eben Norton Horsford in honor of the Norse discovery of America and to affirm his opinion that the Norsemen had landed on the Charles River. Bull was quite simply too tempting a topic to neglect. Thackeray's remark which serves as an epigraph can stand as our excuse for trying a new picture of this most provoking, most enigmatic, and most renowned Norwegian or Norwegian-American in the nineteenth century.

While Bull was a wizard with his instrument, he also had an entrepreneurial genius that was perhaps peculiarly American. He was a child prodigy, a surprising offshoot of the commercial bourgeoisie of Bergen, and he became a unique musician, the hero in a fairy tale that gave Ibsen a model for his *Peer Gynt*. To poet and national novelist Bjørnson he became a beacon of light; to Edvard Grieg, a personal inspiration to seek out the melodies of the Norwegian folk. He also added to the gaiety of nations by trying to influence Norwegian settlement in America with his colony in Pennsylvania known as Oleana. Longfellow found in him a model for the musician in his *Tales of a Wayside Inn*.

In short, he was indeed a "mad-cap," as Thackeray put it. But he was also a genius. His story is well worth the retelling, even now, a century later.

Einar Haugen, Emeritus, Harvard University

Acknowledgments

W E WISH to acknowledge the help we have received from many quarters in writing this book. A number of institutions have furnished us with items from their collections: Bergen Public Library (Nora Constanse Sætersdal); Bergen University Library (Professor Gunnvald Eldevik); Boston Public Library; Harvard University's Widener Library and Music Collection; Kenyon College (which also provided two grants for research and computer searches); Library of Congress; University of Minnesota; New York Public Library, Music Division, sponsored by Astor, Lenox and Tilden Foundations; Oberlin College Library (which provided a brochure by Morand); Oslo University Library (Johanna Barstad) and Oslo University Library Music Collection (Øyvind Norheim); Potter County Historical Society, Coudersport, Pennsylvania (Robert Currin); St. Olaf College Library: The Norwegian-American Historical Association Collection (Professor Lloyd Hustvedt); Smithsonian Institution (Gary Sturm and Stacey Kluck); Sunnmørsposten, Ålesund, Norway (which provided information on Ola Linge); Trondheim University Library (Kari Christensen); and Wisconsin State Historical Society (James L. Hansen). These individuals also have been helpful: Ida R. Corliss, Rockport, Maine; Professor John Daverio, Boston University; Gloria N. Echarte, Key Biscayne, Florida; Øystein Gaukstad, Music Collection, Oslo University Library; Assistant Professor Øyvind Gulliksen, Bø, Telemark; Professor Karl Guthke, Harvard University; Eva Lund Haugen, Belmont, Massachusetts; Knut Hendriksen, Kungliga Teatern, Stockholm, Sweden; Nelly Linge (widow of Ola Linge), Lillestrøm, Norway; Professor Harald Næss, University of Wisconsin–Madison; Sven Nyhus (Hardanger fiddler and music engraver), Oslo; Adrienne Elisha Rubenstein, Kenyon College; Lee Swanson, Wayside Inn, Sudbury, Massachusetts; Arve Tellefsen (violinist), Oslo;

Acknowledgments

Professor Arvid Vollsnes, University of Oslo; Ben E. Watkins (photographer), Boston, Massachusetts; F. Woodbridge Wilson, Curator, Pierpont Morgan Library; Dag Østerberg, University of Oslo; and Professor Orm Øverland, University of Bergen.

Introduction

WE HAVE identified Ole Bornemann Bull with four descriptive terms: "Romantic," "Musician," "Cosmopolitan," and "Norwegian." These terms do not render a complete portrait of Bull, but they will serve to introduce him to readers who are not already familiar with his name.

Romantic. Ole Bull was a romantic in the same sense as Lord Byron (1788–1824) in England, the young Friedrich von Schiller (1759–1805) in Germany, or Victor Hugo (1802–85) in France. In his day he was as famous as they and deserves to be remembered in the same way. If he is not everywhere held in the same respect today, it is due in part to the absence of musical recording in his time. In part it is also the result of his having been a native of Norway, a small country that has played only a modest role in the concert life of Europe.

Romanticism is the name given to a cultural and literary movement that arose in the late eighteenth century in the wake of the American and French revolutions. These shattering events brought to an end the classical and rationalistic outlook that had long been dominant. A wave of sentiment and of emotional writing overwhelmed the art and literature of the western world. Byron, Schiller, and Hugo exemplified various aspects of the movement, and they were followed by a host of others. In Norway the chief protagonists of romanticism were the poets Henrik Wergeland (1808–45) and Johan Sebastian Welhaven (1807–73). Both were admirers of Ole Bull.

Musicians could also become romantics. We need mention only such friends or contemporaries of Bull as Frédéric Chopin (1810–49), Robert Schumann (1810–56), and Franz Liszt (1811–86). These composers had the advantage over literary figures like Wergeland and Welhaven in that their medium of music transcended the national boundaries of language. As a world-famous violinist Ole Bull became the messenger of Norwegian romanticism in all of Europe and America. His extraordinary facility with the violin won him an international audience. His musical inspiration was channeled by admiration for the great Italian virtuoso Nicolò Paganini (1782–1840), who established the role of violin virtuoso. Bull's mastery of the style won him a position as the most celebrated successor of Paganini. In addition to perfecting this Italian style, he adopted the native music of Norway that he had heard in his youth, listening to and learning from the country fiddlers, whose music was quite unknown, not only in Europe, but also in the cities of his own country. Romanticism was at once an international and an intensely national movement. Bull represented both. He embraced Sentiment and Nature; he was colorful, fantastic, and a devotee of national music.

Bull's talent as a performer was not the only source of his popularity with his audiences. He was also handsome, with an irresistible personal charm. In 1838 the Danish fairy-tale author Hans Christian Andersen published an "Episode of Ole Bull's Life" in such a way as to make of him a fairy prince. Bull was not loath to accept the role, and he swayed his audiences by the beauty and vigor of his personality. To the end of his days he retained a litheness of physique and a charisma that won the affection of all who met him, not least his many women admirers. He also retained to the end a childlike naiveté, an amalgam of generosity and simplicity that made him a welcome guest among princes as well as paupers.

Bull's romanticism has indeed created one of the problems for his biographers. He enjoyed amusing his listeners with tales of his life, tales that gradually developed into romances embroidered by his imagination. Disentangling truth from fiction has endlessly complicated any sound retelling of his life. It is obvious that anyone who traveled as far and as perilously as Bull did, in Europe and America and a bit of Africa, by stagecoach and carriage, must have had many adventures. His stamina was immense, and if his tales were occasionally improbable, we must accept them as at least "ben trovato," that is, well told, as the Italians put it.

Musician. Bull was first and foremost a musician. His talent was apparent from his early childhood. At the age of eight he was admitted to the local orchestra as a first violinist. At eighteen he failed his entrance examination in Latin to the University of Christiania (now Oslo), but was immediately appointed temporary conductor of the Christiania orchestra. He was shortly granted leave to visit Copenhagen, ostensibly to develop his skills as a conductor, but in reality to seek out Germany's leading violin teacher, Louis Spohr (1784–1859). He returned disillusioned to Norway, and in 1831, a mere stripling of twenty-one, he left Norway for Paris, the mecca of musicians.

During his early years in Paris, he was constantly in financial difficulty and had little support from home. He was befriended by a French widow, Mme. Villeminot, who rented him a room and, when he became ill, nursed him back to health. In this she found a willing helper in her granddaughter Félicie, who would become Bull's wife in 1836.

Bull made his way through Switzerland to Italy, where in 1833 he achieved his professional breakthrough. Here he came under the helpful influence of the greatest diva of his day, Maria Felicia Malibran (1808–36), and here he began writing his compositions in the Italian opera style. He followed up his success in Italy with a tour of Great Britain and an eventual triumph in Paris. A very favorable review by the French critic Jules Janin (1804–1874) opened the stages of Europe to him.

The reviews of Bull's musicianship, which now grew rapidly in number, remarked on his special sweetness of tone and superb technical skill in improvisation. Critics regularly admired his pizzicati and his trills, as well as his harmonics (overtone pitches). In an effort to rival and even surpass Paganini, he began to work intensively on the construction of the violin. He extended his experimentation to the piano, with less success. Throughout Europe he won the applause of huge audiences, who flocked to hear this "Paganini of the North." In Italy he was made a member of several philharmonic societies, and he was everywhere idolized by kings and potentates.

Despite his success, Bull did not escape criticism. In Germany a new school of musical criticism was rising, one which demanded that virtuosos should perform with restraint and moderation, and should master not only their own compositions but also the works of the famous German composers of the past. Bull did not conform to the standards of some of these new critics, such as the German Gottfried Wilhelm Fink (1783–1846) and the Austrian Eduard Hanslick (1815–1904). Other of these critics characterized Bull as a "charlatan," whose skills were therefore something less than miraculous. While none of this criticism affected his audiences, it gave Bull some personal distress.

In 1843 Bull crossed the Atlantic as one of a handful of European artists who sought a new audience in the West. He was greeted with acclaim in the eastern and southern states which had been settled, and also in Spanish Cuba and French Quebec. Here he wrote compositions using folk melodies of the regions visited. Returning from America to Europe in 1845 for a Mediterranean tour, he came to Africa for the first time. The February Revolution of 1848 drove him back to Norway, where he got involved in the affairs of his native land.

Cosmopolitan. Bull's birth in Bergen, Norway, the most cosmopolitan of Norwegian cities, laid a foundation for his ambition to become a citizen of the world. His desire to escape the provincial atmosphere of the Norwegian capital of Christiania, inspired his early excursions to Denmark, Germany, France, and Italy. Paris offered him an exciting new musical world to explore and introduced him to the French woman who would become his first wife. However, Paris did not provide the employment he sought, and only in Italy did he find the romantic atmosphere that would be his staple throughout life. He won his first target audiences in Great Britain and there took advantage of his opportunity to enlarge the French-Italian world in which he had been immersed by learning English. It became one of his principal languages. His later tours, which took him throughout northern Europe, the Mediterranean, Russia, and back and forth across the Atlantic, granted him the status of a world citizen and increased his awareness of international relations. He warned the French in 1866, for example, of the dangers posed by both the United States and prophetically by the growing power of Prussia.

In 1852 Bull took out first papers for American citizenship in connection with his purchase of a land grant in Pennsylvania which he called "Oleana." He never completed his citizenship, but from 1867 to his death in 1880 he commuted regularly between Norway and the United States, spending summers in Norway and winters in America. His strong ties to America have led some American immigrants to regard him as a fellow "Norwegian-American." It is perhaps as a "Norwegian-American" that his cosmopolitan nature was most fully realized.

Patriot. It may seem ironic that Bull is held by Norwegians to have been a great patriot although he spent more of his life abroad than at home. He often wrote at length to his first wife about establishing a home in Norway, but he was too restless to actually do so. He kept dreaming of the family home at Valestrand, and he finally bought it from his mother and reconstructed it according to his own plans. This was the Norway to which he wished to return, no doubt to relive a happy childhood among its fjords and mountains, where he could hear the fiddlers who had taught him their native melodies. But he had no sooner rebuilt Valestrand than he bought an island south of Bergen named Lysøen. Here he built himself a new residence, a fantastic palace of music that would prove to be his final domicile.

Bull's patriotism was fired by a meeting in 1828 with his contemporary,

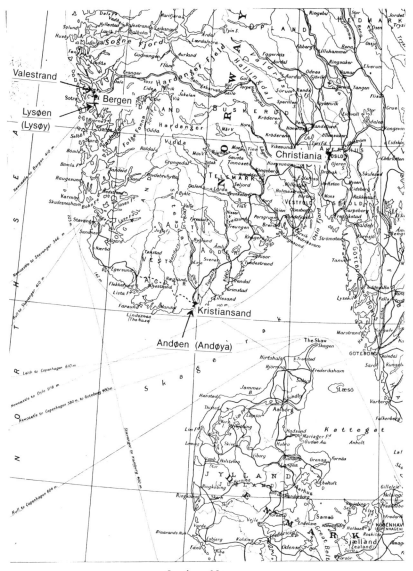

Southern Norway

the poet Henrik Wergeland. They were united in their conviction that Norway should once again be recognized as an independent country. It had been a dependency of Denmark for four centuries and was now united with Sweden under a joint king, with autonomy but not independence. Norwegians of Bull's day were divided between "Pro-Scandinavians" and

"Patriots," among whom Bull reckoned himself. He nursed a life-long aversion to the Union with Sweden, not against the Swedes, but against their domination of Norway. From his first concert in Paris, when he was described as "un violiniste norvégien," to his dying day, he called himself a "Norwegian," not a "Scandinavian."

His first chance to demonstrate these convictions came with the Revolution of 1848, when he joined other Norwegians in Paris in a congratulatory address to the revolt's leader, the poet Lamartine, on behalf of the Norwegian nation. In 1848 there was in fact no Norwegian nation, only a Norwegian people politically tied to Sweden. His return to Norway that same year to found a Norwegian theater was no doubt stirred by the revolution and the hopes for national liberation it awakened in many European peoples.

Aside from his performances, Bull's activities in the years that followed were directed at enhancing Norway's status as a nation. He wrote music based on Norwegian folk melodies. His Norwegian Theater in Bergen, opened in 1850, was deliberately and explicitly directed against the prevalence of Danish actors, speech, and plays in the Norwegian repertoire. When his application to the Norwegian Parliament (the Storting) for a subsidy for the theater was rejected, he emigrated to America in 1852 to build a colony for Norwegian emigrants.

There are traces remaining today of Bull's efforts on behalf of the Norwegian nation. His theater eventually failed, but today it has been reconstructed as the National Stage in Bergen. His American colony of Oleana also failed because of Bull's ineptness in selecting land and in managing financial enterprises. However, nearly a million settlers did in fact follow Bull to make homes in the United States, if not in his Oleana. The Norwegian Music Academy of which Bull dreamed was realized after Bull's death when a music conservatory was founded in Oslo. His homes at Valestrand and Lysøen are today preserved as monuments to Bull and as important parts of Norway's national heritage.

As important as Bull's attempts to create national institutions was the personal encouragement he offered to the men and women who gradually built up a native Norwegian culture. He gave world-famous dramatist Henrik Ibsen (1828–1906) his first chance to learn the art of theater management. He employed Norway's leading poet, Bjørnstjerne Bjørnson (1832–1910), as a director of his theater. He promoted the career of composers like Rikard Nordraak (1842–66) and Edvard Grieg (1843–1907). As Bjørnson said of Bull in his funeral oration of 1880: "Ole Bull gave us self-confidence as a nation when we most needed it."

Ole Bull Chronology

1810	Born in Bergen, Norway, 5 February.
1818	Admitted as "Auscultant" in Harmonien, 19 October.
1822	Begins work under second music teacher, Mathias Lundholm.
1824	Talks grandmother into buying Paganini's *Caprices*.
1828	Leaves Bergen to study at the University of Christiania (now Oslo); fails entrance examination and is hired as a violinist, then temporary conductor of Christiania orchestra. Meets fellow student and poet Henrik Wergeland.
1829	Goes to Copenhagen, then to Cassel to meet violin teacher Spohr, 19 May. Returns to Christiania, 20 September.
1831	Leaves for Paris; arrives 19 August. Meets and takes a room with fellow violinist Ernst.
1832	Finds a room with Mme. Villeminot and granddaughter Félicie, May.
1833	First Paris concert, 18 April. Leaves for Italy via Switzerland, 10 June. Arrives in Milan, 10 August. Seeks out singer Malibran in Bologna.
1834	Farewell concert in Bologna, 5 May. Elected honorary member of the Accademia Filarmonica.
1835	Returns to Paris; concert on 17 June. Concerts at the Paris Opéra, 9 and 22 December. Janin's critique seals Bull's triumph.
1836	Arrives in London, end of April. Successful concerts, 21 May, 1 June, and 15 June. Returns to Paris to marry Félicie, 16 July.
1837	Tours Great Britain, giving a total of 274 concerts. Begins tour in Hamburg that takes him through Germany to Russia.
1838	Reaches Moscow in March; returns to Norway via Finland and Sweden. Celebrated in Christiania and Bergen. Leaves Norway again in October for concerts in Copenhagen and Hamburg. Critiqued by Rosén and Spohr.

1839   Concerts in Berlin and Vienna; critiqued by Fink and Schumann.

1840   Concerts in England; meets and makes friends with Liszt; concerts in Rhine basin.

1841   Concerts in Prague, Warsaw, and St. Petersburg; returns to Norway in June.

1842   Concerts in Sweden, Hamburg, and The Hague; stays at Valestrand.

1843   Travels to Uppsala, Copenhagen, and Bremen; contracts with Schuberth. Leaves Norway for America, November. Wergeland dedicates farewell poem to Bull. Begins first American tour on East Coast; quarrel with Schuberth.

1844   Concerts in the South and in Havana, Boston, Niagara Falls, and Quebec.

1845   Farewell concert in New York, 30 October; departs America, 2 December.

1846   Paris concerts in January; travels through south of France. Crosses Mediterranean to Algiers and back again to Spain.

1847   Concerts in Barcelona, Madrid, and Balearic Islands.

1848   Félicie goes to St. Mihiel; Bull to Paris. Demonstrates on behalf of Norway. Arrives in Norway, 5 November. Buys island of Andøen.

1849   Concerts in Christiania. Composes "Sæter Girl's Sunday" (no. 53a). Launches plan for Norwegian Theater in Bergen.

1850   Opens Theater with great success, 2 January.

1851   Hires Ibsen as stage manager. Petitions Storting for subsidy of Theater; petition rejected.

1852   Arrives in New York, 1 January; gives concerts. Founds Oleana, a Norwegian colony in Pennsylvania, 5 September.

1853   Deeds land for Oleana back to seller Cowan. Settlers disperse to the Midwest.

1854   Travels via Panama to San Francisco.

1855   Involved in a plan for New York opera; spends December at Longfellows in Cambridge.

1856   First visit to Wisconsin. Félicie sends son Alexander to Bull; Alexander arrives in New York, 16 November.

1857   Leaves America with Alexander for Norway, 29 July. Welcomed by Bjørnson. Dismisses theater board; employs Bjørnson as director.

1858   Concerts in Budapest and Vienna; negative review by Hanslick. Concert in Dresden. Meets Grieg, June. Buys Valestrand from mother.

1859	Joins Det Norske Selskab (The Norwegian Society).
1860	Concerts in Christiania; celebrates fiftieth birthday. Travels to Sweden and Germany.
1861	Concerts in Netherlands and England.
1862	Félicie dies in Christiania, 16 February. Bull returns to Norway via Paris and Germany.
1863	Application to Storting for funds for a Norwegian Music Academy rejected. Longfellow includes Bull as "The Musician" in *Tales of a Wayside Inn*.
1864	Summers at Valestrand; winter season concerts in Germany, Vienna, and Prague.
1865	Returns to Norway via Germany; decorated with Order of Adolph. Works on improvements at Valestrand.
1866	Departs for Moscow, tour lasts through winter.
1867	Spring concerts in Warsaw. Travels to Paris to visit Alexander. Summers at Valestrand while preparing for third American tour. Arrives with Alexander in New York, 11 December.
1868	In Wisconsin meets Rasmus B. Anderson and the Thorps, February. Returns to New York for concerts, March. Returns to Norway where work on Valestrand has been completed. Begins fourth American tour in fall.
1869	Tour continues in America. Returns to Norway; summers at Valestrand. Returns to America with Alexander, December.
1870	With Alexander travels via rail to San Francisco; crowned with gold laurel wreath. Travels to Madison to visit the Thorps; courts Sara Thorp. Thorps travel to Norway with Bull and remain for short visit at Valestrand. Bull returns with Thorps to Madison; marries Sara, 6 September.
1871	Daughter Olea born in West Lebanon, Maine.
1872	Performs in Wisconsin State Capitol to raise money to purchase Norwegian books for the University of Wisconsin Library. Travels to Norway with Anderson. Buys Lysøen.
1873	Forms Leif Ericson Monument Committee with Anderson and Johnson. Concerts in Midwest and Norway to raise money for the monument. Spends summer with Thorps at Lysøen.
1874	Climax in quarrel between Bull and Thorp family. Thorps leave for America; Bull joins Bjørnson in Rome.
1875	Tours Sweden, Denmark, and Germany.
1876	Climbs Cheops Pyramid on King Oscar's suggestion, 5 February. Sara effects reconciliation with translation of Norwegian

novel. Gives nine concerts in Boston, the last a fund-raiser for the Leif Ericson monument.

1877   American tour. Returns to Norway; concerts in Belgium, Vienna, and Budapest.

1878   Summers at Wiesbaden before returning to Norway. Performs with Faustina at Trondheim. Last Norwegian concert, 1 August.

1879   American tour. Returns to Norway, May.

1880   Last American tour. Last American concert in Chicago, May. Dies at Lysøen, 17 August. Buried in state in Bergen.

Part 1

LIFE AND
ADVENTURES

1

Nation and Family

I N THE YEAR 1810, when Ole Bull was born, there was a Norwegian
people but no independent state by the name of Norway. Bull was
born a citizen of the dual monarchy of Denmark-Norway, in which
Norway was a secondary partner. Before 1450 Norway had been a king-
dom, whose early history is told in the sagas of Norway's kings, the *Heimskringla,* written in the thirteenth century by the Icelander Snorri Sturluson
(1179–1241). But its dynastic union with Denmark from 1450 to 1814 had
led to the dominance of the more populous country, and for four centuries
Norway was the stepchild of Scandinavia. The Old Norwegian written language was replaced by Danish, and the bureaucrats who governed both
countries were recruited largely from Denmark. Symptomatic of Norway's
secondary status was the renaming of Oslo as Christiania in 1624 after
the Danish king Christian IV (1577–1648). In 1814, when the Great Powers
cavalierly handed Norway over to Sweden, the leaders of the Norwegian
nation met at Eidsvoll and adopted a constitution modeled on the American and French constitutions. In the resulting union with Sweden, Norway won her autonomy, while independence had to wait until 1905.

The capital of the new country was Christiania (since 1924 once more
named Oslo), but the most important city for a long time remained Bergen, a city on the west coast. In the Middle Ages Bergen had grown into
the most significant trade center of the country, largely as a result of the
German Hanseatic merchants' decision to make it an anchor on their northern flank. Christiania remained culturally subservient to Copenhagen, while
Bergen was open to the world—to England, Germany, Iceland, and the
European continent. Its cosmopolitan history made it a special kind of
place, with a population of many strains. In modern Norway it is often
said that the people of Bergen are "not really Norwegians." They are thought
to have mannerisms all their own, a distinctive dialect, a lively tempera-

View of Bergen. Watercolor by J. F. Dreier, 1822.

ment with high-strung tendencies. In short, they are marked by Norwegians as citizens of the world to a higher degree than their compatriots.[1]

Bergen is located at the head of a deep fjord, cozily hemmed in by high mountains. The approach by sea is long and tortuous, but a delightful prospect rewards visitors when they reach the harbor. In Ole's day the harbor was crowded with three-masted vessels and innumerable smaller boats that plied their trade as merchants or as porters from one part of town to another. Houses spread up the hillsides toward the high mountains on either side. They were nearly all built of wood and sat closely together along narrow streets and alleys. The only large buildings were the churches, the governor's residence, and the historic structure known as Håkon's Hall (Håkonshallen). Conspicuous to the visitor was the German Dock (Tyskebryggen), whose Hanseatic buildings are still preserved as historic treasures.

The city was not large in 1820, having only some twenty thousand inhabitants, but it was busy with the traffic of the day. Bergen functioned as the transshipment point for fish from the coast of Lofoten in northern Norway. Ships loaded here were destined for Hanseatic home bases in Hamburg and Lübeck. Bergen offered rich opportunities for young Bull to explore curious corners and hidden nooks and to participate in the boisterous games of the Bergen children.

1. See Christian A. Aarvig, *Den unge Ole Bull: En Violinspillers Ungdomskampe* (Copenhagen, 1934), 7, on this point.

4

The Bull family was by now an old and well-established Norwegian family, though the name must once have been imported, most likely from England. Most Norwegians were at this time still known only by a patronymic cognomen. If the father was named Ole, a son would be called Olsen, that is, the son of Ole, and a daughter, Olsdatter. Family names like Bull were therefore a badge of social status.

The earliest known Norwegian ancestor of the Bull family was Jens Andersen Bull, a pastor in the village of Støren in Trøndelag, who died in 1610. After him came three generations of pastors, followed by some more diversified descendants, several of them military officers. One, Captain Jørgen Andreas Bull (1703–64), was the father of the first Ole Bornemann Bull (1747–1810), whose middle name was a token of respect for Bishop Oluf Bornemann (1683–1747).[2] The first Ole Bornemann Bull, the violinist's grandfather, was an apothecary in Bergen. He married Gedsken Edvardine Storm, a sister of the Norwegian poet Edvard Storm (1749–94). Their son, Johan Storm Bull (1787–1838), was born in Copenhagen but moved to Bergen with his parents when he was a young child. He took his liberal arts degree in Bergen before going to Erfurt in 1804 to study at Trommsdorf's Institute.[3] After receiving his apothecary's degree in Copenhagen in 1807, he returned to Bergen. There he married the daughter of another distinguished Bergen family, Anna Dorothea Geelmuyden (1784–1875), whose family name stemmed from the Netherlands. A local diarist, Bishop Claus Pavels (1769–1822), attended their wedding and noted what he considered to be a tradition curious to Bergen: the bride was the only woman present at the wedding ceremony. The bride's and groom's mothers and the other women presumably enjoyed a party of their own.[4] Johan and Anna Dorothea's first child was the future violinist Ole Bornemann Bull.

One hesitates to describe the Bull family as aristocrats in view of the virtual absence of nobility in Norway. But they were clearly a part of Bergen's upper crust, whose bourgeois life set the tone of Bergen society. As pastors and officials (including apothecaries), they were part of the establishment that ruled the town. They were the educated, cultivated class who

2. Bishop of Bergen from 1732. O. M. Sandvik, "Ole Bull," *Norsk Biografisk Leksikon* 2:407–17 (Oslo, 1925); for further details see Jens Bull, *Den trønderske slekt Bull* (Oslo, 1937) and Arne Bjørndal, "Ole Bull og Valestrand," reprinted from *Frå Fjon til Fjosa* (Stord, 1950), 9.

3. Wolfgang Goetz, "Johan Storm Bull (1787–1838) and Johann Bartholomaeus Trommsdorff (1770–1837)," *Norges Apothekerforenings Tidsskrift* 97.9 (13 May 1989): 256–59.

4. Ola Linge, *Ole Bull: Livshistoria, Mannen, Kunstnaren* (Oslo, 1953), 18. On Linge, see "Sunnmøringen Ola Linge som Ole Bull forsker," *Rogaland* 18 (1947): 11, and "Ole Bull, Utdrag av kritikken over Ola Linges bok: Ole Bull" (Oslo, n.d.).

had opportunities for traveling abroad and gaining a wider world view.

The primary importance of trade made Bergen a highly commercial community, where material values dominated the life and thinking of the people. Perhaps in protest against this commercial atmosphere, some of Bergen's citizens turned to music and the theater. There were as yet no professional musical or theatrical companies in Norway. However, as early as 1765 a musical organization was established in Bergen, called Det Harmoniske Selskab, generally known as Harmonien, and in 1800 a theater was built, at which outside actors, mostly from Denmark, displayed their talents. Ole's parents were members of both organizations and participated in their programs, purely as amateurs. There was an artistic strain in Ole's family, especially manifest in Ole's mother and in her brother, Jens Geelmuyden (1782–1825), who was editor of the city's only newspaper, *Bergens Adressecontoirs Efterretninger,* and a competent cellist. Thus, the family provided a musical environment that would eventually inspire Ole Bull. But no one could anticipate that he would become Norway's first international artist.

2

Musical Prodigy
(1810–1828)

O LE BORNEMANN BULL was born in his family's apothecary on
5 February 1810. It was a square-built house in Strandgaten
known as Svaneapoteket (The Swan). He was the first of ten
children born to Johan and Dorothea Bull. Such large families were not
uncommon in those days, even among the bourgeoisie. Ole's mother survived many of her children.

Ole was very young when he began on a path different from that of
his siblings. For one thing he showed an unusual interest in the family's
musical evenings of string quartet playing. These were occasions when his
uncle Jens Geelmuyden played the cello, and a violinist named Johan Henrich Paulsen (1770–1838) played first violin.

When Uncle Jens saw that Ole at age five was imitating the violinists,
using a plank and a yardstick for a fiddle and a bow, he gave his nephew
a child's violin. "It was as yellow and sour as a lemon," was Ole's later
comment. "When I played on it, the cats would run away from their food
in the little garden pavilion where I practiced."[1] Uncle Jens and his mother
taught Ole to read notes at about the same time as he learned to read letters. He quickly picked up melodies his mother sang. When he was a little
older, his mother taught him to play the piano.

His parents had no idea of a musical career for little Ole. He was destined to follow the same profession as his ancestors, whether as an apothecary like his father and grandfather, or in the ministry of the Lutheran
church, like other reputable forebears. At age seven he was entered in the
regular Latin school, where Latin was still a main subject. In vain, stern

---

1. Ola Linge, *Ole Bull: Livshistoria, Mannen, Kunstnaren* (Oslo, 1953), 19.

The Swan Apothecary, Ole Bull's birthplace.

schoolmasters tried to drill Ole in the mysteries of "*hic, haec, hoc,*" but he was fascinated instead by classical mythology and history, which his friend the poet Henrik Wergeland would later point out, "suited well his imaginative, dreamy nature."[2]

Typical of this imaginative boy were his feelings for his first real violin, which his parents bought from an itinerant French salesman. Bull later reported: "There was one I was quite taken by. It was red as a cherry, and I begged father to buy it." Ole's father did so, but put it away for the following day. That night Ole, thinking of nothing but the violin, sneaked out of his bed. "I only wanted to look at it. I opened the case with a beating heart. There lay the glorious object, shining red and with inlays in mother-of-pearl. I thought it smiled at me, so I had to take it out, stroke it and try the strings. I came to my senses as I heard steps from the other room. It was my father with a candle in his hand. 'What are you thinking about, making such noises at night and waking everybody?' I was so frightened that I dropped the violin on the floor. When I picked it up, it had gotten several cracks. I cried, and while the violin went to the doctor for repairs, it was never the same again."[3]

2. Henrik Wergeland, "Ole Bull: Efter opgivelser af ham selv biografisk skildret," in *Samlede Skrifter,* ed. D. A. Seip (Oslo, 1927), 4.5:184.
3. Linge, *Ole Bull,* 20.

Ole's imagination was further stimulated by summers spent on Osterøen (Oster Island, now Osterøy), some ten miles nearly due north from Bergen, at an estate known as Valestrand. The property had been inherited by Ole's grandfather, and after his death in 1810 it remained the home of his grandmother. It was located by a different fjord from Bergen and opened up to Ole a whole new world, light-years away from the narrow crowded streets of his home. There was a glorious abundance of woods and hills where he could roam freely. In the fjord he could swim and fish and sail at will. Here too his grandmother entertained him with folktales and ballads.

Ole and his siblings played happily in this family summer home.[4] Occasionally he would wander off by himself just to meditate, or listening closely he would try to imitate the sounds he heard in nature. In the neighborhood there were farms where one might hear country fiddling at local weddings or on other occasions. The fiddlers played the Hardanger fiddle, the special west Norwegian rural violin with underlying sympathetic drone strings. On holidays, especially St. John's Day (midsummer), one bridal procession after another would pass the Valestrand estate, with fiddlers playing wedding marches leading the way. The wedding guests were dressed in decorative, colorful costumes, characteristic of their district. Ole was fascinated by these melodious processions and followed them as best he could. He began to form friendships with the fiddlers and to imitate their melodies on his own violin. One of them, Ola Brakvatn (1798–1885), was later given a Hardanger fiddle by Bull.[5] Once, when Brakvatn was playing, Ole patted him on his back and said, "Now play your best, Ola!" Brakvatn shot back, "Yeah, we're both named Ola, and we're both fiddlers!", at which Ole laughed.[6]

Brakvatn was only one of the fiddlers who caught Bull's fancy as a youth. Other fiddlers on Osterøen with whom Bull made friends were Elling Mosevoll (1790–1861) and Magne Kleiveland (1805–92), also known as "Einlidskarden" (from the Einlidskard farm). Kleiveland elaborated his tunes with many variations, and from him Bull learned the folk melody "*Hopparen*" (The Jumper). Bull's favorite country fiddler, however, did not come from Osterøen, but from Telemark, as we shall hear later. All of these

4. Ole's siblings were Knud (1811–89), Johan (1812–83), Edvard (1814–1907), Jens (1815–1905), Anna (1816–72), Johan (1817–73), Gidsken (1819, d. soon after birth), Gidsken (1822–1906), Georg (1829–1917). Knut/Knud, an artist, was arrested in London in 1845 and sent as a prisoner to Australia. He was freed in 1852 and remained in Australia until his death. *Dictionary of Australian Artists,* ed. J. Kerr (Sydney, 1984), 108–9.

5. Arne Bjørndal, "Ole Bull og Valestrand," *Frå Fjon til Fjosa* (Stord, 1950), 27.

6. Ibid., 14.

Osterøen experiences were remote from his parents' urbanized life, and crucial to Ole's own future.

A few members from Harmonien who gathered weekly for musical evenings of quartet playing at the Bull home began to take notice of the young boy's unusual skill in handling the violin. A local, so-called "city musician," Niels Eriksen, promised to give him lessons but soon had to admit that there was nothing he could teach Ole "for now he is teaching me."[7] After this confession, the concert master of the orchestra, Johan Henrich Paulsen, who taught using Giovanni Battista Viotti's (1755–1824) methods, was hired to instruct Ole.

A turning point in Ole's eventual career occurred in 1818, on his eighth birthday. Paulsen, who played the first violin in the quartet, had imbibed a bit too abundantly of the apothecary's freely dispensed liquor so that he was *hors de combat*. Uncle Jens made the joking suggestion that Ole take his part. According to Ole's own later report to Wergeland, his uncle even promised him a piece of candy if he would do it. They happened to be playing a quartet by Louis Spohr, the German master of the violin, which Ole already knew.[8] He played his part to everyone's admiration and not only got his candy, but Uncle Jens bought him his first grown-up violin. It was still a bit too large for him, possibly resulting in Bull's peculiar way of holding the violin throughout his life.[9] As Wergeland put it, Bull "as it were fondles his violin."[10]

Following this impromptu performance, Paulsen eagerly recommended the admission of Ole to full membership in Harmonien. He was admitted, even though it required a change in the rules to read: "For service in the orchestra unconfirmed persons can be accepted." On 19 October 1818, the protocol of Harmonien testified that Ole had been admitted at the age of eight and a half as an "auscultant" (a pupil with access to the orchestra).[11]

In the following year, at just nine years old, Ole made his first public appearance. Bishop Pavels faithfully noted that "the second section of this evening's concert began with a violin quartet (*sic*) by little Bull, the apothecary's son." He added, in a popular quote from the play *Erasmus Mon-*

7. Linge, *Ole Bull,* 20.
8. This quartet was by Franz Krommer (1759–1831) according to Henrik Winter-Hjelm, "Træk af Ole Bulls Liv," *Morgenbladet* (1852).
9. Winter-Hjelm, "Træk af Ole Bulls Liv," *Morgenbladet* (1852).
10. Wergeland, "Ole Bull," 185.
11. The protocol entry is reproduced in Linge, *Ole Bull,* 21.

tanus (1722) by Bergen's own playwright, Ludvig Holberg, (1684–1754): "Well enough, Mamselle, for so young a person."[12]

On his ninth birthday Ole's father ordered for him from Copenhagen a set of *Études* by Federigo Fiorillo (1755–1823),[13] and that winter Bergen was visited by Norway's then leading composer, Waldemar Thrane (1790–1828), for whom Ole played his Fiorillo. Thrane could tell him about Paris, the center of musical art, and especially about its great violin teacher Pierre Baillot (1771–1842). On 21 December 1819, Ole again played a solo, this time a concerto by Giovanni Mane Giornovichi (ca. 1735/45–1804). Bishop Pavels noted it: "At the concert this evening young Bull showed what advances he has made since last winter. He executed strokes which flute player Nicolaysen has said his teacher Paulsen with his stiff fingers is unable to perform."[14]

Ole's scholastic progress suffered from his interest in the violin. He was often absentminded in class and had special problems with German and Latin. One of Ole's teachers, Assistant Rector Winding, disgusted at his inattention, angrily broke out, "Take hold of your fiddle, Ole. Don't waste your time here."[15] Ole's father finally decided that if Ole were to get the degree he needed at the University in Christiania, then Norway's only institution of higher learning, he would need a tutor.

The tutor's name was Musæus, and his methods were antediluvian, to say the least. He maintained discipline by beating his pupils with rulers and canes and by boxing their ears. The boys finally rebelled. One day at about six in the morning, when Musæus arrived, they beat up on him, with Ole, who was the strongest, in the lead. The boys egged Ole on, yelling, "Give it to him, Ole. Don't give up."[16] A maid finally broke up the fight with her fire tongs. Musæus never dared complain to Ole's father.

In 1820, when Ole was only ten, Paulsen left Bergen for Christiania. Two years later Ole got a new and better music teacher, a Swedish violinist named Mathias Lundholm (1785–1860). He had been conductor of the concert orchestra in Gothenburg and had studied with Baillot in Paris for a year and a half. At the Harmonien concerts, Lundholm played solos by Charles Philippe Lafont (1781–1839), Pierre Rode (1774–1830), and Viotti, as well as Baillot and Spohr, many of which he taught Ole to play. In the

12. Holberg was born in Bergen, lived most of his life in Denmark, and died in Copenhagen.
13. Possibly *Étude pour le violin formant 36 caprices*, Opus 3.
14. Linge, *Ole Bull*, 22.
15. Winter-Hjelm, "Træk af Ole Bulls Liv," *Morgenbladet* (1852).
16. Linge, *Ole Bull*, 23.

years from 1822 to 1827 Lundholm must have had an important influence
over Ole, teaching him both the French and German traditions. Even at
this age, however, Ole was already looking for his own ways of playing
and saw Lundholm's methods as rather rigid.

In 1824 Ole read in a music catalog about the 24 Caprices of Nicolò
Paganini. After a conversation with two Italian visitors about their great
countryman, he persuaded his grandmother to buy the music for him. One
day when Ole was working on a concerto by Spohr, Lundholm told him
the Spohr piece was too difficult for him. When Ole nevertheless was able
to play it, Lundholm challenged him with Paganini: "I suppose you think
you can manage this too!" Lundholm was apparently unaware that Ole
had been practicing the very piece he selected to test his pupil on. To everyone's surprise, he played it very well. "Even the cats knew the piece,"
said Bull in reminiscence.[17]

Bull had many opportunities to gain skills in playing chamber music
because the members of Harmonien were not limited to playing in the orchestra. They played trios, quartets, and quintets, especially numbers by
Haydn and Mozart, and on 17 October 1825, young Bull had a chance to
play a quartet (Aria) by Baillot.[18]

During the winter from 1827 to 1828, while Bull was preparing to leave
Bergen for the University in Christiania, he heard concerts by a Danish
violinist named Frederik Carl Lemming (1782–1846). Lemming interested
Bull because he played variations on a Norwegian folk melody, "Stusleg
Søndagskvelden" (Lonesome Sunday Eve). A Swedish newspaper described
his playing as "bizarre." Whether this was because of his method or because he played the folk melody is not known, but his performance could
have sparked Bull's interest in his native music.

By this time Bull was well known as a musical prodigy not only in
Bergen, but through family connections his reputation had preceded him
to the capital. Although his parents may not have known it, Bull's preco-
cious musicianship was not without parallels in his time. Wolfgang Mozart (1756–91), Franz Liszt (1811–86), Felix Mendelssohn (1809–47), Clara
Schumann (1819–96), and Eduard Reményi (1828–98) all had built or would
build reputations at an early age. More than any of these, however, it was
Paganini's reputation that inspired Bull. The supremely popular violinist's
renown as a showman would influence the kind of public image that Bull
eventually found desirable to adopt as his own.

17. Ibid.
18. Adolph Berg and Olav Mosby, Musikselskabet Harmonien 1755–1945, Vol. 1 (Bergen, 1945), 134.

3

Ole Bull Meets Henrik Wergeland
(1828–1831)

C HRISTIANIA, the capital city that was Ole Bull's destination in
1828, is located in southeastern Norway, at the head of a broad
fjord surrounded by small towns and farming communities. At
this time it was not much larger than Bergen, and its cultural atmosphere
was less stimulating. Its importance as a port could not compare with that
of Bergen. Its attraction lay in its being the seat of the Norwegian government. The parliament, known as the Storting, met here, and Christiania
had the makings of a palace. The university dated only from 1811. The
city would eventually surpass Bergen in most respects, except possibly in
charm. In Bull's day it was hardly more than an overgrown village.

Ole's family enjoyed a fairly high prestige in Bergen, but that does not
mean that they were especially wealthy. Their son would have to support
himself while he was at the university, and Ole looked forward to the
possibility of giving violin lessons. He had high expectations, for his family had numerous connections with relatives and friends in the highest eche-
lons of government and the university. He found lodgings with August Bull,
a distant cousin who, like Ole, was planning to study theology. Among
the friends he made was the family of merchant Westye Egeberg (1771–
1830). His son, later Doctor Christian August Egeberg (1809–74), became
Ole's close friend. Christian had a younger sister, Fredrikke, who had musical interests; she played the piano and did some composing. Tradition
has it that there was "something between" her and Ole, but nothing further developed.[1] The family, however, continued to take an interest in Ole.
Soon after his arrival Bull was invited to join the Musical Lyceum, a coun-

1. Ola Linge, *Ole Bull: Livshistoria, Mannen, Kunstnaren* (Oslo, 1953), 26.

terpart to Harmonien in Bergen. He was asked to perform and played a concerto by Spohr. In addition he played quartet soirées in private about town.

Unhappily for Ole, the university examinations proved disastrous, particularly the very stiff requirements in Latin. He was one of more than forty candidates who failed. Ole was distressed at the outcome, so downhearted that he did not eat for several days. He tried to comfort his parents in a letter: "What has happened has happened, and I hope you won't reproach me for it. If fate had been more favorable. . . ." He thoughtfully added, "Who knows what it may be good for?"[2] The remark hints at some reluctance to go on with theology. His friend and biographer Henrik Wergeland, later wrote: "Who knows if this failure was not an elevation towards what he has since become, a powerful hint from the Norns?"[3] Wergeland was here alluding to the Norse divinities of Fate.

Fate did prove to be favorable. Waldemar Thrane, conductor of the Musical Lyceum and of the Theater Orchestra, fell ill. Bull was asked to substitute for him, and he could write to his father that he had received a position in the Theater Orchestra. This would net him the munificent sum of fourteen dollars a month. To this would be added extras for conducting. Now he could not only support himself, but could devote his time to working with music and studying the violin. He wrote joyfully that he had bought two Cremona violins, "which to be sure need some repairs."[4]

On 25 October 1828 Bull saw his first newspaper notice in Christiania, though he was not mentioned by name. The *Morgenbladet* carried a long article about the concert he had conducted. While regretting Thrane's illness, the critic "could only admire the efforts of the management of the Lyceum, for the orchestra was as well manned and as well conducted as one could expect under the circumstances." The writer wished that Bull had selected easier compositions, but "one cannot deny that he succeeded better than could reasonably be expected of one who has so recently taken a post that is not of the easiest."[5] This may seem like faint praise, but at least it was a notice.

About this time Bull met Henrik Wergeland, who was to become his inspiration and hero. Ole mentioned the occasion in a letter of 15 November to his father, but then only in a postscript: "I suppose I have told you

2. Ibid., 27–28.
3. Henrik Wergeland, "Ole Bull: Efter opgivelser af ham selv biografisk skildret," in *Samlede Skrifter,* ed. D. A. Seip (Oslo, 1927), 4.5:186.
4. Linge, *Ole Bull,* 28.
5. Ibid.

that I have become acquainted with the poet Wergeland. Will write more about him in my next letter."[6] Unfortunately, this "next letter" is either lost or was never written, and their momentous encounter was never adequately reported by either Bull or Wergeland. Bull's growth as an advocate of Norway and Norwegian culture is scarcely conceivable without the influence of Wergeland. Wergeland was twenty and Bull eighteen when they met. Here the greatest West Norwegian and the greatest East Norwegian artists of their generation met and united forces in a happy, romantic understanding of the national future of their country.

Henrik Wergeland was the son of Nicolai Wergeland (1780–1848), a pastor and a leading member of the Constitutional Assembly that adopted the Norwegian constitution of 1814. His sister, Camilla Wergeland Collett (1813–95), was an early feminist in Norway and its first important novelist. Henrik grew up in the Eidsvoll parsonage, very near the site of the Constitutional Assembly. He was an enthusiastic supporter of the Constitution and used to say that "he was its older brother."[7] At Eidsvoll the family lived in close contact with the surrounding country folk, and Henrik took an active part in their affairs. He was said by his father to have a "restless and unquiet spirit," and he became a highly controversial figure, a radical opponent of the bureaucratic establishment. Contrary to Bull he got a good classical training and chose to study theology, but he never took a position in the church and devoted himself to authorship, becoming Norway's first and perhaps greatest lyric poet.

Wergeland read widely in the romantic writers of his time. Like many others he went back to Shakespeare as a model for his own writing. He began publishing when he was twenty, and his first collection of poetry, *Digte — Første Ring* (*Poems — First Cycle*), appeared in 1829. When he met Bull, he was at work on a massive poem, a kind of chaotic Divine Comedy entitled *Skabelsen, Mennesket og Messias* (*Creation, Man and Messiah*). He wrote incessantly, producing in his thirty-seven-year lifetime a shelf-full of writings. *Hasselnødder* (*Hazel Nuts*), the memoirs he wrote on his deathbed in 1845, is one of his most affecting works. He retained his humor and sentiment to the last.

Wergeland was a wholehearted advocate of political freedom, national independence, popular rule, a republican form of government, and religious tolerance (especially toward the Jews, who were then excluded from Norway). When Bull spoke of him, as he often did, he cited Wergeland's

6. Ibid., 29.
7. On Wergeland, see Harald Beyer, *Norsk Litteraturhistorie* (Oslo, 1963), 179.

words that had impressed him the most: "Freedom, Republic, Fatherland." Both young men shared a sense of rebellion against the establishment that must have cemented their friendship.

In the biography he would later (1843) write of Ole Bull, Wergeland described his first impression of Bull as "overgrown" (forvoxen), even sickly. "His open face was pale, paler than it now is. His large, clear eyes were deep-set. With his already highly developed nervousness, he was quite neurasthenic, with irritability having a definite dominance in his system. . . . His mind was in a great ferment, like a balloon that tugs and tears at its rope, trying to escape and rise aloft."[8] Wergeland was an admirer of Byron, and as later described by Janet Rasmussen, he appears to have sensed certain Byronic traits in Bull's character.[9] The poet recalled that at their first meetings Bull tried to express in words his plans for great compositions. "Always imaginative, if also fantastic; always magnificently romantic, if sometimes overwrought, full of color and effect—in short just as one might expect it from Bull with his individuality and cultivation, somewhat like a wanderer who walks about in his own thoughts and occasionally picks up something on the way." Wergeland saw in Bull's chaotic thinking a similarity to Schiller's state of mind when he was writing his first play *Die Räuber* (*The Robbers*) (1791). "Bull was also like most great geniuses in combining with a melancholy but mobile temperament a most childlike and trustworthy disposition, and differing from them by having still retained it."[10]

It was an acute observation on Wergeland's part to note Bull's "neurasthenia." Bull complained more than once of his correspondence of depression and a feeling of illness. He wrote to his father: "I am not at all well and am very melancholy."[11] This could have been due to his volatile temperament, but it also could have been a product of the hours he worked, from seven o'clock in the morning until ten or eleven at night. He had regular practice sessions with two orchestras whose future programs he had to map out, and he had pupils. He had his own practicing to do, and he studied harmony. Besides all of this, he had begun composing. "I am working on a symphony," he wrote to his father. "But as I am almost shy towards people, I am afraid my ideas will be just as shy of people."[12] He had also bought a piano on the installment plan. "I often have so much

8. Wergeland, "Ole Bull," 187–88.

9. Janet Rasmussen, "The Byronic Lover in Nineteenth-Century Scandinavian Fiction," *Pacific Northwest Council on Foreign Languages, Proceedings* 29.1 (21–22 April 1978): 121.

10. Wergeland, "Ole Bull," 187.

11. Linge, *Ole Bull*, 30; Ole Bull, *Ole Bull 1810–1910: Et Mindeskrift* (Bergen, 1910), 34 (20 February 1829).

12. Bull, *Et Mindeskrift*, 34 (20 February 1829).

to do that I don't get time to eat. But I still won't give up." Bull never completed the symphony (no. 2) he was then composing.[13] (Numbers given in parentheses following the titles of Bull's compositions refer the reader to the List of Works, where additional details about his works can be found.)

On 26 November 1828, Bull conducted the orchestra of the Lyceum in Spohr's *Overture to Faust* and Ludwig van Beethoven's *Overture to Fidelio.* On 30 December Thrane, only 38 years old, died, and Bull was named titular conductor.[14] He appeared on 14 February 1829, in a violin performance sandwiched between two plays, and for the first time his name appeared in print: "After this performance Concert Master Ole Bull played a *Potpourri* by [Franz Xavier] Pecháček [1793–1840], which he performed to a high degree of perfection. Strength and beauty joined with taste and delicacy to elevate his playing."[15]

Bull now asked his father for permission to visit relatives in Copenhagen, where he planned to give concerts and study harmony. He also requested and got a leave of absence from the Lyceum. He borrowed a hundred dollars from a friend and left for Copenhagen on 19 May 1829. He neglected to tell his father that he intended to go farther afield. In fact he went to Cassel in Germany, seeking instruction from the master violinist Spohr, whose compositions he had been performing. The first his father heard about his plans was in a letter from Hamburg on 26 May. He asked his father's forgiveness, reminding him that Spohr was now his "favorite composer," and as usual in student letters, he asked for money. Whether he got any is dubious in view of Apothecary Bull's growing family.[16]

Bull's visit to Cassel ended in disappointment. Spohr did not accept him as a student, but suggested that Bull go to a music festival at Nordhausen to hear him there. Bull did so and enjoyed what he heard. At the festival he fell into the company of two German students who persuaded him to go with them to the University of Göttingen, where he spent two months. This may be the reason that some accounts of Bull's life list him as having been a student there. He went with the students to nearby Münden, where they played among other things Bull's *Das Gewitter (The Storm)* (no. 3), an improvisation in which Bull "would let lightning crackle and flash on the violin while one of the students would make thunder with the elbows on the piano."[17]

While in Münden Bull accused the second violinist of being out of tune

13. No autograph has been found.
14. In November, Bull had considered writing a *Sørge Cantate (Funeral Cantata)* (no. 1).
15. *Morgenbladet* (14 February 1829).
16. Linge, *Ole Bull,* 32.
17. Wergeland, "Ole Bull," 189.

and called him "ein dummer Junge" ("a stupid youth"). As a result Bull was challenged to a duel, which he described in a letter home. He apparently won the duel after a mutual exchange of blows. This led to another fabulous tale of Bull's having killed a German student. In fact he quietly came back to Copenhagen and stayed there until he returned to Christiania on 20 September. He wrote his mother: "My journey abroad was somewhat adventurous, as you who know my character can easily guess. I have suffered a good deal, but not enough to matter. . . . The worst thing is that I am tormented by creditors. I am up to my ears in debt."[18]

Bull's winter in Christiania was only moderately successful. He sought but did not get the appointment as permanent conductor of the Lyceum orchestra. Then on 20 January 1830, the Lyceum gave a benefit concert for Bull, but the results were indifferent. This was true "even though I played difficult and brilliant variations on Russian themes by [J.] Rüdersdorff (1788–1866), so people now know that I can play something proper."[19] He continued to be productive, however, and his studies in harmony led to his writing two songs for poems by Wergeland, characteristically named "Hymne til Friheden" ("Hymn to Freedom") (no. 4) and "Tordenen" ("Thunder") (no. 5). He also composed music for chorus and wind quartet (no. 6) for a poem by Henrik Anker Bjerregaard (1792–1842) written for Westye Egeberg's funeral in March 1830.

From Christiania Bull made a trip to the city of Trondhjem (now Trondheim) to give a concert, and by the end of June he was back in Bergen. He remained at Valestrand throughout the summer and on 14 September gave his first independent concert in Bergen. We can only speculate how Bull spent the following year in Bergen, how his days were taken up with practice, composing, performing, family, and friends, for there is only a sketchy record of his activities again until 15 June 1831 when he arranged a memorial service for Waldemar Thrane. Thrane's music to Bjerregaard's *Et Fjeldeventyr* (*A Mountain Adventure*) (1824) was performed at the service, and Bull played a concerto by Joseph Mayseder (1789–1863).[20]

Some days following this memorial service, when Bull was out walking, he happened to hear the strains of a Hardanger fiddle through the open windows of a farmer's inn. He dropped in and met one of the most accomplished of its players, Torgeir Augundson (1801–72). Generally known

---

18. Bull, *Et Mindeskrift*, 42 (9 October 1829). Bull's letters to his mother are reprinted separately in Ole Bull, *Min kjære Moder. En kjærlighets erklæring*, ed. Ladislav Reznicek (Bergen, 1980).

19. Bull, *Et Mindeskrift*, 51 (27 January 1830).

20. Linge, *Ole Bull*, 38.

as "Møllergutten" (now Myllarguten, "The Miller's Lad"), Augundson was called by a later writer the "genius of country fiddlers."[21] His encounter with Bull became the subject of a romantic poem, "Møllergutten," by Johan Sebastian Welhaven (1807–73). Augundson was visiting in Bergen, his home being east of the mountains in Telemark, a region famous for its rich folklore. Bull was impressed by Augundson's skill and invited him back to Valestrand, where they spent some days together. There, Bull noted down some of the country fiddler's melodies. With some pride Augundson later told folktale collector Peter Christen Asbjørnsen (1812–85) that in his youth he had played for Ole Bull in Bergen. Bull had asked him to play slowly so he could write the notes, but Augundson answered that he couldn't play slowly, for then he forgot what he would play. "But Ole Bull wrote so fast that it was a terror."[22] At Valestrand Bull surprised Augundson by playing the melodies back to him on Bull's own regular violin. Augundson was later quoted as saying that while Bull played the tunes correctly, "they didn't have the right color."[23] Bull incorporated these melodies into his own repertoire. They fulfilled Wergeland's ideal of authentic native art, and Bull was delighted to acknowledge them as a genuine part of Norwegian folk culture.

When Bull left Bergen for Paris a month later, he took with him a Hardanger fiddle to supplement his two Cremonas. He sailed to Ostende in Belgium on a vessel loaded with lobsters, the *Perceverance,* and then rode the stagecoach from Ostende to Paris, arriving on 19 August 1831. He would not see Norway again for seven years, and a new era of his life was about to begin. As his Norwegian biographer Ola Linge put it, Paris was the beginning of Bull's course "per aspera ad astra" ("through hardships to the stars").[24]

---

21. Leif Lapidus, "Torgeir Augundson, Myllarguten," *Av berømte menns saga* (Drammen, 1944), 45.

22. Peter Christen Asbjørnsen, *Hjemmet og Vandringen* (Christiania, 1847), 107.

23. Linge, *Ole Bull,* 38.

24. Ibid., 40.

4

Paris: Pleasures and Problems
(1831–1833)

PARIS WAS the dream city of every young artist, and for Bull it was, above all, the home of Pierre Baillot. Baillot had been a pupil of Viotti and was now professor of violin at the Conservatory of Music in Paris. Bull was twenty-one, just barely of age. His hopes were pinned to the French capital, but he was utterly unknown, and it seemed unlikely that anyone in Paris could imagine anything significant coming out of the "frozen North."

In his first letter home he wrote in high spirits that he was entering "a whole new world." He found lodgings with a minor official of the Norwegian-Swedish ministry, Kammerherre (Chamberlain) Monrad. Together they visited all the famous sights, from the Tuileries and the Louvre to the Jardin des Plantes and the Magasin des Vins. On 26 August 1831 he wrote to his mother that "in the last two days I have seen more than in my entire life."[1] Bull was well equipped with letters of recommendation from prominent Norwegians to countrymen in Paris, but he found that none of them were in town in the summer. He also had a sum of three hundred dollars from his parents, which he informed them was not likely to last more than five or six months.

He quickly found his way to the Paris Opéra, where he heard the singing of Maria Malibran, the prime soprano of her time. Soon after he went to hear the opera *Moses* (1827) by Gioacchino Rossini (1792–1868). Bull's only comment to his mother was: "I am not downhearted. I have not heard any wizards yet."[2] He also expressed the hope that he might be engaged by the Opéra.

---

1. Ole Bull, *Ole Bull 1810–1910: Et Mindeskrift* (Bergen, 1910), 60 (26 August 1831).
2. Ibid.

Monrad recommended Bull to the Swedish-Norwegian Minister in Paris, the Swedish Count Gustav Carl Løwenhjelm (1771–1856). When Løwenhjelm, who had musical interests and even played the violin, heard that Bull had unusual musical talent and that he was the nephew of Supreme Court Justice Georg Jacob Bull (1785–1854) and a cousin of Bishop Johan Storm Munch (1778–1832), he became interested in the young Norwegian and invited Monrad and Bull to dinner. Bull was pleased, but a bit embarrassed because he was not prepared to appear in fine company. "I had an awful time rubbing out all the spots on my one and only black suit, not entirely new." For the future he ordered "an olive-green dress coat for 50 francs, tails for 30 francs, and a silk vest for 10 francs."[3] These were expensive goods, and one does not wonder that he was constantly in hot water financially!

The first colleague he made friends with was a German virtuoso violinist and composer named Heinrich Wilhelm Ernst (1814–65). He had been a pupil in the Vienna Conservatory of "the famous Ritter von Seyfried [1776–1841] who in turn was a pupil of the immortal Mozart and finally a pupil of the great Paganini," as Bull reported it. Ernst, he wrote, "plays and composes entirely in his [Paganini's] manner. . . . Before my acquaintance with him, I had secured a copy of Paganini's Violin Method book . . . in which I had studied double-stop harmonics,[4] pizzicato, Paganini's famous *Variations on Nel cor più non mi sento* [from Giovanni Paisiello's *La Molinara*], and Paganini's *Duet for One Violin* [*Duo merveille*]." Ernst and Bull played Paganini's *Caprices* together. Ernst also played variations of his own compositions, while Bull "tortured out some bizarre dances on the Hardanger fiddle — and our acquaintance was made."[5] Ernst even volunteered to teach Bull harmony in three or four months for no charge, but Bull declined for fear of becoming too dependent on him.

The two young men found lodgings with the Lippman family, friends of Ernst's at no. 374 Rue St. Denis. Bull assured his father that they were practicing diligently. "I play things by Spohr, on which I have more practice, while he plays things by [Karol Józef] Lipiński (1790–1861), and by Ernst himself. . . . So much is certain," he self-confidently asserted, "that as far as my skill is concerned, I have nothing to fear from the virtuosos of Paris."[6]

3. Ola Linge, *Ole Bull: Livshistoria, Mannen, Kunstnaren* (Oslo, 1953), 43.

4. Harmonics are the upper partials (or overtones) of a string that sound only when it is touched lightly at a node point. They give an ethereal, soft, and pure sound. They were new to the violin technique of the day, and Bull became a master of this technical device.

5. Ole Bull, *Min kjære Moder. En kjærlighets erklæring,* ed. Ladislav Reznicek (Bergen, 1980), 15 (16 September 1831).

6. Linge, *Ole Bull,* 45.

When it came to winning an appointment at the Opéra, however, things looked less hopeful. Director François Habeneck (1781–1849), to whom Løwenhjelm had recommended Bull, informed him that there were no openings. He could wait a month and try for Baillot's position which would soon be vacant. It is not known whether any such application or audition took place. But the evidence appears to indicate that by the winter of 1831 Bull had run out of money, "thanks to your son's former irresponsibility," as a friend wrote to Bull's father (perhaps referring to Bull's gambling).[7] Bull had to move out of the Lippman family's house, and he was lodged for a time on credit in a music school and rooming house operated by Mme. Choron, wife of Alexandre Étienne Choron (1771–1834).

According to Bull's story, while he was living there he was approached by a swarthy gentleman who advised him to visit Frascati's, a well-known gambling establishment. He did so and won a hundred francs by playing a five-franc piece at the roulette table. When a woman tried to steal his winnings, she was stopped by the same dark and mysterious man, who Bull said proved to be the well-known detective spy named François Vidocq (1775–1857). Vidocq was much in the news in 1832, when he was discharged from his post as chief of detectives in Paris, and while it is certain that Bull did gamble it is most improbable that Vidocq had any connection with the destitute violinist.

In Paris the winter of 1831 was desperate; thousands of Parisians were dying of cholera. Bull's parents had broken off with him possibly in disapproval of his gambling. He had pawned the fancy clothes he had bought and was nearly starving. Whether or not he actually attempted to drown himself in the River Seine is not known, but surely the story suggests misery in this period of his life. Another of Bull's unlikely tales from this time is his story of a concert held for the Count of Montebello, where Bull tried out a varnish offered him by one La Cour. It improved the tone of the violin, but spread a horrible odor in the room. In desperation Bull played with such an ecstasy that all listeners were impressed, and the Count invited him to breakfast in the company of Chopin and Ernst. This breakfast supposedly led to a profitable concert that enabled Bull to repay his debts.[8]

We do know that one day in the spring of 1832, Bull was walking in the Rue des Martyres, an ominous name that proved lucky. He was looking for lodgings and happened to see a modest sign advertising a room

7. Ibid.
8. Henrik Winter-Hjelm, "Træk af Ole Bulls Liv," *Morgenbladet* (1852). This story is denied by Linge, *Ole Bull*, 52, 54.

for rent. The landlady was Mme. Villeminot, who received him reluctantly. She was concerned about the safety of her fourteen-year-old granddaughter who lived with her. The girl was pretty and vivacious, and she seems to have felt pity for Bull, who probably looked pale and emaciated. When the grandmother refused Bull's request for a room, the girl whispered, "But look at him, grandmother, he looks like papa!" She had recently lost her father, Alexandre Villeminot, who was a commissaire de guerre with Napoleon.[9] On a second look the grandmother also saw the resemblance and yielded. "Come back tomorrow at noon," she said. Bull responded in his best French, "Merci, Madame, demain a douze heures." He pronounced the "douze heures" in Norwegian fashion so that it sounded like "douceur" (sweetness), which made the granddaughter laugh.[10] In this fashion Bull met the girl who would later become his wife, Alexandrine Félicité Villeminot (1818–62), commonly known as Félicie. He had no sooner moved in than he fell ill and developed a high fever. The two women took care of him and nursed him back to health.

This was in May 1832, and Bull had to live through the coming winter on credit with the Villeminots until he could raise some money. Eventually he turned to his friend Minister Løwenhjelm and persuaded him to write to the Musical Lyceum in Christiania. But the members were able to raise only a hundred dollars. A marine lieutenant named Lous who was returning to Norway agreed to get in touch with Bull's parents and try to reconcile them with their prodigal son. He carried with him not only a letter from Løwenhjelm, but also one from Mr. Bretteville, who had been asked by his son in Christiania to look into Bull's affairs. The son, Christian Bretteville, was a good friend of Bull's who had been alerted to his problems by his appeal to the Lyceum.

Løwenhjelm testified that "M. Ole Bull is cultivating his talent on the violin with the greatest of diligence . . . No one here in Paris is aware of any dissipation on his part. . . . his life here is exemplary and as economical as possible . . . That he, in case he can continue his studies in Paris, will soon enough be notable as one of Europe's greatest violinists, is the opinion of many great connoisseurs—and it is mine as well."[11]

Bretteville reported that Bull's

conduct in Paris deserves the approval of every honorable person. He lodges with a respectable old widow whose acquaintance has been a great good fortune for

9. Linge, *Ole Bull,* 48.
10. Ibid.
11. Ibid., 50.

your son. She has treated him like a son, has watched over him in his dangerous illness, although she is herself poorly, and has paid for both doctor and medicine. . . . I can say that without her loving, motherly care your son would probably have gone to his fathers. . . . It is my firm conviction that it would be quite indefensible not to help your son, and thereby clear the way for him with his talent to take his place among the famous violinists of our time.[12]

These letters were delivered to the elder Bull some time in February of 1833. But times were hard and the Bull family was growing. Apparently no help was forthcoming from Norway. Bull had to borrow from Løwenhjelm, the Egebergs, and others.

Despite his illness and poverty, Bull continued practicing as he pondered his future course. He had plunged deeply into Paganini's work, and the Italian virtuoso and master showman had become a kind of role model for him. He realized that, like Paganini, he had to have his own compositions and decided to work up a piece using Norwegian folk melodies for the Hardanger fiddle. The result was a piece which he called *Souvenirs de Norvège* (no. 7) (later *The Mountains of Norway*). He wrote his mother that it "is quite original in a genuinely Norwegian style. It is dedicated to Count Løwenhjelm and is arranged for *bondefele* [country fiddle, i.e., Hardanger fiddle] with the accompaniment of two violins, viola, cello, double bass, and flute."[13] He also developed some complex variations on a theme by Vincenzo Bellini (1801–35) from his opera *I Capuleti e i Montecchi* called *Fantaisie et Variations de bravoure* (*Bravura Variations*) (no. 8). Bull experimented with novel techniques to match Paganini's variations on a single string, and he flattened the bridge in such a way that it permitted him to play more easily on all four strings at once.

His hope was to establish himself with a single concert, so that he could at least say that he had had a Paris concert. He arranged to play in a musical salon directed by a German named Stoepfel. Two days before the concert the musical journal *L'Entr'acte* carried the following modest notice: "Mr. Ole Bull, a young Norwegian artist, will give a musical soirée next Thursday, which will be of the greatest interest. Mr. Bull's original talent (he will play *Souvenirs de Norvège* on an instrument unknown in Paris) and the assistance of prominent artists will ensure him a numerous and brilliant audience."[14]

The "unknown instrument" was the Hardanger fiddle. The concert was held on 18 April 1833. On the following day the same newspaper carried

12. Ibid., 51.
13. Ibid., 54.
14. Ibid., 53.

a brief review of the concert. Bull's part was summed up as follows: "We must not forget Mr. Ole Bull, who showed an unusual talent. He has such a skill that the greatest difficulties are for him just like a game."[15] That is all. The audience consisted mostly of invited persons who may or may not have perceived anything special about Bull.

Just four days earlier Bull had had his first and only opportunity to hear Paganini play, in Paganini's last Paris concert. It was an occasion Bull had long been waiting for. His next goal was Italy, Paganini's homeland. Paris had disappointed him, but he realized that there was something in the Italian master's style that answered to a chord in himself. Paganini was near the end of his career. There was room for a worthy successor.

15. Ibid., 54.

5

Breakthrough in Italy
(1833–1835)

ULL SOUGHT to hone his performing skills by traveling and giving
concerts, all the while listening and learning. On 10 June 1833,
he left Paris by stagecoach for Switzerland as his first stop on the
way to Italy. He spent the first nights with his countryman the pianist
Hans Skramstad (1797–1839) in Lausanne. He gave a concert in Lausanne's
Casino (a concert hall) on 29 June and a second on 20 July, playing his
Souvenirs de Norvège on the Hardanger fiddle and his *Bravura Variations*
on the regular violin. *La Gazette de Lausanne* commented that "connoisseurs recognize in him one of the most distinguished violinists heard in
Lausanne."[1]

The natural magnificence of Lake Geneva and its environment charmed
Bull and reminded him of Norway. He wrote to Félicie that he dreamt of
living here "in this country where one is free as a bird, together with my
two dearest woman friends, whose names perhaps you know."[2] Here in
Switzerland, where he spent six weeks, he may have written drafts of his
Quartet for Violin Solo (no. 14). He supposedly included a Swiss cow call
(*La ranz des vaches*) and bird song in this unusual piece.

On 29 July 1833 Bull left Lausanne for Geneva. There he wrote his
mother in response to a letter from her "forgiving him for his irresponsibility," a still unexplained transgression on his part. "My tender mother!"
he wrote, "You have made the first step towards reconciliation. Good for
you, good for me. How indispensable for our mutual satisfaction. . . . I
have lost my bodily health, as a consequence of misfortunes, illness, and

1. Alexander Bull, ed., *Ole Bulls Breve i Uddrag. Med en karakteristik og biografisk
Skitse af Jonas Lie* (Copenhagen, 1881), 157 (4 July 1833).
2. Ibid., 158.

overexertion of body and soul. Possibly a most irregular mode of life has contributed to paling my features and changing my appearance. But I feel better here in Switzerland, and I have the hope that the Italian skies will have a happy influence on my health."[3]

Over the following two days, Bull wrote his mother again, telling her that "this year began happily for me. I got pupils and played in many concerts. I began to go around properly clad, and with my concert, which brought in 1400 francs, I was able to pay off my debts."

I have also secured a beautiful violin, a glorious Grand Amati, whose tones are just as pure and soft as your motherly heart. For a connoisseur it has irreplaceable value. It is quite remarkable how much it has contributed to refining my play. I have acquired a fire and a grace in my mode of playing that leaves no one untouched who has heard me recently. But my nerves are irritated to a terrible degree when I play in public. When my solo is over, I can scarcely stand upright, especially when I improvise, something for which I have perhaps a special talent. . . . Oh yes, on the Lake of Geneva I have composed an *Aria appassionata con variationi brillanti* [possibly *Bravura Variations*] and have dedicated it to you, in appreciation of your care for my first musical education. I have played it privately in Lausanne, and up to this time it is the best of what I have composed. . . .

Perhaps I will stay a year in Italy, if I have enough to live on, so I can learn composition without also giving concerts. My renommé and what I can scrape together for the future will be much greater the more time I can spend on the study of composition. I yearn to compose something great. I live as economically as possible in order to take courses in composition and make use of the music library in Milan. It is my hope and my ambition to sweeten your later years with my talent and to die in your arms, but I won't live that long. Your loving son, Ole B. Bull.[4]

Bull's tendency to hypochondria would often break through in his letters home.

From Geneva he returned to Lausanne and went by boat to Vevey "where I attended the great Fête des vignerons (Feast of the Wine Harvest), and where I enjoyed a gloriously romantic day in the company of two Swedish youths, Aaberg and Carlstedt, and the pianist Skramstad, until I entered the stagecoach at 2 A.M. to leave for Milan."[5]

On 10 August 1833 he arrived in Milan, but his plans for study there failed to materialize. There is a notice of a Bull concert at La Scala Theater, which may refer to a gratis concert given for a few invited persons. He also took part in an open-air concert in Milan before going on to Varese

3. Ole Bull, *Min kjære Moder. En kjærlighets erklæring*, ed. Ladislav Reznicek (Bergen, 1980), 16–17 (29 July 1834).
4. Ibid., 17–19 (30 July and 1 August 1834).
5. Ola Linge, *Ole Bull: Livshistoria, Mannen, Kunstnaren* (Oslo, 1953), 58.

to see an Italian friend, and then on to Venice in the winter of 1833. In Venice Bull performed in a concert and he reports that he was called back to the stage five times. He had also mastered a new language. "I now speak fluently German, French, and Italian."[6] After a month's stay in Venice, he left for Trieste.

In one of the towns Bull had visited in all these months of travel in Italy, he succeeded in locating an old violinist of the early Italian school, a ninety-year-old man who had been a pupil of Giuseppe Tartini (1692–1770). "I visited him and asked to see his violin and hear him play. With the greatest kindness he took out an old Amati. The sight of it made my eyes water. And when he drew the bow across the strings, I heard tones that I realized corresponded entirely to Tartini's method, as it must have been according to a letter from the famous master."[7] Bull was still seeking the particular Italian tone quality that eventually would enchant his audiences.

Early in 1834 Bull spent two months in Trieste, giving two concerts at the Great Theater. After the first, the newspaper *Osservatore Triestino* wrote: "As early as in the first strokes of Spohr's *Concerto* we could detect the great master. He played remarkably well the *Variations on the G-String* of the "Austrian Imperial Hymn" by Paganini. But the high point was reached in Paganini's *Variations on Nel cor più non mi sento*. When the selection was finished, a vigorous applause broke out in the hall and Bull had to appear three times to receive the gratitude and ovations of the audience."[8] At the second concert, on 17 February, he played only his own compositions, adding to his *Souvenirs de Norvège,* his *Bravura Variations,* a *Capriccio Fantastico* (no. 10), and a just completed *Concerto in A Major* (no. 9).

Bull had counted on the Italian climate to improve his health, and he did recover, if only slowly. A new way of fingering and a longer bow that required less effort made it easier for him to play. But he could still write his mother, "My nervous system is terribly irritated. Heaven knows if I will ever see you again, dear mother and dear father. . . . In the meanwhile I have done and shall do my fatherland honor, whether I die early or late, famous—honored. . . ."[9] The letter reflects his moody combination of intense vitality and melancholy, a "southern" temperament not easily understood by most Norwegians.

6. Bull, *Min kjære Moder,* 20 (2 February 1834).
7. Linge, *Ole Bull,* 59.
8. Ibid., 60–61.
9. Ibid., 61 (2 February 1834).

In the beginning of March 1834, Bull returned to Venice, where he stayed two weeks to enjoy its art treasures. Then he went through Padua and Ferrara to Bologna, where he played a concert at the local Casino concert hall. One Count di Rangone wrote in his diary early in April about the concert and Bull's part in it: "There was in his playing a mixture of the bizarre and the poetic, and much of Paganini's mode of playing. It was astonishing to hear him perform a two-voiced melody in a single stroke of the bow, with pizzicato, trills . . . and harmonics. He distinguished himself in many other ways also. He is an outstanding violinist, and he won spontaneous and ardent applause."[10]

Bull had heard soprano Maria Malibran in Paris. When he learned that she was singing in Bologna, accompanied by her violinist friend, Charles-Auguste de Bériot (1802–70), whom she later married, Bull sought their acquaintance. In a letter to his father he described their meeting. They asked Bull to play, but he would only play his own violin and so they sent a servant to fetch it. Meanwhile Bériot played some of his own compositions, "quite neatly," as Bull rather drily put it.

I had hardly begun my prelude when Malibran cried, "Ah, how sweet your violin sounds," and to Bériot she said, "His violin has a softer tone than yours. Try it a little." But after some attempts, Bériot returned the violin and said, "Your violin is bewitched."[11] They wanted to know what I could produce on a violin that even Bériot could not handle. I began improvising [no. 11] dark chords, in which all the strings vibrated at the same time, recitatives in octaves, a melody and its simultaneous accompaniment, finally a rushing *Allegro* in minor (my favorite), and I ended with an *Adagio* in major which died away.

Madame Malibran said, "But you will certainly please wherever you go. How is it possible that I have never heard you spoken of?" These words of Madame Malibran, the greatest singer of our age, are dearer to me than the applause of a whole audience. They have given me courage to pursue my path without hesitation. . . .[12]

Throughout the month of April 1834 Bologna was in a fever of musical performances, including operas by Vincenzo Bellini and Rossini. Bull was a constant listener and a frequent guest of Malibran and Bériot. He often stood in the wings at her performances. One evening he was so moved by her singing in *Otello* that he had tears in his eyes. To tease him she thrust out her tongue at him. When he asked her why, she said, "It would have been fine if I too had burst into tears!"[13] Another evening Malibran invited

10. Ibid., 63.
11. Bull had altered the bridge on his violin.
12. Linge, *Ole Bull*, 63–64.
13. Ibid., 64.

The late M.me Malibran de Bériot

She died at Manchester Sep.r 23.d 1836. Aged 28 years

Published by C. W. Fleet St. & Marsh 145 Oxford St.

Maria Malibran (1808–1836). Courtesy of Music Division, The New York Public Library for the Performing Arts, Astor, Lenox and Tilden Foundations.

Bull to her hotel along with guests who expected him to be there. She dressed him in old-fashioned women's clothes and presented him as her elderly aunt. When the guests had waited long enough, Malibran took the bonnet off him and revealed him to the laughing guests.

On 25 April Bull substituted for Malibran and Bériot at a concert in the Casino hall. Bull reported in a letter to his father that he was roused from slumber and appeared at this concert quite unprepared. Without accompaniment he played improvisations on Italian operatic tunes (no. 12). He was enthusiastically received and afterwards accompanied to his lodgings.[14] Bull counted this occasion as his own breakthrough as an artist, and it is probably the performance that became the basis of Hans Christian Andersen's tale "An Episode of Ole Bull's Life."[15] As Andersen told it, "It is a fairytale from our time, a fairytale as only a genius experiences it." It was no small feat to have achieved the status of the hero in a fairytale by Andersen.

Two days later Bull played with Malibran and Bériot at a farewell concert. On 5 May he gave a concert at a theater owned by Emilio Loup, a Swiss. Here he performed *Grand Concerto con accompagnemento a piena orchestra,* divided into three parts: (1) *Allegro maestoso,* (2) *Adagio sentimentale,* (3) *Rondo pastorale* (i.e., his *Concerto in A Major*). He followed with his *Capriccio Fantastico* for violin solo that he claimed as a new invention, an answer to Paganini's *Duo merveille* for violin alone. He hoped it would make a sensation.[16]

The music critic of the paper *Cenni Storici* wrote: "An unusual success. We cannot recount all the qualities that adorn the playing of this young man, who is still less than twenty-five years of age: perfect intonation and extraordinary facility. . . . He touches us with the sweetest, softest tone; he enchants us with the execution of the greatest difficulties. He is the only one we can imagine as the successor of our own renowned Paganini."[17] On the day of the concert Bull was elected an honorary member of Bologna's Accademia Filarmonica. Its "censors" expressed the opinion that "Ole Bull's technique is extraordinary, and we the undersigned are of the opinion that when he can moderate somewhat his fiery temperament, which comes from his youth, he will rank among the first of concertizing violinists." According to Ola Linge, as recently as 1952 there still hung in the concert hall of the Accademia a painting of Ole Bull done in Naples in 1835 by the Italian painter Spiridione Gambardella.[18]

From Bologna Bull went to Florence, where he was assisted in organiz-

14. Ole Bull, *Ole Bull 1810–1910: Et Mindeskrift* (Bergen, 1910), 80 (21 July 1834).

15. Hans Christian Andersen, "En Episode af Ole Bulls Liv. Fortalt efter Kunstnerens egen muntlige Meddelelser (1839)," in *Samlede Skrifter,* 2d ed. (Copenhagen, 1877), vol. 6, 125–28.

16. Bull, *Et Mindeskrift,* 82 (21 July 1834).

17. Linge, *Ole Bull,* 66.

18. Ibid., 66–67. The Academy of Bologna dated from 1666, one of the oldest in the world. Gambardella was later active in London (1842–68).

ing concerts by the Polish Prince and composer Józef Michal Poniatowsky (1816–73). One was held in the local Societa Filarmonica, where Bull was also elected an honorary member. At this concert Bull raised his listeners to a tumultuous ecstasy and understood for the first time what power he could exert on an audience. But he still had moments of despondency. One evening in Florence when he had been practicing for several hours, he sank into a doze. He suddenly thought he saw his father standing before him and saying, "The more you work, the unhappier you will be, and the unhappier you are, the harder you will work." This vision impressed him deeply. He wrote to his father, "As far as my melancholia is concerned, which perhaps worries you, it is not worth much thought. . . . To be sure, it seemed for a time that the mists of unhappiness had penetrated into my nerves. But in this world of artistic and natural riches (like the larva that tosses off its scales and becomes a butterfly) it has been transformed into a constant study of my art."[19]

After his concerts in Florence were completed, Bull left for the village of St. Borgo di Sieve in the Apennines, where he worked for six weeks on his compositions (probably nos. 14–18) and a draft of a Violin Method Book (no. 13). According to Christian A. Aarvig, a Danish musician and biographer of Bull, these weeks gave Bull time for intensive practice that laid the foundation of his violin technique.[20]

Bull was back in Florence by July. Here he finished his *Adagio Religioso* (no. 15), which he also called *A Mother's Prayer.* Bull's American friend Maria Child (see chap. 9) recounted the story Bull told her about its composition. The monks in the Santa Maria Novella Monastery had asked him to compose a piece for them, which he agreed to do. "But progress was slow, and one morning they came to remind me that they had to have it the next day. I had not yet got up when they came. I had been up all night talking with the moon about Norway and other sad things. I promised that they would get it the next day. I got up, took the violin, and it sang my thoughts for me, with the moods from the night. I wrote the melody down, and as I saw before me a mother in prayer before an altar, praying for her child, I called it *A Mother's Prayer.*"[21] It was not unusual for Bull to elaborate on his stories a bit to suit his listeners.

On 1 August 1834 Bull left Florence with Prince Poniatowsky for the bathing resort Bagni di Lucca, known for its mineral springs. This was

19. Ibid., 67–68.
20. Christian A. Aarvig, *Den unge Ole Bull: En Violinspillers Ungdomskampe* (Copenhagen, 1934), 28.
21. Lydia Maria Child, *Letters from New York,* 2d ser. (New York, 1846), 275.

the town where Paganini had been concertmaster in the princely chapel and had given his first concerts in 1799. At the baths were many members of the nobility, among them the Prince of Tuscany and the Dowager Queen of Naples. Bull was presented in a concert to the court in Lucca, accompanied by the Prince's chamber virtuoso, the Austrian pianist Theodor von Döhler (1814–56). At one of their festivities, Bull's appearance was announced, but he remained standing with his violin under his arm. When the Prince asked him why he was waiting, he replied that he did not wish to disturb the conversation. "But everybody is waiting," said the Prince. "Not the lady over there," said Bull. "Oh, the Queen of Naples. I'll tell her to cease." She turned and looked at Bull while the Prince whispered to her. Bull stood looking at the floor, and when all was quiet, he played. The next day he met her in the street. She asked him to come to Naples and play for her when he came. "But you mustn't be so fussy," she said with a smile, "when someone talks while you play."[22]

Bull met Malibran and Bériot again in Bagni di Lucca. When they heard he was to give a concert there, they came to hear him. He returned the compliment, attending their performance. Bull showed Bériot his *Concerto in A Major,* in which he had made some changes. "Bériot assured me," wrote Bull to his father, "that at present he knows no one who would be able to play my Concerto, even if he owned my bow and my violin, as it contains so many hitherto unknown difficulties from beginning to end."[23] He dedicated the *Concerto* to Prince Poniatowsky. At the close of his stay in Bagni di Lucca, a wealthy Norwegian offered his villa in Livorno (Leghorn) to Bull. He stayed there for three weeks before going on to Naples to hear Malibran and Bériot perform at the Opera.

After nearly two years of travel and performances in Italy, Bull gave a concert in Naples on 15 December 1834 that was particularly well received. Two days following this concert, the *Giornale del Regno delle due Sicilie* commented:

A concerto for violin or double bass or waldhorn or oboe is often dangerous for him who plays it and a torture for the audience, a delight only for the few who are or think they are connoisseurs. But on the evening of the fifteenth we were witnesses to an exception to the rule. Ole Bull, born in Norway, professor of the violin, gave a concert in two sections. This young artist showed himself as a modest youth. The audience, which turned out in great numbers to hear him, received him with an encouraging applause that he was soon able to transform into a just reward. He played his *Concerto No. 1* [*Concerto in A Major*] to the accompani-

22. Linge, *Ole Bull,* 69.
23. Ibid.

ment of the whole orchestra and proved to be just as capable in overcoming great difficulties as in playing with moving emotion. After the first section he was called forth three times to vigorous applause. In the second section Bull wished especially to show his skill in mastering the greatest difficulties in playing the violin. The musical connoisseurs redoubled their enthusiasm for him, and the audience again showed its gratitude.

On 20 December the periodical *L'Omnibus* wrote:

Mr. Bull has the bow of an angel in his hands. His instrument, which by its nature is thankless, becomes a human voice when he plays it and not a stringed instrument. If there were a blind person in the theater, he would say that sometimes it was a clarinet, or a lute, or the sweetest voice of a nightingale. About Mr. Bull's style it is to be said that he seems to us the perfect concert player, as he has both mastery and imagination, and withal the right expression and the right variation in his playing. Young as he is, we are sure that in a few years he will surpass all others.[24]

Perhaps equally rewarding to Bull was the praise of his friends Malibran and Bériot following this concert. Malibran sent a message to Bull, summoning him to her loge. There she complimented him and kissed him on the cheek before an applauding audience. Bériot, who was jealous of his success, said: "What in thunder do you have in your violin that can so bewitch the Neapolitans?"[25]

In Naples Bull composed his *Recitativo, Andante amoroso con Polacca Guerriera* (no. 19), his most characteristic composition and the one he played most frequently.[26] It was presumably inspired by the unsuccessful Polish revolt of 1830. Bull had a great sympathy with Poland and all countries that were not wholly free. However, he told Maria Child that the sight of the smoking volcano Vesuvius on a moonlit night gave him the idea.[27] Vesuvius may also have provided his inspiration because he finished most of the composition in Naples. The resemblance between a revolt and a volcanic eruption is considerable, and Bull, whose passionate nature shared something of both, may have been thinking of either while he composed the *Polacca Guerriera*.

Bull left Naples on 5 February 1835, his twenty-fifth birthday, for his last stop on his first tour of Italy, Rome. He later wrote to his mother, "I have sat among the ruins of the great amphitheater, the Colosseum, which can easily seat 80,000 spectators. Under a full moon I improvised at mid-

24. Ibid., 70–71.

25. April FitzLyon, *Maria Malibran* (Bloomington, Ind., 1988), 170–71.

26. Also called *Recitativo, Adagio amoroso con Polacca Guerriera* (usually shortened to *Polacca Guerriera*).

27. Child, *Letters,* 275.

Ole Bull "Violoniste Norwégien," 1830s. Lithograph by Michel Freres after I. P., Bordeaux. Courtesy of Music Division, The New York Public Library for the Performing Arts, Astor, Lenox and Tilden Foundations.

night. Several hundred persons, attracted by the sound of my instrument to this lonely place (inhabited by owls and robbers) woke me with stormy applause to my musical flight. . . . I did not let myself be disturbed and fantasized until the golden rays of the morning gilded the dome of St. Peter's. . . . What I felt? . . . Pain: an endless yearning for an unattainable goal. . . . Alas! It is past! Time, do not fly so rapidly. . . ."[28]

In Rome Bull accepted a distinguished pupil, the nephew of a Vatican librarian, Cardinal Angelo Lansi. The Cardinal gave Bull a violin as part of his fee, a Spadarini from 1662. It was not especially valuable, but it was a memento from Rome. While there, Bull was busy working out the details of the orchestral accompaniment for his *Polacca Guerriera*. He lodged with the Norwegian painter Thomas Fearnley (1802–42). As a joke Bull let Fearnley believe that he was still composing the *Polacca Guerriera* the night before it was to be performed in concert. After Fearnley fell asleep, Bull got up and filled in the missing parts, to Fearnley's great relief when he awoke.

Bull spent several months in Rome deliberating what step to take next in his career. He considered Austria, but a death in the royal family had curtailed concert performances there. Finally, he decided to return to Paris, departing Rome in the spring of 1835. He was happily welcomed home in the Rue des Martyres. His two years of successful concertizing in Italy had brought him a heightened status with audiences. His star was rising.

28. Bull, *Et Mindeskrift*, 89 (20 November 1835, Paris); Linge, *Ole Bull*, 72.

6

Paris and London: Recognition (1835–1836)

ONCE BULL had recovered from the strain of his two-week stage-coach ride by resting up at the Rue des Martyres, he marched off to the musical authorities of Paris. He spoke to Habeneck, conductor of the orchestra, and Edmond Duponchel (1795–1868), director of the Opéra, well armed with notices from Italy. This time there was no hesitation. Bull was granted a chance at a coming concert on 17 June 1835, squeezed in between Rossini's opera *William Tell* (1829) and a ballet by Alcine.

Before this no one had given a violin concert at the Opéra except Paganini himself. Now twenty-five years old, Bull was granted permission to play his *Quartet for Violin Solo* and two movements of his *Concerto in A Major*. His appearance won no advance publicity. He was only an unknown "artiste norvégien," as the program put it. It was a daring venture, a gamble in the face of Paris critics, whose judgment could make or break him. Félicie and her grandmother were there to cheer him on.

That afternoon his bow had broken, and just before the performance the second string of his violin had snapped. On his entry, he tripped on a stage curtain and raised a laugh by his awkward recovery.[1] It was a hot summer evening. There was none of the applause he was accustomed to from Italy. He wrote his mother a description of his nervousness and stage fright. "I strode in like one who goes to the executioner. . . . Twice I lifted my arm to begin, and twice it dropped of itself. . . . I almost fainted. At that moment I caught sight of a triumphant eye of scorn from the orchestra." Then he got hold of himself and let the violin speak. "As my last

---

1. Henrik Winter-Hjelm, "Træk af Ole Bulls Liv," *Morgenbladet* (1852).

37

chords poured forth, ending in harmonics, I heard 'Bravo, bravissimo' from the audience. My Amati had won. The orchestra applauded along with the audience." He went on to play his *Rondo pastorale* from the *Concerto in A Major* with the accompaniment of the orchestra. "I could not hear my last chords through the bravos."[2] The audience was amazed and uncertain: "Could this really be that good?" The critics were divided.

Only one critic, Jules Janin, the chronicler of the *Journal des débats,* expressed real enthusiasm for what he called "ce jeune sauvage." With some surprise he noted that this "sauvage" presented himself as "a civilized person," and with a covert gibe at Paganini, he added, "without charlatanism."

This violin does not resemble any we have heard. It is delicate and soft; it sings vigorously, it sings gently, it sings on four strings, and this is just as difficult as singing on only one. . . . In the *Rondo pastorale* we had to admire the clarity and rapidity of his playing, so beautiful and extended that we had no idea of anything like it. . . . In short, the Norwegian artist scored. His success has made him one of ours. Paris will give him an honorable name that will open all the cities of Europe to him.[3]

Janin's enthusiastic approval and Bull's triumphs in Italy became the basis of the promotional pamphlet written for Bull by F. Morand, presumably a Parisian journalist. This *Notice sur Ole Bull,* dated Boulogne-sur-mer, September 1835, was a survey of Bull's life from birth to age twenty-five, beginning with his "will to free himself from all chains" at the age of five! Morand philosophizes by drawing a parallel between Bull and Voltaire's resistance to parental authority. We learn that Bull hoodwinked his father by pretending to give concerts to benefit the poor. In Morand's version, when Bull arrived in Paris in the midst of a cholera epidemic, his first experience was to be robbed of his money and his violin. "In this miserable situation an artist can either write a masterpiece or commit suicide. Bull chose to leap into the Seine. . . . He was recalled to life; the masterpiece would come later." Bull leaves for Italy, and in Trieste he is declared a genius because he has extended the limits of the violin beyond those set by Paganini. The violinist has never studied composition, we learn, but he has produced his "masterpieces," his *Concerto in A Major,* his *Polacca Guerriera,* and his *Adagio Religioso.* In Italy he is called "the man of sound," as his friend Malibran became "the lady of song." Morand's account is superficial and flowery, with inaccuracies, but it became the

2. Ole Bull, *Min kjære Moder. En kjærlighets erklæring,* ed. Ladislav Reznicek (Bergen, 1980), 20–22.
3. Ola Linge, *Ole Bull: Livshistoria, Mannen, Kunstnaren* (Oslo, 1953), 77–78; cf. Winter-Hjelm, "Træk af Ole Bulls Liv," *Morgenbladet* (1852).

basis of the many accounts of Bull's life that circulated in the press.[4]

During the summer of 1835 Bull pursued his success in the French bathing resorts, ending in Lille, and on his return to Paris he made a contract for two concerts in the Opéra on 9 and 22 December. Yet in the midst of his triumph he wrote to his mother expressing the deepest despair:

At last, after a year's silence I will let you know that I am still alive. . . . alive — oh! My torments and tribulations, my soul's restlessness and the thousand times repeated death pains in my broken heart unhappily remind me that I am still alive. Alas, how dearly bought is the spark of Prometheus!!!

I strove for a name that will survive me. I have attained it. Alas! I did not see the thorns that convulsively entwine my rose, which is ever more so encircled as to be strangled.

I look ahead with courage to my end. I can never become happy. Sufferings are my sustenance. I will give my anxious heart air. Loneliness is my friend, perhaps the only true one that I possess. It accompanies me in my throes of death, on the stage, amidst the applauding public, and sits beside me in my silent chamber at this moment.

It is now midnight. For three weeks I have hardly slept a single night. An inner voice confines me to my compositions until dawn, as if someone were asking me to hurry my labors while there is still time. My ideas arise so clearly to my searching glance that I am taken aback and astonished as if by something supernatural — incomprehensible — What do we understand? Can we grasp why we exist? A riddle. Our fate? An intuition. Justice? A repayment of old gambling debts, which are mostly uncertain and unpaid, yet are made up for the occasion — keep their name and lose their significance. . . . It is already four o'clock in the morning. I must work. Oh mother, mother! You also have your sorrows. We will meet again some time. Farewell! Farewell! Don't forget your Ole.[5]

The letter is a vivid expression of Bull's romantic moods, the ups and downs of his whole life. His despair and preoccupation with death, no less than his exuberance, was an essential part of his artistic temperament and a characteristic of many romantic writers, from Heine to Lord Byron.

The December concerts sealed Bull's triumphs. They were no longer concerts of a Norwegian "sauvage." "All of Paris" was there, King Louis Philippe (1773–1850), dukes and counts, the bestselling author Eugène Scribe (1791–1861), painter Eugène Delacroix (1798–1863), violinist and concertmaster Ferdinand David (1810–73) from Leipzig, and on December 21 even old Talleyrand (1754–1838).

After these concerts Jules Janin extended his former praise of Bull in an article on 14 December 1835 in the *Journal des débats*. It flew like fire to the Norwegian press and at last established Bull's fame among his coun-

4. F. Morand, *Notice sur Ole Bull* (Boulogne, 1835), 9.
5. Bull, *Min kjære Moder,* 20-23 (21 November 1835).

trymen. Once more he proclaimed Bull to be "the great musician." "There are so many tears and so much melancholy in this noble instrument. . . . He sings, he weeps, he is fiery, now drowning out the horns and the trombones, now sighing as softly as an Æolian harp. He is a musician who has not had a famous teacher and belongs to no school. There is something naive, something inspired, with an incredible power." Janin again could not refrain from comparing him with the "charlatanism" of Paganini. "But Norway is like a simple, unassuming girl, honest and straightforward, without makeup. She comes and gives quite naturally all she has in her soul and her heart." Janin stressed Bull's naiveté "which thinks of nothing but following his own good, lovely nature in full daylight, in free, healthy air, in full freedom." He noted that since he had reviewed Bull six months earlier in the Opéra, he had heard him several times in the provinces, and "each time I found again the same talent, the same passionate inspiration, the same naive enthusiasm, and the same fullness of heart." He told of being awakened in Rouen by Bull's "melancholy and tender adagio." Bull had even consoled Janin at the "sea at Dieppe, that horrible sea which makes even healthy people ill." In one provincial town he heard Bull accompanied by a local orchestra "that drove composer Meyerbeer into the sea while holding his hands over both his ears." Bull, Janin claimed, is not a secretive artist "who encloses himself in a room like a thief," but "one who throws his music out as one throws coins to the poor."

He is never happier than when he has a crowd around him to listen, to applaud and weep gratis. . . . If he has not earned much money, he has won honorable sympathies. . . . Young people have come to his concerts, including the poorest, for this musician, himself poor, has opened his door and said, "Enter!" . . . It is necessary to give some lessons in generosity to these egotistical towns in the provinces that do not know it is their duty to encourage a great musician who is passing by. . . . If one has not made Paganini's silver millions, what does it matter when M. Baillot receives you as a brother, [and] back in Paris you can enjoy the services of Habeneck's orchestra?

Other reviewers were equally enthusiastic. For example, *Le Courrier des Théâtres* announced on 10 December 1835: "Ole Bull's playing is full of soul, of energy, of gentleness and charm. He is an artist who deserves all the encouragement to which his talent entitles him." After Bull's second concert, the same reviewer wrote: "He not only showed his skill with difficult pieces, but his violin sang so expressively that one could often believe it was a human voice. On 13 December 1835, *La Revue et Gazette Musicale* wrote "Ole Bull is a great talent who especially shows off in his staccato and in the easy and elegant way in which he executes the most difficult

runs." And on 24 December *La Gazette des Theâtres* proclaimed: "His playing is that of a genius. Only an inspired artist can coax such harmonious
and soulful tones from his instrument."

Encouraged by his success, Bull left Paris in February for Lyons where
he was to give two concerts. After playing them, he became so ill that,
in fear of dying, he sent his profits from the concerts to Félicie. Once he
recovered the strength to travel, Bull returned to Paris only to discover that
a concert engagement in Paris had fallen through because pianist Sigis-
mund Thalberg (1812–71) had usurped his dates by virtue of producing
a letter from the powerful Austrian statesman Metternich (1773–1859). When
Bull demanded an explanation from composer Rossini, who was one of
the directors, Rossini advised him to go to England and seek an engagement from Pierre Laporte, the director (1828–42) of the King's Theatre and
a friend of Rossini's.

Bull followed Rossini's advice and crossed the Channel for the first time.
He arrived in London at the end of April 1836 and was invited to a dress
rehearsal for critics on 10 May at King's Theatre, the auditorium where
Paganini had played some years before. Intrigues reportedly engineered by
the London orchestra's first violinist Nicolas Mori (1796/97–1839) led to
an absurd error that made Bull two hours late. According to Bull's own
account, he picked up his violin and told the orchestra: "You must either
think, gentlemen, that I do not need an accompaniment, or that you are
unable to play one. I can only accept your intention as a compliment and
express my thanks in our mutual language — that of tone."[6] Then he played
his *Quartet for Violin Solo,* followed by a four-part rendition of "God Save
the King" (no. 20), which roused the orchestra to a favorable response.

Bull's regular concerts were scheduled for 21 May, 1 June, and 15 June.
Linge states that "the reviews in the many newspapers would add up to
a whole little book." He lists nineteen articles published just in the period
from 23 May to 7 June 1836. Electrifying passages from the London press
were reprinted in *Den Constitutionelle* in Christiania on 23, 25, and 29
July. For publicity purposes Bull had a dozen of the English reviews translated into French and German and printed as broadsheets under the title
Début de M. Ole Bull au théatre du Roi.[7]

The *Spectator* had written in May: "His performance is one of the
most striking presentations we have ever witnessed. Ole Bull is perfectly
without rival. He expresses the true inspiration and genius of art." After

6. Winter-Hjelm, "Træk af Ole Bulls Liv," *Morgenbladet* (1852), after Wergeland.
7. The German version appeared in H[ermann] B[iow], *Ole Bull: Eine biographische
Skizze* (Hamburg, 1838). Linge, *Ole Bull,* 86–87.

some disparaging remarks about Paganini, the critic enthusiastically declared that

Ole Bull's playing must in many ways be called miraculous. . . . After every piece, applause and cries and wonderment broke out in the whole audience. Some were so excited that they rose in their seats and cried "Bravo" and "Da capo." . . . Ole Bull has made a decided hit. . . . He has eclipsed the transitory fame of all his predecessors in the same musical department. . . . He expressed the whole scale of human feelings and thoughts and made the old legend of Orpheus and his miraculous lyre understandable.

Other newspapers echoed these praises, constantly referring to Paganini and attempting to decide if Bull were greater than the Italian, a problem that on 16 June 1836 the *Morning Post* finally declared was pure nonsense.

Bull had reason to feel happy when he wrote to Félicie on 24 May 1836: "Dearest Félicie, victoria! We have won! I never had a greater success, or hardly as great, as that of last Saturday night. Wreaths, bouquets, and applause! . . . In spite of all intrigues, the journals have pronounced me one of the first violinists of the world." On 26 May he wrote to her again: "Yesterday I played for the Duke of Devonshire; [Giovanni Battista] Rubini [1794–1854] sang, also. The Duke said that I had performed the miracle of endowing the violin with a soul. Many of the finest nobility of England were present, and the ladies were much moved."[8]

The *London Times* of 23 May declared that they "had never attended a more completely successful performance. . . . Perhaps his most remarkable characteristic is the quiet and unpretentious manner in which he produces all his great effects. . . . In long arpeggio passages and others made up of rapid and minute divisions, his bow scarcely seemed to move on the strings; his hand too was almost motionless, yet our ear was charmed with a succession of distinct and sparkling notes."

On 16 June 1836, after the third concert, the *Times* reported that "a more perfect performance can scarcely be imagined." Bull now showed not only confidence in himself, but also in the audience. He played nothing but his own compositions, the *Concerto in A Major,* his *Adagio Religioso,* his *Polacca Guerriera,* and his *Fantasia Solo (Quartet for Violin Solo).* "The great charm, perhaps, consisted in the purity of style with which the whole was given. It was all his own—new, and consistent, and beautiful; not an atom of charlatanism in it; nor was there to be detected any imitation of

8. Both letters are found in Alexander Bull, ed., *Ole Bulls Breve i Uddrag. Med en karakteristik og biografisk Skitse af Jonas Lie* (Copenhagen, 1881), 166, 168.

Félicie Villeminot (1818–1862), after she married Bull in 1836. Painting at Valestrand. Photo by Einar Haugen.

Ole Bull. Stipple engraving after drawing by E. T. Parris, London, 1836. Courtesy of Music Division, The New York Public Library for the Performing Arts, Astor, Lenox and Tilden Foundations.

any other great master. . . ." Bull's country gained recognition through him when, on 19 June 1836, the *Public Ledger* wrote: "Norway can be proud of having fostered such a son. England is glad he came to us."

Ole Bull could feel he had reached the heights. By the time of his London concerts, Paganini had stopped playing, and four years later the old master died. In just two months Bull had earned a net of over 10,000 francs. Now he felt he could afford to marry Félicie. He returned to Paris and signed the wedding contract according to French law on 16 July 1836. They were married on 19 July by pastor Coquerel in the Protestant church L'Oratoire across from the Louvre. He was twenty-six and Félicie, 18; they had known each other for five years. Mme. Villeminot's solicitude for her young granddaughter and for the seemingly impecunious and sickly violinist had been rewarded more happily than she could have ever foreseen.

Bull was in no way marrying beneath him. His young wife's grandfather, Louis Nicolas Villeminot (1748–1827), had been a lieutenant-colonel and a commander of the guard in the French army. Félicie's father, Alexandre (1785–1831), had fought in the war with Spain and became a functionary in the French ministry of finance. Her mother was the daughter of Spanish Count d'Avila, born in Valladolid, who had met Alexandre during the war.

Two days after the wedding, Ole and Félicie left Paris for London. Ole was proud of his bride. She had become a beautiful woman, with her oval face and sparkling eyes. He wrote to his mother that she was "short and slender, black-haired, with large, black eyes, a bearing and face marked by deep seriousness and thoughtfulness. . . . She has a free and natural behavior, and she loves me with all the ardor of a Spanish woman."[9]

9. Ole Bull, *Ole Bull 1810–1910: Et Mindeskrift* (Bergen, 1910), 98 (12 January 1837).

7

Back to Norway via Moscow
(1836–1838)

Now that Ole Bull was married, he had to capitalize on his new-won fame. So he threw himself into a tour of Great Britain, beginning in September 1836. In October in Liverpool he had to replace his friend, the singer Maria Malibran, who had died unexpectedly. Bull lamented her death to Félicie: "Poor woman! After having worked so much for a public that was often ungrateful, she dies as a victim of her own success. She has died of overexertion — A woman endowed with a fiery soul, the most overwhelming passion, an enchanting voice, an acting, a declamation! . . . I remember how I wept in Bologna when I saw her in the role of Desdemona in *Otello*."[1] He went to Manchester to lay flowers on her grave.

The concert in Liverpool proved to be dramatic. The auditorium was faulty, without resonance, so that Bull's violin could hardly be heard except at fortissimo strength. Bull exerted himself so violently that he hemorrhaged during the night. The duke of Devonshire heard of his misfortune and sent a carriage to fetch him to his palatial residence at Chatsworth. Bull wrote to Félicie, who had stayed in Norwood, that the duke cared for him in every possible way, having even forbidden him to play. "I might be taken for a prince, so much consideration and politeness do I receive. . . . It is the most splendid place I know."[2] The duke gave Bull a ring for Félicie, whose absence Bull lamented during his week-long stay at the magnificent estate.

Bull had recovered well under the duke's care, but his constant travel-

---

1. Alexander Bull, ed., *Ole Bulls Breve i Uddrag. Med en karakteristik og biografisk Skitse af Jonas Lie* (Copenhagen, 1881), 180 (27 September 1836).
2. Ibid., 183 (27 September 1836).

ing in England, Ireland, and Scotland taxed his powers. In a year and a half, he is said to have given 274 concerts in Great Britain, traveling night and day by stagecoach and carriage. From Bath he wrote to Félicie: "I fear I may never see you again. I feel so ill at heart and in my head, and often I have a strong trembling. My eyes are so tired and my breast is as if it were slashed by a knife. . . . If my powers should not be equal to my will and I should succumb, remember you have been loved, yea more than loved by your Ole Bull."[3]

Bull's tour extended into Ireland and Scotland in 1837, and Félicie accompanied him for awhile. In both countries, he observed the folk music and composed fantasies on folk melodies. He wrote *Concerto Irlandais* (*Farewell to Ireland*) (no. 21), based on tunes he is said to have learned in 1836 from Thomas Moore, and *Homage to Edinburgh* (no. 23), also called *Scottish Concerto* and *Homage to Scotland*. While touring he also composed *Preghiera Dolente e Rondo Ridente* (*Grieving Prayer and Laughing Rondo*) (no. 22).[4]

On 3 September 1837, Bull wrote from Scotland to Félicie, who had returned to Paris prior to the birth of their first child. He wrote her of his plan to return to Norway and possibly buy Valestrand from his father. He thought of this estate as their future home:

If you should wish to live quietly in this lovely district, we could study agriculture. . . . The climate is very mild, the woods are populated only by deer, rabbits and foxes. . . . The lakes have excellent trout, and the sea will supply us with salmon. Secluded there in our pretty home with our child, what would we lack? . . . . But this is only an idea that ran through my head as I thought of our future marital happiness. . . . We will see. . . .

For my part I am tired of traveling in this way.—I expose my health so that at last it will destroy me if I do not put an end to it. I compose every day here whether I am in bed or not. . . . I am preparing my tourné on the Continent diligently and yearn to live in peace afterwards if I can. . . ."[5]

Their son, Ole Storm Felix (1837–39), was two weeks old when Bull returned to Paris on 30 September 1837. This time he remained in Paris for two months.

While in Paris, Bull had a chance meeting with Paganini on the street. It was a friendly encounter, which ended with a visit to Paganini's quarters. The Italian master showed Bull his violin and complimented Bull on

3. Ibid., 191 (5 December 1836).
4. Henrik Wergeland calls this piece a fantasy on Irish tunes, but that seems doubtful; "Ole Bull: Efter opgivelser af ham selv biografisk skildret," in D. A. Seip, ed., *Samlede Skrifter* (Oslo, 1927), 4.5:207.
5. Bull, ed., *Ole Bulls Breve i Uddrag*, 204–205.

his playing. This was their only personal meeting. Bull wrote to his parents about their encounter, commenting on Paganini's "second position, which is excellent." But he said he was "happy never to have taken anything else from Paganini but his hand."[6]

Although Bull planned to return to Norway, his path home proved to be very roundabout, taking him far to the east and back. The secluded existence he dreamed about would never really happen. Before the year was out, he initiated a grand tour through Germany, Russia, Finland, and Sweden. His companion and secretary was a twenty-two-year-old Danish cellist named Kellermann, who had been studying music in Paris; he acted as agent and accompanist to Bull.[7] The tour began in France at Douai, after which Bull travelled to Courtrai in Belgium. Here he sold his Guarnerius violin to music lover Vermeulen, having bought a new Guarnerius, dated 1744, that became his favorite concert violin for many years.

Bull went next to Hamburg. Upon arriving, he persuaded Hermann Biow, a local poet, to prepare a brochure for publicity purposes, setting forth Bull's merits.[8] It was largely translated from the earlier pamphlet by Morand, with the addition of some notices from London. Biow also included a portrait and a sketch of Bull's life to date, based on English newspapers and what Bull told him. He declared Bull to be a "genius . . . an artistic sun of the first rank."[9] We read the story of Bull's visit to Spohr, of his duel in Münden, and of his "flight," his despair in Paris that caused him to leap into the Seine, where he was saved by some washerwomen! Bull met a person who taught him the secret of a perfume that made a violin more beautiful! Hearing Paganini encouraged him to emulate the master, and he succeeded in surpassing him. Finally, Bull's fame was established by a concert in Bologna. Apparently, this is what Bull wanted his German audiences to believe.

Bull's first concert in Hamburg was on 28 December 1837. He performed, among other works, *Variations on the Hamburg National Song* (no. 24), a piece probably improvised for the occasion. A review that was reprinted in the Christiania paper *Den Constitutionelle* on 22 January 1838 praised Bull's "incomparable virtuosity." The German critic described his personality as modest and straightforward: "In his playing there is exalted, bold geniality, combined with gentle, enrapturing grace. Competence, security

6. Christian A. Aarvig. *Den unge Ole Bull: En Violinspillers Ungdomskampe* (Copenhagen, 1934), 95.
7. Ibid., 38–39.
8. H[ermann] B[iow], *Ole Bull: Eine biographische Skizze* (Hamburg, 1838).
9. Ibid., 6.

Ole Bull. Lithograph by Hermann Biow, 1838. Courtesy of Music Division, The New York Public Library for the Performing Arts, Astor, Lenox and Tilden Foundations.

and elegance, warmth, strength and clarity characterized his performance, and all of it bears the stamp of perfection." He noted that Paganini had exerted a decisive influence on Bull, but "in his playing there is more of the graceful than of the gigantic-fantastic, and in his compositions there is a melancholy, somber seriousness that assumes a milder character."[10]

In Hamburg Bull bought a large English carriage equipped as a bedroom, which he would use on the frigid winter's tour back and forth to Russia. On the way east he was invited to the court of one of Germany's many small dukedoms, that of Mecklenburg-Schwerin. The coachman lost his way in the snow, but Bull slept in his carriage bed, "wrapped in two fur coats." After the concert in Schwerin, the duke called on Bull with tears in his eyes: "My wife has wept the whole time during your playing, and she insists on meeting and speaking with you."[11] Bull was given an audience of three-quarters of an hour with the grand duchess, who told him she had written to her father, the king of Prussia, who was also the father of the empress of Russia, or Czarina, as we would call her.

In Berlin the snow grew obstructive, and Bull had to have runners put on his carriage. He continued to the east, giving concerts in Danzig and in Königsberg; "between these towns I wept all day to Kellermann's surprise."[12] At Riga, Bull's next stop, he met Richard Wagner (1813–83), who was then director of the local theater orchestra. On this sole occasion of their meeting, there was probably little communion. Wagner's musical tastes, for theater and orchestra, were very different from Bull's who preferred virtuoso styles and solo music and whose favorite composers were Mozart and the Italian operatic masters.

At the end of February 1838, Bull and his company arrived in St. Petersburg. He included improvisations on a *Triumphal March* (no. 25) in his program and was rewarded by the orchestra with a diamond ring. His own triumph was somewhat marred by criticism by the German violinist Heinrich Maria Romberg (1802–59), director of the imperial opera, who said: "Bull is a charlatan, a bad imitator of Paganini."[13] From St. Petersburg he plunged on to Moscow, which they reached after two days of hard driving. Here the Russian governor's wife, Princess Galitzin, gave Bull an emerald brooch for Félicie, and the Czarina gave him a ring with eighty little diamonds.

Shortly before he left Moscow, Bull learned that his father had died

10. Ola Linge, *Ole Bull: Livshistoria, Mannen, Kunstnaren* (Oslo, 1953), 99–100.
11. Ibid., 100.
12. Aarvig, *Den unge Ole Bull*, 39.
13. Linge, *Ole Bull*, 102.

Ole Bull, "Sibi par, Plectro nulli secundus," 1838. Lithograph by A. Achilles, Schwerin. Courtesy of Music Division, The New York Public Library for the Performing Arts, Astor, Lenox and Tilden Foundations.

in early 1838, never having heard his famous first son play in public. Ole's brother Edvard reported that their father had often spoken with eager anticipation of Ole's return, knowing that he was on his way back to Norway. Ole grieved bitterly. He wrote to Félicie: "Imagine my sorrow at having to play for Prince Galitzin [Nikolay Borisovich Golitsyn, 1794–1866], the governor of Moscow, on the evening I received this sad news. When I came, all had heard of my sorrow, and the Princess did not want me to play. But I wished to show my firmness of character. When I played Mozart's *G Minor Quintet,* the ladies wept together with my violin."[14] After his father's death, Bull wrote in his letters to Félicie that he was haunted by the thought that he might not see her and their child again.

On the way to Stockholm Bull played in Viborg, Helsingfors (now Helsinki), and Åbo (now Turku) in Finland. In mid-June in Stockholm, he played three concerts. At one he was assisted by a very young Swedish singer, Johanna Maria Lind (1820–87), whose fame, as Jenny Lind, would later rival Bull's fame in America. He also had an audience with King Carl Johan Bernadotte (1763–1844). Bull later reported that the king had asked him what school he had attended to learn such superb playing and that he had replied: "The school of adversity, Your Majesty."[15] Before he left, he had been made a member of the Swedish Academy of Music and had received the Order of Vasa from the king.

Bull reached Norwegian soil at last on 3 July 1838, at Moss near the Swedish border and on 8 July he entered Christiania. The first thing he did was to take two weeks of rest to recover from the rigors of his eastern European tour. He was festively received in Christiania, first feted at a banquet given by the university Student Association on 19 July. Some sixty guests were present, including several professors. Félicie attended the party with him and so got her first taste of Norwegian hospitality. According to the paper *Morgenbladet,* the celebration lasted until 1:00 A.M., after which the celebrants accompanied Bull to his lodgings and hailed him outside his windows. Toward the end of July he announced four concerts to be given in Christiania. They included variations on two Norwegian melodies, "I Rosenlund under Sagas Hall" ("In the Rose Grove under the Hall of Saga") (no. 26) and "Aa kjøre Vatten ("To Fetch the Water") (no. 27). In the meantime Bull had visited his former teacher from his Bergen days, concertmaster Johan Henrich Paulsen. Paulsen was ill, on his deathbed, and living in extreme poverty. Bull played a private program just for him.

14. Bull, ed., *Ole Bulls Breve i Uddrag,* 224–25 (28 April 1838).
15. Linge, *Ole Bull,* 106.

Ole Bull with the Order of Vasa, which he received in 1838. Drawing by A. M. Andersen, 1838. Courtesy of Bergen University Library.

The four Christiania concerts were sold out, and tickets were even scalped. To be so recognized by his countrymen was the realization of Bull's fondest dreams. According to *Den Constitutionelle* he was greeted at the first concert by jubilant cries. The critic wrote:

There is no need of musical knowledge to admire Bull. His artistry is without doubt as remarkable as his genius, for the reason that he speaks a language all understand. . . . The multitude has no idea of how many struggles and defeats and victories, how many waking nights, how many broken ideals and destroyed hopes it costs before the genius is able to become the master of his own strength and prepare the wings for flight. . . . His violin told fairytales; one heard the Alpen horns answering the shepherds' calls from the Norwegian mountains. . . . Most touching seemed to me his "Adagio Cantabile" [from the *Concerto in A Major*]; there was a lament of pain and a haunting melancholy in it that gradually melted away in weeping as his violin sobbed aloud. Then all ended in deep, comforting tones amid scattered sobs.[16]

One of the listeners who was most deeply impressed by the mood of that first Christiania concert was the poet Johan Sebastian Welhaven, who like Bull was from Bergen. Immediately following the concert, Welhaven wrote a poem that opens with the line "Hvor sødt at favnes af Aftnens Fred" ("How sweet to be embraced by the peace of the evening").[17] Called "Til Ole Bull" ("To Ole Bull"), it has since become a classic of Norwegian poetry. The second and fifth stanzas of this poem are given below, with an English translation based in part on the version given in Sara Bull's *Ole Bull: A Memoir.*

Han stod og lytted en Sommerkvæld
og havde stemt sine Strenge,
da gik Akkorden fra Skov og Fjeld,
og over duggede Enge.
Og alle Strenge klang dertil
med underbare Toner,
som Droslens Kluk og Nøkkens Spil
og Suk af Birkekroner.

O, hil Dig salige Toneskald
med Guddomsmagt i din Bue,
fra Dig gaar Jubelens Fossefald,
Du tænder Andagtens Lue.
Naar Verden lytter til dit Kvad
og bæver ved din Vælde

16. Ca. 24 July 1838; cf. Linge, *Ole Bull,* 108–10.
17. J. S. C. Welhaven, *Samlede Digterverker* (Christiania and Copenhagen, 1907), 2: 85–86.

da skjælver Glemmigeiens Blad
af Fryd paa dine Fjelde.[18]

(One summer eve he listening stood,
    His strings all tuned together,
While music rang from field and wood
    Across the dewy heather.
Then all his strings the gift repay,
    With a wondrous echo ringing,
Of thrush's song and elfin's play
    And sigh of birch trees singing.

Oh blessed tone-bard, hail to thee!
    From heaven thy bow was given,
Floods of joy thou hast set free,
    What visions shown of heaven!
To sway the thousands is thy lot,
    Who listen to thy story,
While here each blue forgetmenot
    Would gladly sing thy glory.)

Bull headed from Christiania for Bergen, arriving on 11 August after
a six-day boat trip along the flag-bedecked ports of the south coast. Bergen spread the welcome carpet for him. A dinner was arranged in his honor
by Harmonien, the musical organization that had first awakened his interest in music.

On 19 August Bull's son was baptized, borne to the font by his grandmother Anna Dorothea Bull. He was named Ole Storm Felix after his parents. Ole for his father, Felix for Félicie, and Storm for his grandfather.

On that same evening the first Bergen concert was held, in the quarters
of the Dramatic Society, another of Bull's old haunts. The local paper,
Bergens Adressecontoirs Efterretninger, reported that "everyone was eager
to see the much admired man, who as a child wandered among us without
anyone's suspecting how famous he would one day become."[19] On the following evening, a "Citizens' Dinner" was held, with all of Bergen's prominent citizens present. As usual on Norwegian occasions, there were songs
and speeches, poems and toasts, to which Bull responded with a toast for
the town of his birth.

While in Bergen, Bull visited Valestrand briefly, but even if he had wished
to visit his childhood refuge longer, his parents had not kept the summer
home in good enough repair to permit any lengthy residence. On 26 Au-

18. Sara C. Bull, *Ole Bull: A Memoir* (Boston and New York, 1882), 381.
19. Linge, *Ole Bull,* 113.

gust he gave his farewell concert in Bergen and sailed back along the coast, giving concerts in smaller towns like Stavanger, Christiansand, Arendal, and Larvik. A listener at the concert in Arendal commented that "anyone who does not insist on showing a kind of originality by holding a differing opinion, must feel deeply touched by the melancholy, the attractive, soulful truthfulness, the heartfelt emotion, the youthful power and enthusiasm that breathes through his playing."[20]

Bull had a deep concern for the future of musical education in Norway. In Christiania he donated the proceeds of one concert to "A Basic Fund for the Musical Life of Norway." He agitated warmly for the creation of a music academy, similar to the one he had become a member of in Stockholm. He also considered writing a Norwegian national opera (no. 28) using Wergeland as the librettist.

On 28 October he gave his farewell concert in Christiania. We have a report on it in a letter from Camilla Wergeland (later Collett) to her brother Oscar: "He was ill this evening, giving him a suffering expression, which made his emotion appear even more clearly. In truth he looked transfigured. He did not need to play. In his whole bearing, his gestures and his eyes, there are wonderful melodies. When we came home, my friend Emily and I were going to write reviews of the concert. Mine was very short: 'If I were not Camilla Wergeland, I would like to be Mme. Bull!'" She did not think Bull had been as well received in Norway as he deserved. "We are a singularly hard people. It takes more than sunshine and the mild rains of May to penetrate our icy crust."[21]

Her brother Henrik had already written a farewell poem entitled "Norges Farvel til Ole Bull" ("Norway's Farewell to Ole Bull"). In it Mother Norway is speaking:

> Farvel, min stolte Søn, Farvel!
> Følg Kaldet i din dybe Sjæl.
> Jeg ligner nu en Mark som den
> der ligger her høstblegnet hen. . . .
> Til Dig, min Søn! min Søn som gav
> mig større Glands end Konnings Grav.
> O, vant til Sønners Verdensry
> mit Øie funkler op paany.
> Hvor arm jeg er, man dog Demant
> mer dyr end Glædesblik ei fandt.
> Ak, er der i den Glands ei Glød?
> Blir Dig for koldt i Moders Skjød?

20. Ibid., 115.
21. Ibid., 116–17.

Nei, flyv! udbred din Moders Navn!
Din Hæder trøster da mit Savn.[22]

(Farewell, proud son, farewell!
Follow the Call in inmost cell.
I now am like a field
That lies in autumn without yield.
To you, my son! My son who gave
More glory than of kings the grave.
Oh, accustomed to fame of men,
My eye will sparkle once again.
No matter if I'm poor, a diamond
Dearer than joy I never found.
Ah, does not glory have its glow?
Will mother's bosom be of snow?
No, fly! Extend thy mother's name!
Her comfort will be in thy fame.)

Wergeland and Welhaven were bitter opponents in the cultural life of Norway, and it is interesting that in honoring Ole Bull they could join hands. Their poems were quite different in perspective: Welhaven's was retrospective and elegiac; Wergeland's, forward-looking and inciting.

In October 1838 Bull left Norway for another continental tour. His first goal was nearby Copenhagen, where he had both relatives and friends, and a newly found fame. He won a dear friend and admirer there in Hans Christian Andersen (1805–75). Shortly after they met, Andersen wrote a long letter of friendship:

We have known each other only for some days, but there are characters who do not need a long time to become dear to one another. . . . Thank you for all the poetry that streamed out of your violin. If they could be reproduced in words, we would get a delightful cycle of poems! . . . Even before I met you, I felt a strange sympathy with your genius, and now that we have met face to face and have understood each other, this feeling has been elevated to friendship. It must please you to know that you have won over a soul. Therefore I tell you so, and I am not ashamed of it.[23]

Andersen was ready to crown Bull as fairy prince.

22. Ibid., 117–18.
23. Bull, ed., *Ole Bulls Breve i Uddrag*, 228–29 (4 December 1838).

8

Triumph and Trouble: Touring Europe (1838–1843)

ENMARK WAS an excellent base for what Bull expected would be a triumphal tour. The Danish newspapers were lavishly filled with articles about this new phenomenon of Nordic music. Bull was even presented at court, where King Frederick VI (1768–1839) presented him with a snuffbox set with diamonds. The king asked Bull who had taught him to play, no doubt expecting the name of some famous teacher. Instead, Bull answered: "The mountains of Norway, Your Majesty!" Apparently his answer did not move the king who, after Bull had left, commented: "He's a fool."[1] Actually, Bull's answer contained more than a small element of truth.

Bull gave five concerts in Copenhagen, beginning on 4 November 1838 and several more in provincial towns. He met the leading Danish personalities, such as sculptor Bertel Thorvaldsen (ca. 1770–1844) and poet Adam Oehlenschläger (1779–1850). Andersen put his finger on Bull's appeal to Danish audiences when he wrote Bull describing his own reaction: "I was egotistic enough . . . to imagine and dream that [your violin] was singing for me alone, that I alone heard you tell in fragments the story of your artistic life through your tones!"[2]

1. Christian A. Aarvig, Den unge Ole Bull: En Violinspillers Ungdomskampe (Copenhagen, 1934), 7. According to another version, Bull's answer was much more elaborate, no doubt boring the king; see H. E. Nørregaard-Nielsen, ed., Kongens København (Copenhagen, 1985), 81.
2. Alexander Bull, ed., Ole Bulls Breve i Uddrag. Med en karakteristik og biografisk Skitse af Jonas Lie (Copenhagen, 1881), 228 (4 December 1838); Aarvig, Den unge Ole Bull, 73.

After his last Danish concert, the *Copenhagen Post* commented that Copenhagen audiences were not easy to move. "But in this case they had to yield. Through the whole performance there ran a quality of genius that gave the purest and highest enjoyment of art. There was a moving witchery in the soulful performance of the cantabile passages in the first *Concerto in A Major* and a sobbing pain in several parts of the *Polacca*."[3]

One critic, however, took a negative view of Bull's playing. This was a Swedish pianist and editor of the Swedish journal *For Theater and Music* named Joh. Magnus Rosén (1806–85), whose composition Bull had rejected for performance. Apparently in revenge, Rosén published in Denmark a brochure entitled "Another Judgment of Ole Bull's Value as an Artist." The burden of this attack was that "Bull was dragging the art of music down into the abyss."[4] He condemned both his execution and his compositions, thus establishing a criticism that would plague Bull throughout his European career. Rosén doubted that Bull could play compositions by Spohr, Viotti, or Baillot. In short, he was espousing the principles of the German school against the Italian tradition whose forms Bull had adopted (see chap. 19). Rosén may have sent a copy of this critique to Gottfried Wilhelm Fink, who was soon to write an even sharper criticism of Bull.

After settling his family with relatives in Copenhagen, Bull went on to Germany. He gave three concerts in Hamburg, before proceeding to Cassel, Germany, at Louis Spohr's invitation. This was the same Spohr who had rejected Bull when he sought him out as a nineteen-year-old unknown. Now Spohr wrote that Bull's coming would "awaken great joy among lovers of music." He arranged two concerts and a musical evening in his home at which they played quartets together. One was by Spohr, himself playing first violin, and two by Mozart, in which he yielded first violin to Bull. In a letter to his friend Wilhelm Speyer (1790–1878), Spohr reported that Bull had "enchanted" his audience. "His full-bodied playing and the sureness of his left hand are admirable. But like Paganini he sacrifices too much of the noble instrument to his artifices. His tone in the lower strings is poor; he can use the A and D strings only in the lower range and pianissimo. This gives his playing, when he cannot show off his bravura skills, a great monotony. We experienced this in the two Mozart quartets that he played at my house. Otherwise he plays with great feeling, though not with a cultivated taste."[5]

3. Ola Linge, *Ole Bull: Livshistoria, Mannen, Kunstnaren* (Oslo, 1953), 119 (15 November 1838).
4. J. M. Rosén, *Ogsaa et omdømme om Ole Bulls kunstnerværd* (Copenhagen, 1838), 4.
5. Louis Spohr, *Selbstbiographie* (Cassel and Göttingen, 1861), 2:228.

This somewhat reserved judgment by the German master of the violin was expressed privately. But in Berlin, where Bull arrived at the beginning of February 1839 to give three concerts, he was faced with a more stringent critique. It was written by Gottfried Wilhelm Fink, a music critic of the prestigious Leipzig journal *Leipziger Allgemeine Musikalische Zeitung* (often abbreviated *LAMZ*) and also a teacher at the Leipzig Conservatory (from 1838 to 1843). Fink heard Bull in his second Berlin concert, on 18 February 1839.

In his long, detailed commentary Fink unleashed an attack from the point of view of the German school that would echo widely in the press. He provided ammunition calculated to encourage Bull's rivals, who by this time had begun to be oppressed by Bull's popular success. Wergeland reprinted Fink's critique in his 1843 biography of Bull, sarcastically commenting that "Fink had given it with as much respectable appearance of an old man's and a professor's impartiality as he could muster."[6]

The concert that Fink heard in February 1839 consisted entirely of Bull's own compositions: *Grieving Prayer and Laughing Rondo, Quartet for Violin Solo,* and *Polacca Guerriera.* His critique can be summed up as an attack on Bull's appeal to the public. He described some of Bull's more flamboyant "devices" that deferred to the popular taste. He granted that his playing was "pure" if somewhat thin, and that his harmonics were good, if somewhat overused. "He has skills," the German critic conceded, "but nothing compared with Paganini." Again comparing Bull to the Italian master, Fink argued: "He has obviously chosen Paganini as a model, but he equaled him only in externalities, not in essentials. In his compositions we found no masterpieces of genuine art. They are so strangely combined as suits the modern mode [i.e., the Italian style] that strives only for effects. . . . He knows his time and his people and does not hesitate to use that knowledge."[7] In the end Fink granted that Bull knew how to value true art, for he had proved this by playing without tricks in a private rehearsal before the public concert.

Whatever influence Fink's critique may have had among professional critics, it had no effect on Bull's audiences. If anything, his popularity was stimulated by the knowledge that he had a controversial reputation. That Fink's criticism pursued Bull is evident from a curious document written by one Töpfer on the back of a Bull utterance penned in Berlin on 17 Feb-

6. Henrik Wergeland, "Ole Bull: Efter opgivelser af ham selv biografisk skildret," in D. A. Seip, ed., *Samlede Skrifter,* 4.5:215–18.

7. G. W. Fink, ed., *Leipziger Allgemeine Musikalische Zeitung* 41.12 (March 1839): 237–38.

ruary 1839. Bull wrote out his favorite motto: "Vita bellum, bellum vita" ("Life is war, war is life"). To this he added: "Only through struggle (Kampf) can victory be won; without victory life is nothing, only death is peace. This as a sign of my special respect and devotion." This statement is signed "Ole B. Bull," with the postscript: "Written in fever after the *Polacca.*" On the reverse, Töpfer has written to an unnamed friend living in Potsdam: "I am sending you this souvenir given me by Ole Bull. From this you will be convinced that this great artist is an equally great arrogant and conceited charlatan, the judgment that Rellstab has passed on Bull in today's *Vossische Zeitung:* 'a most remarkable person, full of blustering and oddities, at the same time very smart and clever who knows how to win people.'"[8]

Bull also had friends in Berlin, including the writer Bettina von Arnim (1785–1859), sister of Clemens Brentano, who kept a salon for promising young men. Two letters from Bull to her, probably written in 1839, reflect their friendship. In the first he addressed her formally: "I write to you [*Sie*] from a sorrowful heart, dearest Bettina. My warmest thanks for all that you have done for me." He goes on to ask for her continued friendship. In the second he addressed her informally (*du*), declaring that he has been ill in body and soul. "Ah, you magnificent soul, how could you do what you have done except out of love for mankind, to trouble yourself with anyone as unimportant as me. Yet I feel that I am worthy of you, and I hope to keep your sympathy forever."[9]

When his concerts were completed in Berlin, Bull went on to Breslau, Germany, where he gave five concerts. Here he received a letter from Félicie, who was still in Copenhagen, saying that, after some weeks of illness, their son Ole Felix had died in February. Bull was devastated and wrote her that his sorrows seemed incessant. "I still hope," he wrote, "not for me. No, for you, for mother and family, for my fatherland, my Norway, of whose name I am proud."[10] Félicie met Bull in Vienna and joined him for a time in his travels. In Munich, Bull learned that his grandmother had died. She had been his constant support in earlier days, and her death brought him fresh grief. In the private letters he wrote at this time, his distress is again expressed in the complaints of the hypochondriac, a persona so different from his public image.

8. Berlin, 20 March 1839; in Library of Congress Music Collection, Washington, D.C.
9. Undated, addressed to "21 Unter den Linden"; in Freies Deutsches Hochstift, Frankfurter Goethe-Museum. Bull met her again in 1858. He stayed with her for two days and celebrated her birthday. She died the following year. Cf. Bull, ed., *Ole Bulls Breve i Uddrag,* 390 (2 May 1858).
10. Bull, ed. *Ole Bulls Breve i Uddrag,* 231 (21 April 1839).

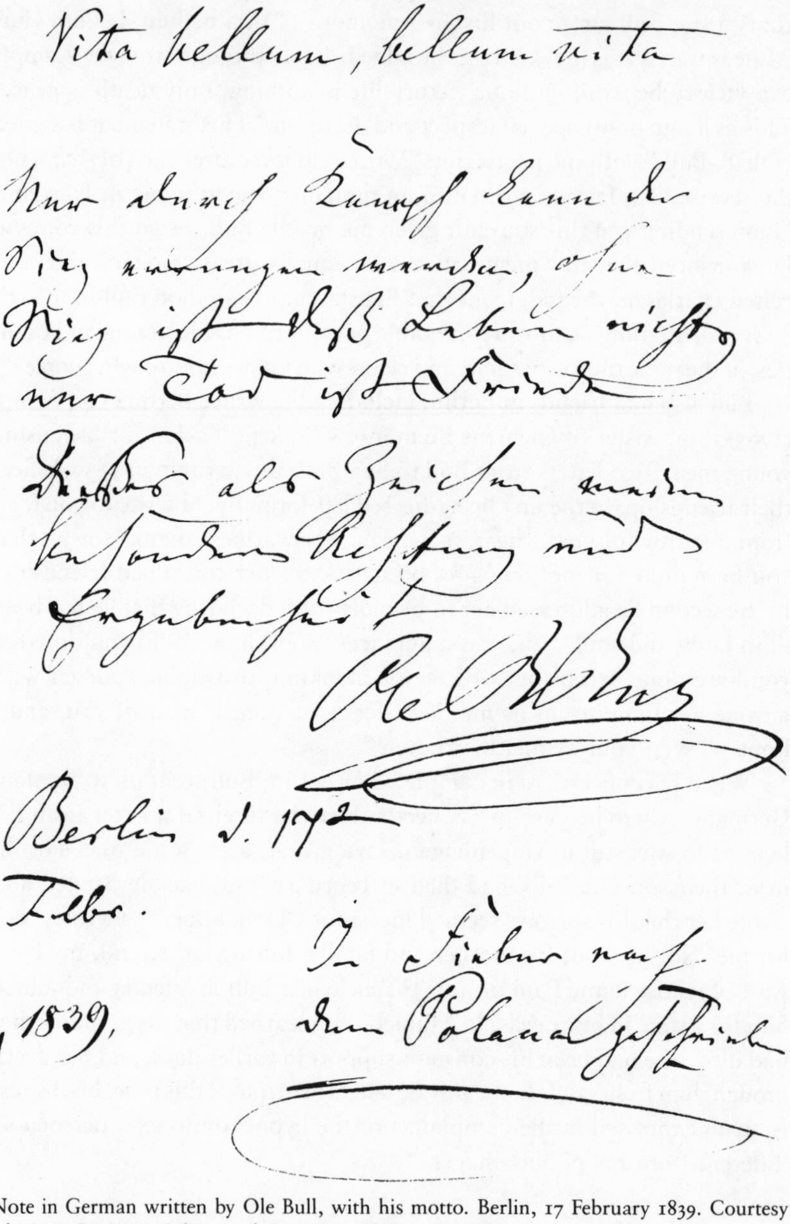

Vita bellum, bellum vita

Nur durch Kampf kann der
Sieg errungen werden, ohne
Sieg ist das Leben nicht
nur Tod ist Friede

dieses als Zeichen meiner
besondern Achtung und
Ergebenheit

Ole Bull

Berlin d. 17t
Febr.
1839.

In Eile nach
dem Polonaise geschrieben

Note in German written by Ole Bull, with his motto. Berlin, 17 February 1839. Courtesy of Music Division, Library of Congress, Washington, D.C.

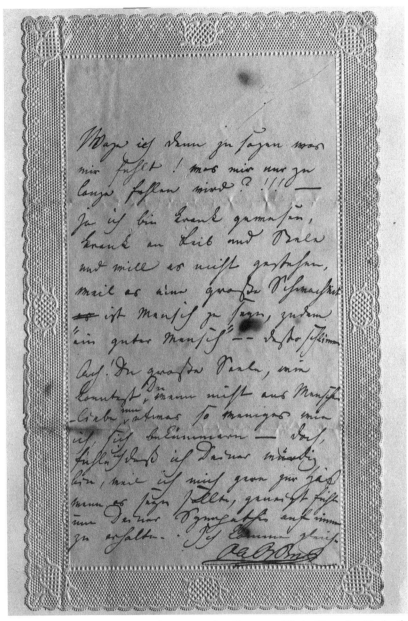

A letter from Bull to Bettina von Arnim, ca. 1839. Courtesy of Freies Deutsches Hochstift, Frankfurter Goethe-Museum.

Ole Bull, 1839. Lithograph by Krehuber, Vienna. Courtesy of Bergen University Library.

Later in Vienna on 2 March 1839, a member of Bull's audience was the famous composer, Robert Schumann. Schumann wrote in a letter to his beloved Clara Wieck (1819–96), later his wife:

Ole Bull gave another brilliant concert. He belongs to the very best and yet he is still a learner. . . . In the most colossal skill and purity he is the equal of Paganini and far above Lipiński. Mayseder is a child beside him, and yet a more perfect human being; Mayseder has understood and resolved his life task. Ole Bull is not yet at his goal and I fear may never get there. His gifts for composition are still quite primitive, but there are some flashing sparks in it. With his many harmonics he would, however, make his way into your heart, of that I am sure.[11]

While in Vienna, Bull was asked to assist at a concert in Salzburg on behalf of a Mozart fund. Constanze, Mozart's widow, was present, and knowing how highly Bull prized the composer, she gave him part of a manuscript written by Mozart. Bull treasured this and later hung it on his wall.

Félicie was beginning to find the travels burdensome, so Bull accompanied her to Paris and then returned to more concerts in the Rhine basin. She spent the summer of 1839 in Paris and in November 1839 sent a joyous letter to Bull informing him of the birth of their second son, one who would be named Alexander Ole Felix Étienne Bull (1839–1914), Alexander for short. "He is your spitting image," she wrote.[12] Bull was so overwhelmed that he went for a walk in the open air before his concert that evening. He wrote thanking her for sending him a lock of the boy's hair and solicitously urged her to take good care of herself. His concert schedule continued in southern Germany until Christmas, when he returned to Paris.

From Frankfurt Bull had written Félicie a long letter, expressing weariness with his work.

Oh, if you only knew, Félicie, how it wearies me to belong to the world, and only for a few moments to myself, you would understand my distaste for it. . . . I have to pull myself together if I am not to seem like a bear (and even then some find me bizarre and strange). In addition I feel the emptiness doubly. I see that all these annoyances are making me bitter and perhaps ungrateful towards fate, but is anything else possible?—Courage, courage! I shout to myself every moment of the day. My head is full of plans. There are so many people around me who fill my ears all at once that I don't know who I should listen to.

Bull listed some of the many people he had to listen to and deal with. He also felt, perhaps with justice, that he was constantly being cheated. His only recourse, a somewhat odd solution, was to drink water and bathe

---

11. Robert Schumann, *Jugendbriefe*, 2d ed. (Leipzig, 1886), 300.
12. Bull, ed., *Ole Bulls Breve i Uddrag,* 235 (5 November 1839).

in cold water every morning and evening. He also urged Félicie and the boy to use plenty of cold water. He ended by saying that he would try to remain in Paris for the winter "if you wish it."[13]

He did spend three winter months in Paris. In December he had bought an Amati violin that pleased him. "It has a ringing tone that makes your spine tingle."[14] During the winter he worked on compositions and gave an occasional concert. That he was still highly reputed in Paris is evident from an article in the Parisian review *Vert-Vert,* which described Bull's "supernatural talent. . . . No one has ever equaled his staccato and never will. His grace, his feeling, his vigor, and rapidity are beyond all expression. His harmonics are like the dying notes of an Aeolian harp."[15] Financially, however, the winter was disastrous, as he complained in later letters.

In March 1840 Bull left Paris for London. After arriving he reported that he had felt a touch of fever and consulted a physician. As usual, his first reaction was alarm: "It is to be despaired about. If I had been alone, I would already have ended my life." But the doctor found that "he had never examined anyone with such muscular strength," and he observed "that I must have an extraordinary sensibility."[16]

The second English tour was to prove no more profitable than the winter in Paris had been. Bull had legal difficulties with an agent named Morandi. He wrote to Félicie: "I am persecuted on every side. That is the fruit of my trip to Paris this winter! What an enormous financial loss for me! And now instead of beginning the labors at Valestrand and arranging my family affairs, I find myself compelled to stay here and risk losing even more."[17] His annoyance at poor concerts in Paris and London, and his experiences with agents in these places, led to some harsh words in his correspondence with Félicie. They were, however, hardly more than the natural differences in expectations one might find in a marriage between two people who lived such different lives. On 15 May 1840 Bull wrote her from London:

Your last letter has given me a moment of ecstasy, but also of sadness at not having you nearby to tell you how much I love you and how proud I am of belonging to you. In my life as an artist you have been my ideal, to whom I have directed my complaints, communicated my joys, babbled loving words. I have, so to speak, probed into your soul in order to become one with you. I have uttered reproaches

13. Ibid., 240–41 (1 December 1839).
14. Ibid., 242 (7 December 1839).
15. "Ole Bull," *Vert-Vert, Revue du Monde Parisien* 8.39 (8 February 1840): 1.
16. Bull, ed., *Ole Bulls Breve i Uddrag,* 257 (30 April 1840) and 259 (5 May 1840).
17. Ibid., 248 (28 March 1840).

Ole Bull, ca. 1840. The earliest photograph. Courtesy of Knut Hendriksen.

as to no one beside my own self, thereby I have honored you above all other fellow beings. . . . In reality we are two hotheads—such as only the most exalted and devoted love can create.[18]

Bull's most interesting encounter in London was with pianist and composer Franz Liszt, "with whom I have in a few days formed a quite extraordinary friendship. . . . We have played together and have both been inspired with admiration and friendship for one another."[19] At a London Philharmonic concert on 8 June 1840, he and Liszt played Beethoven's *Kreutzer Sonata* (Opus 47) together. On 22 June Bull played his own composition, titled *Norwegian's Lament for Home.*[20] Neither he nor Liszt were satisfied with their experiences in London and mutually concluded Germany would be more promising. There they pursued their separate careers. In Darmstadt Bull began his *Concerto in E Minor* (no. 29).

After three months of concertizing in the cities of the Rhine basin, Bull was invited to Berlin, where he gave three concerts in October and November of 1840. On 11 November he gave a special concert of quartets assisted by the best soloists of the opera orchestra. The program was: *Quartet in D Minor* by Mozart, *Quartet in F Major* by Beethoven, and *Quartet in G Major* by Mozart.[21]

The critic reviewing the Berlin concerts and writing in *Die Vossische Zeitung* praised "many elegant, tender, and really beautiful passages," but was displeased with Bull's quartet playing, because "quartet music is so genuinely German that for foreigners it is a strange domain." But in the Dresden *Abendzeitung* the critic reviewed the same concerts with lavish praise: "Ole Bull is great, not only in his own compositions, but also in those of others. Thus we heard him in a violin concerto by Spohr executed so that the severest critics had to marvel." As for Bull's compositions: "All these tone poems were singularly beautiful, with piquant coloring."

After a concert in Leipzig on 20 November Robert Schumann wrote in *Brockhaus'sche Deutsche Zeitung:* "All difficulties are for him just like a game. But he also knows the art of touching the deepest heart strings. Thus [it was] in an *Adagio* of Mozart, which he played quite well and simply, with genuine German feeling."[22]

18. Ibid., 262–63 (15 May 1840).
19. Linge, *Ole Bull,* 128–29.
20. According to Wergeland, "Ole Bull," 220, this composition is the same as *The Mountains of Norway* (no. 7).
21. No further identifying information is given. Linge, *Ole Bull,* 130.
22. Probably an arrangement (no. 30) of the second movement from Mozart's *Clarinet Quintet in A Major* K. 581.

Bull's Gasparo da Salò violin, with angel's head. Courtesy of Bergen University Library.

A memorable event for Bull was his acquisition that winter of a new violin, one made by Gasparo (Bertolotti) da Salò (ca. 1540–1609), one of the earliest Italian violin makers. It was willed to Bull by a wealthy Czech named Rhaczcek, a collector who had been a great admirer of Bull's. Instead of the usual snail-shape, the scroll of this violin was carved into an angel's head with a mermaid beneath. It was said to have been made for an Italian nobleman, Cardinal Pietro Aldobrandini (1571–1621).[23]

23. Both Mucchi and Lütgendorff believe this violin is not a Gasparo da Salò, but a more recent instrument instead; Antonio Maria Mucchi, "L'Ole Bull," in *Gasparo da Salo: La vita e l'opera 1540–1609* (Milan, 1940), 185–93; Willibald Leo, Freiherr von Lütgendorff, *Die Geigen- und Lautenmacher vom Mittelalter bis zur Gegenwart,* 6th ed. (1922; reprint, Nendeln, Liechtenstein, 1968), 2:44.

The musicians of Leipzig, composer Felix Mendelssohn, and Ferdinand David, concertmaster of the Gewandhaus Orchestra, decided to celebrate Bull's receipt of the new violin with a special concert at the Gewandhaus on 20 January 1841. Here Bull, with them and others, played a *Quartet in F Major* from Opus 18 by Beethoven, the *Kreutzer Sonata* by Beethoven, the *Quintet in G Minor* (K. 516) by Mozart, as well as his own improvisation (no. 31) on three tunes: "Serenata" from Rossini's *Il Barbiere di Siviglia,* Act I, "Polonaise" from Bellini's *I Puritani,* and the "Champagne Song" from Mozart's *Don Giovanni,* Act I. It must have been a memorable occasion.

In February 1841 Bull was in Prague, where he played more than twelve concerts in one month. He had great success with an improvisation on a Czech folk song "Sil jsem proso na souvrati" (no. 32).[24] He composed a new piece, *Grüss aus der Ferne* (*Greetings from Afar*) or *Largo Posato e Rondo Capriccioso* (no. 33), and he completed the *Concerto in E Minor* (no. 29), now also called *Erinnerungen aus Prag,* but which was begun in Darmstadt in 1840. This piece was played for the first time at a benefit concert for musicians' families.

From Prague Bull headed once more for Russia, this time via Poland. He hired a pianist named Franz Ulm to accompany him. On 21 March he played in Warsaw for the Russian governor of Poland and on 24 March in a concert at the "Grand Theatre." The *Gazetta Warszawska* wrote that. "calling Bull a unique virtuoso is too little. He is far more, he is a great artist."[25] At the end of the concert, he was recalled seven times.

The Poles overwhelmed Bull with invitations while the Russian authorities took five days to issue his passport to Russia. Bull and Ulm, traveling in the same carriage that Bull had used on his first tour to Russia, made their way through Vilna in Poland to St. Petersburg. On the way, wrote Bull, "my wagon, which is very strong, broke three times. The mud went over the wheels and it took eight horses to extricate it."[26] This was in April, in the midst of melting snows.

He was able to give only one concert in St. Petersburg and was unable to proceed to Moscow because of the weather. He was also ill for some days. He wrote to Félicie: "I am longing so much to get to Norway with you and little Nini [Alexander] and embrace my mother, our family, all our friends, and live in peace and at rest in the bosom of nature. I am ill,

24. Jan Trojan, "Das Brünner Konzertleben in der Zeit der Nationalen Wiedergeburt," *Sborník prací filosofické fakulty brněnské university* 8 (1973): 172.

25. Linge, *Ole Bull,* 133.

26. Bull, ed., *Ole Bulls Breve i Uddrag,* 290 (26 April 1841).

H e u t e
Mittwoch den 20. Januar 1841
Musikalische ·Abendunterhaltung
von
Ole Bull,
im Saale des Gewandhauses.

Erster Theil.

1) Quartett von Beethoven (F - dur, Op. 18), vorgetragen von den Herren Concertmeister *David, May, Wittmann* und *Ole Bull.*

2) Grosse Sonate von Beethoven (A - dur. Kreutzern gewidmet), vorgetragen von Herrn Musikdirector *Felix Mendelssohn - Bartholdy* und *Ole Bull.*

Zweiter Theil.

1) Quintett von Mozart (G - moll), vorgetragen von den Herren Concertmeister *David. May. Inten, Wittmann* und *Ole Bull*

2) **Improvisation** über aufzugebende Motive, vorgetragen von *Ole Bull.*

Herr **Ole Bull** *wird die obengenannten Piëcen auf der vor kurzem erhaltenen berühmten Schatzkammer-Geige (verfertigt von* **Gasparo da Salo** *im 16ten Jahrhundert) vortragen.*

Billets à 20 Ngr. (16 gGr.) sind in den Musikhand-'lungen der Herren **Kistner** und **Hofmeister** und an der Kasse à 1 Thlr. zu haben.

Anfang 6 Uhr. [248]

Concert program, 20 January 1841, Gewandhaus (Leipzig).

I have a fever, a fever that burns and consumes me."[27] To his mother he wrote: "I need quiet after such great exertions. Since we saw each other I have given several hundred concerts and endured cold and heat and sleeplessness. . . ."[28]

On 29 May 1841, Bull left for Copenhagen by steamer and then traveled on to Dresden where he had left Félicie and Alexander since December of 1840. Returning to Copenhagen, the family had a stormy passage to Bergen and arrived at Valestrand in June. They stayed at the family home until November, giving the family its first real vacation in many years. Ole and Félicie's third son, Thorvald Bull (1841–62), was born on 17 August.

In the manner of a true seigneur Bull had ordered abundant supplies from the house of Mumm: three hundred bottles of champagne; fifty bottles of Hochheimer, vintage 1834; fifty bottles of Bordeaux; one cask of common Bordeaux table wine; one cask of Rhine wine; twenty-five bottles of the best Rhine wine; plus various other wines to an amount of 2,800 francs, delivered in Bergen for 3,000 francs, "which is very cheap," as he wrote to his wife. He also ordered fifty live gold and silver pheasants. Félicie did not agree that 3,000 francs was a bargain.[29]

In December 1841, Bull left Félicie and the children in Bergen, where she was anything but happy. She wrote to Bull: "The weather is horrible. It is the worst climate I have ever seen. It is so sad here, the loneliness is frightful, but I must live for my children, who some day will love me, I hope."[30] Bull, on the other hand, was headed for an enthusiastic welcome in Christiania. His tour opened with five concerts in the capital, followed by endless encores. Variations on selected Norwegian folk melodies (nos. 34 and 35) were on his program. *Den Constitutionelle* reported: "He was called forth five times in one evening. Such a thing has never happened to any artist in our theater. Several bouquets were thrown on the stage as Ole Bull left it."[31] On 10 January 1842 a dinner was arranged for him in the Masonic Temple (Logen) in Christiania. Songs and poems were sung in his honor. After Bull had left Christiania, Andreas Munch wrote: "He is no longer playing here and I think that is for the best. He has confounded our heads and emptied our purses. His playing exerts a magic that over-

27. Linge, *Ole Bull,* 133.
28. Ole Bull, *Min kjære Moder. En kjærlighets erklæring,* ed. Ladislav Reznicek (Bergen, 1980), 26 (12 May 1841).
29. Bull, ed., *Ole Bulls Breve i Uddrag,* 283 (12 February 1841).
30. Ibid., 297 (29 December 1841).
31. Linge, *Ole Bull,* 135

whelms our intelligence and throws all misgivings overboard. It is impermissible to play so beautifully."[32]

At this time a harpist named Edvard Pratté (1799–1875), born in Bohemia and raised in Sweden, was attempting to make a career in Christiania. As a fellow musician, he expected free tickets to Bull's concerts, and when none were forthcoming, he wrote a pamphlet attacking Bull, entitled "Upartisk Dom . . ." ("Impartial Judgment . . .").[33] The newspapers refused to reprint it because they considered it scandalous. Instead they printed a critical article by the Norwegian composer Halfdan Kjerulf (1815–68) to show that they did not wish to regard Bull as an "untouchable person." Kjerulf's article had no criticism of Bull as a performer, but gave mixed grades to his compositions.

The attack by Pratté (which he retracted in July 1843) had at least the useful result of producing a Norwegian evaluation of Bull's compositions by Kjerulf. Even more important: it led to Henrik Wergeland's decision to write his 1843 biographical sketch in defense of Bull. Pratté's article is the subject of a special study by Eric Danell, in which Danell explains its background. The attack was based (as were Rosén's and Fink's) on the principles of the German school. The German school, asserting itself against the successes of Italian opera and virtuoso performers in Germany, focused on form and structure (a purity in music) as the most important elements of music (see chaps. 19–20). Pratté had a special aversion to Paris and the French-Italian styles. He aroused Bull's anger by involving Wergeland in what Bull saw as a petty dispute.[34]

In early 1842 Bull engaged Adolph Rosenkilde (1816–82), a Danish actor at the Christiania Theater, as his secretary. In the same old carriage, they made an excursion via Lund in Sweden to Hamburg and on to the Netherlands. Here he gave concerts for the first time in Amsterdam and The Hague, with the court present. At the end of June he returned to Norway and spent a month with Félicie and the children at Valestrand before moving the family to a home in Christiania. *Nocturne,* also called *Til Hende* (*To Her*) (no. 36), and *Villspel i Lio* (*Wild Playing in the Hills*) (no. 37) were performed for the first time after their move to Christiania.

In early 1843 Bull with his family made an excursion into Sweden, giv-

32. Ibid.
33. Anton Edvard Pratté, *Upartisk dom over Violinspilleren Hr. Ole Bulls i Christiania den 10de December givne koncert* (Christiania, 1843).
34. Eric Danell, *Ole Bull och Pratté: Några kritiska randanmärkningar* (Stockholm, 1954), 48.

ing concerts in various towns until he arrived in Uppsala on 18 January. Here he had an unpleasant verbal exchange around midnight with some overly merry students. Bull was offended by their pranks and drove on to Stockholm, instead of giving a scheduled concert in Uppsala. The Uppsala episode was commented on in the Swedish press in a way that required Bull to defend his conduct. He wrote: "It was not anger over the insult endured nor ill will for Uppsala that caused me to leave a city that I wish and expect to see again in more favorable circumstances. For no one recognizes more vividly than I that it is the goal of art to unite, not to sunder."[35] While in Stockholm, he was asked to play at the Royal Palace.

Very shortly after Bull's encounter with the students, Professor Erik Geijer (1783–1847), a leading Swedish historian and poet, invited Bull back to Uppsala as his personal guest, and so Bull returned. One of Geijer's other guests was a Swedish writer, Lotte Dahlgren, who has left a vivid picture of Bull's evening in Geijer's home. Bull, she writes, is a "superb figure, with something of the simplicity and purity of genius over his whole person that give an especially pleasant effect. . . . It was amusing to hear and see him as he spoke, and he spoke much and with unusual liveliness." According to Dahlgren, Bull gave a poetic description of the beauties of Norwegian nature: "There was a life and a force in his presentation that I have never seen equaled. . . . Bull was also quite humorous and told anecdotes. The evening flew as if it had wings." After Bull's concerts, Dahlgren reports, he was followed to his lodgings by the whole audience, more than a thousand persons, singing and shouting "Hurrah!"[36] Bull honored the Swedes with an improvised set of variations on their tune "Liten Karin" ("Little Karin") (no. 38).

From Uppsala Bull headed for Copenhagen, stopping enroute to give a concert in Jönköping, where he met his former teacher Lundholm. In Copenhagen he was greeted by students at a banquet in his honor. The king attended the concert and presented Bull with a ring set with diamonds. Violinist Ernst, Bull's friend from the early days in Paris, and pianist Döhler, with whom he had played in Italy, were both at Bull's hotel. The sister of Bull's secretary, Rosenkilde, recorded an amusing episode that occurred during this visit. It was Döhler's birthday, and in the morning while the pianist was still in bed, Bull entered Döhler's room with Ernst on his shoulders. "Ernst held Bull's violin and used the bow while Bull reached up to finger the strings. Then they gave the honoree twelve gloves for the right

35. Linge, *Ole Bull*, 140; *Svenska Aftonbladet* (28 January 1843).
36. Linge, *Ole Bull*, 141.

hand, in allusion to the fact that Döhler specialized in playing difficult compositions entirely with his left hand."[37]

During these days Ole was anxious about Félicie, who was now living with the children in Paris and about to bear their fourth child. He wrote: "I am in a fever, and if you wish it, I will leave everything to come to you." When he learned in May that Eleonore Genevieve Félicie (1843–1923) had arrived, he wrote: "It is so strange to have a daughter that I can hardly get over it. I think about it all day."[38]

In the same letter Bull told Félicie that he was planning his first tour to America. "I am preparing by writing letters and advertising, for without that and great endurance, courage, and strength, it is impossible to make one's way there, even with the greatest of talent."[39] As might be expected, his wife did not receive the news with equanimity: "I have never been so sad and unhappy as I am now, and I see the future in the darkest light! You are leaving for America and are happy, for you know that you will be taken care of, flattered and feted everywhere, but you do not think of the fact that we may never see each other again."[40]

At a May concert in Bremen, Bull played his *Siciliano e Tarantella* (no. 39), one of his finer compositions, depicting an Italian scene of idyllic folk life. Then he made a quick excursion to Trondheim in Norway. On the way he climbed to the top of Snøhetta, a mountain in the Dovre range then thought to be the highest in Norway. In a typically dramatic and romantic gesture, intended as a farewell to Norway, Bull made his way up the mountain through rain, sleet, and snow with his violin and played from its summit.

Bull visited Félicie in September and decided to start for America in October after farewell concerts in Bergen and Christiania. For the first time, he decided to have some of his compositions printed so that people would have something to remember him by. Julius Schuberth and Co. of Leipzig, Hamburg, and New York published his *Adagio Religioso* or *A Mother's Prayer* (as Opus 1), which Bull dedicated to Félicie, *Nocturne* (as Opus 2), and the *Bravura Variations* (as Opus 3), which he dedicated to King Carl Johan Bernadotte of Norway and Sweden, the "King and benefactor of my native land, Norway."

His last communication in Europe was a letter he wrote to Félicie from Liverpool immediately before departure. He told her that his last concert

37. Ibid., 144.
38. Ibid.
39. Bull, ed., *Ole Bulls Breve i Uddrag*, 314 (19 May 1843).
40. Ibid., 320 (7 August 1843).

in Hamburg had been successful. Even so, he was still upset by certain critics and wrote her that "the newspapers are constantly screaming about charlatanism and wish to prove that my *Tarantella* is no good because castanets are used in the accompaniment. Oh, what philosophers! But it does not matter; they come and they pay."[41]

During the five years before he left for his first tour of America, Bull had given an improbable number of concerts in many different countries, from Dublin to Moscow. He had no doubt overworked himself and neglected the aspects of his profession, such as composing, which would have made his reputation endure. His critics made the most of it, often dismissing him as a mere imitator of Paganini. His main reason for leaving Europe at this time was certainly financial, to derive whatever benefit the new nation in the West could give him. His letters to Félicie during his European tours reflect a constant nagging fear of financial collapse, largely caused by his own lavish life-style and his generosity.[42]

But Bull also chose to go to America because, in spite of his melodramatic complaints and his seemingly frequent bouts of poor health, he was a restless spirit, who found pleasure in travel, in meeting new people, and in experiencing the delights of a virtuoso's life. He had qualities that would help him adapt well in the New World: he was a born entrepreneur and a great showman. The Danish critic Aarvig put it this way: "Bull was a 'selfmade man' of art. Therefore one understands the ease with which he could win the musical public of the New World. . . . Among this people Bull felt at home and here he found his second homeland." Ole Bull, Aarvig wrote, "was a man after the heart of the Americans: self-reliant, courageous, and unafraid."[43]

His old friend Henrik Wergeland, who had followed Bull's career with admiration and reverence, felt moved to write a farewell poem to cheer Bull on his way. He printed "Norge til Amerika ved Ole Bulls Didreise" ("Norway to America on Ole Bull's Departure") as the conclusion of his Bull biography. The poem, spoken by Mother Norway, tied together Bull's reputation in Europe and his anticipated experiences in America. We here include two of its five stanzas. The omitted stanzas express Wergeland's concern about American slavery, which he suggests might be charmed away by Bull's bow, an obviously unrealistic hope. The bitter and bloody American Civil War was to begin in only a few short years.

41. Ibid., 321 (4 November 1843).
42. See, e.g., his complaints about expenses in England (Bull, ed., *Ole Bulls Breve i Uddrag,* 197 [14 December 1836]), Courtrai, Belgium (ibid., 209 [18 December 1837]), and France (ibid., 238 [25 November 1839]).
43. Aarvig, *Den unge Ole Bull,* 106–107, 92.

O, Amerika, betro'd
har jeg dig med ængstlig Ahnen
Ham, min Fattigdoms Klenod,
Ham, mit Hjertes bedste Blod!
—Lad Platanen
kjærligt ham imødebruse,
Alleghannen
ham i venlig Grotte huse,
Susquehannen
som en dæmpet Harpe suse
Ham, min Elskling, ham imod!

Thi hist vest, hvor du vil fly,
er min egen Friheds Kjerne
voxet i Plataners Ly
baaret hid paa svanger Sky.
Derfor gjerne
vilde jeg taknemlig sende
til dens fjerne
Fosterland ved Havets Ende
herlig Stjerne,
og af dem, som hjemme brænde,
straaler ingen med dit Ry.[44]

(Oh, America, to you I have entrusted
With anxious misgivings
Him, the jewel of my poverty,
Him, my heart's best blood!
—Let the sycamore
Whisper lovingly towards him,
Let the Allegheny
House him in its friendly caverns.
Let the Susquehanna
Like a gentle harp resound
To greet him, my beloved!

For in the West, where you would fly,
There the kernel of my own freedom
Grew in shelter of sycamores,
Born hither on a teeming cloud.
Therefore gladly
And gratefully I'd send
To its distant
Fosterland at ocean's end
A glorious star,
And of those that burn at home,
None shines with greater fame.)

44. Wergeland, "Ole Bull," 232–33.

9

American Adventure
(1843–1845)

W HY DID Ole Bull decide to leave Europe and try his luck in
America? Certainly not to join other Norwegian emigrants,
of whom there were still very few. While a shipload of Norwegians had arrived on American shores in 1825, Norwegian settlement
did not begin until the 1830s and 1840s. Most of the first settlers headed
for Illinois and Wisconsin and were still struggling there for a foothold.
The eastern and southern states had by this time long been established,
and they had astounded the western European world by their unprecedented
expansion. However, beyond the Alleghenies the United States was still
quite primitive when Ole Bull first ventured to bring his violin there.

In 1843 America was the great challenge for any European with an adventurous spirit. The criticisms of Fink and others may have discouraged
Bull, and he may have felt that he had pretty well exhausted the European
market for musical entertainment. In America there was a potential new
audience that perhaps thirsted for his musicianship. It was worth a try.
He did not have the skills of the usual Norwegian landseekers, but he had
a desire for adventure comparable to that of early Norwegian pioneers,
such as Cleng Peerson (1782/3–1865), who guided the immigrants to Illinois in 1833, Ole Rynning (1809–36) whose handbook of immigration was
posthumously published in 1839, Ole Nattestad (1807–86) who led immigrants to Wisconsin in 1838, or Even Heg (d. 1850) who founded the Mus-
kego settlement in Wisconsin in 1840.[1] This boyish yearning for adventure
may have played a part in luring Bull to the wild New World, but above

---

1. Theodore C. Blegen, *Norwegian Migration to America 1825–1860* (Northfield, Minn.,
1931), 57–80.

all he saw it as an opportunity to build a fortune to sustain his growing family, a motivation he shared with most of the new landseekers.

Ole Bull was certainly the first Norwegian musician to visit America, but he was hardly the first musician. Alexandre Artôt (1815–45), a Belgian violinist, and Laure Damoreau (1801–63), a French singer, were already performing in New York when Ole Bull arrived there on the steamship *Caledonia* on 22 November 1843, well publicized by his manager Julius Schuberth as "the world's greatest violinist."[2] In December another Belgian, Henri Vieuxtemps (1820–81), a composer and violinist, arrived. All of these musicians perceived Bull as a potential rival and resented the claims being made for him by Schuberth. A French newspaper in New York, *Le Courrier des États Unis,* launched attacks on Bull, both as a person and as a musician. In letters to Félicie, Bull complained about the "plots" devised by the French "clique" in "efforts to reduce me in the opinion of Americans."[3]

The problem was compounded by the fact that Bull had quarreled with his impresario shortly after arriving in the United States and had dismissed him. Schuberth started a suit for breach of contract and took on Vieuxtemps as a client. The matter was not settled for a long time and caused Bull much grief. It was noised about in the newspapers and did in fact give Bull some more or less welcome publicity. When James Gordon Bennett (1785–1872), the editor of the New York *Herald,* urged Bull to defend himself publicly, he replied, "I think it is best that they write against me and that I play against them."[4]

In this decision Bull was right. His first concert was on 25 November, and it won the enthusiastic commentary of the *Herald*'s critic: "It was a tempest—a torrent—a very Niagara of applause, tumult, and approbation throughout the whole performance. The house was crammed from top to bottom. . . . We cannot describe Ole Bull's playing—it is beyond the power of language. . . . At the close of some of his wonderful cadences, the very musicians in the orchestra flung down their instruments and stamped and applauded like madmen."[5]

2. Vera Brodsky Lawrence, *Strong on Music: The New York Music Scene in the Days of George Templeton Strong, 1836–1875.* Vol. 1, *Resonances: 1836–1850* (New York and Oxford, 1988), 200.

3. See, e.g., Alexander Bull, ed., *Ole Bulls Breve i Uddrag. Med en karakteristik og biografisk Skitse af Jonas Lie* (Copenhagen, 1881), 323 (25 December 1843), 327 (24 January 1844), and 331 (14 May 1844).

4. Ola Linge, *Ole Bull: Livshistoria, Mannen, Kunstnaren* (Oslo, 1953), 149.

5. Lawrence, *Strong on Music,* 201–203. Linge, *Ole Bull,* 148, erroneously dates it to 20 November.

Ole Bull. Sketch by F. O. C. Darley, New York, 1843.

Following his third concert in New York, Bull was surprised by being serenaded by the orchestra outside the Astor House. "Thereupon he invited them in to supper, where champagne and wit reportedly flowed in equal torrents."[6]

On 11 December Bull graciously postponed his concert to 13 December in a notice wishing Vieuxtemps all success and "as warm a reception as he himself had enjoyed in America." This concession enabled the New York critic George Templeton Strong to get to both concerts. Strong wrote in his diary that Bull "is a most transcendent player, far superior to Vieuxtemps. His harmonics are admirable, and nothing can be purer and more beautiful than his very high notes; they've all the peculiar quality of the sound of the Aeolian harp. In fact, the instrument loses its character entirely in his hands—the violin is the last instrument one would expect to hear some of his tones from."[7]

Bull could report a great triumph to Félicie. Up to Christmas day 1843, having been in America only a month, he had given fifteen concerts in the cities of the East Coast, several in the same cities. He could report that he had earned a net forty thousand francs, which he had deposited with his banker in Amsterdam.[8] In mid-January 1844 he heard from his wife that she was expecting another child. This caused him to speculate about the future. "Therefore I do everything to earn money. It has cost me a great deal to travel 'en grand', as I do, but my dear, it is necessary." He hoped that he would earn a little fortune that "will permit us to live without cares, so that I can begin to study the theory of the violin."[9]

One writer who was captivated by Bull's playing when she heard him in New York was Lydia Maria Child (1802–80).[10] Born in Medford, Massachusetts, Maria Child (as she was known) was a budding novelist, who was welcomed in Boston's intellectual and literary circles. She and her husband were Unitarians who became involved in the antislavery movement. In 1841 she moved from Boston to New York and began to write a column for the Boston *Courier* called "Letters from New York"; it was essentially a local gossip column. Her columns for the years 1843 to 1845 were eventually published in book form under the same title.

As a liberal and a romantic and a transcendentalist, she felt a spiritual

6. Lawrence, *Strong on Music*, 203, from the *Herald*, 3 December 1843.
7. Ibid., 205–206.
8. Bull, ed., *Ole Bulls Breve i Uddrag*, 325 (19 January 1844).
9. Ibid., 325–26 (19 January 1844).
10. Louis Filler, "Lydia Maria Child," in E. T. Jones *et al., Notable American Women 1607–1950* (Cambridge, Mass.: 1971), 1:330–33.

affinity with Bull that could almost be described as hero worship. Her lyrically enthusiastic writings about him must have eased Bull's way into the Brahmin circles of Boston.

At first she had resisted going to hear Bull, she wrote, because "I never like lions; moreover, I am too ignorant of musical science to appreciate his skill." But on 28 December 1843, after hearing him twice, she discovered that his music

expressed to me more of the infinite than I ever saw, or heard, or dreamed of, in the realms of Nature, Art, or Imagination. . . . Oh, the exquisite delicacy of those notes! Now tripping and fairy-like, as the song of Ariel; now soft and low, as the breath of a sleeping babe, yet clear as a fine-toned bell; now high, as a lark soaring upward, till lost among the stars! . . . his personal appearance increases the charm. He looks pure, natural, and vigorous, as I imagine Adam in Paradise. His inspired soul dwells in a strong frame, of admirable proportions, and looks out intensely from his earnest eyes. . . . While I listened, music was to my soul what the atmosphere is to my body; it was the breath of my inward life. I felt, more deeply than ever, that music is the highest symbol of the infinite and holy.

Child concluded by saying that Bull's "reception in New York has exceeded all preceding stars. His first audience were beside themselves with delight, and the orchestra threw down their instruments, in ecstatic wonder."[11] We must remind ourselves that these words did not come from an adoring teenager, but from a mature forty-year-old woman, "with a mind instinctively opposed to lion worship" but, we might add, prone to romantic rhetoric.

Ola Linge has observed that in America "Bull was in his right element. . . . He was interested not only in music, but in politics, social justice, economic advances."[12] While it was true that he had been concerned with these larger issues, at least since his acquaintance with Wergeland, there is not much evidence for it in Bull's European life. In America, however, his eyes were opened to a new and expanding civilization, where disparities in wealth and power seemed even greater to him than in Europe. Along with all the magnificence, he did not fail to observe the evidence of American violence, especially in the slave states. He wrote to Félicie that a "band of robbers follows me step by step. But I always keep an eye on my things. And I never go out late in the evening. . . . A human life is nothing here."[13]

From Washington he traveled south to Richmond and Petersburg in Virginia and on to Mobile, Alabama, in early 1844. Then he crossed to

11. Lydia Maria Child, *Letters from New York,* 2d ser. (New York, 1846), 23–27.
12. Linge, *Ole Bull,* 151.
13. Bull, ed., *Ole Bulls Breve i Uddrag,* 327.

Havana, which was still under Spanish rule. He reassured Félicie, "I always think of the fact that my life does not belong to me alone," and also wrote her that he had learned the American practice of giving speeches to his audiences. "It doesn't go as badly as one might imagine, since I have no practice in English. But with a firm will one can accomplish a great deal."[14] Just how much Bull had learned through his experiences in England and America is indicated in 1852 in a curious attempt by a Pennsylvania journalist to reproduce his English.[15] It consisted chiefly in replacing the English "th" with "t" and "d," as in "tank" for "thank" and "dis" for "this."

Bull stayed in Havana for seven weeks, giving ten concerts. "To show the people of Havana how grateful I am for their enthusiasm" he wrote to Félicie, "I have composed two pieces, *El Agiaco Cubana* [*Cuban Potpourri*, no. 40] and *Recuerdos de Habana* [*Memories of Havana*, no. 41], in which I have interwoven some of the country's favorite melodies." He praised the beauty of the landscape, "which defies all description." He was amazed and pleased at getting an orchestra consisting almost entirely of blacks: "Their mobile features assume whatever expression the music demands for their passionate feeling. . . . They are the best musicians in America." While he was in Havana, a revolt broke out among the blacks, with violent struggles and terrible punishments. But at Bull's concerts, there was wild enthusiasm, which delighted him: "They have sent me many fine verses and enough flower bouquets to cover the stage. I have saved one of the wreaths for you, my greatly beloved!"[16] Bull added to his repertoire Paganini's *Carnival in Venice Variations* (no. 42), a piece he gradually changed over the years to suit his own technique and finally listed as his own composition.

He had intended to travel to Mexico and Peru but, perhaps discouraged by the Cuban revolt, returned to America instead. On the voyage from Havana back to Charleston, Bull fell asleep on deck and was severely burned by the tropical sun. For a week and more his body seemed poisoned, and he wondered why he did not die. But he applied his usual remedy: "I have treated myself with cold water, eaten little, sweat a great deal, taken cold baths and lots of exercise."[17]

On 15 May 1844 he left Charleston by train for Boston, where he would give five concerts. The first was held in the Melodeon, which seated two

14. Ibid., 326 (24 January 1844).
15. Williamsport *Democrat* (25 September 1852), cited by Mortimer Smith in *The Life of Ole Bull* (Princeton, N.J., 1943), 105–109; thanks to Harald Næss, Madison, Wisconsin.
16. Bull, ed., *Ole Bulls Breve i Uddrag,* 329–31 (14 May 1844).
17. Ibid., 331.

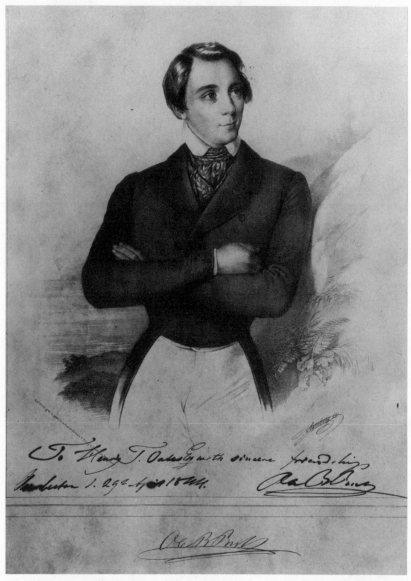

Ole Bull. Drawing by Ramberg, 1841, from Schuberth of Hamburg and Leipzig. Dedicated "To Henry T. Oates Esq. with sincere friendship, Charleston, 1844." Courtesy of Wayside Inn, Sudbury, Mass.

thousand persons. He had an orchestra to accompany him and the assistance of a woman singer. There was a full house, and in the audience sat the poet Henry Wadsworth Longfellow (1807–82) and his wife Fanny (1817–61). In his diary Longfellow succinctly noted, "a great violinist," but Mrs. Longfellow declared in hers that Bull was "a new Orpheus, with a soul in his violin. When we drove home, I seemed to see twelve moons instead of one."[18]

Margaret Fuller (1810–50), along with Longfellow another leading member of the Transcendental School, wrote in her diary: "*The Mountains of Norway* [no. 7], and the *Siciliano and Tarantella* were the great pieces.– He played . . . *Memories of Havana*. . . . I do not know whether the piece was fine or not. I soon forgot it, and was borne away into the winged life."[19] Bull was invited to the Longfellows' home in Cambridge, and met the men and women of their circle.

From Boston Bull proceeded to performances in Hartford and Albany on the way to Canada, where he got as far as Quebec. To Félicie he commented on the conflict between the English and the French. He pitied the latter because they were under the thumb of the Catholic clergy, "who have enriched themselves at the expense of the impoverished population. . . . Priests are called, not doctors" to attend sick children.[20] He admired the Indian craftsmen and bought some of their valuable products for Félicie and the children.

Bull also observed the conflicts in the United States between Protestants and Catholics and deplored their fanaticism. "There are more than a hundred different sects and religions, some of them very strange, I assure you. The Unitarians are without doubt the best of them. They are characterized by good behavior, tolerance, and their simple doctrines: they believe in only one God, not in the Son and the Holy Spirit." He noted that Europeans had no idea of the rapid progress Americans were making in every direction. "Every day one sees new miracles—whole cities springing up from one day to the next."[21]

On the way back to the States, Bull stopped off to see Niagara Falls, "the most magnificent in the world."[22] Here he found inspiration for one of his later compositions, *Niagara* (no. 43). He played in Buffalo and Saratoga, but had to break off the first concert because of a chill, said to

18. Linge, *Ole Bull,* 152.
19. Sara C. Bull, *Ole Bull: A Memoir* (Boston and New York, 1882), 167.
20. Bull, ed., *Ole Bulls Breve i Uddrag,* 332 (29 July 1844).
21. Ibid., 338 (15 June 1844).
22. Ibid., 333 (29 July 1844).

be caused by his drinking several glasses of ice water! He then made his way to a resort in Bristol on Narragansett Bay south of Providence. Here, in June 1844, he got the news of the birth of another son, Ernst Bornemann Bull, who died only a few months later.

Bull continued to send money to Félicie and urged her to make herself as comfortable as possible. "I have suffered terribly at the thought of you, that you are alone, without me to protect and comfort you!"[23] Arriving back in New York, he lamented to her that he had to think of finances. "If only I had been able to gain some sound judgment beside my musical skills. But alas! I have too much neglected money matters, since I was ignorant of the true value of money. This must change—let us hope for the best. I shall persevere."[24] In fact, Bull's mismanagement of his finances never did change.

He hoped to return to Félicie in the summer of 1845 and held out the hope that he would by then have arranged for their stay at Valestrand.

So far we have lived with others, never by ourselves. I would so much like to have the feeling of having a home. It seems to me that would be charming. How our children would enjoy themselves there! How we would seek to arrange things sensibly, without luxury, but pleasantly. . . . We could build and furnish a whole house for ten or twelve hundred francs. We would lay out a beautiful garden, plant fine trees and lovely flowers and make the farm folk around us happy and prosperous. We would perform music, ride and drive in the inner part of Osterøen. We would educate our children, give them an education—at once enjoyable and instructive. And make each other mutually happy. When summer is over, we would spend the winter where we wish. . . .[25]

Bull's second American winter season had already begun in New York in October 1844. He improvised variations on "Yankee Doodle" (no. 45). At the end of December he told Félicie that he had played his new compositions, *Niagara* and *Solitude of the Prairie* (no. 44). He believed that *Niagara* was the best he had ever written, "with quite a new and original structure, not as brilliant as the solo part in *Polacca Guerriera,* but with a more complex accompaniment for the orchestra. I think it will awaken attention in Europe." Even now he still complained about "the French clique" that had used "infamous means" to "destroy me both morally and physically."[26] These laments need not be taken too seriously; we have seen many examples of his occasional paranoia.

23. Ibid., 339 (29 August 1844).
24. Ibid., 340 (15 October 1844).
25. Ibid., 341 (15 October 1844).
26. Ibid., 344 (30 December 1844).

Bull's new American compositions did not receive "the unreserved critical acclaim to which he was accustomed—indeed the work seemed to be an embarrassment to the critics, who apparently did not know what to make of it."[27] James Otis of the *Express* called it "caviare to the million" and suggested that it required "impossibly cultivated listeners."[28] As for *Solitude of the Prairie,* it won no more enthusiasm.

Bull's chief admirer, Maria Child, became the object of a good deal of derision. The *New World* wrote of her:

Mrs. Child is a lady for whose character and talents we entertain a profound respect. . . . she has intervals, however, which are not lucid. Being fond of an occasional ride in the empyrean, she mounts the wild and winged steed of her imagination, and with a fierce huzza, flings the reins upon its untameable neck. Then away she goes—away—away! Who can overtake her? No mortal speed. She is above and beyond this sublunary sphere. What an illustration of this have her high-flown eulogies on Ole Bull afforded! What more could be said of angels? Has language any more elaborately intense superlatives? A very fair fiddler is Ole Bull—very fair! But bless your heart, Mrs. Child, he is no great shake.[29]

Bull's work as a composer received an even more negative critique from George Templeton Strong after a concert in New York on 6 January 1845. He had heard *Niagara, Solitude of the Prairie,* and Bull's *Psalm of David* (no. 47). Strong declared that "which of the three is the greatest humbug, I've not decided. He's a great player, undoubtedly, but that he's no composer one may see by his orchestral parts, of which one can judge better than the solos. They are thin and miserable beyond expression, mere noise, perfectly trivial, and utterly without musical ideas. His theory of the sublime in music would seem to be that it rests on a happy combination of brass and kettledrums." Strong then analyzed the pieces individually and concluded that "he'll have his joke about all this when he gets home, and he'll probably give a series of comic lectures on American characters, illustrated with specimens of these performances and extracts from the newspaper criticisms and eulogies."[30]

From New York Bull headed out once more on the circuit to New Orleans, arriving in Nashville in April of 1845. Here he wrote to Félicie about the violent habits of Americans of the South, where every man went armed, at least with a dagger. He reported that without warning one's enemy would thrust his dagger in one's heart. "I assure you that my trip to Amer-

27. Lawrence, *Strong on Music,* 278.
28. Ibid.
29. Ibid., 279.
30. Ibid., 289–90.

ica has given me more experience of the world than all my journeys in Europe together! . . . My servant Henrik almost became a victim in New Orleans."[31]

From Nashville he would go to Louisville, Lexington, St. Louis, Cincinnati, Pittsburgh, Washington, Baltimore, Philadelphia, New York, and Boston. It would be a grueling tour, but he hoped to be able to tell Félicie that "I have enough to be able to live without being subject to the caprices of the public, partisanship, or national prejudices. . . . Although I have endured many hardships and privations . . . I am stronger than ever."[32]

Two weeks later, Bull wrote Félicie again from St. Louis. He reported on a near accident on the Mississippi during a storm fifty miles from St. Louis. As he entered the boat's cabin, he discovered that part of the deck was gone. The boat almost capsized, and the air was full of lightning. Fire broke out in the boat, but after a half hour the fire was mastered and the danger was over. Bull again observed that human life in America was of no account. "Every day there are accidents with steamers that explode, sometimes with three or four hundred persons aboard. Everything here is on a grand scale. . . . Distances do not matter. There is no nation on the surface of the earth that travels as much as this people — in the winter in the South, in the summer in the North."[33]

This tour would give Bull many equally exciting stories to tell. One was that on a riverboat he fell into the company of some rough customers who offered him a drink of whisky. When he refused, they got angry and wanted to fight with him. He took one of the men on and tossed him on the floor. The man was so impressed that he gave Bull his bowie knife, and after a while Bull accumulated a whole collection of bowie knives. Among the places he visited was the Mammoth Cave in Kentucky. Here, the story goes, he got separated from his party and (in typical Bull fashion) was found only by the others hearing his violin through the caverns.

Another story concerned Bull's fruitless search for the authentic American prairie. In St. Louis he decided that, since he had composed *Solitude of the Prairie* without ever having seen a prairie, he ought to see one. He rode off alone on a horse. The weather was bad, however, and after only two miles he was wet through and had lost the way. He had to spend the night in a nearby inn.

Bull assured Félicie that he had not been idle that spring, but had increased his repertoire, so that he now had some thirty pieces in varied and

31. Bull, ed., *Ole Bulls Breve i Uddrag,* 345 (12 April 1845).
32. Ibid., 346 (12 April 1845).
33. Ibid., 347 (28 April 1845).

novel styles.[34] A new piece he had composed was *In Memory of Washington* (no. 46). In Utica, New York, he complained about the ever-changing weather and the dust that was affecting his eyes. From Syracuse he went to Niagara, Buffalo, Troy, Portland, Hanover, and finally to Newport, Rhode Island. He began preparing for departure and the farewell concerts he would give in the east coast cities in September.

By this time he began to wonder, as well he might, if his wife still loved him: "I feel that you hardly love me as much as I love you. I felt this for a long time, even before I left." In September he wrote that he had more to tell her than he could confide "to this cold paper."[35]

On 30 October 1845 Bull gave his New York farewell concert. Here the grand master of the Masonic Lodge in New York and many of its members were present in full regalia. They gave a speech for Bull and donated to him a set of their regalia in solid gold. He also received a gold medal from The American Institute in New York and another from the Philharmonic Society of Philadelphia. In his speech of gratitude Bull declared that his tribute *In Memory of Washington* expressed the attitude of all Norwegians: "The basic principles for which your people drew their swords and shed their blood inspired the Norwegian people and strengthened them in their struggle for freedom."[36]

Maria Child was there again to comment on Bull's last concerts in New York. She had even composed a poem in his honor, "a wreath of wild flowers to welcome his return," which was published in her 14 October "Letter from New York" for the Boston *Courier.* The first and last stanzas run:

> Welcome to thee, Ole Bull!
> A welcome, warm and free!
> For heart and memory are full
> Of thy rich minstrelsy.

> Of beauty Nature is lavish ever;
> Her urn is always full;
> But to our earth she giveth never
> Another Ole Bull.

In this "Letter" she also speculated on the effect of Norway's natural world on Ole Bull's development as a musician: "On this coast Ole Bull, from childhood, heard the waves roar their mighty bass to the shrill soprano of the winds, and has seen it all subside into sun-flecked, rippling silence.

34. Ibid., 348.
35. Ibid., 350 (17 September 1845), 351 (30 September 1845).
36. Linge, *Ole Bull,* 157.

There, in view of mighty mountains, sea-circled shores, and calm, deep, blue fiords, shut in by black precipices and tall green forests, has he listened to the fresh mighty throbbings of Nature."[37]

In the last letter on Bull from 21 October, she reported her enthusiastic reactions to Bull's *Niagara* and the *Solitude of the Prairie,* and based on these she summed up by dubbing Ole Bull a genius. While she can be pleased by mere skill, she said, "bring me into the presence of genius, and I know it by rapid intuition, as quick as I know a sunbeam." In conclusion she declared that "America, in taking the Norwegian minstrel thus warmly to her heart, receives much more than she can give. His visit has done and will do, more than any other cause, to waken and extend a love of music throughout the country; and when love exists, it soon takes form in science. All things that are alive are born of the heart."[38]

Another who was moved by Bull to write poetry in his honor was Anne Charlotte Lynch [Botto] (1815–91), a transcendentalist writer and literary hostess living in New York. Her poem was tossed to him in a bouquet at his last concert; one stanza reads:

> But, waked beneath thy master-hand,
> Those trembling chords have given
> A foretaste of that deep full life
> That I shall know in heaven.[39]

Bull reappeared in New York on 26 November at the Tabernacle, for an audience of some three thousand persons. He played a novel concerto composed for the widows and orphans of Prague (no. 29) and other popular numbers. He was showered with bouquets, wreaths, and poems. According to the *Herald,* he picked up a nosegay that had been thrown to him, and "bowing low to the audience, he thus bid farewell to New York: 'Ladies and Gentlemen, These flowers will fade, but the spirit that gives them will never die away from my grateful heart'." The *Herald* prosaically noted that, in his two years in America, Bull had netted at least sixty to eighty thousand dollars.[40]

On 2 December 1845, Bull left New York on the sailing vessel *Baltimore.* He expressed his preference for sailing over steam vessels because of the absence of tremor and smoke and his need for rest (and the avoidance of customs officials in England). "I hope," he wrote to Félicie shortly

37. Child, *Letters,* 233.
38. Ibid., 279.
39. Linge, *Ole Bull,* 158.
40. Lawrence, *Strong on Music,* 354–55.

before his departure, "that my long absence and the success and sympathy I have had in America will have an effect in Europe, even in France. My social standing has been greatly enhanced by association with the most distinguished and remarkable men here. My relationship with the Americans is that of an adopted child."[41]

Two years was indeed a long absence, but Bull had enjoyed a reception that could not have been better, in spite of the irksome "cabals" of the French "clique." He was now established as an American personality, indeed as "an adopted child." Aarvig's description of Bull as "a self-made man of art" may well explain his appeal to Americans.[42] Ole Bull's open and outgoing manner, however, is an even better reason why he was so warmly embraced by the American public.

41. Bull, ed., *Ole Bulls Breve i Uddrag*, 353 (30 November 1845).
42. Christian A. Aarvig, *Den unge Ole Bull: En Violinspillers Ungdomskampe* (Copenhagen, 1934), 106.

10

From Algiers to Revolution
(1845–1848)

FTER HIS TWO busy years in America, Bull took a two-month breather in Paris with his family during Christmas 1845. This was his first chance to get to know little Genevieve Félicie, who was only a few months old when he left for the United States. It was also an opportunity to get better acquainted with Alexander, born in 1839, and Thorvald, born in 1841. In one of his letters from New York he wrote: "I have dreamed of Alexander and Thorvald, and my soul is filled with grief over not seeing them."[1] Soon after Bull's return Félicie was expecting another child, who would be called Lucie. Bull had earned a substantial fortune in America, but he still worried about finances, especially in Paris: "Fatal country!" he wrote, "It eats up everything for me."[2]

Bull made his first public appearance since his American tour on 13 January 1846, when his friend, the novelist and drama critic Jules Janin held a musical soirée. The occasion was a repeat performance of the *Festkantate (Festival Cantata)* written for the unveiling of a Beethoven monument in Bonn on 13 August 1845. Janin had written the words, but the music was by Liszt, who was present and performing. Bull was also asked to perform, and according to *Le Monde Musical* he was heard "in one of his eccentric fantasias without accompaniment."[3] Bull must have been pleased at the reunion with Janin and Liszt and happy to meet again the cream of Paris' musical world.

In the course of that spring Bull gave three Paris concerts, one at the

---

1. Alexander Bull, ed., *Ole Bulls Breve i Uddrag. Med en karakteristik og biografisk Skitse af Jonas Lie* (Copenhagen, 1881), 351 (30 September 1845).
2. Ibid., 355 (18 May 1846).
3. Ola Linge, *Ole Bull: Livshistoria, Mannen, Kunstnaren* (Oslo, 1953), 160.

Opéra,[4] a benefit on 27 March for a tenor at the Opéra Comique, and on 16 April a concert at the Théatre des Italiens.

Bull's first concert at the Opéra was attended, among others, by King Louis Philippe and an array of nobility, though the house was not full. *Le Monde Musical* called it a "splendid [*éclatant*] success," noting that "he is one of the greatest and most remarkable violinists in existence with regard to technique, and his cantabile is expressive."[5] *Le Menestral* called him a violinist *"hors ligne"* ("without a peer"). *La France Musicale* averred that "Ole Bull is not one of these elegant little artists who charm a small salon audience with their little coquetry. For this child of the North, filled by a mighty energy, magic dreams, a marvelous fantasy, needs a great public and a hall of large dimensions, in other words, the Opéra and its public." Only one critic, a violinist named Henri-Louis Blanchard (1791–1858), writing in *La Revue et Gazette Musicale,* was displeased. Bull, he declared, was "more pleasing to look at than to listen to," and as for his composing, "his compositions are outside all rules."[6]

On 27 March he assisted at a benefit for Gustave-Hippolyte Roger (1815–79), the first tenor at the Opéra Comique, playing the *Polacca Guerriera* and Paganini's *Carnival in Venice Variations.* According to *La Revue et Gazette Musicale,* "Bull electrified the filled house" and was received with "frenetic applause" for the rendition of his *Polacca Guerriera.* At a *souper* after the concert Bull toasted Roger as "the spoiled child of the public," while one of the guests toasted Bull as "the darling child of the universe."[7]

Bull's major concert was on April 16. This included Liszt's *Cantata,* while Bull performed his *Bravura Variations,* the *Carnival in Venice Variations,* his *A Mother's Prayer,* and his *Polacca Guerriera. La France Musicale* wrote, "We have rarely been witnesses to a more brilliant triumph. . . . It was extraordinary, incredible, unheard of. . . . Never has an artist played like this on a violin since Paganini's days, and perhaps even Paganini himself never had a greater success."[8] The Norwegian violinist could have believed he was still in America.

One observer was the well-known poet, novelist and critic, Théophile Gautier (1811–72). He wrote that Bull reminded him of a Scandinavian who swings his bow "like a bard about to tell of Sigurd the Dragon Slayer or Odin and the Fenris Wolf. . . . And then he tells instead of the Carnival

4. Ibid., 159, reproduces the placard.
5. Ibid., 160 (19 March 1846).
6. Ibid., 161.
7. Ibid., 162.
8. Ibid., 162–63.

in Venice as only Paganini and [his pupil Ernesto Camillo] Sivori [1815–94] could do it. This and the *Polacca* were received with a storm of applause."[9] *La Revue et Gazette Théatrale* spoke of "the brilliant facility of the violinist with his bow that caused noisy outbursts of applause."[10] These snippets from much longer reviews indicate that Bull had finally solidified his standing in Paris.

From Paris Bull proceeded to the south of France, where he gave concerts in Bordeaux, Marseille, and Toulon. He held four popular concerts in Bordeaux; in the words of one correspondent, "No artist, of whatever talent, has been fêted as much."[11] In Marseille he met again his friend the fairy-tale author Andersen. As Bull's biographer Mortimer Smith observed, "There was a great attraction between these two imaginative Scandinavians, the one a teller of fairy tales, and the other himself a living fairy tale."[12] Andersen would use Bull as a model again in a tale called "Pen and Inkwell" (1859), in which he compared the outpouring of the author's thoughts to the notes of a violin, "rolling out like pearls, blowing like a storm through the forest."[13]

Ever restless, Bull fantasized in a letter to Félicie that spring about a possible journey to Chile, but nothing came of it. He told her that people in the south of France "understand music better than in the north, because they really feel it."[14] Only a short time later, however, he complained: "France has at all times been for me a source of poverty and destruction."[15] In other letters he alternately complained about losing money or boasted about testimonials of honor. And early that summer he wrote that he "had been the victim of a nervous agitation, and my exertions during this heat have only increased my suffering."[16]

According to Smith, Bull wrote from Marseille to his wife "that he was never coming back to Paris again, adding that she could live with France and her grandmother and he would live with his violin and his servant." This was too much for the long-suffering Félicie, says Smith, and she retorted with heat that she was no longer naive enough to believe in such phrases—"I know very well that you live with more than your violin, for

9. *La Presse* (19 April 1846).
10. Linge, *Ole Bull,* 163.
11. Ibid., 164.
12. Mortimer Smith, *The Life of Ole Bull* (Princeton, N.J., 1943), 72.
13. Hans Christian Andersen, "Pen og Blækhus," *Samlede Eventyr og Historier* (Copenhagen, 1975), 2:11–12.
14. Bull, ed., *Ole Bulls Breve i Uddrag,* 355 (18 May 1846).
15. Ibid., 356 (28 May 1846).
16. Ibid., 358–59 (8 July 1846).

Ole Bull, 1846, with Gasparo da Salò violin. Drawing by V. Cassier, Marseille. Photo courtesy of Catherine Munch.

you are not one to be satisfied with the contemplative life."[17] While this exchange is possible, there is no evidence for it either in Alexander Bull's collection of letters or in Sara Bull's *Memoir,* so we doubt its accuracy. However, there exists other evidence of their marital discord. One cannot overlook later statements by Bull's good friend Aasmund Olavsson Vinje, who wrote in his journal *Dølen* that "Ole Bull is a marvelously unhappy man in his domestic life. As far as I can tell. . . . he is not responsible for most of it, I can even say that not many would have endured what he has. . . . Novels and comedies could be written such that people have never read the like. I have sat with him and heard tales that Shakespeare could not have invented such madness and humor, and always he has told it with respect for others without hate, beating his giant's chest so it echoed as when one strikes a whole hollow tree with an axe butt."[18] Another good friend, Bjørnstjerne Bjørnson, declared of Bull that "his blood has burned like a fire; his four children are the handsomest in the city; God knows how many children he has around the world."[19] Finally, Bull's reference to friends who "did the worst thing they could do—they aroused a mis-understanding that separated us," in his last letter to Félicie, written in 1862 shortly before she died, indicates how seriously unhappy their mar-riage may have become.[20]

In Marseille Bull appeared to full houses and was praised by the local press: "His place is between Paganini and Liszt. . . ." The critic is in doubt which to prefer, but "admiration is more readily accorded to the frank, modest, unselfish young man, who has given evidence, in many ways, of an excellent nobility of character." He was especially taken by Bull's play-ing of the *Carnival in Venice,* Paganini's old piece. "It is strange enough that the Northman has been able to put more sly cunning and rollicking fun into the scene than the Italian Mephistopheles. . . . Ole Bull ends this composition with a bird song, which is the most surprising imitation one can imagine. Here his instrument is no mere violin, but a gathering of the most charming song birds."[21]

From Marseille Bull shipped across the Mediterranean to Algiers, where he met a friend, General Youssouf, and joined him on a jaunt into the newly annexed French possession of Algeria. He is said to have witnessed a bat-

17. Smith, *Life of Ole Bull,* 72.

18. Aasmund Olavsson Vinje, "Ogso eit Vitnemaal," *Dølen* (25 December 1859).

19. Cited by Carl O. Gram Gjesdal, "Ole Bull," in *Norske Klassikere,* ed. Peter Anker, K. Bækkelund, and E. Straume (Oslo, 1985), 79; source unknown.

20. Bull, ed., *Ole Bulls Breve i Uddrag,* 394 (7 February 1862); see chap. 13.

21. Sara C. Bull, *Ole Bull: A Memoir* (Boston and New York, 1882), 193; translated from *Le Sud.*

tle with the Kabyls, a Berber tribe. He wrote to Félicie that he had given three concerts on a trip with the general to see three towns in the interior, remarkable for their natural beauty and their architecture. He complained of the heat and told her that he had to be on the constant lookout for poisonous insects. He commented on the confusion in the government of Algeria: "If the French lose it, it will be due to their indifference and lack of order. And how many complaints suppressed in injustice!"[22] On his departure the local Swedish-Norwegian consul held a dinner for him where Bull had to endure being called a countryman of Linnæus and other Swedes.

In September 1846 Bull again crossed the Mediterranean, this time to Spain, where he had never been before. He held concerts in Cadiz, Seville, Madrid, Valencia, Barcelona, and in the Balearic Islands.[23] He was everywhere greeted with acclaim. A critic for the *Español* inevitably compared him to Paganini. "Of all the violinists we have heard, Ole Bull approaches most closely to him in performance. . . . This violinist has created the greatest sensation ever known in Madrid." The critic also praised Bull for his work as a composer. "His great *Concerto* has all the qualities of that form of composition."[24] The Valencia *Fenix* declared that "the violin in Ole Bull's hands is a perfect orchestra, and an impetuous torrent of delightful harmonies; it seemed as if the strings multiply, and obedient to the inspiration of the artist, they imitate the human voice as well as the trumpet of the warrior, the song of the maiden, or the lyre of the poet."[25]

Bull responded with enthusiasm. He was delighted with the vocalic quality of Spanish and the fiery temperament of the Spaniards. He bought old violins and seven Spanish paintings, one of them said to be from the eleventh century.

Bull had a special attraction for the sixteen-year-old Queen Isabella II (1830–1904), whose wedding ceremonies he was invited to attend. To honor the queen he composed, as he had done elsewhere, a potpourri of native tunes, bearing the name *La Verbena de San Juan* (*Celebration of St. John's Eve*) (no. 48), and improvised variations (no. 50) on "El Calecero Andaluz" and "La Jota Aragonesa." He also composed *The Guitarist from Seville* (no. 49), in which he simultaneously played the melody and pizzicato accompaniment.

According to Mortimer Smith, the queen's "amorous inclinations were

22. Bull, ed., *Ole Bulls Breve i Uddrag,* 361 (15 August 1846).
23. Smith, *Life of Ole Bull,* 72.
24. It is unclear whether this refers to the *Concerto in A Major* or the *Concerto in E Minor.*
25. Bull, *A Memoir,* 195–96.

already the subject of gossip in royal circles."[26] She heard Bull play and was so struck by the handsome violinist that she commanded him to appear at the palace and play privately for her. He did so and came away with the Order of Charles III and a pin in the form of a vervain with 140 diamonds. Bull claimed that she also offered him a generalship in the Spanish army, an offer he rejected. The inscription on the order was "Pour la vertu." Once when he wore it at the court of Sweden, the Swedish queen laughingly asked him why he had received it. Bull archly replied, "For my virtue, Your Majesty."[27] While it may be true, the story sounds a bit like the tales Bull loved to use to spice his conversations.

During the years from 1846 to 1848 Bull received uniformly enthusiastic reviews, as we see from a broadsheet he had printed in Paris in early 1848, entitled "Compte-Rendu de divers Concerts donnés par M. Ole-Bull" ("Account of Various Concerts Given by Mr. Ole Bull").[28] Of the twelve reviews from France and Algeria we select the latest as a sample, the extravagant and detailed account of *Le Courrier de Dimanche* in Bordeaux from 21 January 1848):

Ole Bull is one of the few artists of the time who show genuine originality. He is the Paganini of the North, the Liszt of the violin. He has filled Europe and the New World with the echoes of his incredible successes, of his unheard-of prodigality, of his innumerable eccentricities. — Ole Bull does nothing like others, he has his own toilette, his own coiffure; he does not know how to turn, to salute, to march like others. He is one of those feverish artists who unceasingly ask of their instrument more than it can give, one sees him sometimes talking to his bow, sometimes struggling against his strings, sometimes bending his ear to his violin, as if inward voices answered him from the interior of the instrument.

Under the mantle of calm, cold and reserved as a man of the North, Ole Bull conceals a burning spirit, a tender and passionate heart. He has an exquisite sensibility, a restless and tormented imagination. He is a true poet—one of those dreamers who everywhere pursue the dream of the ideal.

Ole Bull makes his instrument speak; he makes it weep and laugh and communicates to it a kind of soul. His playing is large, accented, pure, correct, and irreproachable, down to the most spirited transports. Ole Bull possesses to the highest degree the difficult art of nuances, which are the coloring of music. He has the power, the precision, the vigor, the sound quality, the fullness and majesty of style, and this sovereign stroke of the masters who dominate every orchestra. After all, Ole Bull is not just a great performer. He is also, of all composers who have written for the violin, one who has perhaps the greatest value. All he has written is new, original, powerful, the orchestration is rich, the melody abundant, and the

26. Smith, *Life of Ole Bull,* 73.
27. Ibid., Linge, *Ole Bull,* does not include this story.
28. Deposited by Linge in the Oslo University Library.

inspiration appears everywhere. With Ole Bull ideas crowd in, such are his Concertos, his Nocturnes, his *Tarantella,* his *Polacca Guerriera,* and all the beautiful compositions he has let us hear on his first visit to Bordeaux.

It is unknown whether there was any specific reason for the long gap in communication between Bull and Félicie from September 1846, when he arrived in Spain, to 20 July 1847, the date of his first letter home from Barcelona. Félicie appears to have written Bull and complained about his neglect. In his reply he countered her complaints: "Unhappily we do not understand one another; — we both suffer under it."[29] Even after returning to France (via ship to avoid bandits in the Spanish mountains), he was slow to join his wife. She wrote that his long silence had troubled her, and "as I have a tendency always to plague myself with somber ideas, I thought it was indifference on your part, when on the contrary, you were alone and ill."[30]

In April 1848 Félicie moved from Paris to the home of her uncle and grandmother in Saint-Mihiel, a small town on the Meuse River in northeast France, and she pleaded with him to come there, as he apparently did. "The thought of your coming here and spending the summer with me makes me so happy that it is almost a question of life or death for me. . . . Remember that love cannot exist without a bit of jealousy! I have gotten so many stabs in my heart from things that have been spoken to me in all innocence."[31] Félicie perhaps refers here to statements made to her by friends, friends who Bull later complained had aroused a misunderstanding between him and his wife.

Several months before the summer that Félicie hoped they would spend together, the world around them suddenly began to change. On 24 February 1848 Paris erupted in what has come to be known as the February Revolution of 1848. Before long the uprising had spread to other European countries, where young people were impatient with the conservative spirit of their governments. They were eager to rid themselves of the heritage of the Holy Alliance and other bonds on freedom. Only in France did the Revolution succeed in establishing a new government, even though it was far less radical than some enthusiasts had hoped for.

Bull was in Nantes, France, when the Revolution broke out. The news caused him to cancel further concerts and hurry back to Paris. He recalled that the first French Revolution of 1789 had led to Norway's 1814 libera-

29. Bull, ed., *Ole Bulls Breve i Uddrag,* 361 (20 July 1847).
30. Ibid., 366 (28 April 1848).
31. Ibid., 367 (28 April 1848).

tion from Denmark. He no doubt remembered that Wergeland had gone to Paris in 1830 to witness developments after the second, July Revolution. In 1848 many national delegations were streaming to Paris to congratulate the prime minister and leader of the February Revolution, Alphonse Lamartine (1790–1869). A Scandinavian delegation was proposed, but Bull put his foot down. Being in Paris gave him an irresistible opportunity to demonstrate on behalf of Norway. Accompanied by one Captain Rosen, a Norwegian, Bull marched to Lamartine's office and presented him with a "pure" Norwegian flag, a red, white, and blue cross lacking the blue and yellow Swedish colors that had been part of the joint flag since 1814.

Bull then made a speech of greeting on behalf of the Norwegian people to the French Republic. Lamartine, who was a poet and a sympathizer with democracy, replied graciously that "it is a pleasure and an honor for the French Republic to receive representatives from nearly all the nations in the world and to feel this spirit of fraternity which your speaker mentioned, and this enthusiasm for freedom, this honest sympathy that makes all peoples into one family."[32]

In July Bull wrote to Félicie from Paris that life there was still rather grim. "You can hardly imagine the appearance of Paris. We are in a state of siege, and people seem to fear new disturbances. . . . And not a single person who can think clearly, they all lose their heads!"[33]

The summer of 1848 brought Bull his first opportunity to get to know his new daughter, Lucie Edvardine, born in 1846. When he was not with his family at Saint-Mihiel, Bull was living in a Paris hotel and working with an old friend, violin builder Jean-Baptiste Vuillaume (1798–1875): "It is the only way to learn about the structure of instruments." He was eager to improve the quality of the violin, and the instrument that resulted exceeded his expectations. "It has a strong and at the same time soft tone, fits well into the hand, does not tire one and does not resemble any other violin in its tone." He had asked well-known artists to listen to his violin, and "they all agreed that the tone resembles that of an aeolian harp."[34] Vuillaume later told Bull that he was at work on a large double bass which he called an "Octobass," twelve feet in height, with strings stopped by levers.[35]

Meanwhile Bull was planning his next move, a return to Norway. In October 1848 he wrote to Félicie from Amsterdam on his way to Norway

32. Linge, *Ole Bull,* 169.
33. Bull, ed., *Ole Bulls Breve i Uddrag,* 368 (11 July 1848).
34. Ibid., 368 (11 July 1848) and 369 (Saturday, July 1848).
35. Bull, *A Memoir,* 197.

by boat. He had bought property in Norway, sight unseen, Andøen (now Andøya), an island on the south coast of Norway, off the town of Christiansand.[36] As late as April 1849, Félicie was still living with her family in Saint-Mihiel. She wrote to Bull in dismay over his purchase. "I wonder at your delight over Andøen, a property you don't know. It seems to me that you should have looked at it before you bought it." But she was willing to follow his lead. "When I and our children live there, they can at least learn to know you and become fond of you."[37] She arrived at Andøen by May of 1849 and wrote that she was counting the days until he should arrive.

Félicie's letters are entirely innocent of any awareness of the enterprises that would soon take Bull away from Andøen and his family. Bull himself probably had only vague ideas of them when he came to Norway. He only knew that the spirit of 1848 would somehow guide him to a beneficial plan for his beloved land.

36. About Andøen, see Kåre Rudjord, *Oddernes bygdebok* (Kristiansand, 1968), 1:182. For a photograph of the property and information about Bull's brief ownership, see p. 185.
37. Bull, ed., *Ole Bulls Breve i Uddrag,* 371 (6 April 1849).

11

Norwegian Theater and Henrik Ibsen (1848–1852)

AMONG THE ideas Bull was turning over when he returned to Norway on 5 November 1848 was the thought of a Norwegian-language theater. Marie Midling, an actress who later married Edvard Storm Bull (1814–1907), reports that Ole had discussed the idea with his brother Edvard, then in Paris, after a performance at the Opéra.[1] He first revealed it in public at a dinner in his honor arranged by students at the University of Christiania on 10 December.[2] The theater was intended to mark the beginning of a true nationality for the Norwegians, a statement of their national spirit as separate from the Swedes and Danes. Bull had been away from Norway for five years, and now it was necessary to reexplore the terrain.

He began by giving concerts in Christiania on 25 November, 2 December, and 9 December. "Fantasies" (improvisations) on Norwegian tunes (nos. 51 and 52) were included on his programs. He was hailed by *Morgenbladet* with the words: "From the moment Ole Bull sends his first tones out into space, any listener with the least appreciation of music will sense the confidence needed and value it. There stands the great and perfect master who has overcome all difficulties with his mighty arm. For him nothing can fail or go wrong. All is secure and certain."[3]

The dinner the students gave in his honor was replete with speeches

1. Marie Bull, *Minder fra Bergens første nationale scene* (Bergen, 1905), 9.
2. Ola Linge, *Ole Bull: Livshistoria, Mannen, Kunstnaren* (Oslo, 1953), 172.
3. *Morgenbladet* (27 November 1848).

and songs, including one song by Bull's second cousin, the poet Andreas Munch (1811–84). Bull himself gave a long speech telling about the revolution in Paris and his own action on behalf of Norway. He urged that Norway adopt a republican form of government, and in true revolutionary style ended with a playing of the "Marseillaise." Later in the same evening he unfolded his idea of a national theater that would bring Norway's cultural treasures into the limelight. As one such treasure he mentioned Torgeir Augundson, the fiddler from Telemark whom Bull had first met in Bergen in 1831. He should be invited, Bull insisted, to perform in the capital. Following the dinner and after he had promised to memorialize the evening by writing a fantasia to be entitled *December 10,* the date of their dinner, the students carried Bull in triumph to his quarters.

In Christiania Bull became aware of stirrings among the younger generation toward a more active role for national Norwegian values. In the wake of the February Revolution, Norwegian painters like Adolph Tidemand (1814–76) and Hans Gude (1825–1903) were moving home, bringing with them their romantic paintings of Norwegian scenes. Poets like Bjørnstjerne Bjørnson (1832–1910) and Aasmund Olavsson Vinje (1818–70) were creating a new Norwegian literature. Peter Christen Asbjørnsen and Jørgen Moe (1813–82) were collecting folktales and writing them down in a form that would become classic. Ludvig Mathias Lindeman (1812–87) was gathering folk tunes, and pastor Magnus Brostrup Landstad (1802–80) was collecting the oral ballads of Norway. Vinje was an adherent of the radical new folk language (called Landsmål) that Ivar Aasen (1813–96) had devised as a medium of Norwegian expression. The generation active in the 1850s included a number of such "self-discoverers" of unacknowledged national treasures, and Bull would wholeheartedly share in the process.

As a first step he arranged for Augundson to come from his rural home to Christiania and play for a more sophisticated audience than usually heard him. A concert was held on 15 January 1849, with Bull assisting. It proved to be an appealing occasion, even though it was a bit strange to the urban audience. City people were not accustomed to the unusual tunes, the drone basses and the sounds of the extra sympathetic strings of the Hardanger fiddle. Andreas Munch reported on the concert for *Rigstidende,* observing that "by presenting this impoverished country fiddler to the public of the capital and saying to it: 'Listen with good will to this son of the mountains, for I have learned from him,' Ole Bull has honored this audience and himself equally." Munch quoted from Bull's address to the audience: "Do you, the public, understand what I have wanted you to take to heart most of all? You shall dive down into the latent natural poetry [*Den bundne*

Naturpoesi] of your country, as I have done, and honor it so it becomes strong. But you shall not get lost in it and take it raw or dwell only in it alone. In song as in deed you shall rise above the mountain valley by uniting the force and heart of the child of nature with the artistic sense and beauty of cultural life."[4] Munch (and with him Bull) are here clearly distinguishing between natural and cultivated art. While both are part of the national heritage, only the trained artist can rise above the work of the untutored fiddler. It was a doctrine that suited the Romantic Age. Welhaven described the scene in his poem "Møllergutten":

> Og der kom, hvorom han aldrig drømte,
> skjønt han gik saa tankefuld,
> Brev og Bud til ham fra den berømte,
> vidt bereiste Mester Ole Bull.[5]

> (And there came, of which he never dreamed,
> Though he walked about so thoughtful,
> Word and message from the famous,
> Widely traveled Master Ole Bull.)

Bull's invitation set in motion a whole new generation of Hardanger fiddle playing, with competitions and a revival of the rural music.[6]

On 10 March Bull gave his fifth and last concert in Christiania. Here he played his new composition, *December 10*, later retitled *Et Sæterbesøg* (*Visit to the Sæter*) (no. 53).[7] It became his most popular and enduring composition. Its central melody is now known as "Sæterjentens Søndag" ("Sæter Girl's Sunday") (no. 53a) and has become a classic in the Norwegian repertoire. Although it has been commonly thought that Bull wrote the melody to words by Jørgen Moe, it seems that Moe's text appeared after Bull's music. Moe's poem is a sentimental tale about a lonely herd girl who has to watch her flock at the chalet, or mountain farm, while she dreams of her sweetheart going to church in the valley.

The growing national enthusiasm culminated in a series of live scenic "tableaus," a benefit performance for the homeless given in late March 1849.

---

4. *Rigstidende* (21 January 1849).

5. J. S. C. Welhaven, *Samlede Digterverker* (Christiania and Copenhagen, 1907), 3:117.

6. On Augundson, see Meïr Goldschmidt, "Thorgeir Audunsen, Violinspilleren paa Haukelidfjeldet," in *Nord og Syd* (Copenhagen, 1851), 345–61.

7. A "sæter" is a mountain farm used as a summer pasture, similar to the Swiss chalet. The "sæter" was established as a romantic locale in 1824 by Henrik Anker Bjerregaard's romantic play *Fjeldeventyret* with music by Waldemar Thrane (Knut Nygaard, *Henrik Anker Bjerregaard: Dikteren og hans tid* [Oslo, 1966], 102). Bjørnson reported in 1892 that Bull said he had been deeply impressed by this play (Nygaard, *Bjerregaard*, 207).

These were acted versions of the romantic paintings of Tidemand and Gude, with music and choral accompaniments. One of them was the dramatic "Bridal Procession in Hardanger" with words by Andreas Munch and music by Halfdan Kjerulf. (Bull was the model for the fiddler in the painting.) Another tableau was based on Jørgen Moe's poem "Fanitullen" ("The Devil's Dance") which Bull accompanied with his version of the tune (*slått*) by the same name (no. 54). These tableaus were a kind of popular extravaganza that represented the flowering of Norwegian national Romanticism.[8]

Bull soon enough realized that the Danish actors and repertoire of the Christiania Theater were too well entrenched to offer a field for his enterprise. So he turned to his native town of Bergen. Before going there, he settled Félicie, the children, and their French maid, who had all arrived in Norway in May, on his new property on Andøen. He stayed with them only a month, and then headed off to Bergen, where he arrived on 17 June 1849.

There was enormous excitement in Bergen to see Bull again. The Craftmen's Society (*Håndverkerforeningen*) invited him to a festive evening. Their hall was decorated with flowers and leafy branches, and on the wall Ole Bull's name shone in gold letters. The speaker of the evening was Fritz Jensen (1818–70), a painter and later a pastor, who would play a leading role in organizing the theater. That evening he urged Bull "to light the first flame on the altar, and the coming generation will not neglect the worship of its neglected divinity."[9] One newspaper account of the gathering declared that it was impossible to describe the jubilation that greeted Bull and each of his "tone poems." "When he stands before us with his violin in his hand, he is a ruler in the world of the spirit, and the picture we carry away is so intimately fused with his miraculous tones that both are indelibly engraved on the hearers' souls."[10] The company parted in high spirits and not before five o'clock in the morning!

Bull had launched his plan for a Norwegian theater and was meeting with a widespread response. Although the earlier theatrical and musical societies were no longer very active, there were still many who remembered them and wished to see them revived. Bull conferred with interested citizens, including the literary woman who became Ibsen's mother-in-law, Magdalene Thoresen (1819–1903). What they needed was a man of Bull's stature to lead the way.

Bull gave additional concerts, one on 1 July, when he again played his

8. Harald Beyer, *Norsk Kulturhistorie* (Oslo, 1940), 4:328–34.
9. *Bergens Stiftstidende;* Linge, *Ole Bull,* 180.
10. *Bergenske Blade;* Linge, *Ole Bull,* 180.

Ole Bull. Painting by Fritz Jensen, ca. 1850. Courtesy of Bergen University Library.

new composition, *Visit to the Sæter.* A second on 10 July was advertised as a "Farewell Concert," and according to the press, he was hailed as never before. Bouquets, wreaths, and flowers were tossed to him, and after the concert the streets were so crowded that carriages could not pass. When he left Bergen two days later, many hundreds came to see him off. In less than a month, Bull had not only played concerts, but had also prepared the plans for his theater and established a committee ready to undertake its direction. He had rented the old Dramatic Theater and hired his brother Edvard to direct the orchestra.

On 23 July one could read in the press a notice headed "Norwegian Theater in Bergen." Here it was announced that "those ladies and gentlemen who wish to make song, instrumental music, acting skill or national dances a specialty will be able to gain employment. Original dramatic and musical works will be accepted and paid for according to circumstances." It was signed "Ole Bull."[11]

The response was phenomenal. Bull's fellow townsman, Professor Lorentz Dietrichson (1834–1917) reported humorously in his memoirs that "every servant girl who could sing a note, every artisan who had learned a declamation by heart, sang and declaimed and acted for the instructor, and each one thought that he or she would be the obvious choice as first lover or prima donna. . . . No one had dreamt there would be so many talented persons in Bergen; they could apparently be counted by the hundreds."[12] The selection proved to be a nightmare for Fritz Jensen, but in the end he picked eight or nine persons, two of whom became Norway's outstanding actors: Johannes Brun (1832–90) and Louise Gulbrandsen. Bull had no interest or time for such details, but Edvard worked hard at getting the orchestra into shape.

Bull returned to Bergen on 28 October. He found lodgings near the theater and set to work through the fall. He held a private rehearsal on 21 November of *Henrik and Pernille,* a delightful comedy by Ludvig Holberg, the Bergen-born Norwegian author who had lived most of his life in Copenhagen. The major role was performed by Johannes Brun, then only eighteen years old. Marie Midling Bull wrote in her memoirs: "It was a beautiful and unforgettable moment. We were all entranced, we laughed and wept. Ole Bull exulted, 'It's going to work!' He made a little festive occasion for the actors in the foyer. . . . He was inexhaustible in giving

11. Linge, *Ole Bull,* 182.
12. Lorentz Dietrichson, *Svundne Tider. I Bergen og Christiania i 40- og 50- aarene,* 2d ed. (Christiania, 1913), 1:147.

The Bergen Theater in 1908. Photo by Knud Knudsen. Courtesy of Bergen University Library.

enthusiastic speeches, and we were also enthusiastic, in spite of the weariness that followed our great exertion."[13]

Bull planned for an official opening on 26 December but did not actually open until 2 January 1850, which has since been held to mark the beginning of the first Norwegian theater. It is not easy to reconstruct the high spirits of that opening night. Conditions were primitive; for example, there was no heating, so the audience came in their overcoats, as Bull said, "not always of the best quality." The program began with a prelude and a prologue. Then Bull, who had written music for the occasion (no. 55), appeared as the first conductor of the new orchestra. A chorus portraying farm folk (*bønder*) opened with a song urging a renewal of the Norwegian spirit. The orchestra then played Beethoven's *Egmont Overture* (for the first time in Bergen), and finally the curtain rose on Ludvig Holberg's play *Den Vægelsindede* (*The Fickle One;* tr. *The Weathercock*).[14]

The newspaper critics were favorable, and Bull felt that his venture was justified. He wrote to Félicie, who had remained at Andøen: "The whole performance was a marvel." He added: "I work hard. But I don't feel well and can hardly eat. I rarely go anywhere but to the theater. I compose some at night. But it doesn't matter about a bit of work if only I can awaken my countrymen."[15]

13. From Marie Bull's *Minder* as quoted by Linge, *Ole Bull*, 185.

14. Ludvig Holberg, *The Weathercock*, in *Four Plays by Holberg*, trans. Henry Alexander (Princeton, N.J., 1946).

15. Alexander Bull, ed., *Ole Bulls Breve i Uddrag. Med en karakteristik og biografisk Skitse af Jonas Lie* (Copenhagen, 1881), 377 (4 January 1850).

Memorial of the First National Theater; Bull (*top, center*) and company. Photo by A. M. Andersen, Bergen. Courtesy of Bergen University Library.

Félicie was not happy marooned on her island with the children. "The stay here is not very pleasant," she wrote. "The weather is terrible; there is a constant storm, and at night one can't sleep for the howling of the wind, and the house is only a summer structure. . . . 'Poor mother!' you write. 'She's weeping.' I'm also weeping—but there is no one who hears or pities me."[16]

To this Bull replied, "I wish you much happiness, health, satisfaction, and *patience*."[17] The last-named quality was certainly much needed in her life. She wrote a few weeks later to congratulate him on his success, only regretting that she was not there so "at least I could enjoy your triumphs. But it is after all not my lot to have many joys in life."[18] Bull was quite aware of the difficulties with Andøen and reminded Félicie that his work was "necessary for the national honor. . . . The work will endure, it is a national monument."[19] Bull was busy everywhere, overseeing all details. One of the early performances he oversaw and for which he composed some music (nos. 56a–56d) was Wergeland's last play, *Fjeldstuen* (*The Mountain Cottage*) (1845).

In spite of his theater's initial success, it was not long before Bull was involved in unsettling experiences. For one thing he carried on a running battle with the Bergen police, who were accustomed to supervising public performances. They asked for three seats in the orchestra section to be reserved for their men. But Bull had sold out the house and rejected their demand. When they insisted, he set up a sign over some undesirable seats in the rear announcing that "these are the seats for the police." This baiting started as a crude joke, but the police did not enjoy the joke and took him to court. He chose to fight the case all the way to the Supreme Court of Norway, where he finally won his point and gained complete control of complimentary tickets.[20] As he wrote to Félicie, "There are so many affairs and torments that it is a miracle I don't sink to the bottom. But as long as I can, I will work to my last drop of blood for the divine principle of freedom."[21] What started out as a petty dispute about tickets, had risen in Bull's view to a divine principle.

Bull also had his problems with the audiences, who were wont to chat during the music. One evening he suddenly stopped the orchestra in the midst of their playing. While the audience looked baffled, Bull calmly waited

16. Ibid., 375–76 (8 December 1849).
17. Ibid., 376 (22 December 1849).
18. Ibid., 378 (5 February 1850).
19. Ibid., 375 (30 November 1849).
20. C. C. H. B. Dunker, *Ole Bulls Process med Bergens Politi* (Copenhagen, 1851) has a complete account of this episode.
21. Ibid., 380 (17 May 1850).

for silence until the audience got the point. He also added stoves to heat the icy hall and thereby discouraged the use of overcoats. "We have to roast them out of their coats," he said.[22] He also insisted on the audience being dressed in their best. Bull had to face shocked critics, too, who had discovered that the whirling country dancers did not always keep their legs covered. In March and April Bull arranged for Torgeir Augundson to play his Hardanger fiddle at the theater, with Bull assisting, and Augundson had even more success here than in Christiania.[23]

In April 1850, at the end of the first season, Bull bought the theater outright from the Dramatic Society for a sum of 2,800 specie dollars. He did so on the express condition that the building would henceforth be used only for the performances of Norwegian actors and actresses. The conditions of sale were accepted by a bare majority of thirty-five to thirty-four votes, reflecting a nearly even division in the Society between Bull enthusiasts and those who were more skeptical about his program. Bull provided himself with a board of directors and deposited a guarantee of 2,000 Dutch guilders.

The list of plays performed during the theater's first season reflected little in the way of native dramatic talent. Only two of the sixteen plays were by Norwegians, Holberg and Wergeland. But the actors spoke their lines in the Norwegian idiom, presumably that of cultivated speakers from Bergen.

The theatre was in need of funding, so Bull set out on a concert tour. On 19 June he left the Bergen harbor to plaudits from enthusiastic viewers crowded into boats and on to docks, all waving goodbye as a flag-bedecked boat conveyed him to his steamer. It was a lovely, bright northern night, and the citizens of Bergen were applauding their favorite son. Shouts of "Long live Ole Bull!" resounded, while choruses sang. Bull called out: "Long live Norway, old Bergen, and all Norwegian patriots!"[24]

The second season opened 16 October with a slight new play by Claus Pavels Riis (1826–86) entitled *Til Sæters* ("To the Sæter"), written in 1850. For a long time it was a staple of amateur theatricals in Norway. Bull gave two concerts in Christiania, and the newspaper *Morgenbladet,* reviewing his concerts, also offered support for Bull's theater: "In a Norwegian theater the literature of Norway will get a powerful and indispensable support."[25]

22. Linge, *Ole Bull,* 187.
23. Ibid., 192; in June, Bull introduced a new piece, *Ensomhed (Solitude)* (no. 57).
24. T[harald H.] Blanc, *Norges første nationale scene* (Christiania, 1884), 59.
25. This article was authored by Bjørnstjerne Bjørnson according to Linge, *Ole Bull,* 195.

In November Bull went on from Christiania to Denmark, where he gave a series of concerts, and then to Germany, where he played to great acclaim in Hamburg—he had to give seven encores! On the way back he was a guest of the Danish King at Christiansborg Castle. On departure the King gave Bull a handsome snuff box set with diamonds.

Bull stayed at home on Andøen during the summer of 1851. Presumably, he was working on the petition that he submitted to the Norwegian Storting on 2 September 1851. It was an application for a subsidy to his theater of two thousand specie dollars. There were precedents for such subsidies for museums and the like. Bull now presented an elaborate argument for the importance of his request that appealed to national honor and sought independence for the theater. The first season had shown clearly that the theater could not survive without a state subsidy. Today it is taken for granted in Norway that such theaters get generous subsidies, but in 1851 it was still unheard of.

When the petition came up before the Storting on 25 September, Bull's plea fell on deaf ears. Even when the sum was reduced to five hundred specie dollars, there was still a negative majority of eighty to fifty-four. The leader of the Agrarian Opposition, Søren Jaabæk (1814–94), declared that this was not a matter for the State. "If one cannot maintain the nationality and the language in other ways, they will have to go by the board. That Ole Bull has made the name of Norway known throughout the world could not be a reason to pay him, as it were, for it."[26] Times were hard. Most of the Agrarians were also Puritans, who considered the theater a sinful institution. In the ranks of the urban representatives, Bull was held to be either a radical or an irresponsible dreamer.

Bull and his supporters were bitterly disappointed. The poet Vinje wrote an angry and sarcastic poem; two of its stanzas run:

Hvad svare Norges valgte Mænd?
"Gaa med din Sang dit Spil.
Paa Gaden kan du gjerne staa
Og der din Fele gnage paa;
men vi ei lytte vil."

"Hvad nytter Sang og Poesi?
Og Skuespil—O, Gru!
Det skaffer ikke Sild og Brød,
ei Melk til sorten Havregrød.
Det er min Mening, du."[27]

26. Ibid., 198.
27. Ibid., 199.

(What answer Norway's chosen men?
"Go with your song, your play.
Stand in the street as much you will
And saw upon your fiddle,
But we won't listen."

"What good is song and poetry?
And plays—oh horror!
They don't bring bread and herring,
Nor milk for blackened gruel.
That is my opinion, boy!")

Vinje, who saw a good deal of Bull in these days, reported that Bull's nationalistic fervor suffered a setback during this time. He often spoke of leaving Norway for America and assisting Norwegian emigrants in the New World.

Students from the University of Christiania shared Bull's indignation and decided to organize a protest against the action of the Storting. This took the form of a proposal to hold a music festival on 15 October 1851 to raise money for the Bergen Theater. There was a heated debate in the Student Society about this proposal. One of the students spoke disparagingly of the Bergen Theater, its inadequacies and poor prospects. At this point a student named Henrik Ibsen (1828–1906) rose to Bull's defense.

Ibsen's speech was apparently what called Bull's attention to the man who became Norway's most famous playwright. Ibsen was personally a small and unimpressive young man, but he was exactly what Bull needed at this point. Bull had come to Christiania to seek support for his theater and had failed. But, in selecting Ibsen as a "dramatic poet" for the theater, he supplied what it needed more than anything else: a genuine dramatist. In picking Ibsen, Bull chose better than he knew.

The upshot of the October festival was that the students raised three hundred specie dollars for Bull's theater. On this occasion Bull's song for men's chorus and orchestra, *Kunstens Magt* (*The Power of Art*) (no. 58), was premiered.

At this time, like many students, Ibsen was desperately poor, radical in his politics, and uncertain of his future. He had called attention to himself by publishing a drama entitled *Catilina* (1850), based on Roman history. It was not a great play, but it revealed some qualities he would eventually develop in his dramatic work. Also at this time, with his friends Vinje and the critic Paul Botten Hansen (1824–69), he edited a satirical journal called *Manden* (*The Man*). Bull's offer, then, promised Ibsen more financial stability and prestige than he'd ever before enjoyed. He was given a five-year contract, with the understanding that he would produce a play a year to be performed on the second of January each year, the theater's anniversary.

Ibsen came to Bergen and stayed for nearly six years, during which time the theater also provided him with a trip abroad to study theater in Copenhagen and Dresden. Although he never quite fulfilled his contract and was too reticent to be a good instructor for the inexperienced Norwegian actors, he learned the ins and outs of the theater. Bull had performed his most valuable service to the Norwegian theater by appointing Ibsen as its director.

Bull had now done what he could for the theater. He left the management of it to his board and the staff he had hired. He departed Norway on 22 November 1851, stopping to perform in Hamburg, Amsterdam, London, and Liverpool. Here he shipped off to New York and arrived just after New Year's 1852. So began Bull's second visit to the New World, one that would prove to be even more dramatic than the first.

12

Oleana—A Paternalistic Colony
(1852–1857)

HE TALE of Oleana has been told and retold. For Americans it is perhaps the most vivid episode in Ole Bull's life, classic in its rhythm of rise and fall. For Norwegians it became just another example of the artist's lack of grasp on the affairs of the world. Today, Oleana has sunk to be an ironic sidetrack in the great progression of American settlement, leaving merely some minor traces in the woods of Pennsylvania.[1]

Norwegian settlement in America was already underway when Bull returned there in 1852. The Moravians, a sect whose followers had settled in Bethlehem, Pennsylvania, had sent missionaries A. M. Iverson (1823–1907) and Nils Otto Tank (1800–64) to the west, where they helped found a Norwegian colony at Ephraim, Wisconsin, in 1851. Most of the leaders of the Norwegian immigrants chose the fertile lands of the Midwest as the most favorable spot for settlement. There were exceptions, like Johan M. Reiersen, who in 1844 selected Texas. Cleng Peerson (1782–1865), the acknowledged father of Norwegian settlement, also ended his days in Texas, but only after founding settlements in Illinois.

Ole Bull was another exception. He chose the forests of Pennsylvania, and he was already well known, a distinguished and beloved visitor, when he returned to America for the purpose of founding a Norwegian colony. He had hardly landed when he received a letter signed by thirty-seven rep-

---

1. Aside from Ola Linge, *Ole Bull: Livshistoria, Mannen, Kunstnaren* (Oslo, 1953), there are good accounts of Oleana in Torstein Jahr, "Oleana—Et blad af Ole Bulls og den norske indvandrings historie," *Symra* 6 (1910): 2–37, 129–62, 195–216; Anders Buraas, *De reiste ut* (Oslo, 1982); Theodore C. Blegen, *Land of Their Choice* (Minneapolis, 1955); and Theodore C. Blegen, *Norwegian Migration to America 1825–1860* (Northfield, Minn., 1931).

Oleona, Penn., 1990. Photo by Camilla Cai.

resentatives, senators, and officials, headed by the famous politician Henry Clay (1777–1852), and eleven foreign diplomats, urging him to give a Washington concert.[2] He arranged to play there on 26 March 1852 and was so acclaimed that he had to give another concert. In May he gave several concerts in New York, one in Metropolitan Hall, for an audience of three thousand.

By now it was well known that Bull was looking for land to buy. He had inspected some land in Virginia in April and was almost ready to buy it when he was approached by a land speculator named John M. Cowan. Cowan offered him a tract of 11,144 acres in Potter County, Pennsylvania. The price was less than a dollar per acre, a total of 10,388 dollars. He claimed that if Bull should wish to enter a company of buyers, he could produce another 120,000 acres. The land was located in a valley in the Allegheny Mountains, by a creek known as Kettle Creek, that ran into the Susquehanna River. It is virtually certain that Bull had not set eyes on the land when he agreed to enter the deal.

It has been shrewdly suggested by Ola Linge that the poem that Wergeland wrote as a farewell to Bull from Norway in 1843 (see chap. 8) may have run through his mind when he considered this purchase.[3]

2. Linge, *Ole Bull*, 204, reprints the letter, but gives an incorrect number of fifty-seven signatures.

3. Ibid., 205–6.

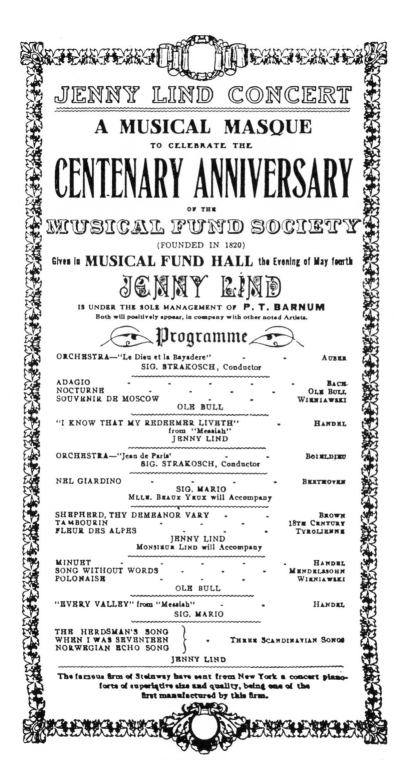

JENNY LIND CONCERT

A MUSICAL MASQUE

TO CELEBRATE THE

CENTENARY ANNIVERSARY

OF THE

MUSICAL FUND SOCIETY

(FOUNDED IN 1820)

Given in **MUSICAL FUND HALL** the Evening of May fourth

JENNY LIND

IS UNDER THE SOLE MANAGEMENT OF **P. T. BARNUM**

Both will positively appear, in company with other noted Artists.

Programme

ORCHESTRA—"Le Dieu et la Bayadere"   -   -   AUBER
SIG. STRAKOSCH, Conductor

ADAGIO -   -   -   -   -   - BACH
NOCTURNE -   -   -   - OLE BULL
SOUVENIR DE MOSCOW   -   - WIENIAWSKI
OLE BULL

"I KNOW THAT MY REDEEMER LIVETH" - HANDEL
from "Messiah"
JENNY LIND

ORCHESTRA—"Jean de Paris"   -   - BOIELDIEU
SIG. STRAKOSCH, Conductor

NEL GIARDINO -   -   - BEETHOVEN
SIG. MARIO
MLLE. BEAUX YEUX will Accompany

SHEPHERD, THY DEMEANOR VARY -   - BROWN
TAMBOURIN -   -   - 18TH CENTURY
FLEUR DES ALPES   -   - TYROLIENNE
JENNY LIND
MONSIEUR LIND will Accompany

MINUET -   -   -   - HANDEL
SONG WITHOUT WORDS -   - MENDELSOHN
POLONAISE -   -   - WIENIAWSKI
OLE BULL

"EVERY VALLEY" from "Messiah" -   - HANDEL
SIG. MARIO

THE HERDSMAN'S SONG ⎫
WHEN I WAS SEVENTEEN ⎬ - THREE SCANDINAVIAN SONGS
NORWEGIAN ECHO SONG ⎭
JENNY LIND

The famous firm of Steinway have sent from New York a concert pianoforte of superlative size and quality, being one of the
first manufactured by this firm.

Concert program, 4 May 1852[?], Philadelphia, with Jenny Lind. Management of
P. T. Barnum. Courtesy of Potter County Historical Society.

117

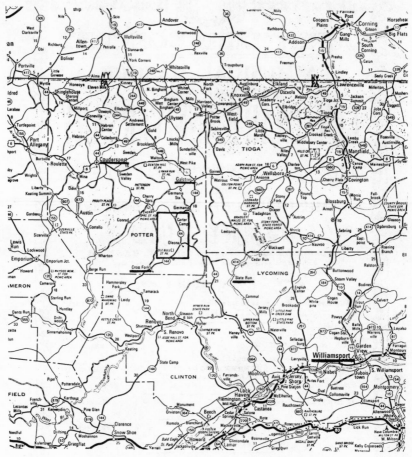

North-central Pennsylvania, showing Oleona, Penn.

— Let the sycamore
Whisper lovingly towards him,
Let the Allegheny
House him in its friendly caverns,
Let the Susquehanna
Like a gentle harp resound
To greet him, my beloved!

Here was his chance to realize Wergeland's poetic prognostication. There may also have been other, more realistic arguments that led Bull to his choice. The terrain was mountainous, resembling the Norway from which the immigrants came. There was healthy air and good outdoor work, with no fear of cholera or fever as in the South or even at this time in the Mid-

118

Kettle Creek in Ole Bull State Park. Photo by Camilla Cai.

west. The approach was arduous, but there was the prospect that a railroad or two would be built. There was even a presumption that beneath the soil were hidden mineral riches. With the rail connection, the New York market would come within easy reach. On paper it was a magnificent idea, worthy of a daring speculator. Bull appointed a New York lawyer and friend, John Hopper, to act as his agent.[4]

In the course of the summer, Bull let it be known in Norway and in the States that there was good land and good pay to be had in his colony for people who wished to work. The citizens in the little town of Coudersport, Pennsylvania (population 250), could hardly believe their eyes when they read that Ole Bull, the world-famous violinist, had arrived there on Sunday evening, 5 September 1852, and that he intended to found a Norwegian colony.

Two days later a group of thirty resolute Norwegians who had arrived in Coudersport on 6 September traveled out to the site of the colony to begin work. They had waited at an agreed-upon place for the arrival of Ole Bull and John Hopper. They were greeted with Bull's private flag, a

---

4. Hopper had been in touch with Bull as early as 1846, as we see from a letter Hopper wrote him about a pistol Bull had ordered in America: "You continue to be much talked about; you entered the hearts of the American people" (3 January 1846) (Bergen University Library).

Norwegian red white and blue cross edged by American stars. The Norwegians may have been dismayed by what they saw in the primeval forest of the Alleghenies, but they fell to with a will, chopping down timber while Bull picked out a site for himself and twenty-five other houses. There was nothing there but a small plain entirely surrounded by tamarack trees (not sycamores!), some of them several feet in circumference, and no structures other than a tiny hotel.

Several wagonloads of food and implements were shipped in from Coudersport, about 30 miles northwest. A fine spruce was trimmed as a flagpole, and the flag was raised over the settlement, to be named "Oleana."[5] Everyone shouted "hurrahs," thirty-one times for each of the States of the Union and three for Ole Bull. Bull gave a speech: "Kind friends meet us on every side, taking us by the hand and giving us welcome to our new homes. Brothers of Norway:—We must not disappoint this confidence, but by lives of industry and honesty show our new brothers that they have not misplaced their friendship." He also reminded the settlers that Norsemen had discovered America before Columbus and said: "We will here establish a New Norway, consecrated to Liberty, baptized in freedom, and protected by the glorious flag of America."[6] With bared heads, the Norwegians promised that they would do their best.

In the evening there was a grand celebration with bonfires, and Ole Bull played his violin in honor of the day. An American who reported on the occasion, Eli Bowen (1824–86), wrote: "No language can describe this music—the auditors, the attendant circumstances, and the occasion, appeared to have given a new and unearthly inspiration to the great artist; he touched every cord of every heart in his audience."[7] Finally they sang a favorite patriotic song of their time, "For Norge, Kjæmpers Fødeland" ("For Norway, Land of Heroes").[8] After the song an American welcomed Bull to Pennsylvania. In this way New Norway was dedicated on 8 September 1852.

A few days later Bull returned to New York to meet the *Incognito,* which was docking with new immigrants, many of them on their way to Oleana. He returned to Oleana on 17 September bringing 105 more colonists. On 24 September the editor of the *People's Journal* in Coudersport exulted on

5. Some American sources call it "Oleona," but we follow the spelling "Oleana" used by Eli Bowen, *The Pictorial Sketch-book of Pennsylvania,* 2d ed. (Philadelphia, 1853).
6. *Clinton Democrat* (2 November 1852), Lock Haven, Penn.
7. Bowen, *Pictorial Sketch-book,* 196.
8. Text by the Bergen bishop Johan Nordahl Brun (1745–1816); melody by the Belgian composer André-Ernest-Modeste Grétry (1741–1813).

Oleana

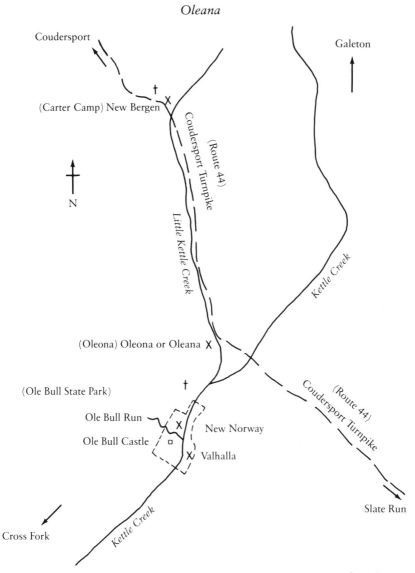

Kettle Creek Valley, Potter County, Penn. (Modern names are in parentheses.)

PART I. LIFE AND ADVENTURES

their coming: "The Norwegians are just what we wanted to subdue our vast forests." Bull and the Oleana colony were also welcomed in an editorial in the *New York Weekly Times* (9 October 1852): "In the formations, products, and animals of this region, the colonists will be continuously reminded of their native Norway." The newspaper foresaw no problems and described Bull's second shipload of settlers as having been "rescued from the grasp of the runners," who preyed on ignorant immigrants.

Among the arrivals was Jacob Aall Ottesen (1825–1904), a pastor who was on his way to a call in Manitowoc, Wisconsin. Bull invited him to come and inspect his colony, and Ottesen agreed to stop off and deliver the first sermon. He later wrote a valuable account of his impressions, noting ominously that the colony was situated sixty English miles from the nearest railroad. It was expected by Bull that two railroads would be built, one from the north and one from the south. Colonists were promised fifteen dollars a month together with food and lodging. Land would be sold at three dollars per acre the first year, rising to five and ten dollars in later years. "It is expected" wrote Ottesen, "that all these impassable woods and steep hills will be turned into cultivated land." But he expressed doubt about its success and advised neither for nor against migrating to Oleana, for he did not know whether Ole Bull would be able to keep his promises. "I truly believe that Ole Bull means very well, but he is not a business man, and furthermore politico-democratic plans en gros are involved in the scheme."[9] Ottesen took a cautious and diplomatic stand, as we might expect from a pastor who was to become one of the fathers of the Norwegian Synod in America.

At the beginning of his settlement project, Bull was not aware that Pennsylvania law required him to declare his intention to become a citizen by taking out "first papers" if he wished to own more than five thousand acres in the state. When he realized what was necessary, he did not, like an ordinary immigrant, go to an office and sign a paper. He demanded and got a public ceremony arranged in Independence Hall in Philadelphia on 25 September 1852. The newspapers gave him all the publicity he could ask for.

A journalist in Williamsport, Pennsylvania, gave Bull an especially enthusiastic welcome. According to his story, Bull declared in Philadelphia that he would definitely become an American citizen, even "a citizen of Pennsylvania." He spoke of having bought much fine land in Potter County and said that he would bring "tens of thousands of my oppressed coun-

9. Blegen, *Norwegian Migration*, 295.

trymen to this free and happy land."[10] He described them as brave, honest, contented, and industrious, and he was proud to think that Americans would like them. Bull then acceded to the welcoming committee's request for a concert, and the journalist's extravagant account describes Bull's playing as "an embodiment of every emotion of the heart—touching the deep wells of affection and reaching the consuming fire of the passions."[11]

In Philadelphia Bull forswore allegiance to the King of Norway and Sweden. With his hand on his heart, he declared (in a grand but essentially meaningless gesture) that he had never sworn any loyalty to the King of Norway and Sweden (neither had anyone else). "I shall value the privilege of citizenship above every other earthly object and shall endeavor to induce hundreds of thousands of my countrymen to so great a boon."[12] He then signed a document and did not overlook the opportunity to tell people about the Norse discovery of America.

Bull spent October and November of 1852 working at Oleana. By the end of the year, there were two or three hundred settlers in the colony, including married persons and children. A schoolhouse and a hotel had been built, and plans were made for three new villages, to be named "New Bergen," "New Norway," and "Valhalla." Bull's house, two stories high and measuring thirty by twenty-four feet, was built on a high slope. It was called "The Castle."

A book published anonymously in Bergen, Norway in 1852, called *Amerika, Ole Bull og det nye Norge* (*America, Ole Bull and the New Norway*) took an encouraging view of Oleana and tried to build enthusiasm for it. Norway's laboring population had, in general, a favorable view, and the labor press hailed Bull's colony. Another book published that year in Norway may also have helped foster a positive attitude toward Bull's American experiment. This was the second major biography written about Bull. Authored by journalist Henrik Winter-Hjelm (1829–59), it was an account of Bull's life up to his second departure for America. It appeared as a series of articles entitled "Træk af Ole Bulls Liv" ("Features of Ole Bull's Life") first in *Morgenbladet* (1852) and then in the periodical *Lillehammer Tilskuer* from 8 June to 5 November. Bull also kept himself in the public eye that year by having his transcriptions of five Norwegian *slåtts* and a folksong published as an appendix (no. 59) to Christian Tønsberg's *Norske Nationaldragter* (*Norwegian National Costumes*) (1852).

Before November had ended, Bull deemed it necessary to arrange a con-

---

10. Williamsport *Democrat* (25 September 1852); see chap. 9, at footnote 15.
11. Mortimer Smith, *The Life of Ole Bull* (Princeton, N.J., 1943), 109.
12. *People's Journal* (8 October 1852).

Retaining wall near Ole Bull's castle. Photo by Camilla Cai.

cert tour to make some money. He chose as his companions the pianist Maurice Strakosch (1825–87), his wife Amalia Patti-Strakosch (1831–1915), a former singer, and her ten-year-old sister Adelina. Adelina Patti (1843–1919) had a marvelous voice that later made her world famous, and she was a good addition to his team. They toured from November to May, but Bull managed to spend Christmas with the Longfellows in Cambridge. It was on this occasion that Bull met William Makepeace Thackeray, who believed the violinist "quite a character for a book."[13]

The winter of 1852 to 1853 was hard on the Oleana colonists, for the road to Coudersport was difficult to keep open. Perhaps to encourage the Norwegians, their American neighbors printed two poems in the local paper that winter. One included the stanza:

> Let the wizard of Norway but sound them one call
> That the wind-spirits taught him far over the sea,
> And the wood sprites will garland each arched forest hall
> And wild and wide shall your welcome be.

The second poem included this hearty greeting:

> Welcome the Norwegian band, a band so freely blest;
> You're welcome to our native land if it will give you rest;

13. James Grant Wilson, *Thackeray in the United States* (New York, 1904), 1:97.

Oleana

View from Ole Bull's castle. Photo by Camilla Cai.

You're welcome to our home so rude, you're welcome to its cheer;
We do not think it an intrude; you are all welcome here.[14]

In March of 1853 the Pennsylvania legislature voted to give Bull dispensation from the citizenship requirement. In Norway, however, it had already been reported that he had given up his Norwegian citizenship, and he was sharply criticized by people who did not understand American law. In any case, Bull did not in fact remain in America the six years required for obtaining a final decree of American citizenship, although by staying five and a half years he was close to meeting the requirement.

Bull and his company carried on their tour from New Orleans to Chicago and Milwaukee. In Buffalo he fell ill, and when he was better, he promptly headed for Oleana. He arrived on the Norwegian national holiday of 17 May, which was celebrated with rockets and dancing.

While he was still on tour, Bull had written a long and enthusiastic letter to his brother Edvard from Augusta, Georgia: "You will have a conception of my activity as artist and leader, and director of my little State in Pennsylvania, only when you know that I am engaged simultaneously in laying out five villages, and am contracting with the Government for

14. Mary E. Welfling, *The Ole Bull Colony in Potter County 1852: One hundredth anniversary observed July 31–August 1, 1952* (Coudersport, Penn., 1952), 6.

125

House built by Norwegian colonists in Oleana. Photo ca. 1904. Courtesy of Potter County Historical Society.

the casting of cannon, some ten thousand in all, for the fortresses, especially for those in California." The city of Philadelphia, he added, had subscribed two million dollars for a new railroad on the south of Oleana, and similarly New York for another on the north of the colony. "So many have applied for land that I have been obliged to look out for more in the neighborhood. I have bought 20,000 acres to the west, and in the adjoining county (MacKean) I have the [right of first] refusal of 112,000 acres. In Lycoming County I am contracting for an old deserted foundry with forests, water power, workshops, and dwellings, and am taking out patents in Washington for a new smelting furnace for cannon." He even invited Edvard to join him in America and offered him 100 acres of land gratis. "You ask me how I thus can play with millions, so to speak! Dear Edvard, when you see it yourself, you will be more astonished. This is only a beginning. My abilities have increased in proportion with the magnitude of the work; my enthusiasm has overcome my despair. My persecutors have themselves provoked my undisputed right to defense, and I answer with facts!"[15]

15. Alexander Bull, ed., *Ole Bulls Breve i Uddrag. Med en karakteristik og biografisk Skitse af Jonas Lie* (Copenhagen, 1881), 382–84 (6 February 1853).

126

According to an account that appeared in *Dwight's Journal of Music,* it was also Bull's intention to build a polytechnical school that would be staffed by European professors, a civil and military institution combined that would be open to the youth of America. The United States needed such a school; why not have it at Oleana? School, foundry, and government would go admirably together. All the government would have to do was buy. Teachers, craftsmen, and laborers would be able to take shares and supplement their salaries by dividends. *Dwight's Journal* claimed that West Point had become exclusive and aristocratic; "the Oleana school would be for the people."[16]

Torstein Jahr, a librarian at the Library of Congress who did the earliest research on Oleana (1910), did not think that this plan was an expression of Bull's "impractical" nature. He pointed out that America at this time did lack just such a school.[17] That there was reason in Bull's venture is suggested by the fact that Pennsylvania later became one of the chief American steel-producing states. In addition, the men who eventually cut down the forests of Pennsylvania earned fabulous fortunes. But these ideas required capital that Bull did not have, even though he and his company worked feverishly to raise funds by their touring. He was expected back in Oleana for the July Fourth festival, but did not come. He was reported to be ill again.

Some of the colonists had already begun to leave, as we learn from a letter of 19 March 1853, in a Christiania paper, written by an Oleana colonist named H. P. Olsen. "There is nothing but big trees, high mountains, and narrow valleys; I have not seen such ugly land in Norway. So God help the poor Norwegians who come to Ole Bull's colony. . . . We have appointed a committee to find Ole Bull or his companions, but so far they have not been successful. . . . When those who are in Ole Bull's colony have received their money they will all leave."[18] Bull had his defenders among the letter writers, but the signs of discontent within the colony were clear.[19] Even so, as late as June 1853, the abolitionist Cassius Clay was sending the colony purebred cattle from his farm in Kentucky.[20]

One of Bull's most merciless critics in Norway was Ditmar Meidell (1826–1900), editor of the humorous magazine *Krydseren.* As early as No-

16. [John Sullivan] Dwight, "Ole Bull and his Colony," *Dwight's Journal of Music,* 3 (28 May 1853): 60–61 (Boston). Blegen, *Norwegian Migration,* 299–300.

17. Jahr, "Oleana," 130.

18. *Christiania-Posten* (19 March 1853); cf. Blegen, *Norwegian Migration,* 297.

19. Other letters are printed in Blegen, *Land of Their Choice,* 230–300.

20. Letter (25 June 1853), Bergen University Library.

vember 1852 he had written: "So far as Ole Bull is concerned, it may be conceded that he can play the violin, but this hardly implies that with his bow he can level the earth, move mountains, and clear primeval forests."[21] On 5 March 1853, Meidell published a ballad that raised a roar of laughter in Norway and became the most celebrated song of Norwegian immigration, even enjoyed by the immigrants themselves who realized that some of the claims made by immigrant leaders and their agents were unrealistic. We include some verses from this essentially scurrilous song:

> I Oleana der er det godt at være,
> i Norge vil jeg inte Slavelænken bære!
>
> Ole — Ole — Ole oh! Oleana!
> Ole — Ole — Ole oh! Oleana!
>
> (In Oleana, there it's good to be,
> Not in Norway, bearing chains of slavery.)
>
> I Oleana der faar jeg Jord for Intet,
> af Jorden voxer Kornet, — og det gaar gesvint det.
>
> (In Oleana there I get land for nothin'
> And the grain grows up without fussin'.)
>
> Aa Laxene dem springer saa lystig i Bække,
> dem hopper selv i Gryden aa roper: dem ska' dække!
>
> (And the salmon leap from the brook
> Crying out to get them a cook!)
>
> Aa Kalvene dem slagter sig hurtig og flaar sig
> aa stejker sig fortere end man tar en Taar sig!
>
> (And the calves do their own slaughter
> And turn to roast while you drink your firewater!)
>
> Ja to Daler Dagen det faar Du for at svire,
> aa er du rektig doven, saa kanske Du faar fire.
>
> (You get two dollars a day for sousing,
> And if you're real lazy, you get more for carousing.)
>
> Ja rejs til Oleana, saa skal Du vel leve,
> den fattigste Stymper herover er Greve!
>
> (Yeah, go to Oleana, you won't have to beg,
> A count they will make out of every yegg!)[22]

---

21. *Krydseren* (20 November 1852); cf. Blegen, *Norwegian Migration,* 302.

22. Norwegian text from Theodore C. Blegen and Martin B. Ruud, eds., *Norwegian Emigrant Songs and Ballads* (Minneapolis, 1936), 192–98.

While this ballad did not cause the collapse of Oleana, it formed a fit-ting finale. It reflected the conservative upper-bourgeois view of Bull's enter-prise, that he was a dreamer who could not be expected to manage a se-rious business. The land had been sold to him with three "reservations," plots of land (totaling 658 acres) that were not included in the deal. This clause seems to have been the source of later conflict. Rumors circulated about Bull's having been swindled by his American contacts. This view is held forth in a letter by lawyer L. E. Bulkley written on Bull's behalf on 21 November 1853, a letter characterized by Ola Linge as incorrect. Linge points out that there is no record of any suit by Bull against his American agents. In any case, on 22 September 1853, Bull deeded back to Cowan the 11,144 acres he had bought, and Bull's money was returned. This did not cover his expenses for Oleana, but at least he was not swin-dled for the land.[23]

What became of the colonists who did settle in Oleana? According to Jahr's very careful investigation in 1910, after Bull had deeded the land back to Cowan most of the few remaining colonists left as soon as they could. At Oleana's height, Christmastime 1852, there may have been as many as three hundred colonists. Only a few were still there in the late 1850s, and a few remained for life.[24] A German physician Bull had met in Havana, Dr. Edward Joerg (1807–73), and his family were one of the few families who remained in Oleana even after Bull had given up on his "New Nor-way." Most of the rest headed west to the new settlements and better land of Wisconsin and Minnesota. As historian Theodore Blegen wrote, in sum-marizing Jahr's results: "The collapse of Oleana did not mean the end of the world for them."[25]

A claim made by Inez Bull, an American "grand-niece" of Bull's, to the effect that "the Ole Bull colonists had been killed by heat and suffocation in a boxcar" appears to be false. She bases it on a story in the Janesville, Wisconsin, *Gazette* for 8 August 1866: "Only 100 out of 800 arrived in Janesville and Beloit, Wisconsin, alive."[26] For one thing, there were never as many as eight hundred colonists. Second, such a stupendous catastro-phe would have been played up in the Norwegian-American press of the time and would have been reported by Jahr as well as Blegen.

23. Linge, *Ole Bull,* 217.
24. See also Welfling, *Ole Bull Colony,* 13.
25. Blegen, *Norwegian Migration,* 307.
26. Inez Bull, *Ole Bull's Activities in the United States between 1843 and 1880: A Biog-raphy,* dissertation submitted to New York University, School of Education (Smithtown, N.Y., 1982), 88. She also states that according to the Chicago *Democrat* (8 August 1854), "seven bodies were taken off the car in Chicago," 88.

Meanwhile, as the colony dissolved, Bull was busy giving concerts. In New Orleans in the late summer, he gave a benefit for the needy who had been impoverished by the yellow fever epidemic. When he learned of the distress endured by his last forty or fifty colonists in Oleana, he gave three benefit performances in New York and Philadelphia for them. On this tour he billed his concerts as "farewells," possibly because he was thinking of returning to Norway, although he did not, in fact, return for another four years.

At concerts held in Washington on 7 and 9 November 1853, President Franklin Pierce and many members of his administration were present. The *National Intelligencer* wrote: "Besides his artistic fame, Ole Bull has shown himself to be a great human benefactor." They especially praised his andante in *Polacca Guerriera* and his playing in *A Mother's Prayer*: "His tone, this full, glorious, moving tone, that he alone can bring forth as if from magic strings, was as lovely as never before."[27]

In March 1854 Bull played for several sold-out houses in Chicago, and following the final concert was a guest of honor at a dinner attended by four hundred Americans and Norwegians. He then headed for San Francisco and, on the way through Panama, caught a tropical fever which took him a long time to shake off. His impresario Strakosch informed the press that Bull had been robbed of money and jewels on the way to San Francisco, but Linge doubts that this was anything but a publicity ploy. Bull performed for two months in California before undertaking the perilous return trip through Panama. Before returning to New York he stopped in Milwaukee, where the Milwaukee *Democrat* (November 1854) hailed "the natural artist whom the tooth of age does not bite . . . who pours out beauty from his noble soul." The writer even indulged in a bit of doggerel:

> Honor to the Fiddle-King
> King by right, divine and holy,
> All the world have crowned Thee, Ole.

In February 1855 Bull foolishly got involved in another grand scheme, this time through the persuasion of Strakosch and impresario Max Maretzek (1821–97), an effort to found an opera in New York. It was a costly error. Bull leased the Academy of Music and opened his season with Verdi's *Rigoletto*. Gross mismanagement by those he hired forced him to close after only five performances, showing that Bull had even yet not learned to guard his own interests. As his second wife, Sara, later wrote of him:

27. Linge, *Ole Bull,* 219.

Ole Bull, 1850s. From an original photograph. Courtesy of Music Division, Library of Congress, Washington, D.C.

"All of Ole Bull's correspondence shows that his friends knew how apt he was to neglect his own affairs, and that they were watchful of his interests and sympathized with him in his reverses."[28] Among those who did so was Maria Child, who wrote him how glad she was that he had given up his idea of a New York opera, "for I always dread to have artists connected with anything that requires financial calculations."[29]

Two years later, in the spring of 1857, when Bull again needed help, Edwin Wallace Stoughton (1818–82), an eminent Boston lawyer and one-time ambassador to Russia, came to his aid. He had read in the day's newspaper that Bull was in trouble. According to Sara Bull, he went into court "at the right moment to save some valuables and jewels, which would otherwise have been lost. A lifelong friendship commenced that day, and Ole Bull often spent weeks together with the Stoughtons."[30] Her statement is confirmed by Bjørnstjerne Bjørnson, who met Stoughton in Boston after Bull's death. Stoughton held Bjørnson's hand and told him about "that bright spirit, that great heart, the loveliest human being he had ever met, the noblest eye he had gazed into."[31] We also learn from Stoughton's letter that in 1857 a judgment of some kind had been obtained against Bull in New York by a Mr. H, possibly his former lawyer, John Hopper. Stoughton wrote to an unnamed colleague asking him to protect Bull from further harassment.[32]

Another friendly letter during these years of financial chaos came from the famous antislavery writer Harriet Beecher Stowe (1811–96). She recalled pleasant hours spent with Bull in Hartford and urged him "not to despair of human nature—nor wholly despair of America."[33] She invited him to "come speak to us of the lovely fjords and dripping waterfalls and glittering lakes of Norway." Even if he couldn't come, she said, their home was a place "where you may at any time, if you choose, come and sleep a day without our troubling you with a word. . . . Nobody shall ask you to play a tune; nobody shall hinder your playing an opera."[34]

Bull also heard again from Maria Child. Sara Bull reports that Child "had heard of his troubles and his need of rest, and wanted him to come to her country home at once." Bull accepted her invitation. He spent twenty-

28. Sara C. Bull, *Ole Bull: A Memoir* (Boston and New York, 1882), 230.
29. Letter (8 March 1855), Bergen University Library.
30. Bull, *A Memoir*, 228.
31. Eva Lund Haugen and Einar Haugen, eds. and trans., *Land of the Free: Bjørnstjerne Bjørnson's America Letters, 1880–1881* (Northfield, Minn., 1978), 65.
32. Bull, *A Memoir*, 229.
33. Linge, *Ole Bull*, 222.
34. Bull, *A Memoir*, 232.

four hours sleeping in one stretch and, Sara reports, "woke refreshed, and, as he said, his reason saved."[35]

In November 1855 Bull visited, possibly for the second time, a former townsman and schoolmate, Peder Anderson. Anderson had immigrated from Norway in 1830 and now lived in Lowell, Massachusetts. Bull was delighted to see Anderson, who had won for himself a position as part owner of a woolen mill and as a skillful artist. Anderson's wife Martha kept a diary. On 3 November 1855 she noted that Ole Bull came to them from Nashua, New Hampshire: "He entertained us with a fund of anecdotes and grotesque imitations, and after smoking a cigar, played *Carnival of Venice* and many Norwegian airs." In conversation with her Bull had said that "the artist must be a compound of burning lava and of ice; his imagination must be on fire, but his reason must be cool and calm, and no passion must be suffered to interrupt the expression of pure feeling." She reported that Bull kept his arms rigid as wood while playing, but after playing he suffered from pain and was physically exhausted. "The very presence of an unfriendly person is painful and any jar upon his feelings will cause tears."[36]

In December 1855 he was again in Cambridge, visiting the Longfellows. On 8 December Longfellow noted in his diary: "Ole Bull and Thackeray and Fields were with us last evening. We had music on the Cremona and a petit souper."[37]

In 1856 Bull received a letter from Phineas T. Barnum (1810–91), requesting an interview of "five minutes only."[38] It is not known if or what Bull replied, nor is it known exactly what Barnum had in mind. The famed circus entrepreneur had brought Jenny Lind to America for a concert tour in 1850 and perhaps wanted to sponsor a tour for Bull as well.

Bull and his company kept up a busy concert schedule through 1856 and 1857. He catered to his American audiences with a *Fantasia on American Airs* (no. 60), introducing "Jordan is a Hard Road to Travel," "Hazel Dell," "Arkansas Traveler," "Pop Goes the Weasel," and "Home, Sweet Home." In July 1856 they got as far as Janesville and Madison, Wisconsin. Jonas Lie reports that by March 1857 Bull was so weak from fever that he had to be helped on to the stage in New York. The quinine he took

35. Ibid., 230–31.
36. Eva Lund Haugen and Ingrid Semmingsen, "Peder Anderson of Bergen and Lowell: Artist and Ambassador of Culture," in Brita Seyersted, ed., *Americana Norvegica* (Oslo, 1973), 4:1–29.
37. Linge, *Ole Bull,* 222.
38. Letter, dated 19 April 1856, Bergen University Library. See program p. 117.

Ole Bull. Photo taken in Minneapolis, Minn., 1856[?]. Courtesy of Bergen University Library.

for the lingering effects of tropical fever was so strong that he could not hear his own tones, and between numbers he had to rest on a sofa and drink port.[39]

In Norway rumors were rife about Bull's unlucky experiences and his illnesses. Félicie received from him neither letters nor funds. Bull had given

39. Linge, *Ole Bull,* 223.

his lawyer friend Bernhard Dunker (1809–70) power of attorney to sell Andøen, and when the money from the sale of Andøen ran out, Félicie sought help from Bull's old friends, the Egeberg family in Christiania. In 1856, on the advice of Fredrikke Egeberg, Félicie sent their son Alexander, who had now reached his seventeenth year, to comfort Bull over the fact, as she wrote, "that you have lost your whole fortune and that you are very depressed. . . . I hope you will receive him as a father, and that he will comfort you as a good son, but above all,—watch over him and protect him with all your might."[40]

Bull was in Chicago when Alexander arrived in New York on 16 November 1856. There Alexander received a letter from his father suggesting that they meet in Albany: "Welcome to me, heartily welcome. You came in time, I hope, to give me a little glimpse of sun on the edge of the precipice. There is now hardly anything left of me,—but it is difficult to overcome one's organism."[41] They did meet and Alexander accompanied him back to Norway and eventually to Félicie after five years of absence from both. Ole's hair had turned gray, and it fluttered in the wind as he went on board the steamer *America* in Boston on 29 July 1857.

Bull's American experience had brought him nearer to his emigrated countrymen. As Jahr put it in 1910: "We Norwegians in America are proud of being able to call him a Norwegian-American."[42] As never before, however, he had good reason to feel doubtful about his reception in Norway. It was probably an encouraging sign that on his return he was met by a German correspondent who interviewed him as "Norway's only famous musician." Although this writer was aware that Bull "has a strong party against him," not only in his native land, but especially in Bergen, this talk was disregarded, and the article was concerned only with Bull as an artist and with his "always original, often striking, sometimes perverse views about art and artists." In the interview Bull offered unusual views on the piano techniques of Liszt and Thalberg, comparing the characteristics of their hand positions and speaking with disdain about "impure hand positions" on the violin. "Art is knowing," he is quoted as saying, "the uninterrupted expression of an enthusiastic, genial will, and the genial will always achieves its purpose." He compared skill in handling the violin to the skill of a master barber, who trims the beard without touching the skin. The picture of Bull that emerges from this interview is not that of

40. Bull, ed., *Ole Bulls Breve i Uddrag,* 385 (9 September 1856).
41. Ibid., 385–86 (12 November 1856).
42. Jahr, "Oleana," 3.

a man who has succumbed to a sense of failure nor suffers ill health. On the contrary, "Ole Bull accompanied all he spoke with extraordinarily lively gestures, which with his Herculean strength and his athletic figure made a deep impression. The whole effect was attractive, and anyone who has spoken with him will no more forget him than anyone who has heard him play."[43]

43. The interview is dated Bergen, 1 September 1857, and is addressed to a Mr. Räde-klau, but it is signed only "O. L." It is in the Stadt- und Universitätsbibliothek, Frankfurt am Main.

13

Ole Bull Meets Bjørnson
(1857–1862)

BULL'S MISADVENTURE in Pennsylvania was no doubt a topic of glee among conservatives in Norway, whose status was being threatened by a rising tide of national and democratic feeling in the populace. From being the unquestioned rulers of the country, the upper bourgeoisie was faced with a growing revolt on the part of a band of young rebels. These were recruited partly from the rural population and partly from the young intellectuals. To them Bull had become a folk hero, both for his attempt to establish a purely Norwegian theater and for his effort to create a Norwegian colony in the United States. The conservatives were tied firmly to the Danish theater and stood in opposition to emigration.

The spokesman of the new generation was a young author and journalist who bore the conspicuously Norwegian name of Bjørnstjerne Bjørnson, a name with two "bears" in it. Some years earlier he had heard Bull play, and now in 1857 he welcomed him home in a lyrical article that occupied much of the front page in his newspaper, Christiania's *Morgenbladet.* The article bore the headline "Ole Bull has Come Home" and was signed only "Bn."

"No one has welcomed Bull," he wrote. "Is this to be the first time? There was a time when the papers had no more precious news than about Ole Bull." Not so strange, "for he had flown out to be our land's springtime messenger in melody."

Even if Bull is in the position of wishing to forget, we are in the position of wishing to remember what he has done for his country and for every single individual. . . . If, like the butterfly who in magic remembrance of the sunlight fluttered toward the candle, only to find that it burned, burned terribly, it is only the more reason for us to receive him with love. Home must be a consolation to one who has suf-

PART I. LIFE AND ADVENTURES

fered, for he has exile in his soul. And if he is lovingly received by us, the painful memories will soon be dispelled in a new poem . . . for this is the poet's way of remembering when one allows him to be a poet."[1]

He ended by saying that if Bull had come to Christiania (not Bergen), he would have been received as in olden times.

Bull was struck by the tone and style of this welcome and soon learned the author's name. He no doubt heard that Bjørnson was a vigorous young man who wrote on art, theater, and politics, and a poet who agitated against Danish performers in the theater. Ibsen's contract had by now run out, and he had become the director of a new Norwegian theater in Christiania. Perhaps Bjørnson was just the man Bull needed to run his theater in Bergen?

As the article suggests, Bull did not immediately join his wife in Christiania, but went from England to Bergen (via Christiansand, where the Merchants' Singing Society had greeted him). He had sent a letter with Alexander to Félicie which she received with special pleasure. It was the first letter in their twenty-one years of marriage, she wrote, in which Bull had addressed her in his native Norwegian. Their entire correspondence had hitherto been in French. She also wrote: "One needs to be lenient with me, for I have suffered much. I recognize my errors, but my head is so weak that I assure you I have moments of absentmindedness—I cannot sleep. I have courage enough, but my strength fails me."[2]

The reason for Bull's decision to go straight to Bergen was no doubt concern about his theater. For one thing, there had been criticism of the actors' adoption of danicisms in their diction. The board had twice written to Bull in America asking him to relinquish his ownership of the theater. He had not answered and was still the formal owner. On his return he immediately began, in his somewhat high-handed way, to introduce changes, and in his eagerness to improve things, he expected the board to pay for the changes. Finally, on 27 August 1857, Bull attended his first meeting of the board. The chairman, Peter Blytt, called Bull's attention to the financial plight of the theater.

Bull paid no heed to the board, and as a result they tried to outwit him by offering the actors a short, two-month contract. This was intended to embarrass Bull by leaving him without actors while a new theater was being built. Bull countered by summarily dismissing the whole board on November 12. The resulting showdown was graphically reported in Blytt's

1. Ola Linge, *Ole Bull: Livshistoria, Mannen, Kunstnaren* (Oslo, 1953), 226–27.
2. Alexander Bull, ed., *Ole Bulls Breve i Uddrag. Med en karakteristik og biografisk Skitse af Jonas Lie* (Copenhagen, 1881), 387 (25 August 1857).

memoirs of the theater some years later. "We expressed our opinions and did not mince words. . . . We maintained that he always placed his own interests, his own personal vanity in the foreground. . . . We told him to his face that his conduct toward us had been hypocritical, even false. . . . Passions were awakened and took form in strong, perhaps too strong words." The members of the board left, while Bull sat "speechless, immobile, with a glitter in his eyes that warned us of enmity, implacable enmity."[3]

Bull's reply to the board was to wire Bjørnson in Christiania: "Come now!" Bjørnson was overwhelmed. "When I stood with this telegram in my hand, I felt it as if I had been taken up to heaven."[4] The theater had been closed for a week, and Bull opened it with a concert on 22 November. Marie Midling Bull reported: "When Bull appeared, a single heckler was heard from the gallery. But the heckler was thrown out, and Bull spoke to the audience in his native Bergen brogue. He told them a parable: 'There was once a man who had won an elephant in a lottery. He couldn't afford to feed it and he didn't have the heart to kill it. So what did he do? He gave it back to its original owner.'"[5] Blytt had to admit that "the whole evening was an unbroken series of ovations. Bull stood as the victor and our defeat was total."[6]

Bjørnson came to Bergen on 29 November 1857. He was now approaching his twenty-fifth year. Bull welcomed him heartily and appointed him director and instructor. The first performance was of Bjørnson's own play *Mellem Slagene (Between the Battles)*, a drama of saga times which had been Bjørnson's début in Christiania and now became the same in Bergen.

Bull stayed in Bergen until the end of February, 1858. On 23 February the singers of Bergen held a concert in his honor with banners, flags, and music, while nearly a hundred torchbearers hailed him at his home. He gave his "Farewell Concert" on the next day. In addition a dinner was held for him with Bjørnson as the main speaker. When Bull left for Christiania, crowds accompanied him to his steamer and a brass band played.

In the capital, however, he got a more reserved welcome. *Christiania-Posten* wrote that "we can only express it as our opinion that only in his quality of being the great violinist of whom Norway can be proud will Ole Bull be received with enthusiasm."[7] He had gotten anonymous letters accusing him of "abjuring Norwegian nationality," but when he appeared in

3. Peter Blytt, *Minder fra den første norske scene i Bergen* (Bergen 1907), 61.
4. Linge, *Ole Bull*, 233.
5. Ibid.
6. Blytt, *Minder fra den første*, 66.
7. Linge, *Ole Bull*, 235.

the Freemasons' Hall no one could resist him. He played Paganini's *E-flat Major Concerto* for the first time in Christiania, and even the composer Kjerulf had to admit that he played "the 'Adagio' as a god."[8] Another source of satisfaction was the creation of the new Christiania Norwegian Theater under Henrik Ibsen. In it, Bull finally saw the fruits of his own idea.

At the end of April 1858 Bull left Christiania for Carlsbad in Bohemia to cure the effects, still lingering, of his tropical fever. On his way through Vienna he saw again Franz Liszt and the dancer Fanny Elssler (1810–84), who welcomed him eagerly. He also went to Budapest, where he gave four concerts in May, followed by one in Vienna.

Here critic Eduard Hanslick treated Bull acerbically, with a critique that is strikingly reminiscent of Fink's twenty years earlier. Hanslick recalled having heard Bull play in 1840: "The pale Nordic youth who had only to take the violin in his hands to excite the most vivid popular sympathy." After (erroneously) summarizing some of the facts of Bull's life, Hanslick went on to say that "having lived for many years as a farmer [*sic*] in the United States, he now suddenly reappears in Europe. . . ."

Ole Bull was always given to a one-sided virtuosity, to a combination of sovereign bravura and bizarre manners, which might be called "Paganinic." Enthusiasm for this kind of thing, which leaves the heart and mind untouched and excites only surprise, has decreased astonishingly during the last twenty years. . . . We demand of a virtuoso, himself insignificant as a composer, that he place his technical abilities at the service of superior music. Now, as he did twenty years ago, Ole Bull plays only his own compositions. . . . Ole Bull's muse is consistent only in two things: inconsistency of musical construction and preponderance of bravura."

Hanslick analyzed the *Polacca Guerriera* from this point of view, saying that Bull's concertos are

similarly formless fantasies, indulging partly in broadly expansive adagios, partly in antiquated bravura. . . . There are two techniques which he favors: harmonics and double stops. Both are executed with brilliant security and purity. . . . Still more brilliant are his staccatos, which he renders unsurpassably, both up-bow and down-bow. . . . His tone has a beautiful softness. By way of summation we can say that his virtues are purely technical. The whole orientation of his playing has become obsolete, and it needs all his personal charm to recall it even partially to a fictitious life.[9]

After a final concert in Dresden, Bull returned to Bergen and Valestrand. While there in June 1858, he rode out to the home of his childhood friend,

8. Ibid., 236.
9. Eduard Hanslick, "Ole Bull," in *Vienna's Golden Years of Music 1850–1900*, trans. and ed. Henry Pleasants (1950; reprint, Freeport, N.Y., 1969), 65.

Consul Alexander Grieg (1806–75). He had heard tell of his promising son Edvard (1843–1907). The fifteen-year-old lad showed Bull his compositions and played for him. Bull discussed the young man's future with the parents and strongly urged that he be sent abroad for study. In the fall of 1858 Grieg was sent to Leipzig to study music. So Bull played a part in furthering the career of the man who would become Norway's best-known composer.

In August and September Bull was back in Christiania. With Vinje as a companion he took a trip to the towns of Hamar and Lillehammer. Vinje wrote in his paper *Dølen* of having known Bull for twelve years and of particularly admiring him "for having awakened an interest in folk music."[10] Bull invited the fiddler Torgeir Augundson also, and they played together. Augundson brought Bull a Hardanger fiddle as a gift. On this trip Bull met an observant young diarist, Elise Aubert (1837–1909), who recorded her impressions of him, noting his "intelligent, handsome face, his clear, beautiful eyes, his modest expression, and his delightful lock of hair."[11]

At Bjørnson's suggestion, the Bergen theater was reorganized as a shareholding company and given the name Den Nationale Scene (The National Stage). Bull's health was now fully restored, and he bought the Valestrand estate from his mother for sixteen thousand specie dollars. After giving some concerts in other Norwegian cities, he came to Valestrand and stayed there with his family through the winter.

On 17 May 1859, the national holiday was celebrated in Bergen with a procession headed jointly by Bull and Bjørnson. One of Bjørnson's best peasant novels, *Arne,* appeared this year and was dedicated to Bull in gratitude for Bull's confidence in him. Bjørnson continued to be active outside of the theater. One of his commitments was to the new Liberal Party (Venstre), which came into being during this time. He helped elect into the Storting (Parliament) all four representatives from Bergen. As a result he was offered the editorship of the paper *Aftenbladet,* which required that he return to Christiania. Bjørnson accepted the offer. In October, when Bull also came to Christiania, it was a matter of course that he should become the baptismal sponsor of Bjørnson's first-born son Bjørn (1859–1942).

In Bergen, without Bjørnson, Ibsen, or Bull the National Stage struggled on but grew weaker with each year. It finally closed on 17 May 1863, its

---

10. *Dølen* (10 October 1858), 11.
11. Elise Aubert, *Fra Krinoline-Tiden* (Christiania, 1921), 81–82.

OLE BULL'
FARVEL-CONCERT
i Festivitetslokalet den 6te Novbr. 1858.

PROGRAM.

FØRSTE AFDELING.

1. Ouverture til "Die Zebrahaut" af *Titl*.
2. Cantabile Doloroso e Rondó Giocoso. componeret og foredrages af *Ole Bull*.
3. "Sævelien" – Gangar
   "Abildhougen" – Springar
   "Rekkveen" – Tougdans
   } udf. af *Thorgeir Audunson* (Möllarguten).
4. En Moders Bön. comp. og foredr. af *Ole Bull*.

ANDEN AFDELING.

5. Krigsmarsch af "Athalia" af *Mendelsohn Bartholdy*.
6. Bravour Variationer over *Bellinis* Romeo ("Ah! jeg elsker Dig höiere end Solen"), comp. og foredr af *Ole Bull*.
7. "De to Systre" – Tougdans
   "Kjivelmöyarne" – Gangar
   "Vosserullen" – Halling
   } udf. af *Thorgeir Audunson*.
8. La Verbena de San Juan (St. Hans Nat i Sevilla). Spansk Musikfest. componeret og foredrages af *Ole Bull*.

Trykt af Bergh & Ellefsen

Concert program, 6 November 1858, with Augundson. Courtesy of Oslo University Library.

fourteenth year. As theater historian Tharald Blanc concluded, for all its shaky beginnings, "Ole Bull's Theater can rightly be regarded as the mother stage of our national scenic art."[12]

On 22 November 1859, some leaders in the national revival movement organized Det Norske Selskab (The Norwegian Society), described as a "society for the advancement of nationality in art and literature." The instigator was Henrik Ibsen, and among the other members were Bjørnson, Bull, Vinje, and Lindeman. Some people still remembered Bull's "abjuration" of nationality, and because of an article in *Drammens Blad,* a concert of his was virtually boycotted in the city of Drammen. At this concert he performed two pieces for the first and apparently only time: *Lørdagskveld på Sætren (Saturday Night at the Sæter)* (no. 61) and *Kringen* (no. 62).[13]

Bjørnson thundered against such "persecution": "I suggest we let all this talk about Ole Bull cease and take him as he is, with all his warmth and impetuosity. . . ."[14] Vinje also expressed his anger: "It is well if we would come to a decision about Ole Bull and all that people criticize him for. It is just as if people enjoy attacking a great man so they can comfort themselves with the thought that he, too, is a sinner. Then the difference between them is not so great. . . ."[15]

In November 1859 Bull gave three concerts in Christiania and won unstinting praise. "Bull has brilliantly shown that he has not, as some would think reasonable, lost ground in his art. . . . And in addition to his vitality and elasticity, which every tone demonstrated, he showed a superior calm and bearing."[16] He no longer limited himself to his own compositions, but played those of others, above all Paganini's music, much of which had now been published. As Bull approached his fiftieth birthday in 1860, he seemed completely restored physically and in some ways revitalized in his playing.

On his fiftieth birthday Bull was inevitably celebrated. He gave a speech for Norway that Rikard Nordraak (1842–66) said "came from the heart and moved everyone."[17] His friend Vinje wrote a heartfelt poem for the occasion; we include two stanzas:

> So er du femti aar idag
> vaar store Ole Bull,
> med ungdom som i andlits drag

12. T[harald H.] Blanc, *Norges første nationale scene* (Christiania, 1884), 340.
13. Linge, *Ole Bull,* 364.
14. *Aftenbladet* (19 December 1859); Linge, *Ole Bull,* 241.
15. *Dølen* (25 December 1859).
16. *Morgenbladet* (15 November 1859).
17. Linge, *Ole Bull,* 243.

og makti like full,
med same elden i din hug
og hugnad i din smil
og med den same gamle dug
til dikt og felespil.

Idag du dine femti naar.
Ver enn deg lengje lik.
Vi faa i fyrste hundrad aar
vist ikkje makan slik.
Det derfor, veit du, naud er paa
at du kan halde ut
til du fær sjaa om vi kan faa
ein annan slik ein gut.[18]

(So now you're fifty years today
Our famous Ole Bull,
With youth in every feature,
Of strength forever full,
With fire still within your soul
And pleasure in your smile
And with the same old gift
for poems and the fiddle.

Today you reach your fifty.
May long you stay the same.
For a hundred years we'll never get
Again the like of you.
So therefore see how great our need
For you to stay alive
Till you can see if we will get
Another lad like you.)

Among those who heard Bull in 1860 at his last "farewell" concert in Christiania was a young composer, Rikard Nordraak, who would write the definitive melody to his cousin Bjørnson's national anthem text. "Divine" he wrote in his diary about Bull's playing. Bjørnstjerne's brother, Peter Bjørnson (1838–1906), who acted as Bull's secretary in 1860 and 1861, asked Bull if he would allow Nordraak to accompany him. Bull was more than willing and two concerts were arranged in Norwegian cities. They played two compositions by Paganini: *Concerto in E-Flat Major* and *Variations on Di tanti palpiti* from Rossini's *Tancredi*. The eighteen-year-old Nordraak was overwhelmed: "When one has stood in his [Bull's] presence, one has

18. Cited by Linge, *Ole Bull,* 243–44.

felt the nearness of God."[19] Unhappily Nordraak died soon after, at age twenty-four.

As the union with Sweden grew less popular in Norway, relations between the two countries cooled. It was therefore feared that Bull would not be well received in Sweden, which was his next goal. But in Sweden he was acclaimed as usual. After his eight concerts in Stockholm, the Stockholm *Dagblad* wrote: "He maintained the great renown he had won here earlier for his extraordinary technique and his characteristic style. His playing even seemed to have won greater perfection in some respects, especially his four-stringed stroke. . . ."[20] The Swedish theater critic August Blanche (1811–68) published a "portrait" of Bull on 17 March 1860. In it he jested about Bull's visiting Sweden just then, "thinking it might be a Norwegian trick to mollify Swedish feelings." He concluded by addressing a lady who admired Bull's jeweled bow: "But what does the jeweler's art have to do with a bow carved by Pan, polished by the Graces, with strings furnished by Pegasus!"[21] While in Sweden, Bull played in Gothenburg (now Göteborg) with Bedrich Smetana (1824–84), who was then conductor of the philharmonic society there.

In the beginning of May 1860, Bull reached Copenhagen and gave five concerts. The Danish paper *Dansk Illustreret Tidende* noted that it was his sixth visit to the Danish capital. "Never has he been received with greater interest. . . . Ole Bull is surely the same as before in originality, genius, and energy. But there is also a sureness and calm about his performance that one sometimes missed earlier."[22] Bull spent the summer at Valestrand, interrupted only by the crowning of Karl XV (1826–72) as King of Norway and Sweden in the Cathedral of Trondheim. On this occasion Bull was a recipient of the Order of St. Olav for "meritorious artistic activity."

In November 1860 he went on another concert tour of Scandinavia and extended it to Hamburg. Bjørnson happened to be in Hamburg and reported on the event on 12 December 1860 in *Aftenbladet:* "No sooner had he taken the first strokes than I had a sense of victory. . . . He tore off with ardent staccatos, single notes full of pain, double harmonics. . . . What applause! What a storm! Called back for encores three times." A Hamburg paper quoted in Christiania's *Morgenbladet* (11 December 1860) declared that "the vigorous applause allows one to conclude that his artistic tour

19. Ibid., 246.
20. Ibid., 244.
21. Aug. Blanche, *Minnesbilder* (Stockholm, 1872), 93–94 (17 March 1860).
22. Linge, *Ole Bull,* 245.

will bring him compensation for his losses in America. The overpowering tone, his daring play with movements and strokes may no longer be present, but his musical understanding has won in depth, which for music lovers was especially revealed in the composition by Paganini [the *E-Flat Concerto*]."

In 1861 Bull performed in several German towns, and many reviews noted that he seemed to have renewed his mode of playing. The tone was less wild and fantastic, calmer, more assured, deeper. When he played in Utrecht in The Netherlands, he was given a silver loving cup. From there he traveled again to London, where he had not performed since 1840. In April and May he gave several concerts in London, and he was happy to meet Adelina Patti again, who now at eighteen was singing in the London Opera. Bull also bought an Amati that he came to love.[23] By the end of July he was back at Valestrand with Félicie for a couple of months. Some new improvisations date from this period (nos. 63–65).

In October Bull returned to England. While he was there he received a letter from Félicie, who was now in Christiania. She complained about her fate and told him that she was ill. To this letter, he responded with a deeply felt letter, in which he countered her complaints with his own feelings of defeat in life:

Pierced by deep sorrow and unspeakable pain I write you these lines. My hope of being able to stay with our children and to bring them up under my loving supervision has given way to discouragement. Whatever I do or how makes no difference. My debt is forever growing and I am defrauded of my receipts. . . . From America I get nothing and poor prospects. Too much compliance on my part and the need to help others, while I forgot my own wants for the sorrows of other people has been much to blame. How I can extricate myself from this painful position I do not know, for there are many machinations against me. At home in Norway I have been persecuted when I was in trouble, for it was only when I could give that I was well regarded. And have I not had all my thoughts fixed on the interests of my native land? Yes, altogether too much. I neglected myself, my family, my affairs and my interests in order to raise the sense of the nationally beautiful. Hate, envy, and slander sought to distort and cripple my every action no matter how unimportant. You could not understand, your friends were not my friends, but neither were they yours, for they did the worst thing they could do—they aroused a misunderstanding that separated us. If only I could come instead of this letter, how gladly I would do so! God bless you and make you strong and healthy! Your devoted Ole.[24]

23. Sara C. Bull, *Ole Bull: A Memoir* (Boston and New York, 1882), 358.
24. Bull, ed., *Ole Bulls Breve i Uddrag*, 393–94 (7 February 1862).

Ole Bull's first family: Félicie Villeminot Bull and children Alexander, Félicie, Lucie, Thorvald. Photo ca. 1860. Courtesy of Foreningen for norske Fortidsmindesmerkers Bevaring.

Written in London on 7 February 1862, this statement of characteristic self-pity mixed with oblique marital concern reached Félicie on her deathbed. According to Jonas Lie, she was too weak to read it. She died in Christiania on 16 February 1862.[25] Bull had already gone on to Paris when he received the news.

When Félicie died at the age of forty-four, some thirty years had passed since the day in Paris when she had first met Bull, a young sick violinist on whom she had taken pity. Her short life had been devoted to their six children, two of whom had died as infants, and all of whom she had raised for the most part on her own. Alexander, the oldest, survived his father and became a violinist, living much of his life, unmarried, in America. At the age of twenty-one, Thorvald, the second son, died very shortly after his mother, from a fall at sea on 26 December 1862. The eldest daughter,

25. A statement by Inez Bull that Félicie died "hopelessly insane from the way Ole Bull was treated in his ill-fated Pennsylvania venture" (*Ole Bull's Activities in the United States between 1843 and 1880: A Biography,* dissertation submitted to New York University, School of Education [Smithtown, N.Y., 1982], 28), citing Sara Bull as authority, is unfounded, as no such statement appears in Sara Bull's *A Memoir.*

Félicie, married Dr. Christoffer Ingier in Blaker, and they had four children. Lucie, the younger daughter, married an attorney, Peter Jacob Homann, in Christiania and died in 1868, only two months following her marriage.

With Félicie's death we conclude a chapter in Bull's life. However little time he had spent with her and their children, she had been an anchor in the life of this vagabond artist.

14

An Academy of Music
(1862–1867)

AFTER A SUMMER of rest at Bad Godesberg in Germany Bull returned to Norway via Hamburg. He wrote his son Alexander about various happenings during that summer of 1862. In Godesberg a young Jesuit had tried to convert him to Catholicism. One morning he embraced Bull so heartily that he broke one of Bull's ribs, and Bull had to spend a week wearing a bandage. A Guarnerius violin he had entrusted to a French repairman had been taken completely apart, and so Bull had to spend hours reconstructing it. Thanks to his having worked with Vuillaume in 1848, Bull was a connoisseur of violins and knew how to repair them. He told Alexander that he now owned three Guarneriuses and a Grand Amati, which he called his "pearl." He further confided: "It is and has been a very hard time for me; I will have to try to keep my courage up. If I go to the bottom anyway, I still have to struggle as long as I can. Perhaps sunshine will come some time when I least expect it."[1]

In 1862 the Danish romantic author Meïr Goldschmidt (1819–87) wrote an account that contributed to the myth surrounding Bull's career. Bull is not known to have had contact with Goldschmidt even though he was a prolific writer and the editor of his own Danish periodical, *Corsaren*. He wrote a survey of Bull's life for the English journal *Cornhill Magazine*, called "A Norwegian Musician." In Telemark, Goldschmidt tells us, Bull met a young woman who had taken out her cittern, a guitar-like instrument, and sung "sweet, simple lays of love and feuds, fragrant with naive faith in a mysterious destiny." Out of this encounter, Goldschmidt suggests,

---

1. Alexander Bull, ed., *Ole Bulls Breve i Uddrag. Med en karakteristik og biografisk Skitse af Jonas Lie* (Copenhagen, 1881), 394–96 (18 September 1862).

came a great representative of nature's music, Ole Bull. In his infancy Bull had apparently unknowingly imbibed the rules of art, not as produced by players, but as proceeding from the instruments playing "with a life of their own." Then, at the age of six or seven, little Ole supposedly heard a bell-shaped blue flower ring, and "fancying he heard nature sing, he began to play the violin."

Goldschmidt includes a fanciful account of Bull's life. Stories are told of his gambling at Frascati's and of his playing with a violin generously rubbed with ill-smelling asafetida, a resin used in folk medicine to prevent disease. His lodging with Mme. Villeminot is pictured as in the house of the Madame Contesse de Faye. There is a brief account of Oleana, repeating the story that Bull was entrapped by swindlers and had to go to court. Finally, says Goldschmidt, in 1862 Bull could "devote himself entirely to his art and his own Psyche, spending his summers in Norway and going towards winter to the south—where the mermaid incessantly calls the Northerner who has once seen her or listened to her."[2] His exaggerated and inaccurate sketch caps the romantic story of Bull and can only be seen as a summary of narratives that stemmed from Bull himself. Those skeptical of Bull must surely have found support for their doubts in this publication.

Bull had returned to Norway in time for the tenth anniversary of the Christiania Norwegian Theater, celebrated on 10 October 1862. Ibsen was still director, although his theater was in bad shape and he was seeking a grant to leave for Italy. The play performed that night was *Til Sæters* (*To the Sæter*), and according to *Morgenbladet* (12 October): "The high point of the evening was Ole Bull, who displayed all his mastery. He was playing not just for the glory of the evening, but for the idea that he has labored for throughout his whole artistic career: the liberation and independence of Norwegian art." *Christiania-Posten* wrote: "It was as if the audience did not want to tear itself loose from its great tone artist who was playing in a place to which he had devoted his most ardent sympathies. He had been its support both directly and indirectly."[3]

The theater anniversary reminded Bull of his struggles for the theater in Bergen, and he decided to try to move the Norwegian authorities once again, this time in behalf of a Norwegian Academy of Music. He had long been concerned about the future of music in Norway. This time he found an ally in novelist Jonas Lie (1833–1908), who was then the editor of the

2. Meïr Goldschmidt, "A Norwegian Musician," *Cornhill Magazine* 6 (23 April 1862): 514–27.
3. Ola Linge, *Ole Bull: Livshistoria, Mannen, Kunstnaren* (Oslo, 1953), 250.

OLE BULL^s

CONCERT

i

Frimurerlogens Festivitetslocale d. 7de October 1862 Kl. 7.

⚬⚬

PROGRAM.

Første Afdeling.

1. Ouverture til Op. "Giovanna d'Arco" af *Verdi*.
2. Concerto i A:

   a. Allegro Maestoso,
   b. Adagio Sentimentale, } componeret og udføres af **Ole Bull.**
   c. Rondo Pastorale,

3. "Til Sverig" af *A. Munch* og *F. A. Reissiger*.
4. a. Præludier af *J. S. Bach*,
   b. La Molinara af *N. Paganini*, } udføres af **Ole Bull.**

Anden Afdeling.

1. Ouverture til Op. "Marco Spada" af *Auber*.
2. Sæterbesøg, componeret og udføres af **Ole Bull.**
3. "Sangerafsked" af *L. Dietrichson* og *F. Abt.*
4. Polacca Guerriera, componeret og udføres af **Ole Bull.**

— ⚬⚬ —

Trykt hos Bergh & Ellefsen.

Concert program, 7 October 1862, Christiania. Courtesy of Oslo University Library.

journal *Illustreret Nyhedsblad*. Lie printed an article signed by Bull, but actually formulated by Lie (according to his statement in the journal).

> My cause in this world is Norwegian music. I am a musician. And as such, people must believe me when I say that I hear a wonderfully deep and characteristic sounding board vibrating within the Norwegian breast. It has been the goal of my life to add strings to it so that it can speak out, so its deep voice can resound in the temple hall. . . . I have offered in vain to direct orchestras and compose for the stage, and in general to do all that an individual can do to break a path for instruction in Norwegian music. But again and again I have encountered the old, well-known gray cliff.

By "cliff" was meant a resistance to artistic causes: "Norwegian artists have constantly encountered 'the gray cliff' in their efforts on behalf of art." The article proposed that Norwegian musicians should "join hands in a common effort to gain the top of the cliff so that we can extend our hands down from above and help other striving artists to rise."[4]

Bull used an invitation to Sweden (for the dedication of a new railroad line) to visit Stockholm and study the organization of the Swedish Music Academy. In Sweden he played seventeen concerts in a month and returned to Valestrand by Christmas.

In a letter of February 1863 to Alexander, Bull wrote that he had spoken to the king and that the Department of Church and Education had recommended a contribution of twelve hundred specie dollars. "I have a great deal to do," he told Alexander, "and I meet with resistance now as usual."[5] He was persuaded, however, that his project would succeed. To show his dedication to the cause of young musicians, he arranged a concert (15 April) with a seventeen-year-old pianist named Erika Lie, playing compositions by Rikard Nordraak, who was then only twenty-one. The royal cabinet presented Bull's proposal in the Storting, but the final result was the same as before. The music academy was voted down by a majority of seventy-two votes. The committee that worked on it even singled Bull out as a reason for rejecting his proposal.

In the same February letter to Alexander, Bull also expressed his grief over the recent death of his son Thorvald. Thorvald had fallen from the mast of his ship in the Mediterranean. Bull consoled himself "with the thought that I did everything in my power to deter him from choosing the sea as his living, but he insisted strongly that he wished to make himself a career."[6]

4. *Illustreret Nyhedsblad,* 19 October 1862; cf. Linge, *Ole Bull,* 251.
5. Bull, ed., *Ole Bulls Breve i Uddrag,* 397 (27 February 1865).
6. Ibid.

In May two new solo songs of Bull's were premiered in Christiania, "I ensomme Stunde" (or "Klage") ("In Moments of Solitude") (no. 66) and "I Granskoven" ("In the Spruce Forest") (no. 67).

In June 1863, a major songfest was held in Bergen. Bull and Bjørnson as well as Ibsen were invited as guests of honor. Over a thousand singers gathered from all parts of Norway. Ibsen wrote a song which three choral groups from Christiania learned for the occasion. The festival marked a significant point in Ibsen's life. He had just published *Love's Comedy,* a verse drama, and was writing a historical drama, *The Pretenders,* both among his first significant plays. Bjørnson used the occasion to praise Ibsen, denouncing those who had compared himself to Ibsen and found Ibsen lacking. Ibsen wrote about the occasion to his host in Bergen, pleased at how kind everyone had been to him: "The festival up there, and the many dear and unforgettable people whom I met, are working on me like a good visit to church, and I sincerely hope that this mood will not pass."[7] We have no account of the meeting from Bull; for him it was no doubt more a matter of course.

After some concerts in Trøndelag, Bull returned to Bergen and offered two concerts at popular prices to whip up enthusiasm for his music academy. His effort was in vain. The Storting was not to be moved. Bull also visited Christiania, where he performed a new fantasy (no. 68) on "Là ci darem la mano" from Mozart's *Don Giovanni.*

In the midst of his disputes in Norway concerning a music academy, a new link with America was being forged by Bull's friend Longfellow. Thackeray's suggestion that Ole Bull was "quite a character for a book" may have germinated in Longfellow's mind as he pondered on the characters to be introduced in his *Tales of a Wayside Inn* (1863). Clearly intending to write an American counterpart to Chaucer's *Canterbury Tales,* Longfellow chose as the site of his tales an old inn in Sudbury, Massachusetts, known as The Wayside Inn. He introduced a series of characters, each of whom tells a tale to entertain the other guests. Ole Bull, whom Longfellow had met in 1844 and again in 1852 and 1855, became one of the figures in Longfellow's fantasy, "The Musician":

> Last the Musician, as he stood
> Illumined by that fire of wood,
> Fair-haired, blue-eyed, his aspect blithe;
> His figure tall and straight and lithe;
> And every feature of his face
> Revealing his Norwegian race,

7. Michael Meyer, *Ibsen, A Biography* (Garden City, N.Y., 1971), 205.

A radiance, streaming from within,
Around his eyes and forehead beamed,
The Angel with the violin,
Painted by Raphael, he seemed.
He lived in that ideal world
Whose language is not speech, but song.[8]

The story that Longfellow assigned to Bull was an Old Icelandic saga from the *Heimskringla,* the saga of King Olaf Trygvason:

And then the blue-eyed Norseman told
A Saga of the days of old.
"There is," said he, "a wondrous book
Of Legends in the old Norse tongue,
Of the dead kings of Norroway,—
Legends that once were told or sung
In many a smoky fireside nook
Of Iceland, in that ancient day,
By wandering Saga-man or Scald;
Heimskringla is the volume called;
And he who looks may find therein
The story that I now begin."
(p. 69)

The tale which the fictional musician then tells, as Andrew Hilen has pointed out, compelled Longfellow, contrary to his usual practice, "to submit to some show of force and violence in his writing."[9] Longfellow followed the general outline of the story as told by Snorri Sturluson in Samuel Laing's translation. The poem is also influenced by Esaias Tegnér's "Fridtjof's Saga" with its gentler, more romantic vikings. Bull is constantly woven into the ancient tale:

And in each pause the story made
Upon his violin he played,
As an appropriate interlude,
Fragments of old Norwegian tunes
That bound in one the separate runes,
And held the mind in perfect mood,
Entwining and encircling all
The strange and antiquated rhymes
With melodies of olden times;
As over some half-ruined wall,

8. Henry Wadsworth Longfellow, *Tales of a Wayside Inn* (Boston, 1863), 14. Subsequent quotations from this poem are from this edition, and page numbers are given in the text.
9. Andrew Hilen, *Longfellow and Scandinavia: A Study of the Poet's Relationship with the Northern Languages and Literature* (New Haven, Conn., 1947), 102.

Disjointed and about to fall,
Fresh woodbines climb and interlace,
And keep the loosened stones in place.

(pp. 69–70)

On the following May 17 (1864) a celebration of the Norwegian constitution was held to commemorate its half-century of existence. Bull went in wholeheartedly for the idea of gathering funds for a memorial statue of Henrik Wergeland and planned but did not complete a *Festouverture (Festival Overture)* (no. 69) for the occasion. At the celebration, a chorus of local singers assisted, and Bull played his *The Mountains of Norway*.

During the summer of 1864 Bull stayed at Valestrand, where the young Edvard Grieg was a frequent visitor. They played Mozart trios together, but they also discussed folk music and nationalism.[10] Bull played folk music and improvised for Grieg.[11] Their acquaintance was very important to Grieg because it introduced him to the tradition of Hardanger fiddle music and suggested a path for his own composing.[12] This direction was further reinforced for Grieg when he later met Rikard Nordraak in Copenhagen.[13] Grieg's first collection of folk songs arranged for piano (Opus 17) was dedicated to Ole Bull in 1869.

In the winter season of 1864 to 1865, Bull traveled to Germany and on to Vienna and Prague. His program was usually Paganini's *E-flat Major Concerto,* his own *Polacca Guerriera* and *Visit to the Sæter,* and Mozart's *Larghetto.* The Dresden *Journal* wrote that "although pure virtuosity has gone out of fashion in the more classical style, it has a rightful position in the hands of a powerful individuality like Ole Bull's, so spiritual, also in his compositions, and with a perfection of mastery and a remarkable sureness." The *Constitutionelle Zeitung* published a long article that emphasized Bull's tone, especially on the G-string, which was "great and of indescribable beauty. . . . The violin, an Amati of the greatest perfection, also has its share in it. But the artistic use he makes of it, his exploitation of its coloration of sound in all nuances, accents, crescendos, his genuine cantilena [songlike] execution, all this is Ole Bull's property."[14]

10. John Horton, *Grieg* (London, 1974), 17.
11. Finn Benestad and Dag Schjelderup-Ebbe, *Edvard Grieg: The Man and the Artist,* trans. William H. Halverson and Leland B. Sateren (Lincoln, Nebr., 1988), 57.
12. Ibid., 58.
13. Folke H. Tørnblom, *Grieg* (Stockholm, 1945), 13–14.
14. Both the Dresden *Journal* and *Constitutionelle Zeitung* quotations are from Linge, *Ole Bull,* 255.

Valestrand, built 1864–1868. Courtesy of Knut Hendriksen.

Bull's tour continued into the Netherlands, where he rested some days in Wiesbaden and at the Duke of Nassau's mansion in the Rhineland. The duke decorated him with the Order of Adolph. In Breslau he was delighted to buy a Gasparo da Salò violin, which became one of his favorite instruments, another "pearl." He returned to Valestrand laden with honors and fame. Bjørnson wrote to Ibsen: "Bull has been rejuvenated by the success he has had in Germany."[15]

Since 1863 Bull had been planning to build a new structure at Valestrand to replace the old family summer home. The new house, designed by Ole's brother, Georg Andreas Bull, an architect, would not be completed until 1868.[16] It was the first structure in Norway to copy the old nordic style, with its cornices and dragon heads. The main hall, a music room, was an attempt to create a chieftain's hall in Viking style.[17] In the summer

15. Ibid., 256.

16. Arne Bjørndal, "Ole Bull og Valestrand," reprint from *Frå Fjon til Fjosa* (Stord, 1950), 3 says 1869.

17. Thanks to Knut Hendriksen; cf. Jens Christian Eldal, "'Bulla-huset'—Nordens eldste sveitserhus?" *Husbukken: Medlemsblad for fortidsminneforeningen* 3 (1990): 10–13 and Eva Sundler, "Ole Bull och den nationalromantiska villan," in Brita Linde, ed., *Studier i konstvetenskap tillägnade* (Stockholm, 1985), 167–80.

of 1865, Bull was much concerned with improving the buildings and grounds at Valestrand. On 2 July 1865, he wrote a long letter to Alexander, saying that he had sent two thousand willows from Amsterdam for planting at Valestrand. Alexander was set to work planting, building a bridge, and moving the office building. Bull hoped that the marsh by the lake would look good sown with oats. "It is such an airy and charming thing in its movements, which remind me of —" and here Bull added a bar of music in the letter that is a variant of the halling "Rotnheims-Knut" (see Example 14.1).[18] He worried about the improved steamship connection with Valestrand, fearing that his estate would no longer remain as private as it had been.

Example 14.1. "Rotnheims-Knut." Letter from Ole Bull to his son, Alexander. Printing error (?) in measure 3.

Bull spent part of 1866 in Christiania, enjoying the company of his mother, his daughters, some of his brothers, and many friends. He saw a great deal of Bjørnson, who now directed the theater in Christiania. In the late fall of that year he left Christiania for Moscow on a tour that proved to be one of the most enjoyable in his life. He stayed in Moscow all winter, while the nobility and other men of means showered him with gifts. He acquired several valuable violins and cellos, and even brought back two Arabian horses. One of the horses died, but the other one, a light yellow Persian-Arabic horse named Caraguese, remained his proud possession for years.

Bull continued to write new music while he toured. He told Johan Hennum (1836–94), an orchestra conductor from Christiania who visited Bull at Valestrand in 1867 following his tour, that in Russia he had composed a piece for the local audience featuring Russian music, as had been his custom elsewhere. He called it *Hommage à Moscou* (*Homage to Moscow*) (no. 70) and ended it with the "Emperor's Hymn." In a letter to Alexander from St. Petersburg, he mentioned a new fantasia composed on a popular Russian song, *Nattergalen* (*The Nightingale*) (no. 71), that was performed as an adieu to the city. "I had to play it twice. It really has no musical value; it is only a mood piece. You may enjoy it, but it is thoroughly sad, and for this reason I will rework it at Valestrand." He also

18. Bull, ed., *Ole Bulls Breve i Uddrag,* 399 (2 July 1865). Arne Bjørndal, *Norsk Folkemusikk* (Bergen, 1952), 269.

Fest for Ole Bull i den norske Forening i Kjøbenhavn.

Celebration for Ole Bull, the Norwegian Society in Copenhagen. *Illustreret Nyhedsblad,* no. 10, 1866.

told Alexander of having had a sound post made of seven-hundred-year-old wood put into his Gasparo da Salò. "I have invented a new way of placing and measuring the post with regard to the structure and playing of the violin."[19] Bull's last Moscow concert, on 10 April 1867, was a benefit for poor students, for which he received in gratitude a silver music stand.

In May of 1867 he gave three successful concerts in Warsaw. The newspaper *Kurjer Warszawski* wrote:

It is now some twenty-five years since he last came. The first time he was in his best youth. Now his hair is gray. Even if his playing does not have the same youthful fire, it now resounds with greater calm and seriousness after many working years. . . . Today as before he stands as the first. . . . In *Polacca Guerriera* the first theme especially was interpreted with such strength of tone and such fire of execution that in spite of his gray hair Ole Bull seemed like a young man. After the *Carnival of Venice* there was endless applause. It is with sorrow we say farewell to the great master.[20]

19. Bull, ed., *Ole Bulls Breve i Uddrag,* 405 (17 April 1867).
20. Linge, *Ole Bull,* 257 (9 May 1867).

Painting of Alexander Bull, Valestrand. Photo by Einar Haugen.

Another Warsaw paper, the *Gazetta Warszawska* expressed similar admiration, adding: "Everything is executed so easily and naturally that only connoisseurs understand what difficulties he has surmounted."[21]

From Warsaw Bull went to Paris to visit his son Alexander, who was studying there. Before leaving Norway for Russia, he had written Alexander a long letter full of advice, with many references to his own early and difficult days in Paris: "Artists there live in general a hollow, miser-

21. Ibid., 258.

able life." Alexander wished him to give a concert in Paris, but Bull had resisted: "How can you imagine that I would be able to break through these wily plots and infamies, about which you have no idea. The coteries are everything, art is a side issue—the cow that gives the milk. In every other place people are less prejudiced than precisely there, where they imagine they are everything." He went on to pontificate about international politics:

Watch out, Alexander! Political events now follow rapidly on one another. The French have an enemy in the United States, who are not to be scorned. The French also have to look out for Germany. Their fleet and finances would be ruined in a short time in case of a war. Times have changed. Now it is the turn of Prussia to play master in Europe. They have worked out their plans and ordered their finances, while in France such things are still in embryo and can easily get out of balance. . . . Watch out—never mix into political conversations; I beg you earnestly.[22]

Bull's opinions were amply borne out by the disastrous Franco-Prussian War of 1870.

Bull spent a pleasant summer at Valestrand, preparing for another American tour, his third, and this time he took with him Alexander, who at twenty-eight had himself become a reasonably accomplished violinist. Together they arrived in New York on 11 December 1867. A new phase of Bull's life was about to begin, one in which his experiences in America would take a novel and surprising turn.

22. Bull, ed., *Ole Bulls Breve i Uddrag,* 403–404 (4 September 1866).

15

A New Life: Norwegian-American
(1867–1872)

B Y 1867, the Civil War had ended and the United States was able
to turn its attention to another American tour by Ole Bull. On this
third tour he chose Josiah Turnbull as his impresario. First there
were some New York concerts, where Bull was heartily welcomed by his
American admirers. From New York he and Alexander headed to Wisconsin, where numerous Norwegians had gone, forming immigrant settlements where he could hope to be received with acclaim.

In 1867 Wisconsin was only a nineteen-year-old state. It was divided
into agricultural land in the south and forested land in the north. The capital city of Madison in the south central part of the state was already the
flourishing center of a state in the making, with a fledgling state university.

Bull's first Wisconsin concert was in February 1868 in Janesville, a small
town to the south of Madison. After this concert a young Norwegian-
American named Rasmus Bjørn Anderson (1846–1936) presented himself
to Bull.[1] Anderson claimed kinship with Bull through his mother, whose
maiden name was von Krogh, a family of noble antecedents in Norway.
She had married a rebellious farm lad from Vikedal north of Stavanger,
Bjørn Andersen Kvelve, who emigrated to Wisconsin with her in 1836 and
became known as Bjørn Anderson. The son Rasmus was a forward and
ambitious young man, who evidently impressed Bull, for he invited Anderson to join him in his carriage to the towns of Stoughton and Madison,
where Bull was performing.

In both places Bull was met by welcoming delegations, in Madison con-

1. Information about Anderson is derived from Rasmus B. Anderson, *Life Story* (Madison, Wis., 1915), Lloyd Hustvedt, *Rasmus Bjørn Anderson: Pioneer Scholar* (Northfield,
Minn., 1966), and personal acquaintance.

PART I. LIFE AND ADVENTURES

sisting of a hundred torch-bearers, who escorted him to his hotel, the Vilas House. Ticket scalpers had jacked up the prices for his concert, so Bull decided to schedule a matinee as an extra concert. After the evening concert, Bull was invited to a reception given by Jeanne C. Carr (1824?–1904) of Madison, the wife of Ezra Carr, a professor of chemistry at the University of Wisconsin. According to Anderson's account, he there introduced Bull to Amelia Chapman Thorp and her daughter Sara, both of whom were to figure significantly in Bull's life. Bull then continued his planned tour in Wisconsin and elsewhere.

Bull reached New York for three "Grand Concerts" in Steinway Hall scheduled for 18, 20 and 21 March 1868. Reports on a broadsheet with articles about his appearances in Wisconsin, Chicago, and Washington give an account also of his earlier adventures in Oleana, following Bull's own account of financial machinations and personal persecution.

About this time John W. Moore wrote a description of Bull for *Western Musical World*. "He is among us for the third time, a happier man than ever before, dear to the affection of his countrymen here and at home, and a firmer friend than ever of our country." Moore "cannot forbear referring to the ravishing division of his consummate arpeggios, forming a finely regulated shower of notes, rich, round, and the most distinct, although wrought out by such slight undulations of the bow, as to leave in something of a puzzle our notions of cause and consequence."[2]

When Bull returned to Norway in the spring of 1868, the house at Valestrand that had been so long in the planning was ready for him. Bjørnson printed a picture of Bull's new home in his journal *Norsk Folke-blad,* seizing the occasion to hail Bull once more: "Ole Bull is the first love this reborn people has had. . . . No one has raised it so high. For he was its own dreams, as the people sat beside its unrevealed folk treasures."[3] Bull's second daughter Lucie, born in 1846, was married that August in the new home at Valestrand.

In the fall of 1868 Bull returned to the United States for the fourth time, and now he stayed a whole year. As biographer Mortimer Smith put it: "The glow of drama which always shone around him continued undimmed."[4] A special friend this time was Robert Ogden Doremus (1824–1906), inventor and professor of chemistry, who was also the president of the New York Philharmonic. Bull was frequently at his home on 70 Union Place in New York. Here he also met the actor Edwin Booth (1833–93),

2. John W. Moore, "Ole Bull," *Western Musical World* 5.5 (May 1868), no page.
3. Ola Linge, *Ole Bull: Livshistoria, Mannen, Kunstnaren* (Oslo, 1953), 261.
4. Mortimer Smith, *The Life of Ole Bull* (Princeton, N.J., 1943), 152.

Bull (*on stairs, wearing hat*) and family at Valestrand. Photo by Knud Knudsen, Bergen. Courtesy of Bergen University Library.

who became a good friend. Another admirer at whose house Bull was frequently seen was Anne Lynch Botto, the American writer who conducted a literary salon.

A dramatic event marking his travels this year was a fire that erupted on his boat going down the Ohio River the night of 4 December 1868. While Bull was walking on the deck, his boat collided with another and burst into flame. Bull hurriedly returned to his cabin, rescued his violin, and swam ashore. He lost his clothes, money, and valuables, including a golden laurel wreath the Masons in New York had given him.[5]

During the winter of 1868 he devoted much time to an idea for an improved piano. He hoped to secure for the piano some of the tone qualities of the violin. He eventually secured as his helper and friend in this work the Swedish-American inventor John Ericsson (1803–89), the designer and builder of the battleship *Monitor,* made famous during the Civil War. Bull wanted "to sustain the sounding board at the ends, leaving the sides free, not permitting the board to be pierced for the insertion of screws to unite

5. Linge, *Ole Bull,* 261; Sara C. Bull, *Ole Bull: A Memoir* (Boston and New York, 1882), 254. How Bull kept his violin dry on the swim ashore is a bit mysterious.

Valestrand. Courtesy of Knut Hendriksen.

the upper and lower framework. . . . The wooden strips employed to strengthen the great surface of the board should . . . be made to help the tone as well, on the principle of the bar in the violin; the whole to be so adjusted that the wood might grow better with use and age."[6]

The first instrument cost Bull fifteen thousand dollars. When Ericsson learned of his problems with the piano, he "made a frame of the right weight and strength. . . . This second piano proved satisfactorily that the theory was sound and practicable." Only two pianos of this type were ever made; one of them is preserved at Bull's later home on Lysøen. Ericsson later wrote that "the great violinist possessed a singularly accurate knowledge of the necessary relations between the capability of resisting the tension of the strings and the elasticity requisite to admit of a perfectly free movement of the sounding board. . . . I regard the independent metallic frame for holding the strings of pianos as an invention which would do honor to any professional mechanic. . . ."[7]

In the summer of 1869 Bull appeared at the Boston Peace Jubilee, an occasion intended to celebrate the conclusion of peace after the Civil War. It was an enormous festival, and Bull functioned as the concertmaster of an orchestra of 1,094 players! After the festival he apparently rested a while at Appledore House on the Isles of Shoals, off Portsmouth in New Hampshire. This was a popular offshore resort operated by the Laighton family. According to Oscar Laighton, Bull played a concert as a benefit for Norwegian fishermen on the Isles, raising 385 dollars and edifying the distinguished guests. Here Bull met the poet John Greenleaf Whittier (1807–92). In a letter to Annie Fields, Whittier would speak of "the great genius of Ole Bull."[8]

Bull returned to Norway, staying for the rest of the summer at Valestrand with visits to Bergen. On 2 November 1869, he was a guest at a dinner given by Vestmannalaget (Society of Westmen), the organization devoted to promoting Aasen's new language of Landsmål (now known at Nynorsk, or New Norwegian). The other guest of honor was his old friend, the poet Aasmund Vinje, who led a cheer for Bull. Bull responded with some words about his own activity on behalf of the national cause: "He hoped the time would come when Norwegians would realize that one could not advance

6. Bull, *A Memoir,* 257.
7. Ibid., 259–60.
8. Oscar Laighton, *Ninety Years at the Isles of Shoals* (Boston, 1930), 74; Lyman V. Rutledge, *The Isles of Shoals in Lore and Legend* (Barre, Mass., 1965), 177; John Greenleaf Whittier, *Letters,* ed. John B. Pickard (Cambridge, Mass., 1975), 3:460–63; Einar Haugen, "Ole Bull and the Isles of Shoals," *The Norseman* 3 (1991): 42–43.

in Music by borrowing from Germany or in Language by borrowing from Denmark."⁹ Actually, Bull himself never used the New Norwegian language. It was the last time Bull and Vinje met; Vinje died in 1870.

In December 1869 Bull was back in America, again accompanied at least initially by Alexander. In February 1870 they took the newly opened Pacific Railroad to San Francisco, happy to avoid the laborious trip across the Isthmus of Panama, with its tropical fevers. His success on the West Coast was as great as ever. According to the San Francisco *Bulletin*, "he possesses the same marvelous strength yet delicacy of touch — the same control of his instrument, the same faculty of throwing his whole soul into the passion of his music. After hearing other accomplished violinists, we are more than ever impressed with Ole Bull's greatness. He stands alone."¹⁰

At his last California concert on 4 March 1870, the daughter of the Norwegian-Swedish consul stepped on the stage and placed a laurel wreath of gold on his head. The wreath was encrusted with pearls and diamonds. At the point of each leaf there lay a pearl, and on the wreath the letters O. B. were engraved with diamonds. In the center was California's coat of arms, and on the back side was carved "To Ole Bull from his Californian friends as a token of their affectionate regards." A General Cobb spoke on behalf of all his friends and named Bull a "King in the Realm of Music." Bull ended his western tour with a concert at Virginia City, Nevada. It is not clear whether Alexander was still traveling with him at this time.

Next he proceeded to Madison, Wisconsin, this time as a guest of the prominent Thorp family. The Thorps had originally come from Oxford, New York, to Eau Claire, Wisconsin. Joseph Thorp (1812–95) had made a fortune cutting and logging the forests of northern Wisconsin.¹¹ When he was elected a state senator, the family moved from Eau Claire to Madison where they set up an elegant household on the shore of Lake Mendota. Their house was admired for its hand-painted ceilings and rose-colored music room. With the finest house in town, on broad lawns facing the north, there was abundant space and the opportunity to display an elegance hitherto unknown in the young capital. Joseph's wife, Amelia Chapman Thorp (d. 1893), proceeded to gain a dominant social position. Their daughter Sara (1850–1911) loved music and was accomplished at the piano.

Before Bull's arrival in Madison, Amelia Thorp wrote him a letter pointedly enclosing a newspaper clipping that hinted at an affair between Sara

9. *Bergenposten,* cited by Linge, *Ole Bull,* 263.
10. Smith, *Life of Ole Bull,* 155.
11. For a biography of Joseph Thorp, see D. I. Nelke, ed., *Representative Men in the United States: Wisconsin Volume* (Chicago, 1895), 623–26.

Ole Bull, ca. 1870.

and Bull. Bull responded in a letter written in what Mortimer Smith has called "his best vein of lush rhetoric and quaint English."[12] In an especially helpless passage he wrote:

I am as a public man always subject to all sorts of pranks, but this hidden attack trying to bring insult upon a family who has received me with a hospitality never to be forgotten is appalling. . . . A terrible blow it must have been to Sara whom I regard as a fairy more than human, and that she, forgetting her own feeling, thinks of solacing the grief of another, and that other my humble self, confirms more than anything my inmost belief. My heart is so burdened that I cannot write and thank her for the beautiful lines she honored me with.[13]

It is hard to know exactly what Bull thought when he wrote this semi-apologetic missive. He seems to treat the clipping as a malicious prank, but he also praises Sara. In the light of later events, one wonders if the clipping could have been inspired by Sara's mother herself.

During his stay with the Thorps, Bull no doubt paid special attention to Sara. It is certain that she was genuinely fascinated by the famous violinist, in spite of the forty-year age difference. He had been a widower for eight years. That a certain attachment grew between them during his stay must have been evident to her family, for Joseph Thorp wrote Bull a letter after his departure. He "warns [Bull], he implores for his child, his only daughter," and he asks Bull "to go out of that universe," that is, Sara's world. Bull quotes these words in his 6 April 1870 letter to Sara, written from Columbus, Ohio. Mr. Thorp was a businessman who did not want his daughter to marry a foreign violinist three times her age and of no certain fortune. But there were more powerful forces at work, namely Bull's loneliness and the social ambitions of Amelia Thorp. In his letter of 6 April Bull ecstatically addressed Sara: "My prayer to the Almighty is embodied in the whisper Sara, my music, my ambition, my love of country, my destiny, my future country, my whole trust hereafter and forever is Sara."[14] Amelia Thorp no doubt saw a marriage between Sara and Bull as a social triumph. She was a woman who knew what she wanted. Later, in Cambridge, she would engineer a match for her son Joseph (1852–1931)[15] with Longfellow's daughter Annie. She also persuaded Longfellow to write his poem on "The Four Lakes of Madison" (1876), though Longfellow had never been west of the Alleghenies.[16] Anderson attributed the relationship

12. Smith, *Life of Ole Bull*, 158.
13. Ibid., 159.
14. Ibid., 160; we have not seen this original.
15. Obituary in Eau Claire paper, 21 May 1931 (clipping).
16. Smith, *Life of Ole Bull*, 157.

between Bull and Sara to Bull's "habit of asking everybody that he met to visit him at his magnificent home, Valestrand."[17] Bull's own letter, however, makes it clear that the relationship between them was already serious before the Thorps' visit to Norway. In any case, Sara Thorp and her parents were on the boat, ready to sail to Norway with him when Bull arrived in New York at the end of his spring tour in 1870.

Robert Doremus in New York and James Reymert, the Norwegian banker who managed Bull's financial affairs, had arranged a festive send-off for him. Mrs. Doremus gave Bull a silk flag from the Philharmonic Society that featured the "pure" Norwegian colors with the addition of the American stars. The New York *Democrat* reported on the occasion, adding: "So thoroughly good and noble, democratic and straightforward as Ole Bull is, he has made millions of friends. No foreigner has won our hearts as has Ole Bull."[18]

In Bergen Bull was just in time for the 17 May celebration. Festivities were held for him, beginning with the traditional parade. Bull led off with the flag he had been given in New York, flanked by two Icelanders who were there for the occasion. At a dinner sponsored by the Workers' Society, Bull could not refrain from speaking bitterly about the theater in Bergen, which now performed nothing but Danish and other foreign pieces. "Who is managing the theater now? Idiots and traitors! If anyone is willing to do something to raise a Norwegian theater anew, I am ready to help."[19]

A little later he proceeded to Valestrand with his American guests, who stayed with him for one or two weeks. Bull then went to Christiania. Since no preparations had been made for welcoming him, Bjørnson wrote on Bull's behalf: "Ole Bull is the greatest one of his kind who has lived among our people. He neither can nor should he be compared with this or that virtuoso who for a time has enjoyed the world's admiration. . . ."[20]

On 9 July Bull gave a concert accompanied by Agathe Backer (later Grøndahl) (1847–1907), one of Norway's best younger pianists and composers. When he was offered tributes, his response was practically a challenge to his compatriots:

When I speak, I prefer to speak through my violin, that is my best friend. I constantly experience that one person after the other is offended by my ideas and my plans, whose execution is important to me because I think they would benefit my native land. Perhaps my conception is mistaken, and perhaps it is beneficial to

17. Anderson, *Life Story,* 107.
18. Linge, *Ole Bull,* 264.
19. Cited by Linge, *Ole Bull,* 265, from Bergen newspapers.
20. Ibid., 266, from *Norsk Folkeblad* (9 July 1870).

our fatherland and me that they do not find support and are not fulfilled. . . .
But I have the hope that these plans will someday be realized; now is not the time,
as I see from the experience I have daily. On the other hand, I cannot adjust my
principles according to circumstances; these have to fit with my principles. For
them I cannot change. It therefore seems to me that at the moment my place is
not here at home. So I am leaving for the place where I feel in myself that I ful-
fill a purpose."[21]

These rather caustic remarks are no doubt a measure of Bull's deep disappointment in Norway's rejection of his theater and music academy. They
express his hope for a better future in America and offer a virtual farewell
to his homeland.

Just what had happened between Bull and Sara during the summer of
1870 remains obscure. He left Norway on 15 August together with the
Thorps. According to Sara Bull's account in her *Memoir:* "The marriage
was delayed in deference to the wishes of others for some months. . . . It
was later decided to have a private marriage. This was consummated in
Norway, and publicly announced and confirmed on the return to the United
States, three months later, in the autumn of 1870."[22]

Mortimer Smith explained the "private marriage" by saying that "in
June they travelled down to Christiania, where they were secretly married.
It was a secret, that is, to everyone save Mrs. Thorp, who entered heartily
into the conspiracy; she was, no doubt, glad of the opportunity to counter
with a *fait accompli* the objections her husband was sure to raise on their
return to America."[23]

Ola Linge is less veiled about the sequence of events: "As soon as they
came to Madison, a notice was sent to the newspapers that Sara and Ole
Bull had been married ('privately') in Norway, but now it would be done
once more according to American laws. This had its good reasons."[24] Then
Linge merely juxtaposes the dates of the American wedding, 6 September, and the birth of their daughter Sara Olea, 4 March, a mere six months
later.

The most pointed account of all is that of Norwegian writer Anders
Buraas in 1982: "In his 60th year he was so unfortunate as to impregnate
a nineteen-year-old girl from Madison, Wisconsin. It led to marriage, but
not a happy one, though it lasted until his death."[25] That Buraas is correct

21. *Morgenbladet* (14 July 1870); Linge, *Ole Bull,* 266–67.
22. Bull, *A Memoir,* 257.
23. Smith, *Life of Ole Bull,* 141.
24. Linge, *Ole Bull,* 267.
25. Anders Buraas, *De reiste ut* (Oslo, 1982), 226.

was much earlier confirmed by historian Albert Barton in Madison.[26] But
an open admission in that Victorian age would have led to public scandal.
Amelia Thorp knew how to handle the problem.

She arranged for a quiet marriage ceremony by a local Madison pastor, the Reverend C. H. Richards, on 6 September, followed by a gala wedding reception at the Thorps' home on 22 September. Eleven hundred invitations were issued, the grounds were hung with Japanese lanterns, and
the rooms filled with displays of flowers. One whole room was set aside
for an exhibit of Ole Bull's trophies received through the years: his gold
crown from San Francisco, a ring from the Queen of Bavaria, a pin of 140
diamonds from the Queen of Spain, a gold snuffbox from the King of
Denmark, and so forth. In the drawing room a long table had been set
up with an array of food, including two gorgeous cakes, one in Norwegian
colors, the other in American. There were ices in animal shapes, and the
caterer had brought his set of solid silver from Chicago, valued at thirty
thousand dollars. The newspapers reported in detail on the clothes worn
by the ladies, while Ole Bull's "plain black" was offset by his "kindly face"
which "looked more radiantly happy even than when the plaudits of entranced audiences followed the strains which he was wont to evoke with
his magic bow."[27]

There is no doubt that the wedding reception was an event in line with
Bull's experiences with European royalty and American entrepreneurs. However, one may question some of the journalistic hyperbole and also wonder just how happy Bull was at having been thus entrapped. Even after
the marriage the Thorps continued to interfere and did their best to clip
Bull's wings. When the time came for Sara to have their baby, Joseph Thorp
bought a cottage in West Lebanon, Maine, where Bull and Sara spent much
of the summer of 1871.[28] It had been the home of Abbie Shapleigh, who
served as a companion to Sara's mother, and who often would function
as a smoother of relations between Bull and the family. Their child, Sara
Olea Bull, was born on 4 March 1871.

From 1870 to his death in 1880 Bull's time was nearly evenly divided
between his life in America and in Norway, first at Valestrand, later at
Lysøen. He adopted the pattern well-known to Norwegian-Americans, if
they could afford the trip, of shuttling back and forth across the Atlantic

26. In conversation with Einar Haugen.
27. Smith, *Life of Ole Bull,* 164.
28. A photograph and an account of their home is in "The Ole Bull Place in West Lebanon," *Down East Enterprise* (August 1970), p. 127, by Frances P. Simister; thanks to George
Ehrenfried.

between the two countries. Norwegian-Americans began to regard Bull with pride as one of them.[29]

Bull had long had a special interest in the relation of Norwegian immigrants to America. In 1870 a plan was launched in Norway for a monument to Norwegian transatlantic migration, to be erected in 1872, the millennium of the uniting of Norway by King Harald Fairhair. Bull proposed a counterpart to the American Statue of Liberty, to be placed at Hafrsfjord in western Norway. But the Norwegian committee rejected his plan, and so Bull turned his interests to Leif Ericson, the Viking-age discoverer.[30]

The best account of Bull's activities on behalf of Norwegian-Americans is found in Rasmus B. Anderson's autobiography. By 1915 Anderson had become the controversial guru of Norwegian-American studies. He had not only founded the first chair of Scandinavian in the United States, but had also been American Minister to Denmark under President Cleveland (1885–89) and later a belligerent Norwegian-American editor. In 1870, however, when he first tried to enlist Bull in a campaign to erect a Leif Ericson monument at the University of Wisconsin, Anderson was still a lowly instructor at the university. In 1872 he conceived the idea of turning to Ole Bull for help in advancing the cause of Norwegian (he did not dare to say "Scandinavian") teaching. He proposed a concert to raise money to buy Norwegian books for the university library. Bull agreed with alacrity, choosing the Norwegian national holiday, 17 May 1872, as the date. Bull secured the assembly chamber in the State Capitol for the concert, and through his playing raised a sum of one thousand dollars for the Norwegian library collection. Then he further offered to pay Anderson's expenses for a trip to Christiania to select his books.

So, in June 1872 Bull and Anderson sailed off to Europe on the White Star steamer *Atlantic*.[31] Sara and little Olea stayed in Madison, either out of concern for the child's health or because of strained relations in the family. Joseph Thorp and his son Joseph, Jr., sailed with Bull, according to Anderson "presumably to keep an eye on his movements and acts."[32] There was no contact between the Thorp gentlemen and Bull on shipboard.

Anderson reported that when the boat came within sight of Norway, Bull sent for him to come on deck. "There he stood with his head un-

29. Torstein Jahr. "Oleana—Et blad af Ole Bulls og den norske indvandrings historie," *Symra* (1910), 6:3.
30. In Old Norwegian, the name was Leifr Eiriksson. "Leif Ericson" is an Americanized version, here adopted because of its common use in American writings on the subject.
31. Anderson, *Life Story,* 150.
32. Ibid., 148.

covered and with tears streaming down his cheeks as he pointed out to me those mountains of his native land that he loved so well."[33] From Christiansand Bull was going to Valestrand, Anderson to Christiania to buy his books.

Before leaving for America in October 1872, Bull gave a benefit concert in Bergen for "Indigent Craftsmen," where he played his *Concerto Romantico* (*Concerto in E Minor*) and two new compositions, *Vision* (no. 73) and *Lilly Dale* (no. 72), a fantasia on an American folk melody. He was now sixty-two years old and, on his return, ready to throw himself into a new project that would demand his energy and the music of his violin, the Leif Ericson monument.

33. Ibid., 155.

16

Second Family—Bull and Madison
(1872–1876)

I N 1872 Ole Bull actually initiated two significant projects, one in America and one in Norway. The first was his sponsorship in America of a monument to Leif Ericson. The second was his purchase of Lysøen (now Lysøya), a 650-acre island lying south of Bergen, a practically uninhabited wilderness of woods and water that rose to a peak with an unobstructed view of the coastal mountains and of the ocean. Bull planned to build a new home on Lysøen, a summer replacement for Valestrand and a supplement to his new home in Madison, Wisconsin.

Bull's commitment to Leif Ericson was strengthened by the rejection in 1870 of his plan for a monument at Hafrsfjord and encouraged by Rasmus B. Anderson, his new protegé in Madison. The early connection between Norway and America was not a completely new interest of Bull's. As early as 1852, in his opening speech at Oleana, Bull had reminded the colonists that the first discoverer of America was not Columbus, but a Norwegian Viking named Leif Ericson.[1]

It is possible that Bull first learned about Leif Ericson in school in Norway, but the subject was not greatly emphasized in the schools of his time. It is more likely that he picked up some crumbs of information during his visits with Longfellow in Cambridge in 1844 or 1845. Ten years earlier in Copenhagen, Longfellow had met the Danish philologist Carl Christian Rafn (1795–1864), who called the American poet's attention to *Thorfinn Karlsefni's Saga*.[2] Rafn gave Longfellow some lessons in Old Icelandic, and Longfellow bought a copy of the *Heimskringla* in the original. By 1844,

---

1. Leif was not strictly a Norwegian, having been born in Iceland, but his father, Eric the Red, came from Norway.
2. In modern Norwegian, "Torfinn Karlsevnes Saga."

Rafn was well known in Cambridge for *Antiquitates Americanae* (1837), his massive work on the evidence in Norse sagas and antiquities for the tenth-century Norse discovery of America. Edward Everett's 1838 review of Rafn's work, printed in *The North American Review,* for the first time brought extensive information to American readers on Leif Ericson.

Longfellow was inspired to write a poem on Scandinavian themes in his rollicking ballad "The Skeleton in Armor" (1839). His romantic tale pictured a shaggy Viking fleeing from the Baltic to New England and leaving behind such dubious relics as the Newport Tower (in Rhode Island) and a suit of copper mail since shown to have come from an Indian grave:

> Three weeks we westward bore,
> And when the storm was o'er,
> Cloud-like we saw the shore
>   Stretching to leeward;
> There for my lady's bower
> Built I the lofty tower,
> Which, to this very hour,
>   Stands looking seaward.[3]

Rafn's apparently authentic relics stood practically unopposed for half a century, until the Norwegian historian Gustav Storm (1845–1903) laid them to rest with his historical research in *Studier i Vinlandsreisene* (1887).

Anderson had first proposed to Bull in 1870 that a campaign be initiated to raise a monument to Leif Ericson on the University of Wisconsin campus. "This would help us to make the University of Wisconsin the chief center of Scandinavian study in the United States."[4] But it was not until 1872, after his return from Norway, that Bull became a sponsor of Anderson's Leif Ericson project. Anderson was also hired that year to teach Sara Bull Norwegian, and he spent much time in taking notes toward a Bull biography.

Anderson secured the aid of a well-to-do Norwegian-American state senator, John Anders Johnson (1832–1901), and by 1873 these three had organized a Leif Ericson Monument Committee, with Bull as president. They published an appeal in the Norwegian-American press and got exactly nothing in response.

Bull decided to try a different approach. He asked Anderson to arrange a series of concerts on behalf of the monument. He did so, and early in 1873 Bull appeared in all the towns of Norwegian settlement from Madi-

---

3. Henry Wadsworth Longfellow, *The Skeleton in Armor* (Boston, 1877), no page.
4. Rasmus B. Anderson, *Life Story* (Madison, Wis., 1915), 190.

son to Decorah, Iowa, with Sara as accompanist and Anderson as speaker. They succeeded in raising some twenty-five hundred dollars. Bull felt that Norwegians in Norway should also contribute to the fund, so they proceeded to Bergen. Bull's new house at Lysøen was ready by this time (1873), and so Sara, and her father and brother, who had accompanied the Bulls and Anderson to Norway, went with Bull to his new home.

Anderson was shipped off to Christiania to bring Bjørnson to Bergen, which he did, traveling over land. The planned concerts were to include performances by Bull with Edvard Grieg's accompaniment and speeches by Bjørnson.[5] At an opening dinner in Bergen, Anderson made a famous speech, jestingly calling for a new coat of arms for Bergen: a dried codfish (*torsk*) under an umbrella, alluding to the two most famous attributes of the city. Not to be outdone, Edvard Grieg jumped up, brought his umbrella to the table and held it over Anderson: "Bergen's new coat of arms!" (with a pun on the word *torsk* to signify also a "fool").[6]

Concerts were arranged in the chief cities on the south coast, Stavanger, Christiansand, and Christiania. The expedition netted somewhere around two thousand dollars according to Anderson's account. This plus the money raised in America was still nowhere near enough for the monument, and the project languished for the moment. In the meantime, however, Anderson had received his appointment as professor of Scandinavian. In 1874 he published a popular book on Leif Ericson with the challenging title *America not Discovered by Columbus*, which by 1930 had gone through eight editions. In 1875 he produced a more substantial book, *Norse Mythology*, which by 1901 had gone through seven editions.

Bull's second project in 1872, the purchase of Lysøen, was successfully completed. He had first visited the island in 1826 and even then was struck by its beauty. He bought the island from a friend, antiquarian Nicolay Nicolaysen, for six hundred specie dollars and in the following year erected the structure now known as "Villa Lysøen." It was built of timber from the island in a style that was a curious mixture of Moorish and Norwegian ("stave church") architecture. A modern art historian, Stephan Tschudi-Madsen, has pinpointed Conrad Frederik von der Lippe (1833–1901) as the architect and a local carpenter, Ingebrigt Bøe (1850–1944) as the master builder. But its numerous and unusual carvings and the turned pillars reflect Bull's own complex personality as a Norwegian patriot and as a cos-

5. See chap. 18 for the program that includes a new piece by Bull, *Yderst mod Vesten ligger et Land (Far to the West there Lies a Land)* (no. 74).
6. Anderson, *Life Story*, 198.

Lysøen, built in 1873. Photo by Knud Knudsen. Courtesy of Bergen University Library.

mopolitan.[7] Comparison of Villa Lysøen with his Valestrand home reveals many elements of the same design.

In the winter of 1872 to 1873, while he was touring America, Bull wrote home to Sara in Madison, Wisconsin:

> How I am longing for Norway, for Lysøen! If you only knew the beauty of the Claustrum vallis lucida,[8] you would pine for it. I have never seen anything that attracts me so mysteriously, so grand, so sweet, so sweeping, so rejoicing! I cannot account for it. The atmosphere there is certainly very peculiar and the woods so variegated, the crevices and ravines, the lakes so many and varied in expression, but the grand views of the mountain must be seen with caution or they will overpower you. They make me feel so thankful to God and weep in prayer for all enemies and friends.[9]

Bull and the Thorps spent most of the summer of 1873 at Lysøen. During this stay Bull sold Lysøen to Thorp, who then proceeded to rent a villa at Menton near Monaco on the Mediterranean for the coming cold season. The role of family man and the company of his in-laws did not

7. Stephan Tschudi-Madsen, "Det var ikke Ole Bull som tegnet Villa Lysø," *Bergens Tidende,* n.d. Clipping, Bergens Offentlige Bibliotek.
8. Latin name of the nearby monastery known as Lysekloster (Monastery of Light).
9. Mortimer Smith, *The Life of Ole Bull* (Princeton, N.J., 1943), 176.

Lysøen. Photo by Knud Knudsen. Courtesy of Bergen University Library.

delight Bull. As the winter in Menton wore on, relations worsened, their differences reaching a climax in April 1874. In Mortimer Smith's words, "The family could not avoid showing their bewilderment and irritation with Ole's inability to act like a conventional and respectable American abroad."[10]

On 4 April 1874, Sara's father wrote in his diary: "Mr. Bull and Sara left this morning—Sara for Florence to meet her mother and Joseph. Mr. Bull to such a place as his desires and conclusions may take him."[11]

In a few weeks the whole Thorp family, including Sara and Olea, sailed for America, and Bull was not to see his wife and child for two years. Part of the quarrel between Bull and the Thorps concerned Sara's future home. Her mother wanted her to remain in America, and Bull wanted her to live in Norway, on Lysøen or at Valestrand.

Bull no doubt felt a constant irritation at the shackles in which his new marriage had bound him. According to the account of Christen Magelsen (1841–1940), a Norwegian artist then in Italy, the Thorp family had locked up Bull's clothes. Bull had to ask a hotel porter to buy him a new set of clothes, and those purchased were too small for him. He traveled to Rome in them anyway and there contacted Bjørnson.[12]

10. Ibid., 182.
11. Ibid.
12. Ola Linge, *Ole Bull: Livshistoria, Mannen, Kunstnaren* (Oslo, 1953), 272.

Lysøen. Music Room. Photo by Knud Knudsen. Courtesy of Bergen University Library.

We have a lively account of the occasion by Bjørnson's son Bjørn (later a theater director and actor).

One morning early, I think it was about eight, our servant Lina came rushing in: 'Heavens, Ole Bull is in the hall, wanting to get in.' Father jumped to his feet: 'Are you letting him stand outside?' 'No, Bjørnson,' laughed Bull, 'I'll get in. There are no doors for me, when I don't want them.' He had had a concert in Florence the evening before and had traveled . . . by night train, sitting up. And now he stood there, lively and happy and wonderful. He was in his mid-sixties, tall and slender. Athletic, but gracious and mobile, full of jest and jollity. Constantly talking, constantly moving. A poseur with a charming embrace and with movements that were often amusing, often with pathos, which gave his words a framework that kept one captivated.

'Dear Bjørnson,' he said as he embraced father, 'the whole world means nothing to me at this moment against the fact that I have you here large as life again.'

The two old friends told stories and were in great good humor. They disagreed about Sweden; Bull told Bjørnson that he was too fond of the Swedes. Bjørnson defended himself by maintaining that the Swedes had to learn to understand the Norwegians. The next morning he sent Bull a letter with Bjørn detailing his views. Bull answered by playing his violin to the fourteen-year-old Bjørn for over an hour until the boy's tears came. "Now," he said,

PART I. LIFE AND ADVENTURES

"You can go home and tell your father that this is my answer to his letter." When Bjørn told his father, Bjørnson said, "That Ole Bull—thank heavens he's Norwegian!"[13]

Bjørnson was delighted at Bull's lively narration of his conflicts with the Thorp family and is said to have doubled up with laughter at Bull's story. "Bull asked father to help him against his new family. He wanted to have his daughter, who was only a couple of years old. He wanted to kidnap the child. He had fantastic plans."[14] Bull had no money, and Bjørnson lent him five lire a day for the six weeks he stayed in Rome. Bjørnson raised enough money to pay Bull's way back to Christiania, and there Bull discovered he had money in the bank which he had totally forgotten.

In Rome he also met Liszt again, and they had many lively discussions. One artist on whom they could not agree was Richard Wagner. "A person who comes out of a Wagner concert," asserted Bull, "is not to be trusted. There is murder in that music, and something that appeals to the lower passions."[15] Such sentiments must have upset Liszt as an ardent advocate of his son-in-law's music.

Before returning to Norway Bull spent some happy weeks in Florence, persuaded by his old friend Prince Poniatowsky to give a concert. Bull raised an electric enthusiasm in his audience by offering them his *The Nightingale, Carnival in Venice Variations,* the *Polacca Guerriera,* and Paganini's *Variations on Nel cor più mi sento.* In delight over their acclaim he later wrote: "My violin did not fail me. I was never more thrilled by its tone myself, and I cannot describe to you the pitch to which the excitement ran or the warmth of my reception. I am so thankful that I have not disappointed my old friends."[16]

On 3 June 1874, Bull wrote to Bjørnson from Florence, mentioning a letter from Mr. Thorp "that fails to discuss our settlement (Opgjør)." He says that Thorp's manner is to treat everything with a "forced smile that you can decorate lettuce with—full of vinegar and oil."[17] Bull spent the early summer of 1874 working at Lysøen. He cleared paths, planted the garden, and completed the furnishing of the house.

13. Bjørn Bjørnson, *Mit Livs Historier: Fra barndommens dage* (Christiania, 1922), 112–17.

14. Ibid., 119.

15. Smith, *Life of Ole Bull,* 184.

16. Ibid.

17. Øyvind Anker, "Ole Bull som økonomisk kannestøper," clipping, no date [1937?]. The letter from Florence is dated 1875, probably an error.

After a tour to the North Cape of Norway, Bull settled into Lysøen for the winter. Then, in July 1875, he again set forth on a concert tour, first as far north in Norway as the town of Tromsø. Here the editor of the *Tromsø Stiftstidende* expressed a wish that Bull would also give a popular concert: "We would like that our workers might for once enjoy something beautiful."[18] Bull then traveled stepwise south to Christiania with his brother Edvard and concertmaster Hennum. In Christiania he assisted in the unveiling of an equestrian statue of King Carl Johan before the palace. On 14 September he performed at a festival in honor of Michelangelo's four-hundredth anniversary, playing his *Siciliano and Tarantella* and *Carnival in Venice Variations* to commemorate the Italian master.

He returned to Sweden in the fall of 1875 and was everywhere received with more acclaim than ever. The newspaper *Nya Dagligt Allehanda* wrote of "the capacity of genius to give significance to whatever forms he uses to reveal his inner life. . . . Ole Bull's appearance yesterday evening was new evidence of the power of this experience."[19]

On this tour Bull was invited to the royal palace at Drottningsholm. Swedish King Oscar II (1829–1907) jestingly said that Bull who had played at the top of Snøhetta Mountain and at Niagara Falls ought to play from the summit of the Cheops Pyramid. "Yes, Your Majesty," said Bull. "On my next birthday I shall play 'Sæter Girl's Sunday' on the Pyramid in honor of my King."[20]

From Sweden he proceeded to Denmark and on to Germany, giving concerts all the way. The Norwegian composer Johannes Haarklou (1847–1925) who happened to be in Hamburg, reported that "old people were moved to tears on seeing him again. . . . There was no doubt that here one had a person of world dimensions, one who enthralls the masses with magic power from his appearance on the stage until he takes his last stroke."[21]

Goby Eberhardt (1852–1926), a German violinist who heard Bull in Bremen, wrote about their meeting: "Ole Bull, the Norwegian Paganini, is one of the most interesting persons I met in Bremen. . . . He played many of his compositions for me on first request. His scales, his broken chords, his staccatos, his harmonics, his single and double stops, all were matchless. . . ." Concerning Bull's first concert in Bremen, Eberhardt wrote: "Bull played his *Concerto in A Major* and his famous *Polacca Guerriera*. . . .

18. *Tromsø Stiftstidende* (18 July 1875), clipping from May Lunde.
19. Linge, *Ole Bull,* 273–74.
20. Ibid., 274.
21. Ibid., 275.

Ole Bull, Berlin, 1876. Photo by E. Milster. Courtesy of Museet Lysøen.

The handsome giant with his striking artist's head, which in many ways is reminiscent of Liszt's, created a stir. And what playing! He played like a young god. Flawless, perfect." Eberhardt called on Bull at his hotel. "He was playing and invited me to come in. I opened the door and there stood Bull in the altogether!" He had no doubt taken one of his famous cold showers and had paid no attention to his attire![22]

From Bremen, Bull went next to Alexandria, Egypt, via Berlin, Switzerland, and Italy. He arrived in Cairo on 4 February 1876, just in time to climb the Cheops Pyramid, as he had promised, on his sixty-sixth birthday. A German writer, Adolf Ebeling (1828–96), reported in his *Bilder aus Kairo:* "Bull was one of the first on the summit of the Cheops Pyramid, and when the violin, carried by Bedouins, reached him, he turned his bare head towards the North. In the still, warm February day the Norwegian mountain hymn rang out over the reverently listening audience and the history-laden Nile Valley."[23] As soon as Bull got back to Alexandria, he wired King Oscar and got a thank-you telegram in return. He did not stay long in Egypt, but did give concerts in Alexandria and Cairo.

In March and April 1876 Bull toured Germany and received a fitting welcome in Bergen on his return in May. On the national holiday, 17 May, he and Edvard Grieg were guests of honor at a performance of *Til Sæters,* which raised money for a new National Stage of Bergen.

Bull had broken his marital bond in what seemed an irreparable way, but he was basically loyal to his commitments, closely tied to his family. After his European fling, the void of his loneliness evidently struck him. He had become a family man at heart, and he yearned for the solace of his young wife and their child.

22. Ibid., 275–76.
23. (Stuttgart, 1878), 139–40.

17

Last Years — Bull and Boston
(1876–1880)

O N 28 January 1875 Bull had written a pathetic letter to Sara, who, he says, had become more necessary for his peace of mind than ever before. He pleaded: "I beseech you to remember that I trust entirely to your own wishes, and then, see my forlorn position. Am I entirely abandoned now? . . . *Come! before too late for your own, for our intensely beloved child's sake.*"[1]

We do not know just how Sara responded to this letter, but we know from Anderson's autobiography that she appealed to him for a solution to their marital problem.

I studied the matter carefully and finally hit on this means of getting the two reunited. I knew Ole Bull's great enthusiasm for everything that would in any way spread the glory and fame of his dear old Norway. . . . I therefore selected the story by Jonas Lie, *Lodsen og hans Hustru* (*The Pilot and His Wife*) (1874) as a book that I would help her translate into English. With this book in her hand I felt sure that Ole Bull would take back his wife with enthusiasm and forget all about her desertion. Besides, this work would keep her mind occupied and help her forget her troubles.[2]

We do not know whether the attempt at reconciliation stemmed from Bull's appeal or from Anderson's ingenuity, perhaps a bit of both.

In the autumn of 1875, when *The Pilot and His Wife* was published, Sara put a dozen copies of the book in her traveling trunk. In the spring of 1876 she left for Norway. As Anderson had expected, Ole Bull was delighted and the reconciliation was complete. The book was dedicated "af-

1. Mortimer Smith, *The Life of Ole Bull* (Princeton, N.J., 1943), 188.
2. Rasmus B. Anderson, *Life Story* (Madison, Wis., 1915), 223.

fectionately to my husband." She brought him back with her to America in the early fall.

The family decided to move to Cambridge, Massachusetts. Here in 1876 they rented "Elmwood," the elegant residence of author James Russell Lowell, who had been appointed ambassador to Spain, later to Great Britain. (It is now the residence of the president of Harvard.) At twenty-six, Sara had finally established her independence from her mother. She took charge of Ole Bull's affairs from that time until his death in 1880. Just how happy this made Bull is not known. Gertrude Fiske, who had known him before his second marriage, contrasted his now gentle demeanor with the worries he had earlier expressed.[3] But Bull's longtime friend Bjørnson, who was her guest in 1880 after Bull's death, found Sara to be "a pin cushion"—"the driest, sharpest thing that God has created." He refused to collaborate with her on a book about Bull because she wanted to "falsify" his story "so that he would stand in the exalted position of the angel Gabriel."[4]

The move to Cambridge brought Bull within walking distance of some of his old friends. He spent Thanksgiving at the Horsfords', Christmas at the Longfellows', and New Year's 1877 at the Fields'. Longfellow received a copy of *The Pilot and His Wife* on 13 November 1876, with a letter inviting him and his daughters to Bull's first Boston concert.

Bull's friend Eben Norton Horsford (1818–93) was a former Harvard University chemist who had made a fortune by inventing baking powder, as well as a popular preparation known as "Horsford's Acid Phosphate," and other products, such as a concentrated biscuit for Civil War soldiers in the field. Horsford took a vigorous interest in the Norse discoveries. He would eventually publish a series of books on the topic and install a plaque at Gerry's Landing near the Charles River, on the spot where he assumed Leif had landed.[5] He also built a stupendous tower on the Charles at Norumbega, a place name on French maps of New England that he associated with Norvegia, the Latin word for "Norway."

Bull's other friend James T. Fields (1817–81) was a publisher and author, for some years editor of the *Atlantic Monthly,* whose home on Charles Street in Boston became a frequent refuge of Bull's.[6]

---

3. Letter from G. Fiske to Sara Bull, Cambridge Historical Society Collections.

4. Eva Lund Haugen and Einar Haugen, eds. and trans., *Land of the Free: Bjørnstjerne Bjørnson's America Letters, 1880–1881* (Northfield, Minn., 1978), 131–32 (letter to Karoline Bjørnson, 16 December 1880).

5. It is still there, moved a little away from the river.

6. A tribute to Bull by Fields appears in Sara C. Bull, *Ole Bull: A Memoir* (Boston and New York, 1882), 397–99.

My dear Mr. Longfellow,

Permit me to send you "the Pilot and his wife" and also request the high honor of seeing yourself and daughters at my first concert to morrow evening and forgive an humble but most ardent admirer of trespassing upon valuable time.

With unvariable gratitude and love yours

Ole Bull

Boston Nov 13th 1876

Letter to Longfellow, Boston, 13 November 1876. By permission of the Houghton Library, Harvard University.

During November and December 1876, Bull gave nine concerts in Boston. Six years had passed since his last appearance there, and the audience greeted him by spontaneously rising and applauding. The last concert (8 December) was organized as a fund-raiser for the Leif Ericson monument. The hall was decorated with American and Norwegian flags. From

PROGRAMME.

PART FIRST.

1.—OVERTURE, "Raymond," - - - - - *A. Thomas*

ORCHESTRA.

2.—TO THE MEMORY OF WASHINGTON, - - - *Ole Bull*

Introduction (Grave), Sorrow and Woe—Allegro agitato, Rising against Oppression—Battle, "God Save the King!" and "Yankee Doodle!" alternately heard—Honor to the Fallen Heroes—(Choral)—Reception of the Victorious Federals, and March in Honor of Washington—Finale.

OLE BULL.

3. { *a*—NECKROSEN (The Water Flower), - - - - *Abt*
{ *b*—SWEDISH NATIONAL SONGS.

SWEDISH LADIES VOCAL QUARTETTE.

4.—BRIDAL MARCH, from "Norse Peasant Life," - - *Edward Grieg*

WM. H. SHERWOOD.

5.—THE MOUNTAINS OF NORWAY, - - - - *Ole Bull*

OLE BULL.

PART SECOND.

1.—SWEDISH WEDDING MARCH, - - - - *Sodermann*

ORCHESTRA.

2.—CARNIVAL OF VENICE, - - - - - *Ole Bull*

OLE BULL.

3. { *a*—SÆTERGJENTEN'S SÖNDAG, - - - · *Ole Bull*
{ *b*—SERENADE, - - - - - - *Sir H. Bishop*

SWEDISH LADIES VOCAL QUARTETTE.

4.—IMPROVISATIONS UPON FAMILIAR MELODIES.

(Themes to be suggested and sent in by the Audience.)

OLE BULL.

5.—MARCH, "Athalie," - - - - - - *Mendelssohn*

ORCHESTRA.

EUGENE THAYER, Organist.   CARL ZERRAHN, Conductor.

Concert program, 8 December 1876, Boston. Courtesy of Wayside Inn, Sudbury, Mass.

187

the stage shone the names of the Vinland Saga: Leif, Thorvald, Thorfinn, plus—George Washington, all in golden letters. That evening, addressing the audience, Bull said:

I see here among the audience stars of the first magnitude. Why should they address me? What am I that I can stand before this audience and address such stars as these? I am but an atom of failure in the universe; yet you are all united with me in that failure in that you have indorsed [sic] me. You belong to me and I belong to you. . . . The name of Washington stands as the greatest pinnacle of glory. It signifies liberty, it signifies every thing that ennobles man.[7]

He concluded by claiming Norwegian ancestry for Washington! Then he fortunately turned to his violin to say the rest. His program included an *Overture* by (Ambroise) Thomas (1811–96), his own *In Memory of Washington,* Grieg's *Bridal Procession* (probably arranged for violin from Opus 19, No. 2), a Swedish wedding march by Johan August Södermann (1832–76), and finally Bull's ever popular *Carnival in Venice Variations* and *The Mountains of Norway.*

After the concert Edward Everett Hale (1822–1909), author and Unitarian clergyman, addressed the audience, expressing the hope that a committee could be formed to realize Bull's idea of a Leif Ericson monument. A committee was indeed created, with Thomas G. Appleton as chairman and a number of eminent New Englanders as members, including Longfellow, Lowell, Charles W. Eliot (1834–1926), and Horsford. The needed funds were speedily raised, and a sculptor named Anne Whitney (1821–1915) was chosen to fashion the monument. Miss Whitney first proposed a shaggy, bearded viking, but the committee preferred a smooth-faced youth, in some ways resembling Ole Bull. The statue was not unveiled until 27 October 1887, seven years after Bull's death.[8]

In January 1877 Bull finally paid a visit to the Thorps in Madison, having apparently reconciled himself somewhat with his father-in-law. Letters from Bull's attorney Turnbull and the children and friends of Félicie give the impression that Bull was not completely comfortable with the Thorp financial dominance that was established in these last years. After Bull sold Lysøen to Thorp in 1873, Thorp deeded it to his granddaughter Olea. After Sara's death, Olea received a fund of thirty thousand dollars for the main-

---

7. *Daily Advertiser,* in Bull, *A Memoir,* 273–74.
8. This elegant Victorian statue mounted on a Viking ship stands in a prominent spot on Commonwealth Avenue in Boston. To this day, it is a rallying point for Scandinavians in the Boston area. It was refurbished and rededicated by the efforts of a Scandinavian-American committee on 9 October 1988, officially decreed as "Leif Ericson Day" by the United States Congress.

Sara Thorp Bull (1850–1911). Courtesy of State Historical Society of Wisconsin.

Ole Bull instructing a pupil. Photo by Mora. Courtesy of Wayside Inn, Sudbury, Mass.

tenance of Lysøen, and in 1973 her daughter Sylvea Bull Curtis in turn donated Lysøen to the Norwegian state. By Norwegian law it was impossible to deprive Félicie's children of Valestrand, which remained in their possession.[9]

After the visit to Madison, Bull set off on a tour arranged by Maurice Strakosch, with the American singer Emma Thursby (1845–1931) as vocal soloist. After four concerts in New York the *Herald* wrote: "Age seems to have been contented with scattering snow upon his head, leaving untouched the fire of his genius. The lithe and agile figure has lost none of its elasticity, and the nerves are as steady as in the noonday of life. . . . Ole Bull, like a prince that had wandered from his own land and returned after a long absence, is restored to the throne he had abandoned by a delighted people; the memory of his great feats is not forgotten."[10] At his last concert of the tour, he was repeatedly recalled after his rendition of an obbligato added to Gounod's *Ave Maria* (sung by Miss Thursby). After the sixth recall he made a little speech, but only after his tenth encore, when he played variations on "We won't go Home until Morning" (no. 75), would the audience let him go. The next morning he sailed for Norway with Sara. Olea was left with the Shapleighs in West Lebanon.

The Norwegian actress Lucie Wolf reported on a meeting with Bull at Lysøen, probably in the summer of 1877. He expressed great admiration for her performance of certain characters speaking local dialect. He suggested that she accompany him to America, where he could promise her at least a million *kroner* in income. "But are you really Norwegian?" he said. "There is a suspiciously warm blood in you, a teeming life that we Norwegians are not used to."[11]

Her day on Lysøen was unforgettable. Bull asked Sara to play an old hymn by Salvini on the organ. Then he asked Lucie Wolf to join him for a walk in the woods. "There he stood in the midst of the light green birchwood on a little height with his bared head thrown back . . . , his handsome face and his eyes alight with the artistic fire of genius. . . . This glorious, perfect figure of Apollo stood shining like an incarnate ideal." Bull played "as only he could play. It was tender, sweetly dreaming, with thunderclaps and waterfalls, laughter and weeping, joy and pain in beautiful union. . . . Never have I lived or will I live through hours like these, no never!"[12]

After the quiet summer of 1877 on Lysøen, Bull and Sara left for Lon-

9. Ola Linge, *Ole Bull: Livshistoria, Mannen, Kunstnaren* (Oslo, 1953), 389.
10. Bull, *A Memoir*, 276–77.
11. Lucie Wolf, *Livserindringer* (Christiania, 1897), 193.
12. Ibid.

don. In Belgium they visited violinist Vieuxtemps, Bull's one-time rival, who had been crippled by a paralyzing stroke. Then they went to Vienna, where Bull gave yet another concert. Critic Edward Hanslick was there again, and while he noted the storm of applause, he still regarded the sixty-seven-year-old Bull's style of playing as antiquated.[13]

From Vienna Bull proceeded to Budapest to visit his old friend from London days, pianist and composer Franz Liszt. Bull wanted to play again a number they had played in England, Beethoven's *Kreutzer Sonata*. According to a student of Liszt's who happened to be present, the results were disastrous. "After no more than a few bars, however, things went wrong," Ilka Horovitz-Barnay recounted. "Liszt glanced up in some surprise, smiled, nodded" and tried again, but "the first movement of the sonata was a series of derailments."

Ole Bull grew ever more flustered and fidgety. Liszt's unimpaired affability seemed only to add to his uncertainty; he groaned and sweated, muttered inarticulately to himself, and with his bow scratched on the music to show Liszt where to begin again. The whole thing was immensely comic, and Liszt laughed like a street urchin. . . . Then, all of a sudden, Ole Bull, his face as red as a beetroot, shrieked, "It's quite impossible to play with you; you can't keep time and you are always playing wrong notes!"

At this, something terrifying happened. Just as a serene sky gives way to a sudden storm, so did Liszt's smiling features change. His whole face altered, lightning flashed from his eyes, his long white hair literally bristled and stood out around his distorted countenance like some fearsome mane. The words came bubbling over his lips like a cataract: "You dare say that to me, you old humbug—to me, Franz Liszt!" . . . Bull hurled insults back. . . . at the end . . . the Master shouted, "Your name will already be forgotten while the world is still kneeling before my memory!" With these words he seized a chair, and in his blind fury . . . smashed it to the floor.

But the next evening, at Ole Bull's recital in the hall of the Music Club, Liszt sat smiling and cheerful in the front row. . . . Liszt applauded conspicuously after every number, and, in thanks, Ole Bull bowed specially to him.[14]

This episode is reported in Mortimer Smith's biography, with the comment that "happily, the two old warriors were not bad friends for long."[15] Sara Bull totally omits the Liszt episode in her biography, quoting only Bull's courteous and friendly letter of thanks for Liszt's hospitality, signed "your devoted admirer and friend."[16]

Both Bull and Liszt were primarily solo performers and had no doubt

13. Linge, *Ole Bull*, 279.
14. Adrian Williams, *Portrait of Liszt* (Oxford, 1990), 554–56.
15. Smith, *Life of Ole Bull*, 196–97.
16. Bull, *A Memoir*, 282–83.

each developed his own style of playing. Neither of them had played many of Beethoven's works and their memory of his music was perhaps rusty after so many years. The report by Liszt's student may have been biased in his favor. It is clear that the two artists had each developed his own idiom (musical idiolect), which here clashed in their old age. Both were especially known as improvisers and were accustomed to occupying the center stage.

After a summer cure at Wiesbaden in 1878, the Bulls returned to Norway for a week's visit at Bjørnson's estate at Aulestad in Gudbrandsdal. Maurice Strakosch came to visit them at Lysøen, bringing with him a singer named Stella Faustina.[17] Together the three gave three concerts in Trondheim. On their return to Bergen, Bull assisted the young Norwegian composer Johannes Haarklou at his first concert. In addition Bull gave two concerts of his own, the final one on 1 August 1878, would prove to be his last concert in Bergen.

In January 1879 Bjørnson received a letter from Rasmus Anderson informing him that Bull had spent Christmas with the Andersons in Madison: "He is fondest of you among all his compatriots." He also mentioned the numerous concerts Bull had recently given. Since returning to America in September Bull had given about thirty concerts with Strakosch and Emma Thursby. Bjørnson immediately wrote and asked Anderson why Bull was still busy giving concerts. "His appearances in America have frightened me. Does he *still* have to make money? . . . He is after all the love of my childhood and youth; he has a marvelous gift, a great heart, the beauty of vitality and genius."[18]

Anderson soberly replied:

Bull is in fine shape. He does not need to give concerts. He has an annual income of 4,000 dollars as long as he lives and Mrs. Bull has 5,000 a year. That he still gives concerts has several reasons. For one thing he is not happy unless he is playing in public, and for another his concerts are so well paid that it is not easy to resist the temptation. For his concerts this winter he has gotten 500 dollars and all expenses. . . . He is daily invited as a guest by the most famous and respected men. . . . I am sorry to say it, but I think it is true that Ole Bull meets more true cordiality and appreciation here than in Norway . . ."[19]

On his birthday in 1879 Bull wrote a long and warm letter to Bjørnson that gave him a chance to express his love for his old friend.

17. Program, no date, Bergen University Library.
18. Unpublished letter in Wisconsin Historical Society Collection, Madison, Wis.; cf. Linge, *Ole Bull*, 281.
19. Cited by Linge, *Ole Bull*, 283.

Ole Bull. Courtesy of Wayside Inn, Sudbury, Mass.

First and foremost my heartiest thanks for what you have acted, spoken, and written for freedom of thought, for elevating society, and exposing the dry rot to the public. We are not as few as before and there will be more when the great conflict comes. . . . I have all my life lived in an age of revolutions and I feel that you understand me better than before. Unfortunately I have not been able to free myself from my Norwegian point of view, but have stubbornly opposed Scandinavianism. As a Norwegian I possess my Ole Viol, who will sustain me when all else fails. He was given me by the Allfather, so that I should believe in Him and have confidence and illimitable love and devotion for Norway.[20]

Here Bull deviated into a political discussion, expressing his concern about the Norwegian parliamentary conflict that would find its solution in 1884: "Why can't the Storting impeach the Cabinet and fetch them with the police?" He then explained that his chief purpose in coming to Madison was on behalf of the Leif Ericson monument, no doubt to discuss it with Anderson. He mentioned that his wife had been ill and that the Thorps were in Brussels with little Olea. "It is better that she stays with her grandparents, whose idyl she is. . . . And you, beloved friend, where you are, I am also, you know that." He signed his letter "Ole" followed by the figure of a violin. This last letter to Bjørnson showed that Bull at sixty-nine was still vigorous and as devoted to his Norwegian friend as ever.[21]

Sara Bull wrote in her *Memoir* that "the summer of 1879 was one of the happiest ever spent by the artist in Norway."[22] On 17 May he was welcomed in Bergen, and as usual he headed the annual parade with his special silk flag. In the evening he enjoyed the presentation of Ivar Aasen's play *Ervingen (The Heir)* at the theater; here was a truly Norwegian play in the New Norwegian language.

On 15 June Bull called on Edvard Grieg to celebrate the composer's birthday at Lofthus in Hardanger, where Grieg did his composing. Bull heard that the Hardanger fiddler Ola Mosafinn (1828–1912) was there, and he asked for him to play, no doubt a great experience for Mosafinn. A plan to celebrate St. John's (Midsummer) was foiled by fog, so Bull invited to Lysøen all the young people who wished to come. Here they were treated to food and drink and violin playing by Bull. At the end of July the railroad from Bergen to Voss was opened, and King Oscar II came to dedicate it. Of course Bull was invited, but uncharacteristically he did not bring his violin; so instead the King sang Bull's "Sæter Girl's Sunday" and gave him his photo.

20. Øyvind Anker, "Ole Bull som økonomisk kannestøper," clipping, no date [1937?], letter dated 4 February 1879.
21. Ibid.
22. Bull, *A Memoir*, 296.

Ole Bull, Boudoir Portrait, 1880. Photo by A. Bogardus, New York. Courtesy of Wayside Inn, Sudbury, Mass.

Once again in America by September, Bull gave another series of concerts. In a Boston concert on 29 January 1880, he performed alongside Ralph Waldo Emerson and Oliver Wendell Holmes to aid the "Old South Preservation Fund."[23] His tour continued through April and May 1880, ending in Chicago.

But he was not feeling well. According to a letter from Professor Storm Bull in Madison, a nephew of Ole Bull's, there was a "major explosion" in the Bull-Thorp household. The family wanted him to stay in America during the summer of 1880.[24] When they nevertheless left for Europe on 30 June, Bull was already gravely ill with cancer. He just barely managed to get to Liverpool, where an English doctor joined them. In Bergen a Norwegian doctor was added to the retinue.

Félicie Ingier, his only surviving daughter by Félicie, visited him briefly at Lysøen. Horsford from Cambridge was one of his last visitors. Horsford, in recalling his final days with Ole Bull, wrote of Lysøen that it was "a very Alhambra of fairy architecture. . . . How often through these galleries, in happier days, had so sweetly thrilled the strains of his favorite Gaspar de Salo [*sic*]!"[25]

On 17 August 1880, Bull asked Sara to play his favorite composer Mozart's *Requiem* on their organ. She played it several times, at quarter past twelve that afternoon, he quietly passed away.

The news of Bull's death was telegraphed to the world, and telegrams of condolence streamed in. It was a loss that all Norwegians could share with many Americans. The funeral was set for 23 August. Family and friends were conveyed to Lysøen in the steamer *King Sverre*. Bergen was clad in black, and the newspapers had columns lined in black margins. Juniper and other greens were strewn in the streets. At Lysøen Edvard Grieg played a prelude on the organ, and pastor Krogh spoke. Wollert Konow (1845–1924), a Storting representative from Bergen, thanked Bull for his contribution to Norway. Eight men from surrounding communities bore the casket. In Bergen harbor all the boats and steamers formed a path for *King Sverre*, and the fortress Bergenhus saluted. A chorus sang Welhaven's poem honoring Bull, "How Sweet to be Embraced by the Peace of Evening," and all the church bells tolled.

On the dock stood not only the officials of Bergen, but also Bjørnson and his wife Karoline, who had come from Aulestad, and the representatives of many societies. Sixteen young women bore his trophies, and the

23. Program printed in Smith, *Life of Ole Bull*, 206.
24. Linge, *Ole Bull*, 393.
25. Bull, *A Memoir*, 312.

Ole Bull's funeral. Bergen Harbor, 23 August 1880. Photo by Knud Knudsen. Courtesy of Bergen University Library.

casket was driven by four black horses. The Brigade Orchestra played Chopin's Funeral March. At the Swan Apothecary, his birthplace, the procession stopped for an observance and sang "Sæter Girl's Sunday."

At the cemetery there were more ceremonies, with Bjørnson giving the main speech, a poetic and masterful oration, beginning: "He was honored, Ole Bull, that we have seen today. He was also loved, and that is greater than being honored." He continued:

Ole Bull became the first and greatest festive moment in the life of this people. He gave it self-confidence, the greatest thing that could be given us. . . . Patriotism was the creative force in his life. When he founded the Norwegian Theater, when he supported Norwegian art, when he helped the National Museum, when his powerful violin sang for other patriotic purposes, when wherever he came, he helped countrymen and others who needed it, it was not so much for the sake of the cause or the person as for the glory of Norway. He always felt as a representative. And if he thought it was needed, at home or abroad, to appear as Ole Olsen Viol, Norse Norwegian from Norway, he never neglected to do so.[26]

Edvard Grieg followed with a brief speech as he laid a wreath on the coffin:

26. Linge, *Ole Bull*, 290–91. Bjørnson's speech was the occasion for an invitation from Sara Bull to visit Cambridge; cf. Haugen and Haugen, *Land of the Free*, 27.

Ole Bull, bust by G. Kitson Forst. Photo by Sarony, New York. Courtesy of Wayside Inn, Sudbury, Mass.

Because more than any other you were the glory of our land, because more than any other you have borne our people with you up towards the bright heights of art, because you were more than any other a pioneer of our young national music, more, much more than any other the faithful, warm-hearted conqueror of all hearts, because you have planted a seed that shall spring up in the future and for which coming generations will bless you—with the gratitude of thousands, for all this, in the name of our Norwegian musical art, I lay this laurel wreath on your coffin. Peace be with your ashes![27]

A final, touching honor came from the country folk around Bergen, who brought their tribute in the form of green boughs, ferns, or flowers and filled his grave to the brim with them. As Bjørnson had said, "Ole Bull was honored, but was loved even more."

Bull was also remembered in America at a memorial service in Boston on 10 October 1880. Cyrus Augustus Bartol (1833–1900), a Unitarian pastor, said of Bull that "for love of liberty for himself and all men he was a living flame."

It was natural he should sympathize strongly with us against secession and slavery in our Civil War. . . . Beyond all else he was humane, cosmopolite, a citizen of the world, and did not distinguish himself, save by genius which he could not help, from other men, but was in union and close communion with all. . . . Money went from him, as it came, like wind or water, being unpractical if not careless to a fault. . . . He was not a professor of Christianity or of religion in any form. He informed me that he got such a shock and revulsion from the doctrines he heard preached in his youth that he was permanently alienated from going to church. . . . But although he had no dogmas to offer, never lived one who accredited more the being of God and immortality of the soul. . . . I judge of men by their treatment of women; and how refined and grand his bearing was to the sex is well known in every country our strange and singular fascinator visited. . . . Aspiring and proceeding, despite his gray locks, he seemed an undeveloped child. Nothing in his mental constitution was fixed or had grown hard. . . . No decay gave hint of an end. . . .[28]

And on Thanksgiving Day in 1880 Alexander McKenzie (1830–1914), a Congregational pastor, said in his sermon, "He found his resting place among the great, on a spot which had been kept for a king—which had found a king. And he wore no royalty but his own great manhood."[29]

27. Jonas Lie, "Ole Bull, hans Karakteristik og Liv," in Alexander Bull, ed., *Ole Bulls Breve i Uddrag. Med en karakteristik og biografisk Skitse af Jonas Lie* (Copenhagen, 1881), 150.
28. His sermon is in Bull, *A Memoir*, 400–406.
29. His sermon is in Bull, *A Memoir*, 407–408. Information on speakers' names and dates is from H. J. Bernouf of Harvard College Library.

Part 2

THE MUSICIAN

18

The Violinist and Folk Music

B ULL PLAYED his violin all over the Western world, poetically put, "from North Cape to the Cheops Pyramid, from San Francisco to St. Petersburg."[1] His first love was obviously performing, and even his composing was totally intertwined with his identity as a performer. His adoring public wrote in newspapers, diaries, and letters about their wonderful, even mystical experiences at his concerts. His critics said that Bull was led astray by this adulation of his public, and that because of it he did not move forward to new challenges. But Bull did not play for the critics; he was rewarded if he had created a fleeting evening of magic for his audience.

One kind of program he gave was directed toward Norwegian events. An example is the concert and speech given on 27 August 1873 in Christiania to raise money for the Leif Ericson statue:

PROGRAM

Yderst mod Vesten ligger et Land (*Far to the West there Lies a Land*) by Ole Bull
Speech by Bjørnstjerne Bjørnson
Visit to the Sæter by Ole Bull
Norwegian Folkmelodies by Edvard Grieg, played by Bull
Lilly Dale by Ole Bull[2]

This program epitomizes the strong Norwegian folk influence on Bull, otherwise a cosmopolitan performer. Three of the four musical selections are specifically Norwegian, two of his own and one by his compatriot Grieg. Bull had a multifaceted musical heritage to draw from, but already in earliest childhood the folk style of Norwegian Hardanger fiddle players cap-

1. Aimar Grønvold, "Med Ole Bulls Billede," in *Norske Musikere* (Christiania, 1883), 123.
2. This program is included in Reidar Mjøen, "Ole Bull," in O. M. Sandvik and Gerhard Schjelderup, eds., *Norges Musikhistorie* (Christiania, 1921), 1:175; *Yderst mod Vesten ligger et Land* (no. 74); *Lilly Dale* (no. 72).

OLE BULL

giver

Onsdag den 27 August 1873 Kl. 5 Em.

med velvillig Assistance en

CONCERT

i Klingenbergs Festsal

til Indtægt for et Monument, reist i Amerika for

Leif Eirikson,

Amerikas Opdager.

PROGRAM.

Yderst mod Vesten ligger et Land, af **Ole Bull.**

Tale af **Bjørnstjerne Bjørnson.**

Sæterbesøg, af **Ole Bull.**

Norske Folkemelodier af *Edvard Grieg.* **Ole Bull.**

Lilly Dale. **Ole Bull.**

Entrée 60 Sk.

Billetter faaes fra Onsdag Morgen Kl. 8 i *Warmuths* Musikhandel og *Cammermeyers* Boglade og ved Indgangen fra Kl. 4.

Trykt hos Bergh & Ellefsen

Concert program, 27 August 1873, Christiania, Norway. Courtesy of Oslo University Library.

tivated him. His urban, "upper crust" family was no barrier to his hearing fiddle tunes *(slåtts)* near his childhood home at Valestrand. This repertoire of *slåtts* became a musical thread throughout his life, and when he used elements of this style in his playing and composing he was expressing in music the emerging nationalism of the Norwegians. His was a romantic view of the fiddler and folk music, and he wanted to teach Norwegians what he felt was valuable in their rural heritage.

One of the first Hardanger fiddle players that Bull heard as a child was Magne Kleiveland, also known as Einlidskarden. Kleiveland noticed young Ole's talent and later said that he had felt even then that Bull was something special.[3] The boy also visited festivities at the home of Ola Brakvatn, another of the great Hardanger fiddle players, and learned more *slåtts*.[4]

In the summer of 1831 Bull met and heard Torgeir Augundson from Telemark, one of the most famous Hardanger fiddle players. The attraction between Bull and Augundson was strong, and they remained lifelong friends. They shared the ability to improvise effortlessly. Augundson liked to make long *slåtts* out of little bits of material,[5] a technique that Bull would also adopt for his own compositions. Bull transcribed from Augundson's playing several *slåtts,* among them a springar called "Nordfjorden" ("The North Fjord") and a halling called "Hopparen" ("The Jumper"). A springar is a dance in 3/4 meter with many quick running steps for the dancer; a halling is an athletic dance for men in duple (usually 2/4) meter. This halling had a text attached "Hev du 'kje hoppa so hoppa du vel no" ("If you haven't leapt yet, you better leap now"). Bull had heard both these *slåtts* from the Oster Island players of his youth (especially Kleiveland), but Augundson's were different versions.[6] In 1849 Bull invited his country fiddler friend to Christiania to perform with him in a formal concert (15 January),[7] and in a private gathering the evening before the concert Bull was already weaving in bits of tunes from Augundson's playing into his own improvisations.[8]

During the spring of 1850 they played six concerts together in Bergen with Bull playing about half, Augundson the rest.[9] Bull considered Augund-

---

3. Arne Bjørndal, *Norsk Folkemusikk* (Bergen, 1952), 251.

4. Ibid., 250.

5. Nils Grinde, *Norsk Musikk Historie* (Oslo, 1971), 96.

6. Bjørndal, *Norsk Folkemusikk,* 255; Arne Bjørndal, *Ole Bull og norsk folkemusikk* (Bergen, 1940), 88.

7. Arne Bjørndal and Brynjulf Alver, *— Og fela ho lét. Norsk spelemannstradisjon* (Oslo, 1966), 47.

8. Bjørndal, *Norsk Folkemusikk,* 256.

9. David Monrad-Johansen, *Edvard Grieg* (Oslo, 1934), 32.

Thorgeir Audunsfon.

Torgeir Augundson ("The Miller's Lad"). Drawing by Adolph Tidemand, *Skilling-Magazin,* no. 27, 1849.

son his equal. Bull played among other things his own tone poem *Visit to the Sæter* which included Norwegian folk tunes. While the joint concerts with Augundson were warmly received in the early 1850s, they were not really understood by the urban population. The novelty of these events wore off, and by 1858 (again in 1860 and 1862) when they played together in Christiania their concerts were a failure.[10]

Bull sought out Hardanger fiddle players throughout his life, and he often used their pieces as encores or as a basis for improvisations within

10. Bjørndal and Alver, *Og fela ho lét,* 47.

The Violinist and Folk Music

his programs. On a tour of the United States in the 1850s Bull got a chance to hear Jens Høgheim (1817–86), the best fiddler in Sogn who had emigrated to the United States. In later years Kleiveland came to Bergen to play for Bull.[11] Bull learned the springar "Store-Mylnaren" ("The Big Miller," besides The Miller's Lad, another name for Augundson) from him; he often played a combination of Kleiveland and Augundson's versions of this *slått* in public.[12]

In the specially arranged playing sessions with Kleiveland, Bull either wrote down the tune or simply learned it by heart. As he learned the piece he did not watch to see how Kleiveland played it, but rather simply listened (sometimes even leaving the room) for the sound and then figured out his own technique to produce the same sounds. Brakvatn, the other fiddler from his childhood, also remained a lifelong friend of Bull's, and was an important source for Bull's transcriptions.[13] Bull learned the Nordhordland bridal gangar "Sylkje-Per" ("Silken Peter") from Brakvatn, and he often played this *slått* in public.[14] The gangar is a folk dance in duple meter (usually 6/8) with dance steps at a walking pace.

Many other fiddlers played for Bull over the years. A few were Elling Mosevoll (1790–1861), Tørris Reigstad (1826–1904), Johannes Horsås (1844–92), and Gunnar Lundekvam (ca. 1816–1912).[15] In Christiania Bull heard and transcribed from Ole H. Kleven (1817–90). He particularly liked the playing of Johannes Fossmark (1812–98), known for his excellent springar style, and of Brynjulf Hefte (1833–1927) because he played in the old Voss tradition. Less appealing to Bull was the mixed style of Per Nilson Bolko (1795–1876), a player who combined Hardanger fiddle styles with flat fiddle (ordinary violin) music, waltzes, and other "civilized" dances.[16]

Bull's collecting of these Hardanger fiddle *slåtts,* as well as his collecting of folk songs, was on a modest level compared to that of Ludvig Lindeman and other collectors of the period. Christian Tønsberg's *Norske Nationaldragter* (*Norwegian National Costumes*) (1852) has an appendix (1851) (no. 59) of six melodies that Bull gathered and arranged for voice and piano, voice and langeleik (Norwegian folk instrument), or piano solo. To some

11. Ibid., 50.
12. The last time he played "Store-Mylnaren" in public was on 17 May 1877 in Bergen. Arne Bjørndal, "Ole Bull og folkemusikken," in Torleiv Hannaas, ed., *Norsk Årbok* (Bergen, 1922), 13.
13. Bjørndal, *Norsk Folkemusikk,* 250–52.
14. The music is in Bjørndal, *Norsk Folkemusikk,* 264.
15. Ibid., 250, 253, 258.
16. Bjørndal and Alver, *Og fela ho lét,* 51, 187, 48.

Bull has added a "præludio" of his own. A few of his manuscript transcriptions still exist (no. B12), but most have disappeared.

Bull toured not only with his two violins but also with his Hardanger fiddle, and for an encore he was always ready to play a Norwegian *slått* on either instrument or possibly a favorite folk song.[17] He played his own version of the *slått* "Fanitullen" in March 1849 in Christiania,[18] and a later transcription (no. 54) survived in the University of Oslo Library (see Example 18.1). The lydian halling "Røysekatten" ("The Weasel"),[19] the halling "Aa so sudla ho mor paa rokkjen sin" ("And then mother is humming with her spinning wheel") (see his *Visit to the Sæter,* chap. 22), and the folk song "Imårå skin solæ so glitrande klår, imårå ri ho Kari te' kyrkje" ("Tomorrow the sun will shine so glitteringly clear, tomorrow Kari would ride to church")[20] were standard in his repertoire. Bull had a mission with the Hardanger fiddle music and other native Norwegian folk music: he wanted to expose the Norwegian people, as well as the whole world, to this folk tradition.

When Bull came home to Valestrand he never missed an opportunity to join in the Hardanger fiddle music, and he kept two Hardanger fiddles there ready to play. On these summer visits he played both his own music and the familiar *slåtts* to the local farmers.[21] During the summer visit of 1864 Grieg was nearby in Bergen, and they met at Valestrand. They discussed folk music, and Bull played Hardanger fiddle tunes. Another summer (1872), when there were seven weddings in one day at the church near Valestrand, Bull himself joined in and played a bridal *slått,* the halling "The Jumper."[22] The Hardanger fiddler, Viking Andreas Gjøstein, who worked at Valestrand from 1872–74, related that he sat with Bull while Bull played old *slåtts* interspersed with his own material. Bull told Gjøstein that the *slåtts* he played came from Augundson.[23] Bull had a chance to hear the fiddler Ola Mosafinn in 1879 on the occasion of Edvard Grieg's birthday; Grieg and Bull again discussed the properties of this unusual

17. Carl O. Gram Gjesdal, "Fra Ole Bull til Sigbjørn Bernhoft Osa," in Ingjald Bolstad, Arnfinn Kyte, and Jostein Mæland, eds., *Norske Tonar. Heidersskrift til Sigbjørn Osa på 75-årsdagen* (Oslo, 1985), 56.

18. Ola Linge, *Ole Bull: Livshistoria, Mannen, Kunstnaren* (Oslo, 1953), 177.

19. Arne Bjørndal, *Ole Bull og norsk folkemusikk,* 85.

20. He played it in the summer of 1861 or 1862 at Valestrand; ibid., 68.

21. Bjørndal, *Norsk Folkemusikk,* 264, 271.

22. Bjørndal, "Ole Bull og folkemusikken," 15–16, gives 1872. Bjørndal, *Ole Bull og norsk folkemusikk,* 26, gives 1871.

23. Bjørndal, *Norsk Folkemusikk,* 273–74.

Example 18.1. "Fanitullen." Because the lower strings are tuned up a whole step (to A and e), all notes written below an a must be read up a whole step. Transcription, University of Oslo Library.

music. Bull then played various Norwegian folk tunes including a springar, probably "The Big Miller."[24]

Bull's invitations to the country fiddlers to play for him and especially his invitation to Augundson to perform in concert with him started a practice of concert performing that continues today among Hardanger fiddlers. These players began to travel more widely and to arrange formal concerts of their own. For this purpose they invented new *slåtts*, different from the ones used for dances and weddings. These new compositions were "program pieces" made up either of several *slåtts* put together or of motives from various *slåtts* strung together with new music.[25] Because this practice is similar to the way Bull built *Visit to the Sæter*—although the framework for his *slått* material was the urban European tradition—this piece came to be considered the model for this new type of *lydarslått* or listening *slått*. Though these pieces consisted of some familiar tunes, they were given new, more encompassing titles. Sjur Helgeland from Voss (1856 or 1858–1924) with "Dei tre budeiene på Vikafjell" ("The Three Milkmaids from Vika Mountain") and Lars Fykerud from Telemark (1860–1902) made such compilations of old tunes and new material under new overall titles.[26]

But Bull was no country fiddler. Although he often used the Hardanger fiddle *slåtts* and folk songs for a special effect as encores or improvisations in his concerts, he was a well-trained urban artist in the central European tradition.

24. Finn Benestad and Dag Schjelderup-Ebbe, *Edvard Grieg: The Man and the Artist,* trans. William H. Halverson and Leland B. Sateren (Lincoln, Nebr., 1988), 234.

25. Bjørndal and Alver, *Og fela ho lét,* 113.

26. Ibid., 56–58. Bjørndal, *Ole Bull og norsk folkemusikk,* 35, gives 1856 for Helgeland's birth; Grinde, *Norsk Musikk Historie,* 97, gives 1858.

19

The Violinist as a Cosmopolitan

THE GROUP that had met in Ole Bull's parents' home to play string quartets had played Beethoven, Mozart, Haydn, and Pleyel. Paulsen, a member of that group, had been trained especially in Viotti's methods. Viotti was one of the founders of the French school of virtuoso violin playing. Bull learned Fiorillo, Giornovichi, and Viotti's music under the tutelage of Paulsen. He also learned from Paulsen the German literature, especially Spohr's music. Spohr, though a brilliant violin virtuoso, had followed German classical principles in his compositions, using abstract musical ideas, as exemplified in Haydn, Mozart, and Beethoven. At the same time, Spohr's concertos displayed a new romantic flavor by including dramatic recitative (No. 6 in G Minor, Opus 28) and even opera scene construction (No. 8 in A Minor, Opus 47). While Bull's later attempt to study with Spohr was a bad choice—they were opposite in temperament and in their approach to music—he had already learned Spohr's style.

Bull, who was an individualist and a free-form idealist about music, took well to the direction he received from his second teacher, the Swedish Lundholm. Lundholm had been trained by Baillot, and with him Bull studied much of the virtuoso literature of the French violin school: Lafont, Rode, Baillot, as well as more Viotti and Spohr.

Bull, however, was already intrigued by Paganini's pieces, which belonged to the Italian tradition. Italian styles were sweeping Europe in the 1820s and 1830s, coming as far north as Norway. Paris, in particular, was having a love affair with Italian opera that especially focused on Rossini's works. Europe was reveling in the *bel canto* (beautiful singing) style and the art of the coloratura soprano—a light, airy, colorful ornamentation surrounding melodies of pure, singable quality. Audiences were buying simplified arrangements of their favorite opera arias (often called fantasias)

PART 2. THE MUSICIAN

to play at home on parlor pianos with their family and friends singing or playing along. Musicians, in order to make a bit of money, turned out these popular arrangements by the dozen for the most unusual combinations of voices and instruments.

The same public flocked to hear the instrumental virtuoso performers who gratified the public taste with their arrangements of favorite operatic arias and with diabolically difficult variations on those popular melodies. The audience got opera with its beautiful, familiar melodies and virtuosity of variation, all in one. The easy-to-understand, singable melodies, the intense emotional pull on the heartstrings from the performer's swoops and wide dynamics, the dazzling display of technique, the personal mystery and magnetism of each performer made for an exciting emotional and musical experience for the audience. Of course they adored and supported their heroes and heroines of the stage.

Bull already had an extraordinary technique when he came to Paris in 1831. Like Liszt, without extensive training he was soon a match for the Paris virtuosos.[1] "If he wanted to learn a new piece he read it through thoughtfully, put it aside for a bit, and in the meantime paced back and forth. Suddenly he stopped, looked up, took hold of his violin and played the piece from memory."[2] Rehearsing Paganini's music with his new friend and colleague in Paris, the virtuoso violinist Ernst, was probably just the extra polishing Bull needed. The famous French orchestra director Habeneck further encouraged Bull's Italianate tastes and direction,[3] and the favorable Paris review of 1835 by Jules Janin in *Journal de débats* clinched Bull's reputation as a master of the virtuoso literature. Bull was stepping into the same arena as Paganini and Liszt, and the timing was excellent because Paganini had just retired.

According to Robert Schumann, Bull was an equal to Paganini.[4] In Warsaw in 1841 another reviewer gave him the ultimate compliment: "Paganini is great, Bull is greater. Ole Bull has Paganini's technique, but Paganini does not have Ole Bull's warmth and heartfelt style."[5] Bull, at thirty-one, had reached the pinnacle of his profession. Where could he go from here? He needed bigger mountains, bigger audiences to conquer, and he shrewdly

1. Reidar Mjøen, "Ole Bull," in O. M. Sandvik and Gerhard Schjelderup, eds., *Norges Musikhistorie* (Christiania, 1921), 1:176.
2. Bull's daughter Eleonore Félicie Ingier (1922) quoted in Arne Bjørndal, *Norsk Folkemusikk* (Bergen, 1952), 275.
3. Mjøen, "Ole Bull," 1:176.
4. Robert Schumann, *Jugendbriefe*, 2d ed. (Leipzig, 1886), 300.
5. Mjøen, "Ole Bull," 1:179.

chose the United States. "The land of milk and honey" was to reward him with an adoring public. Audiences were eager for the latest in European fashions, and Bull's Italianate repertoire and style of playing were just what they wanted to hear.[6] His willingness to travel the great distances of the United States gave him an enormous public. Since no audience heard him frequently, he could use very similar programs from year to year and still maintain his popularity. In fact the very repetition of pieces from earlier concerts was a plus because audiences liked to hear their favorite pieces again and again. (Traveling performers today often plan their concert programs in similar fashion. They become known for certain pieces and the audience hopes, even expects, to hear some of those pieces again.) Bull, a seasoned performer by 1843, began his first tour of the United States. For the next thirty-seven years he continued to tour everywhere in the Western world to constant and almost invariably enthusiastic public acclaim.

Bull played the "public's heart strings,"[7] and they responded with innumerable accounts of his playing. Often wildly enthusiastic, sometimes lyrical, occasionally even offered in poetic form, these accounts do not usually further our knowledge of what Bull really did on stage or what he actually sounded like because they generally convey only the listeners' feelings and reactions. It is from the critics that we learn the most about his playing style.

Bull had excellent technical skills and was often praised for an especially clean and facile technique. His left hand was very sure on the fingerboard.[8] His intonation was pure and his tone, bell-like. His trills were completely even, regardless of which pair of fingers he used. His scales were also accomplished perfectly in rhythm and were smooth in tone quality. When he played consecutive thirds, sixths, and octaves in both diatonic and chromatic scales, a correspondent to *Leipziger Allgemeine Musikalische Zeitung* called them "a pleasure to the musical ear."[9] One can guess that the double-stop scales were both in tune and very rapid. He could shift from low to very high positions without effort, and his left-hand pizzicato also seemed effortless. His excellent tremolo and *sautillé* effects showed the flexibility of his wrist.[10]

6. Ibid., 1:172.

7. G. W. Curtis (1852) cited in Ola Linge, *Ole Bull: Livshistoria, Mannen, Kunstnaren* (Oslo, 1953), 348.

8. Louis Spohr, *Selbstbiographie,* Vol. 2 (Cassel and Göttingen, 1861), 228.

9. Linge, *Ole Bull,* 332 (letter to *Leipziger Allgemeine Musikalische Zeitung,* 1841).

10. Walter E. Colton, cited in Sara C. Bull, *Ole Bull: A Memoir* (Boston and New York, 1882), 347–48.

Bull's staccato techniques—and he had several kinds—supposedly made it possible to get in more than 350 notes in one bow stroke![11] Johannes Haarklou's description was more moderate but still amazing if it is true; he said that he heard 110 staccato notes in one down bow in a concert in Hamburg in 1875, when Bull was sixty-five years old.[12] Bull could maintain his amazing control of these staccato effects both up-bow and down-bow, and even in arpeggios he kept the staccato effect clean.[13] He had designed a special bow that was heavier, stiffer, and longer (by two inches) than the standard bow, and because it was heavy and stiff it could bounce back from the strings rapidly, making it easier to play the fast staccatos. The bow could be worked simply with its own weight on the strings; Bull did not have to press down as much as other violinists did. The extra length meant that more notes could fit into a single bow stroke.[14]

One of the difficult tricks that he borrowed from Paganini was to play whole passages on the G string alone. Critics often compared his music to Paganini's in this respect, one of the few direct comparisons that critics explain in any detail. However, Bull went beyond Paganini to develop his own special brand of virtuosity. He was particularly praised for his playing in polyphonic movements. The three or four linear strands of music were apparently fully audible and all handled with excellent phrasing. In other words, his double, triple, and quadruple stops were well executed, in tune and integrated into the musical fabric. Such extensive polyphonic playing was possible because Bull had developed a very flat bridge of his own design. According to Spohr, this bridge construction meant that he could use the middle strings, the A and D strings, only in the lower positions and only *pianissimo*.[15] Not only did he alter his violin's bridge to aid polyphonic playing; he also tightened his bow hair to a lower tension than usual. The flat bridge and the loose bow hair together made it easier to play several strings simultaneously.[16] It is possible that the flat bridge design and heavy bow were ideas Bull had gained from studying the Hardanger fiddle which has just such characteristics to aid in playing several strings at once.

11. Linge, *Ole Bull,* 332 (letter to *LAMZ,* 1841).

12. In Bull's *Concerto in A Major;* Johannes Haarklou, "The Life of Ole Bull. From the Danish of Johannes Haarklow [*sic*]," *Music* 21.1 (December 1901): 50.

13. Eduard Hanslick, "Ole Bull," in *Vienna's Golden Years of Music 1850–1900,* trans. and ed. Henry Pleasants (1950; Reprint, Freeport, N.Y., 1969), 67.

14. It was difficult to get horse hair long enough for this bow, according to Arne Bjørndal, *Ole Bull og norsk folkemusikk* (Bergen, 1940), 60.

15. Spohr, *Selbstbiographie,* 228; see chap. 8.

16. Nils Grinde, *Norsk Musikk Historie* (Oslo, 1971), 122.

Bull was also unusually skilled with harmonics, double harmonics and trilled harmonics. (Natural harmonics are the upper partials of a string that sound only when a string is touched lightly at a node point.) The thin strings used in Bull's time facilitated harmonics. These became a special feature of his playing, and one that particularly distinguished his style from Paganini's. Bull employed harmonics especially when he improvised. Since using extensive double, triple, and quadruple stops and using many kinds of harmonics were new in his time, reviewers frequently mention these effects, and they always agree that Bull was a master of them. However, the conservative reviewers invariably criticize him in the same breath, calling these techniques cheap effects.[17]

Bull's modified violin bridge and bow were only two of the devices that aided his masterful technique. His playing position was also important to his unique style. The anatomy professor Alpheus Benning Crosby (1832–77) who studied Bull in 1877 gave a description of Bull's playing position.[18] Bull stood with his weight on his left foot, the right somewhat forward for balance. He did not incline his head to the left as violinists generally do nor did he use his chin to anchor the violin in place. Instead the elbow of the supporting left arm was well forward of the body and the whole arm raised high so that the palm of the left hand rose *above* his collarbone. The violin neck rested on the "palmar surface" of the left thumb and sloped *downward* toward the collarbone. (This angle, with the violin sloping downward into the collarbone, was and is the reverse of usual practice.)

Violinists generally use the head and chin to anchor the violin so that the left hand does not need to support the instrument's weight, but Bull let the entire weight of the violin rest on his left-hand thumb. Since he did not seek additional support by gripping the violin between his left-hand thumb and fingers, his four fingers were free to perform their activities on the fingerboard. His remarkably flexible left hand made it possible for him to change positions quickly. Bull discovered that the most comfortable position for these fingers to touch the strings was at an oblique angle, not as most violinists did, with the fingers vertical to the fingerboard. His supporting left thumb would slide inward under the neck of the violin toward

17. Linge, *Ole Bull,* 336.

18. Alpheus Benning Crosby, "The Anatomy of the Violinist, Mr. Ole Bull: His Pose and Method of Holding the Violin," appendix to Sara C. Bull, *Ole Bull: A Memoir* (Boston and New York, 1882) gives perhaps the most complete account of Bull's playing posture (pp. 329–46). See also chap. 23. The drawings of Bull's hand positions were made by James Stuart. For his nine additional drawings on a poster, see next page.

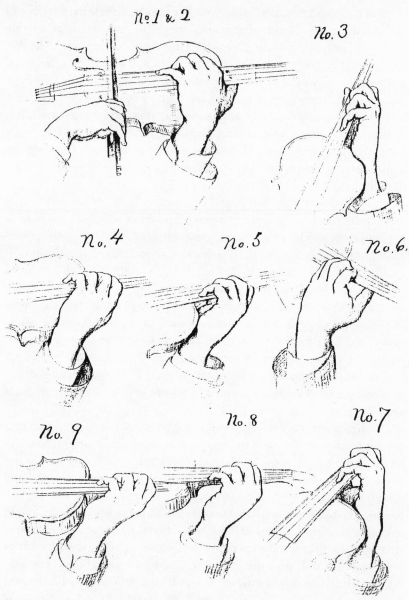

The Hands of Ole Bull. Drawn from life by James R. Stuart. Courtesy of Music Division, Library of Congress, Washington, D.C.

its body to accommodate different hand positions (placements of the hand that divide the fingerboard into sections thus allowing the hand to reach all the points on a given string). In the highest position (closest to the body of the violin) Bull raised the neck of the violin even more to accommodate his supporting thumb up against the body of the violin. Crosby's illuminating account remained incomplete, and as a result there is no good description of Bull's bow arm (the right arm). Arthur Abell says of Bull's bowing: "He did not hold it in the ordinary way, but grasped the stick higher up with the thumb some distance above the frog, claiming that this gave him greater strength and command."[19]

An important result of Bull's unusual playing methods was his characteristic tone. It has been described as sweet and pure, or clean and clear, and interestingly, as a small or soft tone. This description of "small" is in comparison to the German school of Spohr and later Joseph Joachim (1831–1907) because the term "small tone" was used for Paganini's sound also. This sound was partly the result of the thin gut strings on Bull's Amati and Gasparo da Salò violins, his main performing instruments. The contrast of string type became more noticeable in later years when Joachim, using heavier strings, was Bull's main competition.[20] Joachim himself said of Bull, "His tone is pleasantly soft and full of feeling."[21]

Bull's ability to make a singing tone in *cantabile* movements—especially at private gatherings—was renowned. His high notes, often at the climax of a phrase when he played with a full tone, were also especially pure and clean. To this clear, pure tone quality he added his ability to play simple, slow melodies with great feeling.[22] Adagios were his specialty. Bull's shadows and nuances, accents and crescendos, made melodies seem to stream out of the instrument.[23] He would form small details with beautiful musicality but sometimes would do so at the expense of the big, overarching melodic line.[24] "He uses music as color," said one reviewer.[25]

A gift of Bull's was his ability to improvise. His nephew reports, "Ole Bull often engaged in fanciful improvisation when he played for the family

19. Arthur M. Abell, "Ole Bull," in "Famous Violinists of the Past, VII," *Musical Courier* 57.10 (1908): 5.
20. Linge, *Ole Bull,* 334.
21. Henry T. Finck, "Masters of the Violin," in *The Mentor,* 4th ser., no. 5 (New York, 1916), 6.
22. Grinde, *Norsk Musikk Historie,* 122.
23. *Die Constitutionelle Zeitung* (1840), cited by Linge, *Ole Bull,* 341.
24. Grinde, *Norsk Musikk Historie,* 123.
25. G. W. Curtis, *New York Tribune* (24 May 1852), cited by Linge, *Ole Bull,* 348.

or among musical friends; it came naturally and easily for him."[26] This skill at improvising helps to account for his popularity with audiences. The excitement of watching and hearing music being newly created in the moment can be especially intense. The demands of the Italian performing style made this skill an imperative, but, as mentioned before, Bull also used folk melodies as the basis for improvisation. Bull in fact improvised on anything. Even when he played Mozart quartets he could not restrain himself, and this made it difficult for the other players to follow him.[27]

Bull's extravagant personality was a most important element in his concerts. In his early years in French salon society he had shown that he was capable of commanding a performance as well as any "salon-lion." He could hypnotize or spellbind his audience simply with his stage presence. Later he used this in-the-moment magnetism successfully with all his audiences. He had a certain appealing naiveté combined with an intensity or fervor that he conveyed to the audience. He was described as sometimes warm and passionate, other times strong and wild.[28] Aasmund Vinje used the word "subjective" to summarize these qualities.[29] Bull had an aura that some called a magic spell, others a godlike presence, and part of the aura had its roots in his Norwegian-ness. Bull was considered a wild native son both at home and abroad. His appeal was, like that of Liszt and Chopin, a national style that was a bit foreign and therefore excitingly exotic.

The term charlatanism was never far from the lips of critics. Some said Bull could lack musicality; others said he had little taste, that he was not "well-bred" on stage. They would gleefully cite the example that Bull would continue a bow stroke even when not touching the string to make a visual, but not audible, *ppp* effect.[30] Few performers, however, are truly free from such moments of showmanship. Often these are devices used to create or sustain a mood. Bull's continuing the bow stroke, for example, would be

26. Finn Benestad and Dag Schjelderup-Ebbe, *Edvard Grieg: The Man and the Artist,* trans. William H. Halverson and Leland B. Sateren (Lincoln, Nebr., 1988), 57.

27. [Catharinus Elling], "Ole Bull," in Gerhard Gran, ed., *Nordmænd i det nittende aarhundrede* (Christiania, 1902), 489.

28. G. W. Curtis, cited in Linge, *Ole Bull,* 348.

29. Vinje considered Vieuxtemps, Laub, and others "objective," meaning distant or cool; *Dølen* (13 May 1860).

30. G. W. Fink, ed., *Leipziger Allgemeine Musikalische Zeitung* 41.12 (3 March 1839): 238–39. Theodore Thomas, a discerning musician and conductor in New York, was so impressed with this effect that he taught his orchestra to make "an effective *diminuendo* at the end, finishing with a *piano, pianissimo, à la Ole Bull.* This was altogether a new effect," he said. Theodore Thomas, *A Musical Autobiography,* ed. George P. Upton (New York, 1964), 334.

used to avoid jarring the audience out of a quiet mood at the end of the piece. The distinction here between the art of illusion and charlatanism is often in the eyes and ears of the beholder.

Criticisms of Bull's playing sometimes stemmed from episodes that had nothing to do with an actual performance. Critics in Sweden, for example, said he was not good enough to play the quartets of Beethoven and Haydn, but this was said after Bull had rejected invitations to play with an amateur Swedish quartet.[31] Bull in fact had no hesitation about performing in quartets when they were of the high quality that he found in Cassel, Berlin, London, and Copenhagen.[32]

Critics complained regularly about Bull's choice of concert repertoire.[33] His countryman Halfdan Kjerulf, for example, noted the absence of "serious" works on his programs.[34] Such criticisms came most strongly from critics who preferred the abstract ideals of German instrumental music, ideals that generally embodied opposition to coloratura (ornamented vocal style) melodies, opposition to text- or story-influenced music, and opposition to folk elements or nationalistic suggestions in music. These followers of Spohr, espousing conservative German attitudes, looked particularly to the repertoires of Beethoven or earlier composers for their ideal models. Such pieces, however, did not generally fit with Bull's goals for programming a concert. He sought to make programs in which the virtuoso and *cantilena* (singing) aspects of music were primary.

For this Bull needed his own works or the virtuoso works by his contemporaries, pieces that allowed for these qualities. Improvisation and ornamentation were also important to this style of playing, and any performer choosing this route in the 1820s or 1830s had to conform to the public's expectations. Only in the 1840s did public taste in central Europe begin changing. As these audiences began to seek new styles, either turning to the past masters (Mozart and Beethoven), or to "serious" contemporaries (Schumann and Mendelssohn), Bull directed his attention to the American and other outlying markets where he found a public still enamored of the Italian virtuoso and *cantabile* styles. This public remained faithful admirers of the style throughout Bull's lifetime.

A concert evening with Bull was usually in two parts. A fairly standard program from the middle of his career comes from Hamar, Norway, for 23 September 1858.

31. *Nya Dagligt Allahanda* (1838), cited by Linge, *Ole Bull,* 349–50.
32. Linge, *Ole Bull,* 352.
33. Grinde, *Norsk Musikk Historie,* 122.
34. Mjøen, "Ole Bull," 1:178.

OLE BULL
gives
Thursday September 23 1858 7 o'clock in Hamar a
CONCERT
with the following pieces:
I.
1. *The Mountains of Norway* composed and played by Ole Bull
2. *The Rose,* a solo for cello by L. Spohr played by H. Nicolaysen
3. *Le Streghe* (The Witches), composed by Paganini, played by Ole Bull
II.
4. *Visit to the Sæter* composed and played by Ole Bull
5. *Meditation on a Theme by Sebastian Bach,* composed for cello by Gounod, played by H. Nicolaysen
6. *Carnival in Venice* with Introduction composed and played by Ole Bull

Concerts were advertised as Bull's, but he typically played only four numbers. Other interspersed pieces (from two to seven) were for pianists, singers, or as in the above program, a cellist. If there was an orchestra, each half of the concert would begin with an additional overture, usually from an Italian opera. At the concert described above, which was given in the small town of Hamar, Bull was probably accompanied by only a piano. Bull generally concluded his program by playing one of his own virtuoso crowd pleasers, followed by several encores.

His programs occasionally included the "serious" composers. On at least one occasion (1862), Bull played *Præludier* (*Preludes*) by Bach. No less a pianist than Franz Liszt accompanied him in Beethoven's *Kreutzer Sonata* (Opus 47) at London's Philharmonic Society Hall in 1840, and Felix Mendelssohn also accompanied him in the same piece in 1841 at a concert in the Leipzig Gewandhaus.[35] There is no evidence that Bull played other Beethoven violin sonatas publicly, but he did play a piece identified as *Quartet in F Major* (Opus 18, No. 1), and the concerto Opus 61, identified in an 1864 program only as a concerto with "Allegro non troppo," "Larghetto," and "Rondo" movements.[36] The pianist, Aubertine Woodward Moore who accompanied Bull in Madison, Wisconsin, in 1879, said Bull was impatient with Beethoven.[37] A letter from Bergen partially explains Bull's impatience. It states: "Bull placed Mozart above Beethoven. To him the former is more genial because he is closer to the source [of inspira-

35. On Liszt, see Linge, *Ole Bull,* 352; on Mendelssohn, see "Ole Bull," *Nation* (3 May 1883).

36. Linge, *Ole Bull,* 130. An Opus 49 (probably an error for Opus 47) violin sonata appears in an 1863 program.

37. Aubertine Woodward Moore, "The Real Ole Bull: Personal Reminiscences," *Etude* 30.4 (1912): 251.

giver

Torsdag den 23de September 1858 Kl. 7 i Hamar en

CONCERT

af följende Indhold:

I.

1. "Norges Fjelde" componeret og foredr. af Ole Bull.
2. "La Rose", Solo for Violoncel, af L. Spohr, foredrages af H. Nicolaysen.
3. "Le Streghe" (Hexene), comp. af Paganini, foredrages af Ole Bull.

II.

4. "Et norsk Sæterbesög" componeret og foredrages af Ole Bull.
5. "Méditation sur un thème de Sebastian Bach", comp. for Violoncel af Gounod, foredr. af H. Nicolaysen.
6. "Carnevalet i Venedig" med Introduction componeret og foredrages af Ole Bull.

Indgangen aabnes Kl. 6½.

Concert program, 23 September 1858, Hamar, Norway. Courtesy of Bergen University Library.

tion]. The latter struggled with difficult problems, among them the instruments, especially the bassoon and clarinet; he went against things [that would be] in accordance with their nature and made them sound raw, hollow or shrieking."[38]

Bull was particularly drawn to the lyric and vocal aspects of Mozart's melodies. As mentioned before, he learned the quartets of Haydn and Mozart while still a child from playing them on evenings in his parents' home that were devoted to string quartet music. In later years, he often performed Mozart quartets, for example a *Quartet in D Minor* (K. 421?) and a *Quartet in G Major* (K. 387?), with fellow musicians in private chamber concerts. Wherever he went on tour, from Bologna to Wisconsin, such private occasions gave him great pleasure. He especially liked to play Mozart's *String Quintet in G Minor* (K. 516); he played it, for instance, in 1841 at a soiree in Leipzig at which Felix Mendelssohn and Robert and Clara Schumann were present.[39]

Bull performed the first movement of Mozart's *D Major Concerto* (K. 211 or K. 218) on one occasion in New York (8 January 1870), and he played the violin sonatas in private settings, for example, in Madison, Wisconsin, in 1879.[40] He also selected isolated movements from various Mozart works and arranged them himself. On his concert programs these are enigmatically labeled "Adagio" or "Larghetto," in one case we know the "Adagio" came from a Mozart clarinet piece;[41] in another, the "Adagio" came from a string quartet.[42] He even used Mozart's music for his improvisations. He invented a violin version of the *Don Giovanni* overture when he played for Augundson,[43] and Haarklou describes a concert in which Bull played a section of the same overture as a four-voiced composition.[44] In the 1860s Bull performed variations on "Là ci darem la mano," also from *Don Giovanni* (no. 68).

Excluding Bull's own compositions, which are discussed in chapter 20, his programs usually included pieces from the contemporary virtuoso literature. In his early performances, for the most part, he played music he

38. Letter to Rädeklau from O. L. [?], Bergen, 1 September 1857, in the Stadt- und Universitätsbibliothek, Frankfurt am Main.

39. Robert Schumann, *Haushaltbücher*, ed. Gerd Neuhaus (Leipzig, 1982), 707n209.

40. George C. D. Odell, *Annals of the New York Stage* (New York, 1936), 8:659; Moore, "The Real Ole Bull," 251.

41. Henrik Wergeland, "Ole Bull: Efter opgivelser af ham selv biografisk skildret," in D. A. Seip, ed., *Samlede Skrifter* (Oslo, 1927), 4.5:220. The "Larghetto" was probably from the clarinet quintet K. 581 (no. 30).

42. Abell, "Ole Bull," 5.

43. Elling, "Ole Bull," 472.

44. Johannes Haarklou, "The Life of Ole Bull. From the Danish of Johannes Haarklow [sic]," *Music* 21.1 (December 1901): 50.

had studied with his teachers, Spohr (for example, *Concerto in Modo di Scena Cantante,* Opus 47), Viotti, Pecháček pieces, and the Paganini *Caprices.* On his own he learned Paganini's *Variations on Nel cor più non mi sento* and *Duo mervielle* (a duet for violin alone) as well as some virtuoso pieces by Rüdersdorff (*Variations on Russian Folk Melodies*), Mayseder (concertos), Ernst, and Lipiński.[45] In 1845 Bull told Félicie that he had about thirty pieces actively in his repertoire.[46] At about the same time, programs first show him playing Paganini's *Carnival in Venice Variations* (Havana, Cuba). Apparently this piece became his own little by little (no. 42) because, by the late 1850s, programs began to list the work as partially or completely by Bull (see the wording in the 1858 program above). Bull's version seems to have ended with a bird-song imitation.[47] About this time (1860), he also included a *Hungarian Fantasy in Gypsy Style* by Redleij Kohne.

Paganini, however, was Bull's favorite virtuoso composer. As Paganini's works were published he began adding more of them to his repertoire. From about 1860 on, his programs were quite regularly structured to include three pieces of his own and one by Paganini. Paganini's *E-flat Major Concerto No. 1* (often transposed to D Major) was a favorite showpiece. Others were *I palpiti* (variations on "Di tanti palpiti" from Rossini's *Tancredi*), *Variations on the G String on the Austrian National Hymn, Moto perpetuo, Le Streghe* (Heksedansen or The Witches' Dance) (unaccompanied), and the *B Minor Concerto.*[48] As time passed, some critics commented that his repertoire was dated.[49]

In planning his programs Bull was particularly generous to younger Norwegian composers. The only time he and Edvard Grieg performed together (11 August 1873), they played two selections from Grieg's violin pieces.[50] On 27 August of the same year, he played Grieg's *Norwegian Folkmelodies,* probably a version of Opus 17.[51] On 7 August 1878 in Bergen, he played Johannes Haarklou's *Adagio Religioso* in Haarklou's debut

45. Christian A. Aarvig, *Den unge Ole Bull: En Violinspillers Ungdomskampe* (Copenhagen, 1934), 65–66.
46. Alexander Bull, ed., *Ole Bulls Breve i Uddrag: Med en karakteristik og biografisk Skitse af Jonas Lie* (Copenhagen, 1881), 348.
47. Linge, *Ole Bull,* 360.
48. Bull played the entire concerto and listed it in his programs as *Concerto Campanella.*
49. Grinde, *Norsk Musikk Historie,* 122.
50. Benestad and Schjelderup-Ebbe, *Edvard Grieg,* 151, say the "Minuet" was movement 2 to Grieg's violin sonata Opus 8, and the "Gavotte" was the published Opus 22, no. 2 for violin and piano. Linge, *Ole Bull,* 270, says they are from Grieg's *Holberg Suite* though that was not published until after Bull's death. Mortimer Smith, *The Life of Ole Bull* (Princeton, N.J., 1943), 178, says they both came from Grieg's Opus 8.
51. Mjøen, "Ole Bull," 1:175.

concert as a composer. Haarklou's piece, composed specifically for Bull, had the same title as one of Bull's own pieces. To have interested the great Ole Bull was an important accomplishment for the young composer, and Bull commented to a friend, Lars Holst, that Haarklou's "violin solo is a bit overstated, but there is a spirit's power in his music. This man has a future."[52]

Bull also added sentimental songs to his repertoire. A popular tune, "Leggenda Valacca" ("Angel's Serenade") by Gaetano Braga (1829–1907), originally for voice with cello or violin obbligato but often found in other arrangements, was the last piece Bull played before he died.[53] Other such popular pieces that he played from 1860 to the end of his life were Bach-Gounod's "Ave Maria" or "Méditation" (a violin obbligato),[54] Rossini's "Li Marinari" ("Seaman's Song") from Les soirées musicales (an 1864 program), and Rossini's duet "Quis est homo, qui non fleret" from Stabat Mater (for the first time on the 1864 program).

Bull must be seen as one of the most brilliant representatives, perhaps a genius, of the nineteenth-century cantilena techniques, of bravura techniques, and of improvisation. Those who heard him reacted strongly, either with adoration or condemnation, but these passionate reactions obscure his real musical contribution. Only by understanding the three-fold accomplishments of this nineteenth-century musician can we begin to measure his genius. First, Bull was an improviser creating music in the moment. Second, he was a performer presenting works in re-creation in order to show his ability at interpreting musical thought and emotion. And third, he was a composer writing music that would be preserved for posterity. Because the first two elements, improvising and recreating music, are lost, Bull's (or, for that matter, Liszt's, Paganini's, or Malibran's) concerts live only in the words of others. In the next chapter, we look at the evidence of his work that Bull did leave behind, his written works. They are an incomplete but very important source from which we can learn much about him as a musician and an artist.

52. Finn Benestad, Johannes Haarklou: Mannen og verket (Oslo, 1961), 10.
53. Linge, Ole Bull, 356; opening bars of the music are given by Linge on p. 369.
54. Ibid., 286.

20

The Italian Style

WALTER E. COLTON (a violin maker who repaired Bull's instruments in later years) speaks about the intimate relationship between performing and composing for Bull. "In his compositions the various motives are always well worked out, and abound in broad and beautiful effects. As they were written for himself, they exemplify his peculiarities of fingering and bowing. Like Paganini's, they are almost unplayable; for, apart from the difficulties of *technique,* without the *vis viva* of the master they lack their greatest charm."[1]

Almost everything Bull wrote was intended for his own performances, and therefore he composed to emphasize his abilities in the *cantilena* (singing) and *bravura* (virtuoso) styles. His pieces are mostly for violin solo or for violin with orchestra or piano. In the matter of accompaniment, Bull was very practical about the conditions under which he knew he would have to perform. Since he could never be sure of finding an orchestra in outlying towns, either in Europe or the United States, he often included a piano accompaniment with the score. At times he had to play without any accompaniment at all. While most of his compositions are for violin, he also wrote a few songs, choral pieces, and orchestral works for occasions of national significance to Norway (see chap. 22).

Only three of Bull's approximately seventy compositions received opus numbers. Schuberth of Hamburg and Leipzig published these works in 1843: Opus 1, *Adagio Religioso, pour violon avec orchestre ou piano (A Mother's Prayer)* (no. 15); Opus 2, *Nocturne* (no. 36); and Opus 3: *Fantaisie et Variations de bravoure, sur un thème de Bellini pour violon, avec orchestre ou piano (Bravura Variations,* no. 8). Another work, *Siciliano and Tarantella* (no. 39) was given to Schuberth but never published by them.

---

1. Sara C. Bull, *Ole Bull: A Memoir* (Boston and New York, 1882), 348.

It was unusual in the nineteenth century for a musician as popular as Bull not to use the opportunity to publish more. Income from publishing was usually an important way for musicians to earn a living, and Bull's pieces certainly would have sold. Possibly he did not consider it important to publish or did not want to take the time to ready his manuscripts for publication. More likely, he became hesitant about entering into further publishing contracts after his publishing experience with Schuberth ended in hostility.

His failure to publish more of his works is even more surprising because audiences clamored for copies of his music. Unauthorized versions were made for amateurs to play at home, as reminders of Bull's concert performances. Particularly attractive melodies were taken from his larger works and arranged for new combinations of instruments or voices. Sometimes texts were added to the tunes; for example the famous song "Sæter Girl's Sunday" (no. 53a) was originally for violin. Other arrangements, none of them by Bull, reorganize his music and sometimes alter or simplify his harmonies. It is often from these arrangements that people have attempted to form an impression of Bull's music, yet these arrangements are most likely dim pictures of Bull's original.

Bull's greatest skill was in writing beautiful melodies, not surprising considering his interest in both folk melodies and the Italian melodic style. His phrase structure is particularly clear. In folk-style tunes it is regular, balanced, and solid (see chap. 22). In Italianate melodies it often spins itself out in long spans, a kind of additive phrasing typical of the *bel canto* style. In these Italian-style melodies he left room for improvisation by the soloist, especially at the cadenzas. These moments rely on the ingenuity and skill of the performer.

Numerous, heavy-handed criticisms of Bull's compositions have been made, particularly concerning his handling of form. It has been called "loose and uncertain" or "lacking coherence."[2] Halfdan Kjerulf said Bull "is sailing without compass and gropes in the half darkness."[3] Only a bit more charitably, he suggests that the compositions are "potpourri works."[4] Robert Schumann felt that Bull shifted moods back and forth so suddenly that the listener was ill-prepared for what would come next.[5] Other critics

2. Nils Grinde, *Norsk Musikk Historie* (Oslo, 1971), 122–23.
3. Ola Linge, *Ole Bull: Livshistoria, Mannen, Kunstnaren* (Oslo, 1953), 343.
4. Halfdan Kjerulf (1860), cited in Reidar Mjøen, "Ole Bull," in O. M. Sandvik and Gerhard Schjelderup, eds., *Norges Musikhistorie* (Christiania, 1921), 1:178.
5. Robert Schumann, *Neue Zeitschrift für Musik* (5 April 1839), cited in Linge, *Ole Bull*, 339.

pointed out that there was little working through of ideas, that the counter-point was loosely handled, and that Bull's harmonies were simplistic. Some said the compositions did not follow the basic rules of composition and needed more direction. The composer Johannes Haarklou felt that these weaknesses were a result of Bull's weak technical schooling,[6] while the Swedish press, even less sympathetic to Bull, unfavorably compared his compositions to Beethoven.[7]

Those who criticized Bull's taste in performing (see chap. 19) were the same people who found his compositions objectionable. Much of the criticism derived from expectations about German methods of composing, an approach that required musical unity and coherence—thematic, formal, harmonic, and rhythmic—as a basic tenet of musical logic and musical excellence. Beethoven was the nineteenth-century's model for just this type of unity. The criticisms of Bull's work as having incoherent or unorganized form, simplistic harmonies, unsophisticated orchestration, needless ornamentation, and emphasis on melody alone were complaints that the same critics leveled at the operas of Bellini, Rossini, and Gaetano Maria Donizetti (1797–1848).

Here, in Bull's words, is the opposing camp's view of German composing methods: "Beethoven placed the idea, the motive of polyphonic movements, higher than the actual sounds; he consciously sacrificed them to the controlling presence of the ideas." Bull was also unsympathetic to the many notes in Wagner's orchestrations: " . . . in the eyes of the composer they present themselves excellently on the paper but [they] certainly can't be listened to—whereas in Haydn and Mozart, how simple, almost poverty-stricken it looks and how rich in effect it sounds."[8]

Opera composers became Bull's models. He twice labelled pieces with a traditional classical form—his two concertos—but even they show great flexibility of form in ways which indicate that Bull preferred the freer but no less specific forms of Italian opera. His technical training was amply sufficient to emulate these models, and criticisms to the effect that he could not harmonize his own compositions are not borne out by the autograph scores of surviving pieces, for example, *Siciliano and Tarantella* or the *Concerto in E Minor*. His harmonic progressions are simple and graceful, but not adventurous, as is to be expected given his operatic models where melody is the driving force. In reassessing Bull's works, the modern writer Nils

6. Finn Benestad, *Johannes Haarklou: Mannen og verket* (Oslo, 1961), 62.
7. Linge, *Ole Bull*, 351.
8. Letter to Rädeklau from O. L. [?], Bergen, 1 September 1857 in the Stadt- und Universitätsbibliothek, Frankfurt am Main.

Grinde criticizes an occasional overuse of the diminished seventh chord, but otherwise finds the harmonic structures well formed for this style.[9]

Three issues make it difficult to study Bull's works in detail. (1) Based on concert programs and descriptions, it appears that a single work was given different titles and was significantly altered over the years. (2) Many works were lost, either because the manuscript has disappeared or because the work was never written down. (3) The surviving versions often do not include all the notes that Bull played in concert and are therefore sometimes skeletons of performances rather than completed compositions.

Accepting these limitations, we shall look first at Bull's pieces that were composed specifically for the international audience, those without Norwegian ethnic intent or content. When Bull went to Paris, he began writing pieces to perform on the world stage he was preparing to conquer, and for these compositions he specifically avoided Norwegian characteristics. His influences for these works derived from three sources: Paganini's music, Italian operas, and Bull's early classical training in the works of Spohr and Viotti.

Bull began playing Paganini's music when he was a teenager, and by 1833 and 1834, when he was a young violinist at the beginning of his career, Paganini had become both his idol and his most feared competition. Bull actually heard Paganini in concert only once, but rivaling and surpassing the Italian virtuoso became his driving ambition as he traveled through Italy in 1834. Thus inspired, Bull wrote his answers to Paganini's *Duo mervielle* (a duet for violin alone) that were to become trademarks of his technical prowess. Expanding on Paganini's idea of continuous double and triple stops, Bull wanted a piece devoted to quadruple stops. To that end he wrote the *Capriccio Fantastico* (*Capriccio, Fantasia Capriccio, Capriccio ma moderato*) (no. 10) and the *Quartet for Violin Solo* (no. 14).

The *Capriccio Fantastico* was first performed in Trieste in 1834, and the *Quartet* in Naples in the same year. A reviewer said that in the *Capriccio Fantastico* one could hear alphorns.[10] Another said that the *Quartet* included a Swiss cow call;[11] and one said Bull "produced three tones quite clearly with the bow and the fourth with the finger."[12] None of these effects appear in the surviving album leaves, two short unrelated fragments from

9. Grinde, *Norsk Musikk Historie*, 123.

10. Henrik Winter-Hjelm, "Træk af Ole Bulls Liv," *Morgenbladet* (1852).

11. *Metropolitan Magazine*, cited in Linge, *Ole Bull*, 360.

12. *London Times* (23 May 1836), cited in Christian A. Aarvig, *Den unge Ole Bull: En Violinspillers Ungdomskampe* (Copenhagen, 1934), 83.

Example 20.1. *Quartet*

the *Capriccio Fantastico* and a brief "Grave sostenuto" from the *Quartet*.[13] The *Quartet* fragment is a section in four-part homophony in G major. Written on four separate staves (score notation), all four parts continue throughout, thereby justifying the name *Quartet* (see Example 20.1). The *Capriccio Fantastico* fragment in G minor, written as triple and quadruple stops (violin notation), has a slightly more open texture, a melody against one or two slower moving harmony notes (see Example 20.2).[14] Since Bull did not play the four-part texture as broken chords (i.e., one note after the other), of necessity he could have accomplished this brilliant technical feat of four simultaneous pitches only by pressing down on his flat bridge

13. The 1839 *Capriccio Fantastico* fragment is at the Deutsche Staatsbibliothek, Berlin, and the 1837 "Capriccio ma moderato" fragment is at the British Library; the 1837 autograph of the "Grave sostenuto" from the *Quartet* is in Signor De Begnis' autograph book (Boston Public Library).

14. The "Capriccio ma moderato" fragment (British Library) is in A minor with a cadenza.

Example 20.2. *Capriccio Fantastico*

with the loose bow hair. This ability to play four-part harmony became one of Bull's most important and distinctive stylistic features.

Biographers have overlooked the importance of Italian opera and specifically of Maria Malibran, the famous coloratura soprano, in determining the course of Bull's composition. Even more than Paganini's works, Bull's close friendship with Malibran and their common love of the Italian opera were pivotal in forming his ideas about musical composition and musical style. Bull first heard Malibran sing Italian opera in 1831 when it was the rage of Paris. Later, from 1833 to 1835, he traveled in Italy, absorbing even more Italian opera. During this time, Bull became close friends with Malibran and he spent precious months in her company and that of her violinist friend Bériot (see chap. 5). They even traveled and performed in concerts together. Bull heard Malibran sing in opera after opera, music by Bellini and Rossini. He heard how she improvised and ornamented melodic lines; he heard her pure tone quality and lyric style. Bull's Italian style melodies evolved from this operatic coloratura tradition, as exemplified by Malibran. A violin's intimate, melodic sound lends itself particularly well as a substitute for the light, cantilena Italian voice of the 1820s and 1830s. In addition, the virtuosic displays possible on the violin match the agility of the Italian coloratura passages of this period. The two solo instruments could be almost interchangeable.

Critics and supporters alike have been led astray in their descriptions of Bull's musical form because they have not understood its derivation from Italian opera of the 1820s and early 1830s. The critics, by calling his works formless and without a definite plan, imply that instrumental works should be sonata types with formal movements, motivic development, and interconnecting ideas. Furthermore, by indiscriminately labeling his pieces fantasias, rhapsodies, potpourris, and mosaics,[15] these same critics do not distinguish between the nationalistic works and the ones using Italian compositional methods. While Bull's nationalistic works are indeed potpourris or mosaics of tunes strung together (see chap. 22), the other works are not. The confusion in terminology arises because some of Bull's works in Italian style are titled fantasia, for example, *Fantaisie et Variations de bravoure, sur un thème de Bellini.* Here, the term is applied in its nineteenth-century sense which means only that the piece belongs to the virtuoso tradition; the term does not provide a description of the composition's formal design.

Bull's Italian-style works use the flexible formal model of the *scena ed aria* from Italian opera of the 1820s and 1830s. A *scena ed aria* is a single unit of music in an opera, sometimes casually, but not quite correctly, translated as a scene. Simply described, it has a broad formal pattern, in which the recitative is usually followed by a lyric section. This songlike section may be called by various terms such as *cantabile, cantilena,* or *cavatina.* The form concludes with a *cabaletta,* the bravura or virtuosic section usually in an AA' form.[16] A cantabile and cabaletta together would be called the aria. There may also be an orchestral introduction, expansions within the lyric section and a *tempo di mezzo* (a choral link between the lyric section and concluding cabaletta).

Bull's works that suggest this form, partially or completely, are his *Polacca Guerriera* (no. 19), *Bravura Variations* (no. 8), *Siciliano and Tarantella* (no. 39), *A Mother's Prayer* (no. 15), *Nocturne* (no. 36), *Greetings from Afar* (no. 33), and *Grieving Prayer and Laughing Rondo* (no. 22).

Recitativo, Andante amoroso con Polacca Guerriera (no. 19), composed in Naples and Rome in 1835 during Bull's first visit to Italy, fits the *scena ed aria* model well. The violin soloist (who replaces the operatic solo singer) is accompanied by orchestra or when one is not available, by the piano. The opening orchestral fanfare for brass instruments establishes the military character of the piece. The fanfare idea, though not always using this rhythm pattern ♪♪♪ ♩exactly, provides an extra bit of unity to this instrumental *scena ed aria.*[17] This fanfare introduces the operatic recitative for solo violin. In an opera the recitative would provide a place for the action of the story to unfold. The musical style would tend toward short phrases,

15. Linge, *Ole Bull,* 343, 346.
16. The AA' form may be separated by a short mid-section, but it generally remains entirely in the tonic key.
17. The examples are taken from the violin and piano version published in Christiania by Carl Warmuth in [1886].

Example 20.3. *Polacca Guerriera:* Cavatina, mm. 76–81

Example 20.4. *Polacca Guerriera:* Polacca, mm. 111–15

some with coloratura elaborations, but without a lyric or forward moving theme. The music would instead follow the text's phrasing and inflections. Bull borrows this musical type using the solo violin to "speak" an imaginary text in short phrases while the orchestra accompanies with sustained chords or with a slow harmonic motion.

A transition (Andante) leads directly into the "Andante Amoroso" (or "Adagio Amoroso") which parallels the song portion (or cavatina) of the *scena ed aria*. In this section a singer would exhibit the lyric or *bel canto* qualities of the voice. Bull used a simple cantabile D-major violin melody with thirds and sixths in order to display his famous sweet, clear violin tone (see Example 20.3).

The following transition ("Più stretto un poco Allegretto") uses the fanfare rhythm (see above) to announce a "Polacca" in A major. The "Polacca" or polonaise, originally of Polish origin, was a popular dance during this period, and a similar "Polacca" appears in Bellini's *I puritani* of the same year, one of the operas that Maria Malibran sang and that Bull knew well. Bull's "Polacca" demonstrates his bold spirit as well as his scalar passagework (see Example 20.4). The following E-major 3/4 "Arietta" ("Poco più Lento") (see Example 20.5) of a passionate character (*cantabile appassionato*) continues the lyric section and lets Bull display his intense emotional abilities, concluding with three fermatas that allow the possibility of an improvised cadenza.

In the transition ("Più mosso" in C meter), Bull increases the tempo, shows his technical ability with thirds, sixths, staccatos, and trills, and brings

Example 20.5. *Polacca Guerriera:* Arietta, mm. 167–74

Example 20.6. *Polacca Guerriera:* Final theme 1, mm. 219–27

back the fanfare style to announce the equivalent of the concluding cabaletta in a *scena ed aria.* For the singer, this brilliant section in AA′ form would have been the place for virtuosity, improvisations, and ornamentation of all kinds.

Bull's final section with its A major theme ("Moderato" only in its basic beat) fulfills these operatic norms (see Example 20.6). The first time the violin includes octaves for ornamentation. Then a transition (Meno Allegro) builds up the technical fireworks — arpeggios, triple and quadruple stops, octaves, scales, thirds, staccatos, and chromatic scales with orchestral fanfares in the background (see Example 20.7) — all in order to lead into the final statement of the theme. That statement, in true cabaletta fashion, lets the soloist ornament with brilliant technique, continuous staccato sixteenth notes, while the theme itself appears only in the orchestra (see Example 20.8). Fanfare material for the orchestra, now ♫ ♪, concludes the piece while the violin continues with rapid triple and quadruple stops rushing toward the end (see Example 20.9). An operatic soprano could not have invented a more brilliant close.

Of Bull's pieces influenced by the Italian operatic tradition, the *Polacca Guerriera* was the best known. He played it constantly, perhaps more than any other piece, knowing that his audiences would respond enthusiastically every time.[18] By the mid 1840s there were various arrangements of it available to the public. For example, one solo piano version, arranged

18. Linge, *Ole Bull,* 346.

Example 20.7. *Polacca Guerriera:* Transition, mm. 261–68

by Charles Grobe and published in Philadelphia in 1845, includes only the "Polacca" and "Arietta" theme transformed into an ABA form using the "Polacca" theme for the A section. This arrangement was given the new title *Bellone: Polonaise à la Militaire.* Many copies of it were sold to the delighted amateur public in the United States who had just heard Bull perform for the first time.

Bull's *Fantaisie et Variations de bravoure, sur un thème de Bellini pour violon, avec orchestre ou piano (Bravura Variations,* no. 8), his Opus 3 composed in Paris in 1832 and 1833, also uses the *scena ed aria* structure,[19]

19. The overarching key scheme and large-scale design resemble the "Introduzione e scena" and "Duetto" (Dormono entrambi/Deh! con te) of Bellini's *Norma,* Act 2. They both have

Example 20.8. *Polacca Guerriera:* Final theme 2, mm. 287–91

but with a variations form superimposed on it. The theme for the varia-tions is "L'amo, ah l'amo, e m'é più cara" from the opera *I Capuleti e i Montecchi* by Bellini. The piece opens in D minor with an orchestral in-troduction which contains a prefiguration of Bellini's theme (see Example 20.10).[20] With the stabilization of F major, the recitative begins and the violin soloist enters (see Example 20.11).

A transition (Più vivo) uses virtuoso passagework and a cadenza to ar-rive at the dominant of A major, the key of the coming Bellini theme. Bellini's theme (Moderato quasi Andante), which opens the cantabile section, func-tions as the lyric *bel canto* melody within the *scena ed aria* (see Example 20.12), and it cadences with a nine-measure orchestral closing. The lyric section continues as the violin again states the theme in Variation 1 (Più lento) but with added staccato scales, leaps, and arpeggios (see Example 20.13). This variation is followed by the same orchestral closing.

Variation 2 is an example of Bull's emphasis on improvisation. It is im-portant to note that Bull was one of the last performers in the nineteenth century to practice extensively the art of improvisation; more and more composers were writing out every note that they expected of the performers.

two different melodies within the lyric section, and both have the second one in the key of the cabaletta.

20. The examples are from the 1843 Schuberth edition.

Example 20.9. *Polacca Guerriera:* Conclusion, mm. 331–43

Example 20.10. *Bravura Variations:* Introduction, mm. 20–23

Example 20.11. *Bravura Variations:* Recitative, mm. 47–52

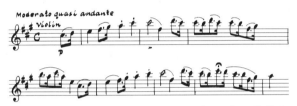

Example 20.12. *Bravura Variations:* Theme from Bellini

Example 20.13. *Bravura Variations:* Variation 1

This variation is not written out in the score at all, and the orchestra has twenty-five measures of rest during which Bull would have improvised alone. The unusual lacuna at this early point in the piece (as opposed to the fermata for a concerto movement cadenza) shows how important and essen-

Example 20.14. *Bravura Variations:* Variation 2

Example 20.15. *Bravura Variations:* Variation 3

tial Bull considered improvisation to the execution of his pieces. Only in the separate violin part do the notes for this variation appear, suggesting that the performer could vary it for each performance without causing the orchestra any surprise. In this Variation 2, because it is still within the lyric section, Bull has chosen to use triple and quadruple stops in a smooth manner to express the much varied theme in minor mode (see Example 20.14).

Variation 3 (Allegretto giocoso) again allows the melody to be clearly heard in the violin part, this time embellished with staccatos and repeated notes. This variation concludes the first portion of the cantabile section (see Example 20.15).

The following orchestral interlude of new music (Allegro vivo) changes the A major tonic into the dominant of D major. This harmonic redefinition heralds the beginning of an "aria" in D major, called "Andante Arioso." It has a completely new melody (see Example 20.16).[21] This melody acts as a continuation within the operatic lyric section and yet is also in effect a substitute for a Variation 4. Thus, although the piece is on the surface

---

21. Bjarne Kortsen has published Variations 4 ("Andante Arioso") and 5 ("Moderato") as a separate piece titled *Arioso* (Bergen: Edition Norwegica, 1978). He has based his edition on the incomplete autograph manuscript in the University of Oslo Library. His editor's notes suggest that he did not know it belonged to the *Bravura Variations*.

Example 20.16. *Bravura Variations:* Andante Arioso

Example 20.17. *Bravura Variations:* Moderato (Variation 5)

a theme and variations, it conforms here to the operatic model that per-
mits new music for its various parts. In fact, for Variations 4–7 (paralleling
the "aria and cabaletta"), the violin never again clearly states the Bellini
theme. In the following "Moderato" (Variation 5), the theme is almost lost
in a violinistic display of octaves, thirds, and sixths (see Example 20.17).
The "Moderato" concludes in a cadenza which causes a final pause in the
motion and closes what would be an opera scene's lyric portion.

The tempo changes to "Allegro moderato" and the meter to 4/4, force-
fully beginning the final section. In this Variation 6 or "cabaletta," the
flutes and clarinets finally bring back an altered but recognizable Bellini
theme (see Example 20.18). "Più animato" (or Variation 7) completes a
two-part operatic "cabaletta," but because of the violin's triple and quadruple stops in sixteenth notes, it has no possibility for including the theme
from the variation form (see Example 20.19).

To summarize, during the first part of the lyric section Bellini's theme
was brought out clearly and treated both tenderly and in lightly orna-

Example 20.18. *Bravura Variations:* Variation 6

Example 20.19. *Bravura Variations:* Più Animato (Variation 7)

mented fashion by the violin, while in the "aria" (Andante arioso and Moderato) and the "cabaletta" (Allegro moderato and Più animato) the Bellini theme was secondary or absent. Thus, as the *scena ed aria* structure spins itself out, the variation form disintegrates.

Adagio Religioso, pour violon avec orchestre ou piano (no. 15) is an instrumental cavatina. This piece lacks a concluding cabaletta, just as might be the case in an opera, particularly in tender or reflective moments where it would not seem dramatically appropriate. Bull's alternate title for Opus 1, *A Mother's Prayer,* immediately suggests that such a fast section would be superfluous.[22] The piece has an orchestral introduction (Adagio grave) on the dominant of G minor. The solo violin becomes the "voice" of the following recitative (in octaves), using the expected short phrases of recitative style, and concludes with a short cadenza.

A transition (Andantino) prepares the instrumental cavatina. This "Andante Religioso," is pure song in *bel canto* style: it is a long-breathed, seamless melody doubled in thirds and sixths in G major and in an ABA' construction. In an operatic cavatina of this construction, the A' repeat would have new text, and the music would begin the same as A but soon be significantly varied.[23] Bull carries out this plan, and the A', beginning after a cadenza, is enriched with harmonics, ornamentation, and octaves. Bull even uses flutes and oboes in thirds and sixths to support the melody (see Example 20.20). This creates the "sweet" texture of woodwinds so familiar from Rossini's arias. Throughout the piece, the orchestral parts

22. Bull composed it in Florence in 1834, and it was published by Schuberth in 1843 as an orchestra score that included the piano part. Example 20.20 is from this score. Bull was still playing this piece to American audiences in 1844 and 1853. See Linge, *Ole Bull,* 219, and Lydia Maria Child, *Letters from New York,* 2d ser. (New York, 1846), 23.

23. Bellini's cavatina "Meco all' altar" from *Norma,* Act 1 is such an example [A 4 + 16)–B–A'].

Example 20.20. *A Mother's Prayer*, mm. 74–81. The violin plays entirely using harmonics.

are the picture of simplicity, designed, as in Italian opera, to serve as a backdrop to the *bel canto* vocal line.

The *Nocturne* (no. 36), Opus 2 published in 1843, is also a simple, instrumental cavatina in *bel canto* style.[24] Comparison of surviving sources, an autograph score in the University of Oslo Library and the printed orchestra/piano score (Schuberth, 1843), provides an excellent example of the problems with the Bull source material. In the autograph the orchestration is not completely written out in many places, and the violin part is

24. The form is A (8 measures)–A'–B–A", a typical cavatina structure. The *Nocturne* had its first performance in Christiania in 1842. It may well be the same as *Til Hende* because Winter-Hjelm describes a *Notturno til Hende* as new in September of 1842; *Morgenbladet* (1852). Possibly it is also the same as the piece titled *Nocturne amorosa*.

Example 20.21. *Nocturne*, mm. 51–60. Autograph, Oslo University Library; Printed score, Schuberth, 1843

often just a skeleton of the published version. Particularly noticeable is a ten-measure outline of a violin melody (the final return of A) in the autograph score that becomes rich three- and four-part harmony for unaccompanied solo violin in the printed score and contains a melody change in m. 56 (see Example 20.21 above). Comparison of the two sources also shows changes of orchestration in the published version. For pieces lacking a printed version, this suggests how much has been lost, particularly of the violin part, in Bull's hastily written scores.

The slow to fast (lyric to cabaletta) formula of the *scena ed aria* extends to Bull's *Siciliano and Tarantella* (no. 39), one of his most effective showpieces. This composition remained unpublished because of difficulties with his publisher Schuberth in 1843.[25] Nevertheless, Bull played this piece in 1843 in Bremen, Copenhagen, and Christiania before he left for

25. Linge later bought this autograph manuscript from Schuberth and sold it to the University of Oslo Library. This orchestra score without the violin solo part and an autograph of the violin and piano arrangement are at the University of Oslo Library. They differ in small ways from one another. A violin and piano version with some simplifications in the violin part and minor changes in the piano part was published by Ola Linge (Oslo: Edition Gamma, 1948).

Example 20.22. *Siciliano,* mm. 23–31

the United States and continued to play it often on his first American tour.[26] It remained in his repertoire until his death; he performed it in Madison, Wisconsin, in 1879 with his wife Sara at the piano.[27]

The Siciliano is a quiet, flowing D-major melody (see Example 20.22) that is connected by a short recitative featuring violin harmonics and an accelerating passage to the lively Tarantella in G major.[28] The Tarantella (Allegro assai) is in rondo form which replaces the very different cabaletta form of the operatic formula. In the Tarantella the theme comes three times (twice in quadruple stops for violin) separated by interludes in related keys,

26. Child, *Letters,* 272.

27. Albert O. Barton, "Ole Bull and his Wisconsin Contacts," *Wisconsin Magazine of History* 7 (1924): 441.

28. A (8 measures)–A'–B is the form of the *Siciliano*'s main melody. Example 20.22 is from the incomplete orchestra score with the violin part added from the violin-piano arrangement.

and the tempo gets faster with each new appearance of the theme.[29]

Greetings from Afar (no. 33) (*Grüss aus der Ferne, Largo posato et Rondo capriccioso, En fjern Hilsen,* and even *Concerto dramatico*), composed in Prague in 1841, preserves the slow-fast design of a *scena ed aria,* but like in *Siciliano and Tarantella* the form is balanced toward the longer fast section. The "Largo posato," a slow melody with ornamentation, thus acts as a cavatina in D minor, while the "Rondo capriccioso" substitutes in tempo and position for a cabaletta. The latter is lively and divided into several sections (D major with one middle section in G major). Because the surviving sources—an incomplete autograph score, a few parts (oboe 1, bassoon 2, bass drum), an incomplete organ arrangement, and a one-page

29. As paraphrased by Linge, Bull described this piece as follows: "The *Siciliano*—in the evening light a couple whisper tenderly about their love. The *Tarantella*—a festival begins and the two dance together until they collapse with exhaustion and joy." Ole Bull, *Siciliano e Tarantella,* ed. Ola Linge (Oslo, 1948), no page. See List of Works, no. 39.

album leaf—do not add up to a common version, the design of the rondo cannot be reconstructed with certainty.[30] The principles of rondo form are present: the primary material (D major) returns, and there is contrasting material in a lyric section (G major) and in a "Più vivo" section (D major, the "Cantabile" of the album leaf). However, the order of sections and the structure of the conclusion remain in doubt. Typical for Bull's use of operatic cabaletta principles, the final section (D major) is a virtuosic buildup to the end, and it does not bring a return of the main rondo theme.

The *Grieving Prayer and Laughing Rondo* (no. 22) (*Preghiera dolente e Rondo ridente;* later *Cantabile doloroso e Rondo giocoso*) seems also to be based on the slow-fast formula of the *scena ed aria,* but the three surviving orchestral parts reveal little else. The album leaf written in Prague in 1841 presents only the opening measures of the "Rondo giocoso."[31]

One piece remains that, without further information, does not fit clearly into the above categories. Ola Linge arranged for piano and voice a *Barcarolle* (no. 76). His version derived from two of Bull's drafts (location unknown). This seems to be an early Italian-style song, which suggests that it might have been composed between 1833 and 1835 when Bull was on his Italian tour,[32] yet the Norwegian melodic formula—the second-third intervals in the same direction as heard in "Sæter Girl's Sunday"—appears in mm. 24–28 (see Example 20.23).

Example 20.23. *Barcarolle,* mm. 24–28

30. The incomplete score is in Copenhagen at Det kgl. Bibliothek. The organ arrangement titled *En fjern Hilsen* is mostly without the violin solo. The album leaf (1842) titled "Cantabile" is a part of the rondo. These last two and the orchestra parts in a copyist's hand are in the University of Oslo Library.

31. The three orchestra parts in a copyist's hand are in the University of Oslo Library; the location of the album leaf is unknown.

32. The awkward piano accompaniment suggests that Bull's drafts were early working copies. However, the problematic moments could result from the combination of Bull's two sketches. Linge's notes to the edition do not make it clear how they were combined.

Bull's concertos also do not take up classical German models, but rather show strong operatic influences similar to those in Spohr's unusual Opus 47, *Concerto in A Minor in Modo di Scena Cantante.*[33] Bull's *Concerto in A Major* (no. 9) (or *Grand Concerto*), written in 1834, was a piece he played often, and it was considered among his best works.[34] Reviewers sometimes referred to the piece by its movement titles, "Allegro maestoso," "Adagio sentimentale," or "Rondo pastorale," as if it were three separate entities because in concert Bull did not always play all the three movements as a unit.

Only three orchestral parts (oboe 1, bassoon 2, and bass drum) of the concerto survive, but this barren skeleton reveals some important points about the structure of the piece.[35] Bull used the concerto form in a loose way as did many nineteenth-century composers, but even for a nineteenth-century composer the key scheme is unexpected. The third and last movement is in E minor/major, when both the title, *Concerto in A Major,* and opening movement of the piece (A major) suggest that the piece should also conclude in A major. This unusual choice of final key suggests that Bull was applying a principle of relatively free key choice, perhaps justified by the freedom in these matters often exhibited in Italian opera.[36] A *scena ed aria* structure is suggested by the pattern of tempo and key changes within this third movement; how the "Rondo" form, as it is titled, would be carried out remains unclear. Without further discoveries of source material, little else can be said about this piece.[37]

The *Concerto in E Minor* (or *Concerto Fantastico*) from 1841 (no. 29), another of his major works, reveals in more detail Bull's concerto structure. All three movements survive in an autograph score, and the second movement ("Adagio") is preserved in a posthumously published violin and piano version.[38] This E-minor concerto uses a free double-exposition form

33. This composition of Spohr's (1816, published 1820) was a deviation from his usual concerto form, being constructed like an opera scene. Bull learned this piece during his early years of study. In 1839 Spohr reversed the "influence" by including an ironic reference to Ole Bull in his Concerto No. 14, Opus 110.

34. Kjerulf, cited in Linge, *Ole Bull,* 343.

35. These parts in a copyist's hand are in the University of Oslo Library.

36. The *Concerto in E Minor* uses the same principle. See below.

37. The second movement's tempo markings, "Adagio" followed by "Andantino," would also seem to signify operatic conventions, possibly a recitative followed by a cavatina, but melodic lines do not survive to allow certain identification.

38. The autograph score, dated Prague, 12 February 1841, is in the University of Oslo Library. This score is Bull's almost complete working copy. There is a marking for an insertion (now lost) to movement 1, and the only extant part (bassoon 2) in a copyist's hand at the University of Oslo Library indicates that the insertion was twenty-seven measures long.

for the first movement, and it includes a slow introduction.[39] The second theme, as the most immediately distinctive, acts as a unifying formal device. It is an Italianate cantabile melody stated in E major in the orchestral exposition by the flute (m. 34), in G major in the violin exposition (m. 98), and finally in E minor by the cellos and basses, significantly varied, for the recapitulation (m. 142). This last statement is placed in reversed position; it stands as the *first* theme of the recapitulation.

Movements 2 (Adagio sostenuto or Grave à la Preghiera) and 3 (Rondo vivo scherzoso, Rondo scherzando, or Rondo marcato) are connected with the words *attacca subito* ("begin immediately"). Movement 2 is an AB-A′C lyric section, the first half in G minor, the second half in G major. The opening of the third movement provides the smooth transition via the dominant seventh chord to C major.

Using the unexpected key of C major (instead of E minor) for the final movement corresponds to the unusual key choice for the A-Major Concerto's third movement. By not returning to the key of the first movement (also the title of the piece), Bull reinforces the possibility of operatic influences for both these pieces. Indeed, the "Rondo" title is not carried out; nothing returns in the manner of a traditional rondo. Instead the form, all in C major, is made up of three discrete sections; the spirited opening connects to a lyric "Moderato molto" melody and concludes with a short, driving "Animato e vivace." It is comparable perhaps to an operatic ensemble finale with a lively concluding *stretta*. Thus, Bull's concertos show signs of operatic influence.

Ole Bull's written music remains today fragmentary and mostly unpublished. Yet even these bits of his non-Norwegian work give the picture of a composer very well versed in the Italian opera tradition. He fully understood its formal construction, its various melodic styles, and its harmonic underpinnings. His melodies are diatonic, using scales and arpeggios in rapid sections and predominantly adjacent seconds and thirds in the slower

The conclusions to movements 1 and 3, not fully worked out in the score, show some deviations from the later bassoon part. The autograph's second movement agrees with the bassoon part. In the 1886 published version of this movement, the piano accompaniment is rhythmically simplified and the violin solo somewhat changed.

39. The solo violin entrance in E minor (m. 61) would be the beginning of the second exposition with theme 1 vastly altered. The piece then modulates to G major for the second theme (m. 98). The brief development starts at the "Tempo Moderato, Minore" with rhapsodic material (m. 120), and the recapitulation begins with the second theme in E minor (m. 142). Only a rhythmic motive from the first theme follows at "Quasi tutti" (m. 166). Measure numbers are according to the autograph score, not the bassoon part. Our description bears little resemblance to Grinde's in *Norsk Musikk Historie*, 123.

sections. His harmonic vocabulary is also diatonic, avoiding modal relationships and any extensive use of chromaticism.

Rather than fantasias, as his Italian works are so often incompletely labeled, he wrote untexted opera scenes of careful design. The overlay of performance considerations, of improvisation, of technical fireworks, and of the sweet, singing violin tone seduced his listeners, and the fact that the pieces did not sound organized to his German listeners indicates their bias against Italian opera, not an inherent weakness of design in Bull's compositions.

The added improvisation found in all of these works was a custom of the times, one necessary to the virtuoso performer. Concert performances were considered creative events of the moment, not, as concerts have become today, almost exclusively reinterpretations of past masterpieces. Performers of imagination today could take Bull's pieces and rediscover his flights of creativity, but they would have to learn to participate actively in the improvisational process. Just as the recent crop of coloratura sopranos has rediscovered the ornamented singing of Bellini and Donizetti's operas, so a violinist would have to relearn the art of *bel canto* playing and bravura improvisation to render these pieces effectively.

21

Music for the Public

BULL FIT neatly into the breach where the European art-music came to overlap with popular or vernacular music. Nineteenth-century audiences attended not just prestigious symphony concerts and opera performances, but eagerly sought out the popular styles of music at theatrical shows, in the music halls, and in the ballrooms of both Europe and America. European spas stirred with popular music events, and in the United States the public flocked to circus performances and minstrel shows. Europeans enthusiastically embraced popular dances and tunes as they swept from country to country, and Americans devoured these latest fashions as soon as they crossed the Atlantic. In a matter of months, people thousands of miles away could dance to a waltz by Johann Strauss or hum a polka by Joseph Lanner. These large, mostly untutored audiences responded emotionally rather than intellectually to their musical experiences, and a style would succeed or fail based on its first impression with them.

Vernacular or popular music was available everywhere. Military bands played marches in the town square. "Salon" orchestras and wind bands entertained with light selections and played for dance evenings. These orchestras and bands played medleys of opera melodies, arrangements of popular tunes, variations on national melodies and, of course, dance music. Soloists of great virtuosic skill were often engaged to perform with these groups. Singers, violinists, trumpeters, flutists, clarinettists, all got a chance to show off their talents with "concertos" that were really sets of variations on familiar tunes. These pieces were meant as vehicles for technical display, high-wire circus acts to dazzle the public.

This circus or "show" aspect was crucial to the success of these solo performers. P. T. Barnum, the gifted American promoter, for example, cleverly sought out such European virtuosos because he understood that the American public wanted flashy entertainment with an exotic foreign flavor. Barnum would weave these virtuoso players or singers into a show filled with a wide variety of amusing acts. Then he would advertise the show shamelessly; the Swedish singer Jenny Lind, for example, became "The Swedish Nightingale." Although Bull was engaged only one time by Barnum, Bull's managers used similar advertising techniques, and when Otto Lessmann (1844–1918) in *Musical America* criticized Bull, he railed mostly against what he considered Bull's massive and tasteless advance publicity.[1]

If the eager but untutored audience were to sit still for a solo performance, the music needed to be either technically brilliant or openly sentimental, painting its picture with a broad and sweeping brush. The repetition of favorite tunes was a direct way into the hearts of this audience. A tune could be humorous, catchy or sentimental, but it always needed to be simple, built of regular and predictable phrases. Soloists who wanted to succeed would not hesitate to use songs such as "Yankee Doodle," "For He's a Jolly Good Fellow," or even "Mary had a Little Lamb" for their variations.

Bull was proud of his role as a purveyor of this vernacular style. He could not fathom "why the Germans bang away with their mechanical exactness and endless harmonies, but they neglect the purer, sweet melodies which reach the heart of the people. The majority of the public have no time to read between the lines. . . . Why, if the people pay their money to hear me play 'Lucy Long,' and 'The Arkansas Traveller,' why should I not gratify them? I should feel that I had cheated them if I did not consult the taste of my audience."[2]

And that is exactly what Bull did. On his travels throughout the world, he incorporated familiar melodies of the lands he visited. These pieces were meant as crowd pleasers. It is no longer possible to say to what extent they included genuine native material or to what formal models they adhere because so few survive. Among the lost pieces were, for example, works described as a fantasia with Irish folk tunes, *Farewell to Ireland* (*Concerto Irlandais*) (no. 21) from 1837, a fantasia with Scottish tunes, *Homage to Edinburgh* (*Scottish Concerto* or *Fantasy on Scottish Folk Melodies*) (no.

1. See Otto Lessmann, "How Ole Bull Made a Music Critic," *Musical America* (4 March 1911). Clipping New York Public Library, concerning performances Lessmann had heard in the 1860s.
2. Dexter Smith, "Reminiscences of Ole Bull," Boston *Herald,* no date. Clipping, New York Public Library.

23) from 1837, and pieces with American material, *Solitude of the Prairie* (*Solitude de la prairie*) (no. 44) and *Niagara* (no. 43) from 1844.[3] *Niagara* is especially intriguing for Bull described it as having "quite a new and original structure, not as brilliant as the solo part in *Polacca Guerriera,* but with a more complex accompaniment for the orchestra."[4] Much later, 1872, he wrote another fantasia on an American folktune, *Lilly Dale* (no. 72).

The tour of Cuba in 1844 yielded *Cuban Potpourri* (*El Agiaco Cubano* or *El Ajiaco Cubano*) (no. 40) and *Memories of Havana* (*Recuerdos de Habana* or *Minner fra Havana*) (no. 41). Both pieces were first performed in the spring of 1844 in Cuba[5] and later that same year in New York.[6] Bull wrote that in *Memories of Havana,* "I have braided in some of this country's most loved melodies."[7] More about this piece we do not know.

Cuban Potpourri has been described as a rhapsody or medley on Cuban melodies,[8] and a Cuban review from 1844 describes it as a fantasia on motives from a dance called "La Pepilla" composed by Ulpiano Estrada.[9] The only surviving section, a *Grand March taken from Ole Bull's Celebrated Spanish Airs 'Agiaco Cubano' and Arranged for the Pianoforte by Adolphe Kurs,* does not indicate any Cuban influence.[10] This simple march has a sectional structure (AABACA DD EE ABA); section C contrasts on the subdominant major, section D on the submediant minor. The harmonies are simple; the rhythms traditional for any march.

From Madrid in 1847 comes *The Guitarist from Seville* (no. 49), a piece that has been described as a Spanish folk song in bolero rhythm with a mandolin-like accompaniment, all of it played by the violin.[11] Here too we are tantalized by what may be a partial version, a *Guitar-Serenade* that Anders Heyerdahl wrote down from his own memory of Bull's playing.[12] This fragment is a virtuoso passage containing triple stops interspersed with a few scalar passages and the rhythmic pattern ♫ ♪ ♪; it is al-

3. There are reports that he played all four pieces in New York in 1844. Lydia Maria Child, *Letters from New York,* 2d ser. (New York, 1846), 231, 232, 272.
4. Alexander Bull, ed., *Ole Bulls Breve i Uddrag. Med en karakteristik og biografisk Skitse af Jonas Lie* (Copenhagen, 1881), 344 (30 December 1844).
5. Programs from Cuba, 1844, University of Oslo Library.
6. Child, *Letters,* 308.
7. Bull, ed., *Ole Bulls Breve i Uddrag,* 329 (14 May 1844).
8. Ola Linge, *Ole Bull: Livshistoria, Mannen, Kunstnaren* (Oslo, 1953), 365.
9. Unidentified clipping. University of Oslo Library.
10. New York: John F. Nunns [1846].
11. Linge, *Ole Bull,* 346.
12. *Norske Danse og Slaatter for Violin,* 2d ed. (Christiania: Oluf By's Musikforlag, [written between 1856 and 1861, printed 1905]), 14.

most without melodic substance or harmonic interest. Another piece with Spanish effects from 1847 is *Celebration of St. John's Eve* (*La Verbena de San Juan, Spansk Sankt-Hans-Natt*) (no. 48).

From Moscow comes *Homage to Moscow* (*Hommage à Moscou*) (no. 70) for violin, chorus, and orchestra and *The Nightingale* (*Nattergalen*) (no. 71), a fantasia on a Russian popular song by A. Alyabiev; both were first performed in Moscow in April, 1867. Some of these popular or folk melody pieces may have been on-the-spot improvisations, while others were compositions quickly written down for a single series of concerts. Perhaps these were not pieces Bull expected to play again, and therefore he made no attempt to preserve his manuscripts. About *The Nightingale,* for example, he wrote to Alexander, "It really has no musical value . . . I will rework it at Valestrand."[13] There is no record that he ever did.

Improvising on a tune was something Bull had done throughout his life with all the material that came his way. It had begun with ornamenting Norwegian *slåtts* and folk songs (see chap. 18 and 22). Then in Bologna in 1834, when he was asked to improvise on operatic tunes suggested by party guests, he showed off by weaving all three suggested tunes into one piece (no. 12), a feat he repeated in Leipzig in 1841 (no. 31) using the "Serenata" (Ecco ridente il cielo) from Act I of Rossini's *Il barbiere di Siviglia,* a "Polacca" (Son vergin vezzosa) from Bellini's *I Puritani,* and the "Champagne Song" (Fin ch'han dal vino calda la testa) from Mozart's *Don Giovanni,* Act I. In the 1841 program the piece was listed as *Improvisations on Given Motives.*[14]

In England in 1836 Bull improvised on the spot a four-voiced version of "God Save the King" (no. 20) just to show off his fabulous quadruple stops.[15] He improvised on the Czech folk song "Sil jsem proso na souvrati" (no. 32) in Prague in 1841.[16] And in New York in 1844, he topped off a concert with a spur-of-the-moment improvisation on "Yankee Doodle" (no. 45).[17]

Bull invented variations on "El Calecero Andaluz" and "La Jota Aragonesa" (no. 50) in Spain in 1847.[18] A *Fantasia on American Airs* (no. 60) introduced "Jordan is a Hard Road to Travel," "Hazel Dell," "Arkansas

13. Bull, ed., *Ole Bulls Breve i Uddrag,* 405 (17 April 1867).

14. Program is given in Linge, *Ole Bull,* 131.

15. Henrik Wergeland, "Ole Bull: Efter opgivelser af ham selv biografisk skildret," in D. A. Seip, ed., *Samlede Skrifter* (Oslo, 1927), 4.5:204.

16. Jan Trojan, "Das Brünner Konzertleben in der Zeit der Nationalen Wiedergeburt," *Sborník prací filosofické fakulty brněnské university* 8 (1973): 172.

17. Child, *Letters,* 23.

18. Henrik Winter-Hjelm, "Træk af Ole Bulls Liv," *Morgenbladet* (1852).

Traveler," "Pop goes the Weasel," and "Home, Sweet Home," in Bloomington, Illinois (1856?)[19] and in New York in 1877 Bull's last encore was
variations on "We Won't go Home until Morning" (no. 75).[20] These pieces
must have been exuberant show pieces intended to bring down the house.

Bull always built his concerts to please and excite his audiences. A typical non-Norwegian concert program would be the one designed for his
American audience on 15 November 1853. This concert was boldly advertised as intended specifically "for the Western States" (the Midwest today)
and as Bull's last concert before retiring (Bull was only 43 years old!):

First and Only Grand Concert

1. *Grand Fantasie de Concert,* or favorite airs from the *Child of the Regiment,*
   composed and performed by Maurice Strakosch
2. *Happy Birdlings of the Forest,* Wallace bravoure song, composed for Kate
   Hayes, sung by Adelina Patti
3. *The Mother's Prayer,* a Fantasia Religiosa, composed and executed by Ole Bull
4. *Ah, Non Giunge,* celebrated Rondo Finale from La Sonnambula, sung by
   A. Patti
5. Paganini's famous *Witches' Dance,* performed by Ole Bull

Part II

1. *The Banjo,* a new Capriccio Characteristique, composed and performed by
   M. Strakosch
2. *Comin' Thro' the Rye,* favorite Scotch Ballad, sung by A. Patti
3. *Grand National Fantasie* for violin alone, performed by Ole Bull, dedicated
   to the Senate and Congress of the United States at their request and performed
   on the occasion of his first concert in Washington
4. Jenny Lind's *Echo Song,* sung by A. Patti
5. *Carnival of Venice,* by Ole Bull[21]

Bull's program was a lively variety show. Strakosch, the manager, was
the pianist or conductor for the evening. Adelina Patti, the ten-year-old
child prodigy, was the coloratura, singing in both Italian and English. Bull,
who played only four works on the whole program, was the heralded violin virtuoso playing both Paganini's and his own works. Two of his works
were from earlier European tours, but the *Grand National Fantasie,* most
likely *In Memory of Washington* (no. 46), was specifically tailored to please
his American audience. It was a multipart work for violin and orchestra.

19. Program in the Bergen University Library.
20. Linge, *Ole Bull,* 279.
21. Program in the Boston Public Library.

Bull had composed it during his first tour in the United States, dedicating it to the memory of George Washington, whom he saw as the leader of an independence struggle similar to the Norwegian one. The piece was first performed in 1845. In this 1853 concert he seems to have played an unaccompanied version. An even later (though undated) Boston program gives a vivid description of the work:

To the Memory of Washington   Ole Bull

Introduction (Grave), Sorrow and Woe—Allegro agitato, Rising against Oppression—Battle, *God Save the King!* and *Yankee Doodle!* alternately heard—Honor to the Fallen Heroes—(Choral)—Reception of the Victorious Federals, and March in Honor of Washington—Finale[22]

In Memory of Washington seems to have the same construction as the Norwegian potpourri or medley pieces (see chap. 22). The only extant music is a partial selection, a piano arrangement titled *Grand March* and first published in Philadelphia in 1845 (see Example 21.1).[23] The march, as it appears in this arrangement, is built exclusively of four-bar phrases that make an AA' BABA CC'DD' pattern. Faint suggestions of an Italian-style accompaniment appear in the B (mm. 9–12) and C phrases with the triplet subdivisions of the quarter-note pulse. Also the turn of phrase at mm. 10 and 12 hints at Italian melodic cadential formulas, but any suggestion that this piece might originally have been written for violin is absent from the arrangement. Also there is nothing particularly American about the piece except the sentiment behind its composition.

Although Bull published little and did not write down all of his music, others wanted to remember it. Friends and audience members sometimes wrote down what they remembered of Bull's playing, for example the *Guitar-Serenade* mentioned above. Still others wrote out only a melodic line or two, probably for their own use.[24] Some of these are the Norwegian *slåtts* that Bull played as encores. Others come from the best-known pieces, like *Polacca Guerriera,* still others from lost pieces, and some may not have been by Bull at all.

One tune traveled far. *Ole Bulls Polka* (no. B3) comes from a "wan-

22. Program at Longfellow's Wayside Inn, Sudbury, Massachusetts.

23. No arranger is listed. It also appeared as *Marsch af 'Washingtons minde'* (*March from 'In Memory of Washington'*) in *Ole Bull's Favorit Compositioner* (*Ole Bull's Favorite Pieces*), ed. F. A. Reissiger (Christiania: Warmuth, 1880), and in an arrangement for janissary (brass) band in a hand copy (Bergen Offentlige Bibliotek).

24. Some examples are in the University of Oslo Library. See the List of Works, especially section B.

Example 21.1. "Grand March" from *In Memory of Washington*

derer" who arrived one day sometime before 1865 at the Olsen farm and taught the tune to Olsen's father, himself a young boy at the time.[25] According to the son, Christian Olsen, who wrote the tune down, it derived originally from Paganini. From Paganini to Ole Bull to the "wanderer" to Olsen senior to his son Christian Olsen, one can only wonder what is left of Bull in this piece.

Many were eager to exploit the popularity of Bull's name. In the years after his highly successful first tour of the United States from 1843 to 1845, the American public, ready to buy anything with Bull's name on it, fell victim to commercial gimmicks. From 1844 and on into the early 1850s, there appeared in Philadelphia, Boston, and New York various editions of music that capitalized on Bull's name. Joseph Labitzky (1802–81) published *Ole Bull's Waltzes, as Performed at the American Institute, with Enthusiastic Applause, by Ole Bull* (New York, 1844) (no. B4). These waltzes were written by Labitzky, and it is not likely that Bull had any part in their publication.

An *Ole Bull Violin Instruction Book* appeared from Keith's Music Publishing House (Boston, 1845) (no. B5). There is no indication that the violinist had any part in this method book either. Rather, because the collection contains many "Ethiopian" melodies—"Negro Jig," "Old Joe," and "Pea Patch Jig," a repertoire appropriate for a minstrel show—another composer may be responsible for this book. Frederick Buckley, who played violin, viola, melophone, and "tamburini" and called himself "Ole Bull, junior" or "Master Ole Bull,"[26] is possibly that author. He was a member of the minstrel troupe called the New Orleans Serenaders or New Orleans Operatic Serenaders. While most publications give his name as "Ole Bull, junior" or "Master Ole Bull" (nos. D1-D7) and thus at least marginally differentiate him from the famous violinist Bull, the delicate distinction could easily have been lost on the public.

It will suffice to mention only one example of Master Ole Bull (Buckley's) limited craft, a song with piano accompaniment, "Awake my Love for Me: A Serenade" (no. D7) with a three-verse text by James T. W. Coffroth and a dedication to Miss F. T. Barnard (Boston, 1850). The song structure is of the simplest type, a verse (4 + 4 bars) and a refrain (4 + 4 bars) with an eight-bar introduction and four-bar coda for piano. The melody is in sentimental, popular style, and the harmonies never leave the tonic and dominant. The piece contains nothing of violinist Ole Bull's style; the

---

25. It was published in Torpelund par Eskebjerg, Denmark, by Christian Olsen, 1926.
26. George C. D. Odell, *Annals of the New York Stage* (New York, 1931), 5:490, 498.

melody is neither operatic nor folklike in origin, and it does not even display any distinctive features of its own.

Ole Bull's first tour of the United States brought other hangers-on. American publishers, capitalizing on his fame, issued easy-to-play piano arrangements of his best-known tunes. (Later the Norwegian publisher Warmuth, with "Sæter Girl's Sunday," did the same thing by issuing nineteen different instrumental arrangements.) Three of these American commercial editions have already been mentioned, the march from *Cuban Potpourri,* the march from *In Memory of Washington,* and a piece newly titled *Bellone,* really the polonaise from *Polacca Guerriera.*

Another arrangement of the same sort, a waltz called *La Belle Fanny* (no. B1) arranged by A. Foreit, cannot with certainty be identified as originally by Bull himself.[27] However, because the melody later appears in two hand-written collections[28] made by Norwegians, Ole Tobias Olsen and Anders Moestue, this piece probably belongs among the violinist's works. Its tune was probably extracted from one of Bull's larger, now lost works.

Bull tailored his music to the differing publics all over the world and gained monumental success doing so. A measure of that success was in the hand-copies that admirers like Olsen and Moestue made of the melodies they enjoyed. Music publishers and enterprising individuals like Master Ole Bull saw a very different angle to Bull's successful public image, its financial potential. They, in turn, capitalized on his name and his image, not always in ethical ways, and in so doing furthered their own commercial enterprises.

27. Boston: G. P. Reed, 1845. It has been catalogued under both Ole Bull and Ole Bull, junior.
28. In the University of Oslo Library.

22

The Norwegian Style

B ULL'S INTEREST in Norwegian music was active throughout his life. Not only did he play the *slåtts* he had learned from country fiddlers (see chap. 18), he also composed in the Norwegian idiom. These pieces have a different purpose from his international works, emphasizing as they do his national heritage. They were intended to fire up Bull's Norwegian audiences and to educate his international ones to the cause of Norway.

Among these Norwegian works are the only pieces Bull wrote that are not for violin, as well as many composed for his own violin performances. These compositions use a potpourri organization, relying on the straightforward phrase construction and appeal of folk or popular tunes and sometimes on a story to organize and color this music. They seem to resemble most closely the ethnic works discussed in chapter 21, and there are similar problems in studying these Norwegian works. Many compositions are lost; surviving ones have varying titles, and many do not include everything that Bull actually played in his concerts.

For these Norwegian works Bull used either genuine folk tunes or invented ones in the style of the folk music. Since he had learned Norwegian folk music directly from the Hardanger fiddle players, he understood the many alternate tunings necessary to play their tunes. He had learned their several types of pieces: *huldreslåtts* (tunes from *huldre* or mountain creatures), hallings, springars, and gangars; and he had absorbed the various characteristics of these tunes: their modal basis, their raised fourths and flatted sevenths, their varied repetition of phrases, their repetitions that formed sequences, their simple harmonies made up of intervals of open fourths or fifths, and their frequent drone basses. The folk style also included elaboration through improvised ornamentation. Bull included these characteristics in his nationalistic compositions. At home in Norway, these folk traits encouraged nationalistic enthusiasm, while abroad the same compositions had a special exotic flavor for his foreign audiences. With their melodies interlaced with modal or pentatonic folk formulas but accompanied by diatonic harmonies, these compositions sounded completely different from his Italian-style pieces (see chap. 20).

Bull did not really have enough time in his busy life to assimilate folk music fully,[1] and it was never an object of serious, consistent research nor an overriding principle in his composition. He used folk tunes, rather, as statements of nationalism, as vehicles for improvisation, or simply as encores to his concerts.

The Norwegian influence was the earliest one on his compositions. These native nationalist leanings show already in his choice of texts for his early songs. These songs, composed in Christiania in 1829, have nationalistically based texts: "Hymn to Freedom" (no. 4) and "Thunder" (no. 5) by Wergeland. They are mentioned in a letter to his father but are apparently lost.

How Bull exhibited *musically* his personal call to the cause of Norwegian nationalism can be seen in the first surviving works. Probably influenced by his contact with Augundson in 1831, he wrote *The Mountains of Norway* (no. 7); it included the Hardanger fiddle and its folk melodies. This piece was first named *Souvenirs de Norvège* (1832–33) and is probably the same piece called *Norges Fjelde* or *The Mountains of Norway* after 1833.[2] He also later titled it *Fjeldenes Echo* (*Mountain Echo*), *Norwegers Traum und Heimweh* (*A Norwegian's Dream and Homesick Longing*),[3] *Norwegian's Lament for Home*, *Norske Fjeldtoner* (*Norwegian Mountain Tones*), and *Reminiscenses de mon berceau* (*Remembrances of my Childhood*). In the first version the Hardanger fiddle was accompanied by string quartet, double bass, and flute. Bull played this piece often on his tours and varied it as the years went by. In the reworkings he changed the Hardanger fiddle part to a violin part, and in some concerts he was accompanied by piano or even played unaccompanied. He composed this piece for his earliest triumphs in Italy and was still playing it nearly fifty years later (at his last public concert, 22 May 1880). The piece exists only incompletely: of the later violin and orchestra version there survives only

1. Kristian Lange and Arne Østvedt, *Norwegian Music: A Brief Survey* (London: 1958), 25.

2. Herman Severin Løvenskiold (1815–70) used the title *Les Souvenirs de la Norvège* in 1831. See Ole Nørlyng, "Les Souvenirs de la Norvège: Om Komponisten Herman Severin Løvenskiolds norske Klaverværker opus 3, 1831," *Studia musicologica* 8 (1982): 159.

3. Henrik Wergeland, "Ole Bull: Efter opgivelser af ham selv biografisk skildret," in D. A. Seip, ed., *Samlede Skrifter* (Oslo, 1927), 4.5:210, 220.

the oboe 1, bassoon 2, and bass drum parts; the solo violin part and remaining accompaniment parts are lost.[4] Based on these few parts, *The Mountains of Norway* seems to be a sectional piece—a medley, a mosaic, or a potpourri are perhaps the best descriptions—of folk tunes. Two dance tunes can be identified, a halling and a final springar. A "Polskdands" (published separately for piano but titled as part of *Norges Fjelde*) seems to fit into the nineteen-measure "Più lento" section in the orchestral parts, although the cadence must have been altered for the piano arrangement. The orchestral parts indicate that there is one accompanied "variation" of a tune and another unaccompanied "variation" for violin alone, the second one was perhaps to be an improvisation. Finally a fermata near the end of the piece allows the performer to insert a cadenza in order to demonstrate technical brilliance.

The surviving treasure which corroborates that Bull's folk-melody works were medley or potpourri pieces (as Kjerulf called them) is *Visit to the Sæter* (*Et Sæterbesøg*, no. 53). This piece became one of Bull's most frequently performed works. His most dramatic performance of it was atop the Cheops tomb in 1876 where (as might be expected) he played it as an unaccompanied solo; it is otherwise a violin and orchestra piece. This composition was first titled *December 10* because it was written after the occasion on 10 December 1848 at Det norske Studentersamfund in Christiania where Bull had played a single halling and whetted the audience's appetite for more folk music.[5] At its first performance on 10 March 1849, the piece was still called *December 10,* but already in the summer of 1849 it had acquired its final title, *Visit to the Sæter.*

The music of the first version is lost, but it must have been somewhat different from the surviving versions (an 1865 orchestra score and a violin-piano arrangement).[6] Handwritten copies of the concluding Nordhordland halling transcribed to show how Bull played it in the early years differ from the later full versions of the piece.[7] These two later versions are alike in structure and probably reflect Bull's 1864 revisions.

4. The surviving pages are in the University of Oslo Library in a copyist's hand. They come from the same incomplete orchestra-part collection as the *Concerto in A Major.*

5. See List of Works, no. B10. A transcription of that particular halling is in the Bergen Offentlige Bibliotek.

6. Both are in a copyist's hand. There are also surviving orchestra parts. All are in the University of Oslo Library. The violin-piano arrangement was posthumously published in 1885 by Warmuth.

7. The halling was transcribed twice by Sophonias Christian Krag who heard the whole piece played on 29 March 1849, and once by Ivar R. Eide. These manuscripts are in, respectively, the Bergen Offentlige Bibliotek and the University of Oslo Library.

Visit to the Sæter brillantly captures the Norwegian spirit. The violin's gangar melody is particularly characteristic of Hardanger fiddle *slåtts* in its rhythm, melodic shape, and motivic connections. Two of the subsequent tunes are actual folk songs, "Eg ser deg ut'for gluggen" ("I See You Outside the Window") and "Den bakvendte visa" ("The Backwards Song"). "Aa so sudla ho mor paa rokkjen sin" ("And Then Mother is Humming with her Spinning Wheel"), a Nordhordland halling that Bull learned in his childhood, closes the piece.[8] Bull composed one melody of his own for this piece which was later called "Sæter Girl's Sunday" (no. 53a). It too is in folksong style with characteristic rising fourth intervals for weak-beat cadences (mm. 130 and 134) (see Example 22.1). Another folk feature of this song is the frequent use of the melodic shape: adjacent intervals of a third and a second moving in the same direction (mm. 127, 128, etc.). (This device is also prevalent in Grieg's folk-style melodies.) The song has a traditional

Example 22.1. *Visit to the Sæter:* "Sæter Girl's Sunday," mm. 126–34

8. Arne Bjørndal, "Ole Bull og folkemusikken," in Torleiv Hannaas, ed., *Norsk Årbok* (Bergen, 1922), 14.

folk-song structure: five four-bar phrases balanced in an AA′BAA′ plan.[9]
Visit to the Sæter loosely tells a story by linking the melodies succes-
sively. According to a newspaper account based on Bull's description, the
piece opens with cow bells and the cuckoo in the mountains.[10] The sæter
girl sings longingly of her love. Then her love is heard playing a halling,
but "den Gamle" (an old man) who opposes the match is asleep in her
cottage. The girls warns her love by singing "I See You Outside the Window," and he goes away unhappily singing "The Backwards Song." When
the old man leaves, she sings again, now a song "with characteristics of
an authentic mountain tune" (Bull's own description of his "Sæter Girl's
Sunday") and a halling at the end represents the joyous arrival of the young
lover.[11] A similar version of this story appeared in the concert program
of Christian Suckow who performed this piece in 1879. A Norwegian audience would have been able to follow the story in a general way because
they would have recognized the folk tunes and known the texts for them.

Although *Visit to the Sæter* is made of successive melodies, one mark
of musical unity is the reminiscence of the opening cuckoo motive. Another unifying bit of material is the plaintive oboe theme that opens the
piece in minor and then evolves into the 6/8 gangar melody in major (see
Examples 22.2 and 22.3). The opening oboe theme's mm. 13–14 are also
similar to the Violin I accompaniment to "I See You Outside the Window"
(see Example 22.4).[12] This song alternates with the dance tunes until the
central moment of the piece, where there is a violin cadenza. The improvisa-

13

Example 22.2. *Visit to the Sæter:* Introduction, mm. 9–14

Example 22.3. *Visit to the Sæter:* Gangar, mm. 23–29

9. In most arrangements it is shortened to AA′BA′. Sometimes it is lengthened to
AA′BA′BA′. Example 22.1 is from the violin/piano edition of 1885.
10. *Morgenbladet* (10 March 1849).
11. Ola Linge, *Ole Bull: Livshistoria, Mannen, Kunstnaren* (Oslo, 1953), 176–77.
12. Examples 22.2–22.4 are from the copyist's orchestra score. For Example 22.3, the
score has an extra measure after m. 25. It is deleted in the example. In Example 22.4, m. 55,
third eighth-note, the copyist incorrectly had c″ in the melody.

Example 22.4. *Visit to the Sæter:* "I See You Outside the Window," mm. 53–58

tion and expansion by the violinist is followed by three remaining tunes which balance the opening material. The final lively halling concludes with a violin flourish.

Bull's most famous composition, "Sæter Girl's Sunday" (no. 53a), is derived from *Visit to the Sæter* (see mm. 126–134 shown above). Jørgen Moe's text, "På solen jeg ser" ("I Look at the Sun"), was added soon after the piece was first performed, and as a separate song it has become a national treasure. The same melody also appeared as a solo song under the title "Norsk Frihedsmarsch" ("Norwegian Freedom March") with a text by Tønnes Rolfsen, "Fædreneland! fra fjeldtop til strand" ("Fatherland! from Mountain Top to Shore"). This version was used for the festivities of 17 May 1850.[13] The melody has appeared with many other titles, for example "Til Sæters" ("To the Sæter"). As "Die Sonne scheint Hell" ("The sun shines clearly") (Cologne, 1926), it was arranged for men's chorus with soprano solo; and as "Solitude on the Mountain" (Boston, 1919), it was arranged for organ. Wilhelm Hansen of Copenhagen published at least nineteen such arrangements including one for cello and harmonium! Bull's own freedom with this melody is shown in a comment from his accompanist Aubertine Woodward Moore. Moore said that Bull sometimes improvised on the tune unaccompanied and other times asked Moore to join in by indicating verbally which chords he wanted to support his improvisations.[14]

Bull's free approach to his own melody shows that he treated it in the same manner as a folk tune. A long list of such genuine or composed folk tunes appears on his programs or as encores. Some were arranged in advance; others were improvised on the spot. These works are different from

13. A photograph of the 1850 version is in Linge, *Ole Bull,* 369; also see Ola Linge, "Når skrev Ole Bull melodien som blev 'Sæterjentens Søndag'?" *Aftenposten* (10 November 1934), and C. H. Barth, "Har 'Sæterjentens Søndag' vært 17-mai marsj?" *Morgenavisen* (16 May 1950).

14. Aubertine Woodward Moore, "The Real Ole Bull: Personal Reminiscences," *Etude* 30.4 (1912): 251. The story attributed to Grieg—that he was amazed when Bull could not harmonize his own "Sæter Girl's Sunday"—is puzzling since Bull would have already harmonized the tune for the violin-orchestra piece *Visit to the Sæter.*

his medley or potpourri works in that they use a single tune to display Bull's skill at variation and improvisation. The tunes were well known to his Norwegian audiences: "I fjor gjæt' eg gjetinn" ("Last Year I Herded the Goats") (no. 51),[15] "For Norge, Kjæmpers Fødeland" ("For Norway, Land of Heroes") (no. 34),[16] "Liten Karin" ("Little Karin") (a Swedish folk song; no. 38), "Kjæmpeslåtten" ("Giant's Folkdance") (no. 65),[17] and "Aa Kjøre Vatten" ("To Fetch the Water") (no. 27).[18] In the programs and written descriptions, our only sources for information about these pieces, they are described as fantasias, improvisations, or variations. These showpieces were generally unaccompanied, and when playing them Bull used his famous four-voiced (quadruple-stop) harmonies, rapid staccatos, doubled-harmonics, and arpeggios. Throughout Bull's life he improvised such pieces on Norwegian themes.

Besides his medleys and his improvisations on Norwegian tunes, in December of 1849 Bull composed some incidental music for an intensely nationalistic play, *Fjeldstuen* (*The Mountain Cottage*) by Wergeland. This play was ideal for Bull's new Norwegian theater in Bergen (at a time when Bull himself still felt complete loyalty to Norway) because it opposed emigration and glorified Norway. The play had originally contained melodies borrowed from Thrane and Bjerregaard's *Fjeldeventyret* (1824) (*Mountain Adventure*) (for example, "Aagot's Mountain Song") as well as folk tunes.[19] Bull's new music (no. 56), first used for the 13 January 1850 performance, included an orchestra overture (lost) and music for chorus and various songs. The surviving music consists of four songs in an autograph at the Library of Congress.[20]

"Afsted over Hav!" ("Away Over the Ocean") (no. 56a) for treble chorus in unison is accompanied by an orchestra: strings, flutes, clarinets, bassoons, trumpets, French horns, trombones, and timpani. Like the "Huldresang" ("Huldre Song") (no. 56d) that closes the play, it has a short instrumental introduction. Next is a separate brief chorus for women

---

15. 1848 program; Linge, *Ole Bull*, 353–54.

16. Ibid., 135.

17. Program 1861.

18. 1838; Linge, *Ole Bull*, 112.

19. Theodore C. Blegen and Martin B. Ruud, eds., *Norwegian Emigrant Songs and Ballads* (Minneapolis, 1936), 78.

20. The two choruses (nos. 56a and b) are duplicated in another hand on a single leaf at the Theater Archive of the University of Bergen. The melody to "Sigrid's Song" (no. 56c) (Bull's hand) with piano accompaniment (Otto Winter-Hjelm's hand?) is on a single sheet at the University of Oslo Library, and according to Linge, *Ole Bull*, 365, the melody is also in draft at Lysøen.

singing in unison "Holdt nu, Lensmand" ("Stop Now, Mayor") (no. 56b). This chorus is accompanied by strings, and in the "Efterspill" ("Postlude") there is an oboe motive. In the third song, "Sigrids sang" ("Sigrid's Song") (no. 56c), Sigrid pledges to wait for her love with the text "Her, hvor i alt" ("Here, Where in Everything"). In the Library of Congress manuscript, it is titled only by these first words of text and is for female solo voice with strings, flutes, clarinets, and bassoons. Only one verse of text is included, but the song clearly has three verses because new music is provided for a third-verse ending. "Sigrid's Song" later became popular enough to be arranged for men's chorus by Johan Didrik Behrens (1820–90) with the title "Den forladte" ("The Abandoned One"). Finally, the "Huldre Song" (no. 56d) with the text "Saa ganger nu ind" ("Go in Now") closes the play with the hope that the emigrants will return to Norway. The song is Bull's arrangement of an existing "Air Norvégien" (a folk melody) for female solo voice (the *huldre,* a female spirit), strings, flutes, clarinets, bassoons, and timpani.[21]

These four simple, tuneful songs are completely in folk character, three of the four with lilting 3/8 or 6/8 meter and three of the four in minor. Prominent use of the sixth and seventh degrees of the minor scale, the raised fourth of the major scale, and cadences on weak beats with rising fourth melodic intervals are characteristic of the folk coloring (see Example 22.5, mm. 3, 4, and Example 22.6, mm. 2, 3, 5). These melodies have been harmonized smoothly and simply with diatonic chords that are sometimes enriched with repeating chords or arpeggiation. In these simple songs (nos. 56a–56c) and the song arrangement (no. 56d), Bull shows that he had absorbed the shape and character of Norwegian folk song.

A few other individual songs (like "The Abandoned One," the retitled "Sigrid's Song") have become part of Bull's legacy with Norwegian choruses. As arranged by Behrens they have become in effect composed folk songs. *Kunstens Magt (The Power of Art)* (no. 58) was originally for men's chorus and orchestra and was composed for a fund-raising event in Christiania (15 October 1851) for Bull's Bergen theater. "I ensomme Stunde" ("In Mo-

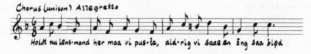

Example 22.5. *The Mountain Cottage:* "Stop Now, Mayor"

21. This "Air Norvégien" with Wergeland's text is included in the first edition of Wergeland's *Fjeldstuen* that was published in 1848.

Example 22.6. *The Mountain Cottage:* "Sigrid's Song" ("Here, Where in Everything"). Autograph, Music Division, Library of Congress, Washington, D.C.

ments of Solitude") (no. 66)[22] and "I granskoven" ("In the Spruce Forest") (no. 67) were first heard as solo songs, sung by H. Brun and accompanied by Erika Lie, in one of Bull's own concerts (Christiania, 1863).[23] "In Moments of Solitude" has been arranged again and again, not only for men's voices but even for mandolin and piano. It is best known in a string quintet arrangement by Johan Halvorsen (1864–1935) retitled "La mélancolie." This simple folk-style melody with slightly irregular phrase structure (4–4–3–4–4 bars in an AA'BCD pattern) is in minor with the seventh degree using both sharp and natural forms (see Example 22.7).

22. The possibility exists, since this melody is preserved in the midst of a set of Bull's folk tune transcriptions (no. B12), that it is a folk melody and not by Bull.

23. Øyvind Anker, "Et ukjent Manuskript av Ole Bull," *Norsk Musikkliv* 15 (1948): 16–17.

Example 22.7. *In Moments of Solitude,* page 1 of 2. Autograph, Oslo University Library.

Bull's Norwegian musical style, both in the pieces written for himself and in those written for others, ran like a thread through his tumultuous life and career, continually reaffirming his pride in his Norwegian heritage. He wrote these pieces in order to serve the cause of the Norwegian people, to boost their confidence in themselves and identify them to the world as a people. His Norwegian works were never the mainstay of his professional existence and concert giving. Yet, for Norwegians and Norwegian-Americans today, it is this small body of musical literature that preserves Bull's musical reputation. His Norwegian song melodies "In Moments of Solitude" and "Sæter Girl's Sunday" are still taught to Norwegian schoolchildren, and modern Norwegians and Norwegian-Americans esteem "Sæter Girl's Sunday" as a well-worn, well-loved folk song. Perhaps most indicative of its pervasiveness in Norwegian culture today is that "Sæter Girl's Sunday" is one of the background themes for Norwegian broadcasts on international short-wave radio, surely a sign of Ole Bull's success in composing music that would reveal the face of his beloved Norway to the world.

Part 3

EPILOGUE:
THE MAN
AND THE MYTH

23

The Man

THE LYRICAL extravaganzas of journalists who have portrayed Ole Bull leave little room for sober consideration of his physical appearance as a human being. Dr. Alpheus Benning Crosby, professor of anatomy at Bellevue Hospital Medical College in New York City, wrote an anatomy of Bull in 1877 analyzing his physique in detail, with special attention to the way he held his violin.

The pose of Mr. Bull when playing is a model of manly grace. He rests his body centrally over the left leg as a firm column of support, while the right foot is advanced and the right leg forms an oblique brace. . . . The figure is singularly erect, nor does the head incline like that of the ordinary violinist. . . . The bust, which has been superbly developed by a lifetime of musical gymnastics, measures on full inspiration forty-two inches; and although the years have increased, the waist measure remains exactly the same. Mr. Bull's height in his stocking feet is five feet eleven and a quarter inches. As he stands before an audience waiting for his accompaniment, with his narrow waist, his superb bust, his finely cut face, and the carriage of a prince, he is the incarnation of Magnus Apollo.[1]

Bjørnstjerne Bjørnson offers a more poetic portrait of the violinist in a letter he wrote in 1859:

His entry into a room strikes everything else down, and yet it is modest. But it is so wonderfully undaunted, so cheerful, so self-contained, so smiling, so confident — and modest. His eyes are so unfathomably warm, dreamy, expressive, changeful, his eyebrows like a forest, but gloriously formed; no portrait of him but is wooden. His face cannot be grasped; you can only imagine with what force he is present in any idea he has conceived. His mouth is ironic but melancholy, his chin small, cleft, sage, coquettish; it has dimples. Around his eyes are marked protuberances, as on all Nordic faces; his forehead is roundish without a single projection, broad, curved like the back of a violin. . . . He is slender, broadshouldered, narrow as a virgin around the waist, and the chest from the arms to

1. Sara C. Bull, *Ole Bull: A Memoir* (Boston and New York: 1882), 330–31.

271

the hips is round as if he were turned on a lathe. He has the strength of many men, his arms are like steel, you can't insert a finger or a line, his hands are sinewy, energetic and so expressive that I have never seen such a revelation of character in a hand, it must be because they serve his spirit so faithfully. . . .[2]

There is little we need add to Bjørnson's portrait except to say that Bull had reddish-brown hair in his youth, turning to grayish-white in his forties, and his smile was apparently very winning.

Because he had associated with many southern Europeans, Bull had a special way of being attentive to women that some Norwegians regarded as affected. On a trip across Lake Mjøsa he met the twenty-one-year-old author Elise Aubert, who wrote about him to her mother:

He is gallant like a Frenchman. He talked nonsense to a fare-thee-well, spoke compliments and fished for compliments back. . . . But his appearance is delightful — his intelligent, handsome face, his clear, beautiful eyes — his modest expression, and his delightful lock of hair — the figure, the position, the way in which he has lined his cloak with silken velvet — the virtuosity with which he saw to it that the public could observe the large diamonds on the buttons of his sleeves — it all gave the impression of something extraordinary.[3]

Bull's perhaps most noticeable trait of character was a streak of childlike innocence, a personal nonchalance that was highly appealing. In 1843 Adam Oehlenschläger, the Danish poet and dramatist, met Bull as a fellow passenger on the boat from Copenhagen to Christiania. In his *Erindringer (Memoirs)* he wrote: "When Bull had displeased me once by too exaggeratedly picking away at the Swedes, I went over and sat on a bench. Soon after he came crawling on all fours towards me, barking like a dog. This was an original and charming way of bringing about a reconciliation and getting the offended person to laugh."[4] Bull's capacity for childlike enthusiasms often surprised and charmed people, even those who did not know him well. A New Orleans book dealer, for example, who sold tickets for Bull's concerts reported that he went up to Bull's hotel room only to find Bull happily playing on the floor with his vocal soloist of the evening, ten-year-old Adelina Patti.[5] She had gotten him to play a game of pick-up-sticks with her. The American writer Eleanor Hallowell Abbott (1872–1958), who grew up as a neighbor to the Bulls in Cambridge, told a similar story of his playfulness. She recalled that as a four-year-old she arranged

2. Ola Linge, *Ole Bull: Livshistoria, Mannen, Kunstnaren* (Oslo, 1953), 295–96. Bjørnstjerne Bjørnson, *Brev*, ed. Halvdan Koht (Christiania, 1912), 1:82.
3. Elise Aubert, *Fra Krinoline-Tiden* (Christiania, 1921), 81–82.
4. Linge, *Ole Bull*, 299.
5. Ibid., 300.

a "bazaar" with Bull before the livingroom fireplace. He "not only played but he sang! He not only sang but he danced! Free and untrammeled as a gypsy he wove, foot, fiddle, and voice, his fantastic, folk-lorish sort of rhapsody in and out among the enchanted company."[6]

Bull's temperament was as labile as a child's, moving from humor, jests, and play to depression and tragedy. In many of his letters there is evidence of what can only be described as a form of emotional hypochondria. At the age of nineteen he wrote to his father from Christiania: "No wonder if I am sometimes shaken by hard blows which often strike me and threaten to destroy me (I hope to my advantage and benefit). I will not lose my courage, but believe that we are not put into this world to dance on roses. . . . Do not scold me for seeing the world from too dark a side. I comfort myself by thinking that a crust will form around my heart, but when it is torn away, the pain is so much the greater."[7]

This pain was sometimes overwhelming. In 1834, fearing that he was somehow at death's door, he wrote: "My nervous system is terribly irritated. Heaven knows if I will ever see you again, dear mother and dear father. . . ." In November 1835 he wrote to his mother: "I can never become happy. Sufferings are my sustenance. I will give my anxious heart air. Loneliness is my friend, perhaps the only true one I possess. It accompanies me in my throes of death, on the stage, amidst the applauding public, and sits beside me in my silent chamber at this moment."[8]

Even after his triumphs in Paris he wrote of similar feelings. Immediately after his marriage to Félicie he wrote to her from Bath in a melancholy vein: "I fear I may never see you again. I feel so ill at heart and in my head, and often I have a strong trembling. My eyes are so tired and my breast is as if it were slashed by a knife. . . . If my powers should not be equal to my will and I should succumb, remember you have been loved."[9] One wonders how the young bride received such laments. Eventually she must have learned to discount them.

There is no doubt that Bull enjoyed calling attention to himself. In view of his acknowledged physical strength, his health, and his survival into his seventieth year, he probably exaggerated the physical pain he may have had. His complaints seem rather to be an expression of his abnormal sen-

---

6. Eleanor Hallowell Abbott, *Being Little in Cambridge, When Everyone Else was Big* (New York, 1936), 150.

7. Linge, *Ole Bull*, 35–36 (9 December 1829).

8. Ibid., 61 (2 February 1834) and 79 (21 November 1835).

9. Alexander Bull, ed., *Ole Bulls Breve i Uddrag. Med en karakteristik og biografisk Skitse af Jonas Lie* (Copenhagen, 1881), 191 (5 December 1836).

sitivity and awareness of feeling and emotion, particularly the dark side.

Another expression of this sensitivity can be found in his many quarrels and court cases. He tended to see plots and what he called "cabals" all around him, beginning with his years in Paris. There is evidence of this in his quarrel with Morandi in England, in his conflict with the French artists in New York, in his defiance of the police in Bergen, and in the falling out with his impresario Schuberth in America. His extraordinary skill with the violin no doubt built up in him a sense of complete mastery and control, and consequently other matters perhaps easily caused annoyance if they did not go smoothly for him. In spite of Bull's hypochondria and suspicions and quarrels, however, he was extremely generous in giving benefit concerts to help others. And he valued friendship. In later years he kindly looked up former associates and friends, for example, his old music teacher Paulsen or even his former rival Vieuxtemps in Belgium.

One trait that runs through Bull's career is his impracticality, particularly his irresponsible handling of money. His American protégé Rasmus B. Anderson told of a trip with Bull to a bank in Norway. Bull had a bundle of money wrapped in a daily newspaper and gave it over to Anderson while he (Bull) went for a walk. When he got coins in change, Bull "handed a part of it to me and put the rest inside his vest pocket. The bag containing the rest of the gold he threw carelessly into his valise among his linen and underwear."[10]

Most of the enterprises he undertook that involved monetary transactions, like his Norwegian Theater, his Music Academy, the New York opera, or his Oleana colony, were financial disasters. In part this was due to inadequate preparation; Bull simply tossed out bright and impulsive ideas with little notion of what they might lead to. Their failure also resulted from his impatience; he easily abandoned his projects in mid-course. If he had been foresighted and disciplined, he perhaps would not have been the butt of so many pranks. But his impulsive and impractical nature was also the force that stimulated and drove his efforts toward Norwegian national advancement.

Bull can be characterized as a typical romantic visionary. He was not dreamy, sentimental, or reticent, like Chopin or Schumann. He was more active, more revolutionary, like Wergeland, Shelley, Byron, Hugo, or Liszt. Already by the age of twenty-six, he had declared his romantic code of honor to his father: "Independence is not too dearly bought for a proud man—. Life is freedom, slavery is death. Without battle no victory, with-

10. Rasmus B. Anderson, *Life Story* (Madison, Wis., 1915), 149.

out victory no freedom. 'Vita bellum—bellum vita' is my motto."[11] Throughout his life, he remained vigorous in defense of the principle of freedom, even though he made enemies by his agitation and despite the fact that this behavior deviated from bourgeois American norms and upset his later American family.

At the age of thirty-one, when he had been married for five years, had become a father and lost his first son, and had known his first brilliant success in Europe, Bull offered this slightly reformulated view of life in a guest book dedication for the Polish writer Edmond Choieck in Warsaw: "Those who are slaves of the material life, who strive for honor and let themselves be daunted by mishaps, those who know nothing but unworthy or indifferent vices, they say that life is but a dream. But the god-fearing man who believes in progress and sacrifices himself working for humanity, shows clearly by the happiness he gives to others that life is a reality."[12]

Although Bull presumably speaks here of himself as a "god-fearing man," it is not clear how prominent a role his religious beliefs played in his life. As a child he was brought up as a Lutheran and remained so until he was confirmed. In letters to Félicie he emphasized the power of prayer and his reliance on God, but in later life he evidently became a pantheist after the model of Victor Hugo. He seems to have felt some kind of connection with supernatural spirits, but there is no evidence of any deep reality of these in his life.[13]

For all Bull's magnetism as a violinist, he was not a great orator. Even so, he enjoyed giving speeches, especially on festive occasions, and he was proud of his voice, whose carrying power he would often demonstrate. On the occasion of Bull's fiftieth birthday, composer Rikard Nordraak transcribed the following speech, which is typical of Bull's enthusiasm on such occasions. He told his audience to be happy about being born as citizens of Norway.

I know of no people more favored by divinity in having been given their own laws in agreement with their wills and character. . . . If God grants me, a humble sinner, some years still to live among the mountains of Norway, I shall always strive to attain what has been my highest goal, that Norwegians should understand my art, for this would give me full assurance of being national, for which I have always struggled. Therefore I thank God who has let me drink my mother's milk and grow up here in Norway, which inspired me with the direction in music that I have followed. May Norway in the future foster many sons of art who will be able to glorify her name![14]

11. Linge, *Ole Bull*, 313 (Birmingham, 1836).
12. Ibid., 316, cited from La Mara, *Briefe hervorragender Zeitgenossen* 1895 (1 April 1841).
13. Linge, *Ole Bull*, 308–309.
14. Nordraak in 1860; cited in Linge, *Ole Bull*, 316.

Bull was especially concerned about the welfare of the common people, which in Norwegian politics made him a supporter of the liberal (Venstre) party. In 1849 a local Bergen paper wrote that "Ole Bull has been flattered by high and low, even the highest, but the elegant life of the salon has not been able to win him for the views of the aristocrats. Royal orders and expensive presents have not made him an adherent of princely power. His heart beats for the people. He is a democrat in the word's noblest sense; though he abhors mob rule and the red republic just as much as the red reactionaries and the absolute power of kings."[15]

As far as his work for Norway is concerned, he constituted a living link between the work of Henrik Wergeland and the writings of Bjørnstjerne Bjørnson. Inspired by Wergeland, Bull recognized in Bjørnson a disciple who would follow in his footsteps. The Norwegian author Christian Gierløff (1879–1962) has written that these three men constituted a "powerful harmonic chord of nationality."[16]

Bull's work on behalf of Norway was at the same time work on behalf of music, and through music of humanity. In the United States he was even more loved than in Norway, and while he always emphasized his Norwegian roots, he was a powerful force in bringing music and musical knowledge to every corner of America.

Finally we may ask whether we are justified in calling Bull a genius. One of the most striking images of Bull's personality is found in his first biographer Jonas Lie's comparison of him to the frigate bird.

This is the world's largest and most powerful bird. It can fly from Africa to South America. . . . It has incredible sharpness of sight, but its feet are too short to catch its prey except by rapid swoops. Ole Bull was such a frigate bird, whose genius had given him the wing power to fly from San Francisco to Odessa. Everywhere he earned money and honor, fame and flowers were strewn on him as for one of the few chosen ones of art; but everywhere he also bore with him the consciousness that his musical skill for this life was not quite mature enough to seize the big compositions, the universal musical views, which actually lay unborn and sang and dreamed for life in his soul. Now and then this need broke through like a volcanic geyser into a new and original melody or a tonal sequence that contained the basic kernel of a composition which he would never be able to make wholly transparent.[17]

15. *Bergens Stiftstidende* (19 July 1849); cf. Linge, *Ole Bull,* 317.
16. Linge, *Ole Bull,* 319.
17. Bull, ed., *Ole Bulls Breve i Uddrag,* 8–10; cf. Hans Midbøe, *Dikteren og det Primitive* (Oslo, 1964), 13–14.

24

The Myth

THE FIGURE of Ole Bull retained an aura of magic for a long time, an aura that has not yet been entirely dispelled, even in America. He lived in an era when public dissemination of information was still extremely limited. It was chiefly spread through newspapers or journals that appeared at intervals and with a small readership. The Bull mythology grew from numerous other sources, but part of it did come through the limited media of his day.

Bull did not begin his public self-advertising until well after his triumphs in Italy in the early 1830s. His first use of it was the French pamphlet written for him in 1835 by F. Morand. This referred to his contacts with Bériot and Malibran and included Janin's enthusiastic first review. Morand alluded facetiously to the Villeminots' street address in Rue des Martyrs: "Martyr, heaven awaits you" and announced that "in Trieste was born the man of genius."[1] There Bull had surpassed Paganini by first executing "quadruple staccatos" (quadruple stops), and in "Italy he was called 'the man of sound,' as Malibran was 'the lady of song.'"[2] According to Ola Linge, "it is from this brochure that most of the erroneous 'stories' have come that are repeated in biographies and in all reference books in all countries."[3] This puff preceded Bull's September concerts in Paris, after which Janin's praise rang out all the way to Norway.

Morand's pamphlet was followed in 1838 by Hermann Biow's Hamburg brochure, which included a handsome picture of Bull, engraved by Biow himself. He also included a sketch of Bull's career, followed with German translations of a dozen notices from the English press on Bull's 1836

1. F. Morand, *Notice sur Ole Bull* (Boulogne, 1835), 11.
2. Ibid., 14.
3. Ola Linge, *Ole Bull: Livshistoria, Mannen, Kunstnaren* (Oslo, 1953), 11.

tour of Great Britain.⁴ These had already appeared in French translation on a broadsheet of that year.⁵ In 1839 Hans Christian Andersen published his version of "An Episode of Ole Bull's Life," "told according to the artist's own oral account."⁶

This amount of self-generated publicity inevitably aroused criticism in the musical circles of Scandinavia. The opposition stemmed from Sweden, first from editor Rosén in 1838 and then from harpist Pratté in 1843 (both printed in Danish), as we have recounted above (see chap. 8). In 1839 Rosén's critique was taken up by the German musical editor Fink (see chap. 8) who also adhered to the stricter canon of the German style of composition (see chap. 19).

It was to refute these critiques that his old friend and fellow Romantic Henrik Wergeland took up the cudgels for Bull in 1843. The result was a full account of Bull's life, based in part on news stories of Bull's concerts and partly on Bull's own narrative. Wergeland's biography became a friendly farewell on the eve of Bull's departure for America.

Wergeland's biography was followed in 1852 by an extended account of Bull's career written by journalist and friend Henrik Winter-Hjelm, who was literary editor of the journal *Norsk Tidskrift for Videnskab og Litteratur* from 1853 to 1855. Winter-Hjelm copied parts of Wergeland's biography, moderating much of Wergeland's poetic enthusiasm. Wergeland had emphasized the value for Norway of Ole Bull's international fame, so that "in Europe Norway should be known otherwise than as a home of barbarians, and in America not only by runaway sailors and ragged emigrants."⁷ Winter-Hjelm's account appeared serially in Norwegian periodicals, not in book form, and it included reports of Bull's American tour.⁸

Another contemporary who often wrote about Ole Bull was his friend from youth Aasmund Olavsson Vinje. As early as 1858 he wrote an account in his journal *Dølen* about their common tour to Hamar and Lillehammer. Vinje admired Bull especially because "he is the first who has artistically used and once again awakened our own music."⁹ When

4. H[ermann] B[iow], *Ole Bull: Eine biographische Skizze* (Hamburg, 1838), 13–36.
5. *Debut des Herrn Ole Bull auf dem King's Theatre*, Paris, n.d. [1836?]; in French, *Début de M. Ole Bull, au Théatre du Roi.*
6. Hans Christian Andersen, "En Episode af Ole Bulls Liv. Fortalt efter Kunstnerens egen muntlige Meddelelser (1839)," in *Samlede Skrifter*, 2d ed. (Copenhagen, 1877), 6:125–128).
7. Henrik Wergeland, "Ole Bull: Efter opgivelser af ham selv biografisk skildret," in D. A. Seip, ed., *Samlede Skrifter* (Oslo, 1927), 4.5:182.
8. Henrik Winter-Hjelm, "Træk af Ole Bulls Liv," *Morgenbladet* (1852).
9. Aasmund Olavsson Vinje, "Olaf Bull reiser til Heidemork," *Dølen* (10 October 1858), 9, 11.

he heard Augundson play in Christiania, Vinje wrote a comparison of the two violinists. "One can weep and laugh, but the other can also add joy to his weeping and sadness in his tone; one gives life, as it is, and the other explains it; one is, in other words, Nature and the other is Art."[10] In a later article Vinje compares Bull with a new German virtuoso, Laub, but he did not find "the same pleasure in Laub's playing as in Ole Bull's." He found that Laub and other German violinists are "objective," while Bull (and Paganini) are "subjective," i.e., they "sin here and there, but they also do so much good that it makes up for its weakness and then some."[11]

In 1862 the Danish romantic author Meïr Goldschmidt also managed to contribute to the myth of Bull's early career through his survey in the English journal *Cornhill Magazine,* under the title "A Norwegian Musician."[12] His account summarizes the fanciful narratives that stemmed from Bull himself. By this time Bull had become his own fairy prince.

The first author to depict Bull as a character in literature was his American friend Longfellow in 1863, possibly at the suggestion of Thackeray. Bull appears as "The Musician" in several sections of his *Tales of a Wayside Inn* (see chap. 14). Although it is not known whether Bull ever visited the Inn, his name is preserved by the proprietors of the Wayside Inn in Sudbury, Massachusetts. There are pictures of Bull on the wall, some signed by him, a piece of music with his signature, and a small archive of mementos.[13]

A second author to seize upon Bull's life and treat it fictionally was the romantic French novelist George Sand (1804–76). Her story *Malgrétout* (1870) takes the form of a letter written by a Miss Owen to her friend Mary, with whom she had been raised to the age of eighteen. She recalls their youth together at an estate named Malgrétout, on the river Meuse in the north of France near the Belgian border. One day, she says, the girls heard a violin being played in the woods, and soon the violinist appeared as "a young man dressed as a tourist and with an agreeable appearance." The player repeated on his violin a tune Miss Owen had been humming, "rendered with a truly admirable improvisation . . . sweet melodies that varied and repeated the theme . . . with the most touching and elevated inspiration."[14]

10. Aasmund Olavsson Vinje, "Myllarguten og Olaf Bull," *Dølen* (14 November 1858), 25.
11. Aasmund Olavsson Vinje, "Nokot um Felespil," *Dølen* (13 May 1860), 328.
12. Meïr Goldschmidt, "A Norwegian Musician," *Cornhill Magazine* 6 (23 April 1862): 514–27.
13. Kindly displayed to the authors by the archivist, Lee Swanson.
14. George Sand, *Malgrétout* (Paris, 1870), 39.

The violinist proves to be "the famous Abel, the incomparable violinist, so refined, so rich, . . . so overwhelmed with gifts from all the sovereigns of Europe, and of whom one said that his bow brought him a hundred thousand francs a year. . . ." Miss Owen is much taken with Monsieur Abel: "I look, I think, I talk, I act, and I work to break with all that is the rule in the world's etiquette." Abel has a companion named Monsieur Neuville, "who did not have like Abel the gift of happy improvisation, the creative fire, the idea in itself. . . . Abel is the greatest prince, the only great prince of the earth! It is magnificence allied with simplicity, the ingenious prodigality of Providence. . . . The following year he traveled through America and earned enough to pay for his instrument, for they trusted him on his word, which was known to be sacred and inviolable."[15]

The story of Abel goes on in a different direction from the life of Ole Bull, but there is reason to suppose that Bull was the model for Sand's Abel. It is not known whether she ever met Bull, but she could have heard him or heard about him from her lover Frédéric Chopin or from Liszt, who did know him. Bull's wife Félicie (and Bull) spent some time on the Meuse in 1848, but Sand's story is from much later.

A third author who was fascinated by the figure of Bull was the Norwegian novelist and teacher Kristofer Janson (1841–1917). He emigrated to America in 1879 and became a Unitarian pastor among the Norwegians in Minnesota.[16] Like Bull, Janson came of an upper-class family in Bergen, but contrary to Bull he early adopted Aasen's rural New Norwegian language as his medium. He had a number of popular novels to his credit before his emigration. One of them, entitled *Den Bergtekne* (*The Spellbound Fiddler*) (1876), is based on events from the life of Torgeir Augundson.[17] An episode from real life—when Bull invited Augundson to perform in the city—figures prominently in the book.

The Bull myth was perpetuated not only in literature, making his life into fiction, but also fictional Ole Bulls began to spring up in real life. During his lifetime and afterwards, his name was appropriated by others for their own gain (see appendix A). There were also numerous personal accounts by people who had met him, sometimes only once. These continued to appear in newspapers and journals for years after his death, and memorabilia of all kinds also served to keep his name before the public. The most valuable such object is the Ole Bull Stradivarius, now belonging to

15. Ibid., 44.
16. Nina Draxten, *Kristofer Janson in America* (Northfield, Minn., 1976).
17. The book was translated into English by Auber Forestier (Aubertine Woodward Moore) in 1880 as *The Spell-bound Fiddler,* with an introduction by Rasmus B. Anderson.

"Ole Bull" Stradivarius from 1687. From the Herbert R. Axelrod Quartet. Courtesy of Smithsonian Institution.

the Herbert Axelrod Quartet of Stradivarius instruments housed at the Smithsonian Institution (see appendix B for additional examples).

Ole Bull was also remembered during his lifetime and afterwards in lithographs, photographs, paintings, drawings, and statues. Many are pictured in this book and also described in appendix C. Musical works were dedicated to him by friends and admirers, and even as late as 1920 the

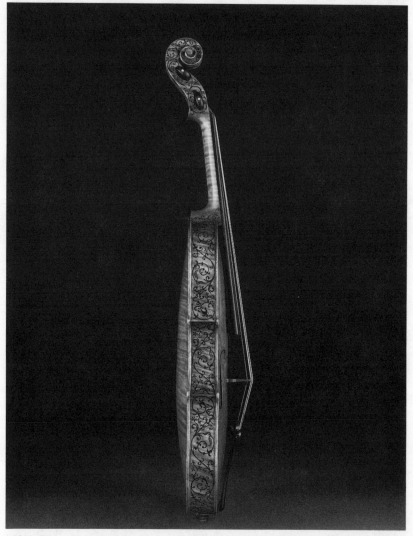

"Ole Bull" Stradivarius from 1687. From the Herbert R. Axelrod Quartet. Courtesy of Smithsonian Institution.

American composer, Will George Butler, wrote a piece in his honor, *Visions of Oleona*. An extensive list of such works dedicated to Bull appears in appendix D. Scholarly and popular books, journal articles, and lexicon entries have kept the facts and legends of Ole Bull alive in Norway and the United States. These works are described in appendix E.

Perhaps the place Ole Bull is best remembered in the United States to-

Ole Bull statue, Loring Park, Minneapolis, Minn., 1897. Sculptor Jakob Fjelde. Photo by Theodora Ingerson.

Ole Bull statue, Bergen, 1901. Sculptor Stephan Sinding. Photo by Knud Knudsen. Courtesy of Bergen University Library.

day is Potter County, Pennsylvania. The Ole Bull State Park, established on lands the state took over from the Lackawanna Lumber Company in 1908 (1909?), has kept Bull's name before the public. New Norway, Walhalla, and Bull's "Castle" fall within the park's boundaries. Up on a hill past Kettle Creek and Ole Bull Run are a cellar hole and a piece of a retaining wall that constitute the remains of his castle; there are no other signs of Bull's colony. A graveyard near the park contains the graves of some of the first settlers, members of the Olson and Andresen families. Oleona (the American spelling of Oleana) is today an open field area at a crossroads with a few houses, and New Bergen (about 8 miles away) is a small settlement called Carter Camp.

In 1920 and again in 1952 major celebrations were held at the park to honor Bull, but the State of Pennsylvania has rejected petitions to rebuild Bull's castle. Potter County is a forested area which began lumbering in earnest only after Bull's time and which remains today a mostly unsettled, idyllic mountainous area, used for hunting and fishing, dominated by state parklands.

Ole Bull's plans for a Norwegian Academy of Music were not realized in his lifetime. A music academy was finally founded in 1883 when the composer L. M. Lindeman founded a school for organists, which, in 1892, became the Music Conservatory. In 1973 it was named Norges Musikkhøgskole (Norway's Music School), and in 1978 it became a state-run institution.

An even more specialized academy was initiated in Voss, Norway, bearing Bull's name: Ole Bull Akademiet (The Ole Bull Academy). It was established by a well-known master player on the Hardanger fiddle, Sigbjørn Bernhoft Osa (1910–90), who in 1973 conceived the idea. Modest contributions from the government enabled him to begin offering courses in Norwegian folk music in 1977.[18] Osa's plan was to bring country fiddlers in as instructors and role models, and to practice folk dancing and the telling of folktales and singing of ballads. Students at the University College of Music were given a chance to visit the college in Voss as part of their coursework. While this did not directly refer to Bull, it was very much in his spirit.

The Bull family has helped to preserve Bull's property. Alexander Bull, Ole's only son to survive his father, inherited Valestrand. Alexander turned it over to his sister Félicie. Félicie Bull (Ingier) had four children, of whom

18. Gunnar Stubseid, "Ole Bull Akademiet: Ein spelemannsdraum vert røyndom," in Ingjald Bolstad, A. Kyte, and J. Mæland, eds., *Norske tonar: Heidersskrift til Sigbjørn Osa på 75-årsdagen* (Oslo, 1985), 130–36.

Ole Bull statue, Bergen Theater, 1909. Sculptor Ambrosia Tønnesen.

only one, Lucie Jonassen, had children. Lucie's daughter Anne Margrete (Hendriksen) and opera singer Arne Hendriksen lived in Stockholm. Their two children are Knut (b. 1944) and Nils (b. 1945), and their families spend summers at Valestrand. Lucie Jonassen's other daughter, Lucie, married a Bjerke and lives (1989) in Oslo.

A certain conflict arose over Bull's fortune, which proved to be greater than had been believed. In 1873 Bull sold Lysøen to Joseph Thorp, Sr., no doubt to finance his villa there. Thorp willed it to his granddaughter Olea Bull Vaughan. During her last years Sara Bull fell under the influence of an Indian sect named Rajah Yogi and willed a large part of her estate to its members. After her death in 1911 Olea was forced to go to court to have the will annulled on the grounds of insanity because of "undue influence." Newspapers in Boston and New York had a field day reporting on the case.

A part of the will that was accepted by Olea was a trust fund of thirty thousand dollars "for the purpose of preserving, maintaining and making improvements upon Lysøen, the home of her father, Ole Bull as a memorial to his memory." Sylvea Bull Curtis, who inherited Lysøen after Olea's death, was an informally adopted daughter, born a Shapleigh. Technically, she had no right to bear the name Bull, as is made abundantly clear in correspondence from Bull's granddaughter Anna Ingier in the Bull archives in Bergen. Anna Ingier carried on a hostile letter campaign to all members of the Thorp family. Sylvea eventually donated Lysøen to Norwegian authorities in 1973 and thereby removed a deep Norwegian grievance.[19]

We have now surveyed the shadow cast by Ole Bull long after his death. It is evident that, in Bjørnson's words at his funeral, "he was much more than a fiddler."

As a musician he sounded his violin everywhere in what was then the "civilized" world and to some extent even out of it. He started as a musical prodigy before going to school and developed through life an unexampled mastery of the violin. Coming from a remote, unrecognized corner of the world this young man found himself following in the footsteps of Paganini and became a man of the world. He outdid the master in the length of his career, in his persistence, and in the distances he traversed, as well as in the originality of his performance. Greeted by French critics as a "sauvage," he won the plaudits and rewards of crowned heads throughout Eu-

---

19. A detailed account is found in *Innstilling om Lysøens framtidige bruk.* . . . (Bergen, 1975), 46–48.

Bull and Thorp families. Sara Thorp Bull is second from left. Courtesy of Cambridge Historical Society.

rope, from London to Moscow. He was the ideal Romantic in a romantic age, who could cause women to swoon and men to weep.

This man "with the magic bow" was accused of being a charlatan because of his dexterity, which made listeners think of the wizards of old. His range of musical expression included the tenderest adagios as well as the crashing of thunder. He could cradle his bow like a mother over her child, play on all four strings at once, and imitate sounds from the birds of the woods to the shepherd's flute. He learned early to take his violin apart and put it together again to achieve better resonance.

While he was crowned more than once as "king of the violin," he was withal modest in his manner. He had a rich fund of anecdotes and could entertain a company of friends. He was a born showman, whose skill as an entertainer was appreciated by his listeners, whether they were Polish noblemen or American cowboys. But he could also be temperamental, and in his correspondence it is often apparent that he suffered from a hypochondriac strain. He often wrote as if he were on the brink of disaster, expecting to die at any moment, yet he was obviously strong as a giant.

Although he spent most of his adult life away from his native land, he never forgot that Norway was his home. His childhood among Norwegian country folk on Oster Island, between sea and mountains, left an

Sylvea Bull Curtis. Courtesy of Oslo University Library.

indelible impression. He overlooked no occasion to remind people that Norway, Scandinavia's stepchild, was a sovereign nation, even in a dynastic union with Sweden. His attempts to create a Norwegian theater, or a Music Academy, or to found a Norwegian colony in the United States were financial failures, but they sowed seeds in Norwegian soil that led to independence in 1905. His eye was also constantly on the lookout for artistic talent in his people, from Torgeir Augundson to Henrik Ibsen, Bjørnstjerne Bjørnson, and Edvard Grieg.

Yet Ole Bull found a second homeland in the United States. He almost became an American citizen, and he married an American wife. In his last ten years he commuted annually between Norway and America. He celebrated his last birthday in the company of such men as Longfellow and Holmes, among the brahmins of New England. Only by defying his American family did he force his last trip back to his "Island of Light" in Norway. When he died shortly after his return, his demise was mourned not only in Norway but also in America. All his life he had been an advocate of freedom, of political liberalism, and the rights of humanity.

We have followed his trail to the end. A citizen of the world, a hero of Norway, a man of many moods and exquisite sensibilities.

List of Works

Appendices

Bibliography

Index

List of Works

A. WORKS

This list is drawn partially from Ola Linge, *Ole Bull: Livshistoria, Mannen, Kunstnaren* (Oslo, 1953), 358–69 (about fifty items) and from Øystein Gaukstad, "Fortegnelse over Ole Bulls komposisjoner," (a typescript listing eighty-one items) in the University of Oslo Library (UOslo). Christian A. Aarvig, *Den unge Ole Bull: En Violinspillers Ungdomskampe* (Copenhagen, 1934), 104–105, lists thirty-six items. Some of the separately listed works may be the same piece, and certain similarly titled pieces listed together may be different works. Not enough information is available to describe them with certainty. Most of Bull's surviving music manuscripts are at the University of Oslo; much of his correspondence is at the Bergen University Library.

CHRISTIANIA 1828–1829

1. *Funeral Cantata* (*Sørge Cantate*) (projected)
DED.: Waldemar Thrane
SOURCE: letter to father, 15 November 1828
SEE: Ole Bull, *Ole Bull 1810–1910: Et Mindeskrift* (Bergen, 1910), 31

2. *Symphony* (possibly the same as the projected *Variations on the National Song for Orchestra*)
WORKED ON: Christiania, February–March 1829
SOURCE: letters to father, 20 and 28 February 1829
SEE: Bull, *Et Mindeskrift,* 34, 36

3. *The Storm* (*Das Gewitter*)
FOR: violin and piano
DESCRIP.: improvisation
1ST PERF.: Münden, Germany, Summer 1829
SEE: Henrik Wergeland, "Ole Bull: Efter opgivelser af ham selv biografisk skildret," in D. A. Seip, ed., *Samlede Skrifter* (Oslo, 1927), 4.5:189; Alexander Bull, ed., *Ole Bulls Breve i Uddrag. Med en karakteristik og biografisk Skitse af Jonas Lie* (Copenhagen, 1881), 27; Christian A. Aarvig, *Den unge Ole Bull: En Violinspillers*

Ungdomskampe (Copenhagen, 1934), 104; Henrik Winter-Hjelm, "Træk af Ole Bulls Liv," *Morgenbladet* (1852)

4. "Hymn to Freedom" ("Hymne til Friheden") (Text: Henrik Wergeland)
COMP.: Christiania, 1829
FOR: voice and piano
DESCRIP.: "I am composing in a new genre for two of Wergeland's poems"
NO KNOWN PERF.
SOURCE: letter to father, 30 November 1829
SEE: Bull, *Et Mindeskrift*, 46; Linge, *Ole Bull*, 36, 358

5. "Thunder" ("Tordenen") (Text: Henrik Wergeland)
COMP.: Christiania, 1829
FOR: voice and piano
DESCRIP.: "I am composing in a new genre for two of Wergeland's poems"
NO KNOWN PERF.
SOURCE: letter to father, 30 November 1829
SEE: Same sources as at no. 4 above

CHRISTIANIA 1830

6. *Cantata for Westye Egeberg's Funeral* (*Cantate ved Grosserer Westye Egebergs Gravlegging*) (Text: Henrik Anker Bjerregaard)
COMP.: Christiania, 1830
FOR: chorus and wind quartet (trombone, French horn, two bassoons)
DESCRIP.: a choral piece, a quartet, two songs?
DED.: Westye Egeberg (died March 1830)
1ST PERF.: 1830
SOURCE: letter to father, 6 March 1830
SEE: Bull, *Et Mindeskrift*, 52; Linge, *Ole Bull*, 36, 359; John Bergsagel, "Ole Bull," in Stanley Sadie, ed. *The New Grove Dictionary of Music and Musicians* (London, 1980), 3:447.

PARIS 1832–1833

7. *The Mountains of Norway* (first as *Souvenirs de Norvège;* after 1833, much revised, probably became *The Mountains of Norway* (*Norges Fjelde*) (1838). With probable further revisions called *Fjeldenes Echo* (1838), *Norwegers Traum und Heimweh* (1839), *Norwegian's Lament for Home* (1840), *Norsk Fantasi* (1840), *Recuerdos de mi infancia, Fantasie* (1844), *Reminiscenses de mon berceau* (1847), *Norske Fjeldtoner* (for violin solo, 1863)
COMP.: Paris, 1832–33
FOR: Hardanger fiddle accompanied by two violins, viola, cello, double bass, flute; later violin and orchestra; later unaccompanied violin or with piano
DESCRIP.: medley piece of *slåtter* and folk songs
DED.: Count Gustav Carl Löwenhielm
1ST PERF.: Paris, April 1833

HAND COPIES: "Polskdands" melody in two copies by Sophonias Christian Krag, 29 March 1849 (Bergen Offentlige Bibliotek); orchestral parts to *Norges Fjelde ou Reminiscenses de mon berceau,* oboe 1, bassoon 2, bass drum only, used 1847–51 (UOslo)
ARRANG.: for piano, "Polskdands af 'Norges Fjelde'" arranger unknown, in *Musikalsk Løverdagsmagazin,* part 2, vol. 3, no. 5; "Polskdands" also published separately
SOURCE: letter to mother, Lausanne, 4 July 1833
SEE: Bull, ed., *Ole Bulls Breve i Uddrag,* 68, 157, 252, 256, 276; Wergeland, "Ole Bull," 210, 220; Winter-Hjelm, "Træk af Ole Bulls Liv," *Morgenbladèt* (1852); *Den Constitutionelle,* 15 January 1843; Linge, *Ole Bull,* 54, 129, 359

8. *Bravura Variations,* Opus 3: *Fantaisie et Variations de bravoure, sur un thème de Bellini pour violon, avec orchestre ou piano;* possibly the same as *Aria appassionata con variationi brillanti* for violin solo (1833)
COMP.: Paris, 1832–33; revised 1839, 1840
FOR: violin and orchestra, violin and piano
DESCRIP.: variations in *scena ed aria* form on "L'amo, ah l'amo, e m'é più cara" from *I Capuleti e i Montecchi* by Bellini
DED.: King Carl Johan (Bernadotte) of Sweden and Norway
1ST PERF.: 29 June 1833, Lausanne
AUTOGRAPH: *Arioso,* an incomplete score of Variations 4–5, 5 is in simplified form (UOslo)
PUBL.: Hamburg and Leipzig: Schuberth, 1843 (orchestral score including piano part, separate violin part with Variation 2, separate piano part, orchestral parts)
MODERN ED.: for violin and piano, *Arioso* ("Andante Arioso" and "Moderato" only), ed. Bjarne Kortsen (Bergen: Edition Norvegica, 1978)
ARRANG.: for cello and orchestra by Rob. E. Bockmühl, Hamburg and Leipzig: Schuberth [ca. 1850]
SEE: Bull, *Et Mindeskrift,* 74–75; Ole Bull, *Min kjære Moder. En kjærlighets erklæring,* ed. Ladislav Reznicek (Bergen, 1980), 18; Bull, ed., *Ole Bulls Breve i Uddrag,* 157, 242, 268; Winter-Hjelm, "Træk af Ole Bulls Liv," *Morgenbladet* (1852); Wergeland, "Ole Bull," 208; Linge, *Ole Bull,* 55, 61, 127, 367

ITALY 1834

9. *Concerto in A Major (Grand Concerto, Concerto 1)* (movements: Allegro maestoso, Adagio sentimentale, Rondo pastorale)
comp.: Trieste, February 1834; revised 1864
FOR: violin and orchestra
DED.: Prince Poniatowsky
1ST PERF.: Trieste, February 1834
OTHER PERF.: Loups Theater, Bologna, 2 May 1834
HAND COPY: orchestral parts to *Concerto in A Major,* oboe 1, bassoon 2, bass drum only, used 1847–51 (UOslo)
SOURCE: letter to father, Florence, 21 July 1834
SEE: Bull, *Et Mindeskrift,* 81, 90–91; Winter-Hjelm, "Træk af Ole Bulls Liv," *Mor-*

genbladet (1852); Wergeland, "Ole Bull," 196, 211, 212; Linge, *Ole Bull,* 70, 75, 83, 85, 88, 94, 100, 343, 359–60

10. *Capriccio Fantastico* (*Capriccio* [1836], *Fantasia Capriccio* [1836], *Capriccio ma moderato* [1837]; different works?)
COMP.: Trieste and Bologna, February 1834
FOR: solo violin
DESCRIP.: called Bull's answer to Paganini's *Duo merveille;* includes "alphorn sounds"
1ST PERF.: Trieste, February 1834
AUTOGRAPHS: album leaf "Capriccio ma moderato" in A minor ending with a cadenza (1837) (British Library); album leaf "Capriccio fantastico" in G minor to Aloys Fuchs (28 June 1839) (Deutsche Staatsbibliothek, Berlin)
SOURCE: letter to mother, 2 February 1834
SEE: Bull, *Et Mindeskrift,* 81, 90; Winter-Hjelm, "Træk af Ole Bulls Liv," *Morgenbladet* (1852); Bull, *Min kjære Moder,* 22; Linge, *Ole Bull,* 56, 61, 65, 75, 84, 88, 110, 130, 360. See also no. 14 below

11. "Improvisation"
FOR: solo violin
DESCRIP.: Recitative, Allegro, Presto in minor, Adagio maestoso in major
PERF.: private, Bologna 1834
SOURCE: letter to father, 21 July 1834
SEE: Bull, *Et Mindeskrift,* 79–80

12. *Improvisations on Given Motives*
FOR: violin solo
DESCRIP.: Italian opera melodies from *Norma* and *I Capuleti e i Montecchi* by Bellini, *Le siège de Corinthe* by Rossini
EARLY PERF.: Bologna 1834
SEE: Bull, *Et Mindeskrift,* 80; Wergeland, "Ole Bull," 197; Winter-Hjelm, "Træk af Ole Bulls Liv," *Morgenbladet* (1852)

13. *Violin Method Book*
WORKED ON: St. Borgo di Sieve, July 1834
SOURCE: letter, 1834
SEE: Bull, *Et Mindeskrift,* 83; Wergeland, "Ole Bull," 198; Bull, ed., *Ole Bulls Breve i Uddrag,* 44, 398; Linge, *Ole Bull,* 68. See also *Violin Notes* in Sara C. Bull, *Ole Bull: A Memoir* (Boston and New York 1882), 347–77; and in John Broadhouse, *How to Make a Violin. The Violin . . . Notes by Ole Bull,* rev. ed. (London, [1910?]), 117ff.

14. *Quartet for Violin Solo*
COMP.: Florence, 1834
FOR: solo violin
DESCRIP.: called Bull's answer to Paganini's *Duo merveille;* includes Swiss cow call
1ST PERF.: Naples, Autumn 1834

List of Works

AUTOGRAPH: album leaf "Grave sostenuto," from *Quartetto per un [violino] solo* in G major (Dublin, 25 February 1837) (Boston Public Library)
SOURCE: letter to father, Florence, 21 July 1834
SEE: Bull, *Et Mindeskrift,* 82; Bull, ed., *Ole Bulls Breve i Uddrag,* 43, 71, 342; Wergeland, "Ole Bull," 198, 204; Winter-Hjelm, "Træk af Ole Bulls Liv," *Morgenbladet* (1852); *Leipziger Allgemeine Musikalische Zeitung (LAMZ)* (March 1839); Linge, *Ole Bull,* 56, 83, 85, 360; Zinken Hopp, *Eventyret om Ole Bull* (Bergen, 1945), 50. See also no. 10 above.

15. *A Mother's Prayer* (Opus 1, *Adagio Religioso, pour violon avec orchestre ou piano* (*En moders bøn, Preghiera d'una madre,* sometimes *Andante Religioso*)
COMP.: near Florence, 1834
FOR: violin and orchestra, violin and piano
DESCRIP.: Italian opera style
DED.: Félicie Bull
EARLY PERF.: London 1836
AUTOGRAPHS: score as *Adagio Religioso* (Christiania, 30 July 1838) (UOslo); incomplete organ part (from the arrangement for violin and organ) (UOslo); album leaf with four measures "Recitativo" (Leipzig, 14 January 1841) (Deutsche Staatsbibliothek, Berlin)
HAND COPY: complete organ part (from the arrangement for violin and organ), differs from score (UOslo)
PUBL.: Hamburg and Leipzig: Schuberth, 1843 (orchestral score including piano part, separate violin part, separate piano part); later ed. for violin and piano as *En moders bøn, Andante Religioso,* Christiania: Warmuth, n.d., differs from 1st ed.
ARRANG.: for piano, Christiania: Warmuth; for piano, Stockholm: Elkan; for piano, Christiania: H. Neupert; for orchestra, in hand copy (Musikaliska Akademiens Bibliotek, Stockholm); for cello, by Rob. E. Bockmühl, Leipzig: Schuberth [ca. 1850]; for violin and piano, by Emil Kross, Cologne [1914?]
SOURCE: letter to mother
SEE: Bull, ed., *Ole Bulls Breve i Uddrag,* 43; Wergeland, "Ole Bull," 198; Winter-Hjelm, "Træk af Ole Bulls Liv," *Morgenbladet* (1852); Linge, *Ole Bull,* 68, 88, 343, 360, 367

16. *Fantasia pastorale* (*Fantasie*)
COMP.: 1834
SOURCE: letter to mother, Florence, 21 July 1834
SEE: Bull, *Et Mindeskrift,* 83

17. *Duet for Organ and Violin*
COMP.: 1834
1ST PERF.: St. Marks Church, Florence, 1834
SOURCE: letter to mother, Florence, 21 July 1834
SEE: Bull, *Et Mindeskrift,* 84

18. *Trio for Violin*
COMP.: 1834?

DESCRIP.: composed for practice
SEE: Bull, ed., *Ole Bulls Breve i Uddrag*, 44; Wergeland, "Ole Bull," 198.

ITALY 1835

19. *Polacca Guerriera*, full title: *Recitativo, Andante amoroso con Polacca Guerriera* ("Andante amoroso" also called "Adagio amoroso")
COMP.: Naples and Rome, 1835; revised 1864
FOR: violin and piano, violin and orchestra
DESCRIP.: lyric and virtuoso piece in Italian style with a polonaise
IST PERF.: Rome, 1835
AUTOGRAPHS: album leaf to Aloys Fuchs (28 June 1839) (Deutsche Staatsbibliothek, Berlin); album leaf with two melody lines to F. Bohm (8 December 1860) (UOslo)
HAND COPIES: orchestral parts to *Polacca Guerriera*, oboe 1, bassoon 2, bass drum only, used 1847–51 (UOslo); "Moderato Cantabile" melody in two copies by Sophonias Christian Krag, 29 March 1849 (Bergen Offentlige Bibliotek)
PUBL.: violin and piano, *Polacca Guerriera pour violon avec accompagnement de piano*, Christiania: Warmuth [1886]
ARRANG. OF SELECTED MELODIES: for piano, Christiania: Warmuth; for piano as *Bellone: Polonaise à la Militaire* by Charles Grobe, Philadelphia: George Willig, 1845; for piano in hand copy as "Ole Bulls Drøm: Vals Sentimental" by Engebret Aasgaard, 1862 (UOslo); for cello and piano or orchestra, by Charles Werner, Leipzig: Schuberth; for orchestra in hand copy, by Harald Heide (Harmonien, Bergen); as choral song, text added to "Polacca" melody by Andreas Munch (10 January 1842)
SEE: Wergeland, "Ole Bull," 198, 199, 209; Winter-Hjelm, "Træk af Ole Bulls Liv," *Morgenbladet* (1852); *LAMZ* (March 1839); Linge, *Ole Bull*, 71, 73, 85, 88, 94, 103, 343, 361, 368

ENGLAND, IRELAND, SCOTLAND 1836–1837

20. "God Save the King" Improvisation
FOR: violin solo
DESCRIP.: four-part harmony
IST PERF.: London, 1836
SEE: Wergeland, "Ole Bull," 204; Winter-Hjelm, "Træk af Ole Bulls Liv," *Morgenbladet* (1852)

21. *Farewell to Ireland* (*Concerto Irlandais*)
COMP.: Dublin, 1837
DESCRIP.: rhapsody or variations on Irish folk melodies
SEE: Bull, *Et Mindeskrift*, 92–93; Wergeland, "Ole Bull," 207; Winter-Hjelm, "Træk af Ole Bulls Liv," *Morgenbladet* (1852); Bull, ed., *Ole Bulls Breve i Uddrag*, 59; Linge, *Ole Bull*, 95, 362; Gaukstad, "Fortegnelse," 2

22. *Grieving Prayer and Laughing Rondo* (*Preghiera dolente e Rondo ridente;* later *Cantabile doloroso e Rondo giocoso*)

List of Works

COMP.: Dublin, 1837, revised Darmstadt, 1840
FOR: violin and orchestra
DESCRIP.: Italian operatic form; Wergeland, "Ole Bull," 207 calls it a fantasy on Irish national tunes, doubtful
EARLY PERF.: Berlin, 18 February 1839
AUTOGRAPH: Album leaf, Prague, 5 March 1841 (location unknown: facsimile in Ladislav Reznicek, ed., *Tilegnet Ole Bull 1980. 1810. 1880* (Oslo, 1980)
HAND COPY: orchestral parts to *Cantabile Doloroso e Rondo Giocoso*, oboe 1, bassoon 2, bass drum only, used 1847–51 (UOslo)
SEE: Wergeland, "Ole Bull," 207; Bull, ed., *Ole Bulls Breve i Uddrag*, 59, 71, 276; Winter-Hjelm, "Træk af Ole Bulls Liv," *Morgenbladet* (1852); *LAMZ* (March 1839); Linge, *Ole Bull*, 343, 363

23. *Homage to Edinburgh (Homage to Scotland, Scottish Concerto, Skotsk Concerto, Fantasy on Scottish Folk Melodies)*
COMP.: Edinburgh, Fall 1837
DESCRIP.: fantasy on Scottish folk melodies
SEE: Wergeland, "Ole Bull," 207; Winter-Hjelm, "Træk af Ole Bulls Liv," *Morgenbladet* (1852); Bull, ed., *Ole Bulls Breve i Uddrag*, 59; Linge, *Ole Bull*, 86, 130, 362; Bergsagel, "Ole Bull," 3:447.

TRAVELS 1838

24. *Variations on the Hamburg National Song (Das Hamburgische Nationallied: Auf Hamburg Wohlergehe)*
COMP.: 1838
DESCRIP.: improvised variations
SOURCE: letter to father from Callmeyer
SEE: Bull, *Et Mindeskrift*, 106

25. *Triumphal March Improvisation (Triumfmarsch)*
DESCRIP.: improvisation on a theme, "ends with a pianissimo"
PERF.: St. Petersburg, 16 March 1838
SOURCE: letter to Félicie, 17 March 1838
SEE: Bull, ed., *Ole Bulls Breve i Uddrag*, 219

26. Variations on "In the Rose Grove under the Hall of Saga" (*"I Rosenlund under Sagas Hall"*)
DESCRIP.: improvised variations
PERF.: Christiania, 23 July 1838
SEE: Linge, *Ole Bull*, 111

27. Variations on "To Fetch the Water" ("Aa kjøre vatten")
DESCRIP.: improvised variations
PERF.: Christiania, 27 July 1838
SEE: Linge, *Ole Bull*, 112

28. Norwegian nationalist opera (projected) (Wergeland, projected librettist)
SEE: *Morgenbladet* 279 (6 October 1838); Linge, *Ole Bull,* 107

TRAVELS 1840–1843

29. *Concerto in E minor (Erinnerungen aus Prag [Remembrances from Prague],*
Gran Concerto, Concerto Fantastico, Secondo Concerto romantico [?], *Concerto*
pathétique [?]; movement titles vary slightly: La notte, L'aurora, Il giorno)
COMP.: Darmstadt, 1840 and Prague, February 1841
FOR: violin and orchestra
1ST PERF.: Prague, 14 February 1841 (still incomplete)
AUTOGRAPH: score as *Concerto Fantastico* dated Prague, 12 February 1841 (UOslo)
HAND COPY: orchestral part to *Concerto in E,* bassoon 2 only, used 1847–51 (UOslo)
PUBL.: *Adagio tirée de concerto,* movement 2 only, for violin and piano, differs
from score, Christiania: Warmuth [1886]
SOURCE: letters to father, 10 August 1840 and 18 February 1841
SEE: Bull, *Et Mindeskrift,* 83; Wergeland, "Ole Bull, 223; Winter-Hjelm, "Træk af
Ole Bulls Liv," *Morgenbladet* (1852); Bull, ed., *Ole Bulls Breve i Uddrag,* 276, 285,
400; *LAMZ* (1842), 101; Linge, *Ole Bull,* 137, 269, 362, 364; Hopp, *Eventyret,* 50

30. Arrangement of "Adagio" by Mozart
DESCRIP.: probably "Larghetto" (movement 2) from Mozart's *Clarinet Quintet in*
A Major, K. 581
PERF.: 1840, 1841
SEE: *LAMZ* (1840), 1009 and (1841), 266; Wergeland, "Ole Bull," 220

31. *Improvisation on Given Motives:* "Serenata"\(Ecco ridente il cielo) from *Il bar-*
biere di Siviglia Act I by Rossini, "Polacca" (Son vergin vezzosa) from *I Puritani*
by Bellini, and "Champagne Song" (Fin ch'han dal vino calda la testa) from *Don*
Giovanni, Act I by Mozart
PERF.: Leipzig, 20 January 1841
SEE: Linge, *Ole Bull,* 131

32. "Improvisation" on "Sil jsem proso na souvrati"
DESCRIP.: improvisations on a Czech folksong
PERF.: Prague, February 1841
SEE: Jan Trojan, "Das Brunner Konzertleben in der Zeit der Nationalen Wieder-
geburt," *Sborník prací filosofické fakulty brněnské university* 8 (1973): 172.

33. *Greetings from Afar (Grüss aus der Ferne, Largo posato e Rondo capriccioso*
[1842], *Ein ferner Grüss, En fjern Hilsen, Concerto dramatico* [1843])
COMP.: Prague, February and March 1841
FOR: violin and orchestra, violin with piano and organ
DESCRIP.: Italian operatic form
AUTOGRAPHS: unfinished score as *Grüss aus der Ferne, Largo posato e Rondo ca-*
priccioso, dated Prague, 27 February 1841 (Det kgl. Bibliothek, Copenhagen); as

En fjern Hilsen, incomplete organ arrangement (UOslo); album leaf "Cantabile" to Thora Olsen (20 October 1842) for violin and piano (UOslo)
HAND COPY: orchestral parts to *Grüss aus der Ferne, Largo posato e Rondo capriccioso,* oboe 1, bassoon 2, bass drum only, used 1847–51 (UOslo)
SOURCE: letter, 1 March 1841
SEE: Bull, ed., *Ole Bulls Breve i Uddrag,* 286; Wergeland, "Ole Bull," 223; Winter-Hjelm, "Træk af Ole Bulls Liv," *Morgenbladet* (1852); *Den Constitutionelle* (15 January 1843); *LAMZ* (1841), 261; Linge, *Ole Bull,* 132, 362, 366

34. Variations on "For Norway, Land of Heroes" ("For Norge, Kjæmpers Fødeland")
DESCRIP.: improvisation
PERF.: Christiania, 28 December 1841
SEE: Bull, ed., *Ole Bulls Breve i Uddrag,* 296; Linge, *Ole Bull,* 117, 135

35. Variations on Norwegian Folk Melodies
DESCRIP.: improvisation
PERF.: Christiania, January 1842
SEE: Linge, *Ole Bull,* 135

36. *Nocturne, pour violon avec orchestre ou piano,* Opus 2 (*Til Hende* [*To Her*] = *Fantasia e notturno, Nocturne amorosa*)
COMP.: Christiania, September 1842
FOR: violin and orchestra, violin and piano
DESCRIP.: serenade or cavatina
1ST PERF.: Christiania, 1842
AUTOGRAPH: *Notturno,* incomplete score, 4 December 1842 (UOslo)
HAND COPY: for violin and piano, 27 May 1850 (UOslo)
PUBL.: Hamburg and Leipzig: Schuberth, 1843 (orchestral score including piano part, separate violin part, separate piano part, orchestral parts); as *Nocturne in D Major* in *The Complete Soloist for the Violin,* ed. Edgar Haddock (The Concert Room, pt. 5567)
ARRANG.: for cello and orchestra or piano by Rob. E. Bockmühl, Leipzig: Schuberth [between 1844 and 1851]
SEE: Wergeland, *"Ole Bull,"* 224; Winter-Hjelm, "Træk af Ole Bulls Liv," *Morgenbladet* (1852); Bull, ed., *Ole Bulls Breve i Uddrag,* 84; *Den Constitutionelle* (15 January 1843); Aarvig, *Den unge Ole Bull,* 105; Linge, *Ole Bull,* 363–64, 366

37. *Wild Playing in the Hills* (*Villspel i Lio*)
COMP.: 1842; revised 1860
DESCRIP.: many dissonances, national melodies, possibly a medley piece
1ST PERF.: Christiania, 10 December 1842
SEE: Bull, ed., *Ole Bulls Breve i Uddrag,* 84; *Den Constitutionelle* (15 January 1843); Wergeland, "Ole Bull," 224; Winter-Hjelm, "Træk af Ole Bulls Liv," *Morgenbladet* (1852); Linge, *Ole Bull,* 363–64.

38. Variations on "Little Karin" ("Liten Karin")
DESCRIP.: improvisation on a Swedish folksong

PERF.: 17 February 1843
SEE: Bull, ed., *Ole Bulls Breve i Uddrag,* 88; Winter-Hjelm, "Træk af Ole Bulls Liv," *Morgenbladet* (1852); Aarvig, *Den unge Ole Bull,* 104; Hopp, *Eventyret,* 126

39. *Siciliano e Tarantella (Siciliano and Tarantella)*
COMP.: 1843 (Linge speculates in his modern edition of 1948 (see below) that the piece was begun in Italy in 1833–34, but there is no evidence for this.)
FOR: violin and orchestra, violin and piano
DESCRIP.: Italian style, one connected piece, Tarantella in rondo form
1ST PERF.: Bremen, May 1843
AUTOGRAPHS: score without violin part (UOslo); violin and piano arrangement with some changes (UOslo); album leaf "Siciliano" (Wiesbaden, 30 April 1878) (Deutsche Staatsbibliothek, Berlin); album leaf "Siciliano" (Altona, 1876) (Universität Hamburg, Zentrum für Theaterforschung, Hamburger Theatersammlung)
PUBL.: Schuberth bought rights but did not publish
MODERN ED.: for violin and piano, slightly simplified, ed. Ola Linge, Oslo: Edition Gamma, 1948 (score and parts were available from Gamma)
SEE: Bull, ed., *Ole Bulls Breve i Uddrag,* 91, 321; Wergeland, "Ole Bull," 229; *LAMZ* (1844), 58; Winter-Hjelm, "Træk af Ole Bulls Liv," *Morgenbladet* (1852); Linge, *Ole Bull,* 144–45, 147, 363, 368; Albert O. Barton, "Ole Bull and his Wisconsin Contacts," *Wisconsin Magazine of History* 7 (1924): 441.

THE NEW WORLD 1844–1845

40. *Cuban Potpourri (El Agiaco Cubano, El Ajiaco Cubano)*
COMP.: Havana, February 1844
FOR: violin and orchestra
DESCRIP.: rhapsody or potpourri of Cuban melodies; fantasia on motives from a dance called "La Pepilla" by Ulpiano Estrada
1ST PERF.: Havana, 20 March 1844
AUTOGRAPH: Bull's photograph with two lines of melody to Senora Joerg, no title, identification highly uncertain, in C minor (Havana, 15 April 1844) (Consistory, Coudersport, Penn.)
ARRANG.: for piano by Adolphe Kurs, *Grand March taken from Ole Bull's Celebrated Spanish Airs, 'Agiaco Cubano,'* New York: John F. Nunns [1846]
SEE: Bull, ed., *Ole Bulls Breve i Uddrag,* 329; Winter-Hjelm, "Træk af Ole Bulls Liv," *Morgenbladet* (1852); Linge, *Ole Bull,* 151, 365

41. *Memories of Havana (Recuerdos de Habana, Erindringer fra Cuba* [1848])
COMP.: Havana, February 1844
DESCRIP.: Cuban melodies included
1ST PERF.: Havana, 10 April 1844
SEE: Bull, ed., *Ole Bulls Breve i Uddrag,* 329; Winter-Hjelm, "Træk af Ole Bulls Liv," *Morgenbladet* (1852); Linge, *Ole Bull,* 365

42. Arrangement of *Carnival in Venice Variations* by Paganini (*Recitativ og Variationer over en neapolitansk folkemelodi 'Carnival i Venedig'* [1848], *The Carnival*

de Venice: Explanation, Introduction and Cadence Theme [1853], *Recitativ og Carnival de Venezia* by Bull [1865])
FOR: violin solo
DESCRIP.: a gradually made arrangement of Paganini's piece; later programs generally list it as by Bull alone; Italian folk melody
EARLY PERF.: as by Paganini only, Havana, March 1844; as by Bull only, 1856; as by Bull-Paganini, 1858
SEE: Linge, *Ole Bull,* 257, 360

43. *Niagara*
COMP.: New York, October 1844
FOR: violin and orchestra
DESCRIP.: "after my own opinion, the best composition I have written and with quite a new and original structure" (letter to Félicie, in Bull, ed., *Ole Bulls Breve i Uddrag,* 344); includes popular song "Long Time Ago"
1ST PERF.: New York, 18 December 1844
SEE: Bull, ed., *Ole Bulls Breve i Uddrag,* 108, 110, 341, 344; Winter-Hjelm, "Træk af Ole Bulls Liv," *Morgenbladet* (1852); Linge, *Ole Bull,* 153, 364; Vera Brodsky Lawrence, *Strong on Music,* vol. 1, *Resonances: 1836–1850* (New York and Oxford, 1988), 278, 289–90; New York *Spirit of the Times* (8 March 1845)

44. *Solitude of the Prairie* (*Solitude de la prairie, Præriernes ensomhed, Ensomheden i prærierne*)
COMP.: 1844
FOR: violin and orchestra
1ST PERF.: New York, 23 December 1844
SEE: Bull, ed., *Ole Bulls Breve i Uddrag,* 343, 344; Winter-Hjelm, "Træk af Ole Bulls Liv," *Morgenbladet* (1852); Linge, *Ole Bull,* 153, 364; Lawrence, *Strong on Music,* 279, 290

45. Variations on "Yankee Doodle"
DESCRIP.: improvisation
1ST PERF.: New York, 1844
SEE: Bull, ed., *Ole Bulls Breve i Uddrag,* 104

46. *In Memory of Washington* (*Washingtons minde, Grand National Fantasie* [1853], *To the Memory of Washington*)
COMP.: New York, 1844–45
FOR: violin and orchestra, occasionally violin solo (1853)
DESCRIP.: medley piece intended as a tone painting to express United States' independence struggle, including "Yankee Doodle," "God Save the King," and ending with "Hail Columbia"
DED.: George Washington
1ST PERF.: New York, 16 October 1845
ARRANG. of march only: for piano as *Grand March to the Memory of Washington,* Philadelphia: A. Fiot, 1845; for piano as *Marche tirée d'une fantaisie pour violon,* Christiania: Warmuth, 1886; for piano as *Marsch af 'Washingtons minde'*

List of Works

by F. A. Reissiger in *Ole Bull's Favorit Compositioner,* Christiania: Warmuth, 1880; for piano in *Løverdags-Magazin, Musikalsk,* no. 9; for janissary band, hand copy (Bergen Offentlige Bibliotek)
SEE: Bull, ed., *Ole Bulls Breve i Uddrag,* 116, 333, 352; Winter-Hjelm "Træk af Ole Bulls Liv," *Morgenbladet* (1852); Linge, *Ole Bull,* 156, 157, 364; Mortimer Smith, *The Life of Ole Bull* (Princeton, N.J., 1943), 149; Lawrence, *Strong on Music,* 354

47. *Psalm of David (Davids Salme)*
COMP.: 1845
FOR: violin and orchestra
DESCRIP.: "full of devotion and sincerity in the oriental-religious spirit, like a hymn and a prayer," *Morgenbladet* (11 December 1848); from Psalm 78
1ST PERF.: New York, 6 January 1845
AUTOGRAPH: album leaf with melody from "Largo maestoso," New York, 26 June 1845 (Boston Public Library)
SEE: Bull, ed., *Ole Bulls Breve i Uddrag,* 112; Winter-Hjelm, "Træk af Ole Bulls Liv," *Morgenbladet* (1852); Linge, *Ole Bull,* 155, 364; George C. D. Odell, *Annals of the New York Stage* (New York, 1931), 5:147; Gaukstad, "Fortegnelse," 4a; Lawrence, *Strong on Music,* 289–90

MADRID 1846–1847

48. *Celebration of St. John's Eve (La Verbena de San Juan, Spansk Sankt-Hans-Natt, St. Hans natt i Sevilla. Spansk musikfest* [1858])
COMP.: Madrid, April 1847
DESCRIP.: potpourri of Spanish tunes, Spanish motives, a fandango
DED.: Queen Isabella
1ST PERF.: Madrid 1847
SEE: Bull, ed., *Ole Bulls Breve i Uddrag,* 119, 362; Winter-Hjelm, "Træk af Ole Bulls Liv," *Morgenbladet* (1852); Linge, *Ole Bull,* 166, 365

49. *The Guitarist from Seville (Guitarspilleren fra Sevilla)*
COMP.: Spain, April 1847
FOR: violin solo?
DESCRIP.: bolero-like folk tune with mandolin effects (pizzicato) for accompaniment
ARRANG.: possibly *Guitar-Serenade* for violin solo as remembered by Anders Heyerdahl in his *Norske Danse og Slaatter for Violin,* 2d ed., Christiania: Oluf By's Musikforlag, [written between 1856 and 1861, printed 1905], 14.
SEE: Linge, *Ole Bull,* 166, 345, 365

50. Variations on "El Calecero Andaluz" and "La Jota Aragonesa"
PERF.: Spain, August 1847
SEE: Winter-Hjelm, "Træk af Ole Bulls Liv," *Morgenbladet* (1852)

NORWAY 1848–1849

51. Fantasies on "Last Year I Herded the Goats" ("I fjor gjæt' eg gjetinn")
DESCRIP.: improvisation

PERF.: 25 November 1848
SEE: Linge, *Ole Bull,* 345–46, 353–54

52. *Memory of the Miller's Lad (Minde om Møllergutten)*
DESCRIP.: fantasy
PERF.: 1 December 1848
SEE: Linge, *Ole Bull,* 172

53. *Visit to the Sæter* (first titled *Den 10de December [December 10], Et Sæter-besøg* [1849], *Et norsk Sæterbesøg, A Mountain Vision*). See no. 53a below.
COMP.: 1848–49; revised 1864
FOR: violin and orchestra, violin and piano
DESCRIP.: medley or potpourri piece of folk tunes including Bull's own melody "Sæter Girl's Sunday" without text (see no. 53a below)
DED.: Det norske Studentersamfund
1ST PERF.: Christiania, 10 March 1849 as *December 10*
AUTOGRAPHS: album leaf of melody, Chicago, 8 January 1868 (New York Public Library at Lincoln Center); album leaf of melody, New York, 17 April 1868 (UOslo); album leaf of melody, Richmond, 21 November 1872 (Library of Congress, Washington, D.C.); album leaf of melody, Copenhagen, 16 November 1875 (UOslo); album leaf of melody, Berlin, 11 December 1875 (J. B. Muns Catalogue, Musical Autographs List 90-2); original autograph burned before 1868 by Johanne Margrethe Hagerup Bull (sister-in-law)
HAND COPIES: orchestral score, Trondheim, 22 June 1865 (UOslo); orchestral parts in A minor and D minor (UOslo); for violin and piano, as *Fantasia für Violine & Pianoforte Begleitung, Et Sæterbesøg,* n.d. (UOslo); "Halling" melody only in two copies by Sophonias Christian Krag, 14 April 1849 (Bergen Offentlige Bibliotek); "Halling" melody only by Ivar R. Eide (UOslo)
PUBL.: for violin and piano, Christiania: Warmuth [1885] (by Alexander Bull)
ARRANG.: for violin and piano, *Sæterbesøg* by Kristofer L. Framstad, hand copy (UOslo); for piano, as *Reminiscenzer fra Sæterbesøget* by F. A. Reissiger in *Ole Bull's Favorit Compositioner,* Christiania: Warmuth, 1880
SEE: Bull, *Et Mindeskrift,* 124; Winter-Hjelm, "Træk af Ole Bulls Liv," *Morgenbladet* (1852); Linge, *Ole Bull,* 173, 176, 181, 362; T[harald H.] Blanc, *Christiania Theaters historie 1827–1877* (Christiania, 1899), 132; Arne Bjørndal, *Ole Bull og norsk folkemusikk* (Bergen, 1940), 83

53a. "Sæter Girl's Sunday" ("Sæterjentens Søndag," "Til Sæters," "Le dimanche de la bergère," "Die Sonne scheint Hell," etc.) (Text added: "På solen jeg ser," Jørgen Moe)
FOR: voice and piano
DESCRIP.: originally part of *Visit to the Sæter* (no. 53 above)
ARRANG.: for nineteen different combinations (including voice and piano) as harmonized by Johan S. Svendsen (various arrangers) titled *Solitude sur la montagne / Sæterjentens Søndag / Sehnsucht der Sennerin,* Copenhagen: Wilhelm Hansen, also by Christiania: Warmuth; other arrangers include Nicolai Hansen, C. B. Roepper, Ella Faber, Joh. Pohly, Thomas Beck, F. A. Reissiger, Konrad Ramrath, R. Nathusius, Konrad Grimstad; several hand copies (UOslo); in many collections; as

List of Works

solo song "Norsk Frihedsmarsch," new text by Tønnes Rolfsen "Fædreneland! fra fjeldtop til strand" for 17 May 1850 (UOslo)
SEE: Linge, *Ole Bull,* 369; *Aftenposten* (10 November 1934); *Morgenavisen* (16 May 1950)

54. Arrangement of "Fanitullen" ("The Devil's Dance")
DESCRIP.: violin solo
PERF.: Christiania, March 1849
HAND COPY: by Ludwig von Malthe, "as Ole Bull played it" (UOslo)
SEE: Linge, *Ole Bull,* 177

NORWAY 1850–1851

55. Music for the Prologue
DESCRIP.: (1) music to accompany a prologue; (2) piece for men's chorus
DED.: for the opening of Bergen's theater
1ST PERF.: Bergen, 2 January 1850 (with *Den Vægelsindede* by Ludvig Holberg)
SEE: *Morgenbladet* (7 January 1850); Linge, *Ole Bull,* 186

56. Music for *The Mountain Cottage* (*Fjeldstuen* by Henrik Wergeland). See nos. 56a–56d below.
COMP.: Bergen, 1849–50
FOR: orchestra, chorus, soloists
DESCRIP.: overture (lost), choruses, songs; incidental music for the play
1ST PERF.: 13 January 1850
AUTOGRAPH: score for two choruses and two solo songs, December 1849 (Library of Congress, Washington D.C.)
SEE: Bull, *Et Mindeskrift,* 125; Bull, ed., *Ole Bulls Breve i Uddrag,* 374, 376, 377

56a. "Away Over the Ocean" ("Afsted over Hav!")
FOR: unison female chorus and orchestra
DESCRIP.: text in Theodore C. Blegen and Martin B. Ruud, eds., *Norwegian Emigrant Songs and Ballads* (Minneapolis, 1936), 85–86
AUTOGRAPH: score (Library of Congress, Washington D.C., missing one folio)
HAND COPY: melody only (Theater Archive, Univ. of Bergen)

56b. "Stop Now, Mayor" ("Holdt nu, Lensmand")
FOR: female unison chorus, strings, oboe
AUTOGRAPH: score (Library of Congress, Washington D.C.)
HAND COPY: melody only (Theater Archive, Univ. of Bergen)

56c. "Sigrid's Song" ("Sigrids sang") (also as "Den forladte" or "The Abandoned One") Text: "Here, Where in Everything" ("Her, hvor i alt")
FOR: female solo voice, orchestra
DESCRIP.: strophic song, text in Blegen and Ruud, eds., *Norwegian Emigrant Songs,* 88–90
AUTOGRAPHS: score as "Her, hvor i alt," December 1849 (Library of Congress, Washington D.C.); as "Sigrids sang," melody in draft at Lysøen; as "Den forladte: Her,

306

List of Works

hvor i alt," melody only in Bull's hand (UOslo), accompaniment by Otto Winter-Hjelm? (UOslo)
PUB.: Steenske Bog- og Nodetrykkeri (of original version?)
ARRANG.: for men's chorus as "Den forladte" by Johan Behrens in *Firstemmig Kor-og Kvartet-Sangbog for Mandsstemmer*, no. 8, and *Skole-Sangbog*, vol. 1, no. 13
SEE: Linge, *Ole Bull*, 365, 368; Bergsagel, "Ole Bull," 3:448

56d. "Huldre Song" ("Huldresang"). Text: "Go in Now" ("Saa ganger nu ind")
FOR: female solo voice, orchestra
DESCRIP.: arrangement of an "Air Norvégien" (published in Henrik Wergeland *Fjeld-stuen* (Christiania, 1848); text in Blegen and Ruud, eds., *Norwegian Emigrant Songs*, 96–97
AUTOGRAPH: score (Library of Congress, Washington D.C.)

57. *Solitude (Ensomhed)*
1ST PERF.: Bergen, 16 June 1850
SEE: Linge, *Ole Bull*, 365

58. *The Power of Art (Kunstens Magt)* (Text: "Lægger du dit øre" by Henrik Ibsen)
COMP.: 1851
FOR: men's chorus and orchestra
DESCRIP.: strophic song
DED.: to raise money for the Bergen theater
1ST PERF.: 15 October 1851 by Studentersangforening, Christiania
AUTOGRAPH: score (UOslo)
ARRANG.: for men's chorus by Johan Behrens in *Firstemmig Mands-Sangbog*, no. 27; for men's chorus, printed by Edvard Winther's lith. Institut with J. Behrens corrections (UOslo)
SEE: Linge, *Ole Bull*, 366

59. *Norwegian Mountain Melodies (Norske Fjeldmelodier)* published as Appendices I–III (1851) to *Norske Nationaldragter (Norwegian National Costumes)*, Christiania: Christian Tønsberg, 1852. Contents: App. I. Halling fra Hallingdal (piano). App. II. (1) Gammel Tougeslaat fra Silgjord (voice and langeleik); (2) Tougdands: Haugtusslaaten (piano). App. III. (1) Springar fra Thelemarken (piano). (2) Folke-'vise fra Orkedalen "Ifjol gjætt' e gjeitinn" [sic] (voice and piano). (3) Vosserulla (piano)
DESCRIP.: five Norwegian *slåtter*, one folk song; brief preludes by Bull
AUTOGRAPH: score of App. I and App. II, no. 2, Christiania, 20 October 1850 (UOslo); score of App. II, no. 1, as "To piger," Christiania, 22 October 1850 (UOslo)
HAND COPY: melody only of App. I by Ole Olsen, "Halling according to Bull's notations" (UOslo)

UNITED STATES, 1852–1857

60. *Fantasia on American Airs,* introducing "Jordan is a Hard Road to Travel," "Hazel Dell," "Arkansas Traveler," "Pop goes the Weasel," "Home, Sweet Home"

307

List of Works

PERF.: Bloomington, Ill., 1856?
SEE: 1856? program (Univ. of Bergen Library)

NORWAY, 1859

61. *Saturday Night at the Sæter* (*Lørdagskveld på Sætren*)
COMP.: uncompleted
PERF.: Drammen, December 1859
SEE: Linge, *Ole Bull*, 364

62. *Kringen*
COMP.: uncompleted
PERF.: Drammen, December 1859
SEE: Linge, *Ole Bull*, 364

NORWAY, 1861–1862

63. *Grand Folk* (*Storfolk*)
DESCRIP.: improvisation?
PERF.: Valestrand, Summer 1861 or 1862
SEE: Bjørndal, *Ole Bull og norsk folkemusikk*, 68

64. *A Fight in Hollender Street in Stettin* (*Et slagsmål i Hollendergaten i Stettin*)
DESCRIP.: improvisation?
PERF.: Valestrand, Summer 1861 or 1862
SEE: Bjørndal, *Ole Bull og norsk folkemusikk*, 68

65. *Giant's Folkdance* (first as *Kjæmpedans, Kjæmpeslåtten* [1862])
COMP.: 1861, revised 1865
DESCRIP.: fantasy
PERF.: Christiania, September 1861
SEE: Bull, ed., *Ole Bulls Breve i Uddrag*, 400; Linge, *Ole Bull*, 365

NORWAY 1863–1864

66. "In Moments of Solitude" ("I ensomme Stunde" or "Klage") (Text: Marcus Jacob Monrad, added later)
COMP.: 1863?, possibly an extant folk melody (see no. B12 below)
FOR: violin and piano, voice and piano
IST PERF.: Christiania, 2 May 1863, as solo song
AUTOGRAPHS: violin and piano (UOslo); melody as "Klage" (location unknown; facsimile in Hopp, *Eventyret*, facing p. 45)
TEXT PUBL.: *Tvende Texter af Job Spillemand [M. J. Monrad] til Melodier af Ole Bull. 1. I ensomme stunde. 2. I granskoven* (two texts by Job Spillemand [Monrad] to melodies by Ole Bull), *Illustreret Nyhedsblad*, 1863, no. 18
ARRANG.: for men's chorus by Johan Behrens in *Sangbog for Mandssangforeninger*, no. 32, and *Udvalgte Folkeviser og Sange*, no. 36; for mandolin or violin and piano

as "In Lonely Moments" by Hjalmar O. Anderson, 1903; for string orchestra (also violin and piano) as *La mélancolie* by Johan Halvorsen, Copenhagen: Wilhelm Hansen, 1914; for piano by F. A. Reissiger in *Ole Bull's Favorit Compositioner,* Christiania: Warmuth, 1880; also hand copies
SEE: Linge, *Ole Bull,* 78–79, 366, 367; Nils Grinde, *Norsk Musikk Historie* (Oslo, 1971), 122; Øyvind Anker, "Et ukjent Manuskript av Ole Bull, *Norsk Musikkliv* 15 (1948): 16–17.

67. "In the Spruce Forest" ("I granskoven") (Text: Marcus Jacob Monrad, added later)
COMP.: 1863?
FOR: voice and piano
1ST PERF.: Christiania, 2 May 1863 as solo song
AUTOGRAPH: melody only (UOslo)
TEXT PUBL.: *Tvende Texter af Job Spillemand [M. J. Monrad] til Melodier af Ole Bull. 1. I ensomme stunde. 2. I granskoven* (two texts by Job Spillemand [Monrad] to melodies by Ole Bull), *Illustreret Nyhedsblad,* 1863, no. 18
ARRANG.: for men's chorus by Johan Behrens in *Firstemmig Mands-Sangbog,* no. 73, and *Udvalgte Folkeviser og Sange,* no. 75
SEE: Linge, *Ole Bull,* 366; Anker, "Et ukjent Manuskript," 17

68. Fantasy on "Là ci darem la mano" from *Don Giovanni* by Mozart
FOR: violin solo
PERF.: Christiania, 17 July 1863
SEE: 1863 program (UOslo)

69. *Festival Overture (Festouverture)*
DESCRIP.: projected for the Norwegian theater, 17 May 1864
NO PERF.
SEE: Linge, *Ole Bull,* 254

RUSSIA 1867

70. *Homage to Moscow (Hommage à Moscou)*
COMP.: Moscow, 1867
FOR: violin, chorus, and orchestra
DESCRIP.: ended with the "Emperor's Hymn"
1ST PERF.: Moscow, April 1867
SEE: Bull, ed., *Ole Bulls Breve i Uddrag,* 401; Linge, *Ole Bull,* 365; Bergsagel, "Ole Bull," 3:448

71. *The Nightingale (Nattergalen)*
COMP.: Moscow, 1867
DESCRIP.: fantasy on the Russian popular song "The Nightingale" ("Solovei") by A. Alyabiev
1ST PERF.: Moscow, April 1867
AUTOGRAPH: manuscript (?) in 1868–69 scrapbook of Bertha Collins

SEE: Bull, ed., *Ole Bulls Breve i Uddrag,* 405; Linge, *Ole Bull,* 365; *The Herald-News,* 21 July 1970

UNITED STATES 1872

72. *Lilly Dale (Lily Dale)*
COMP.: 1872
FOR: violin and piano
DESCRIP.: fantasia on an American folk tune with variations
PERF.: Bergen, October 1872
SEE: Bull, ed., *Ole Bulls Breve i Uddrag,* 407, 408 (nos. 72 and 73 as separate pieces); Linge, *Ole Bull,* 269 (as two pieces), 366 (as one piece)

73. *Vision*
COMP.: 1872
FOR: violin and piano
DESCRIP.: four distinct motives in the Finale
PERF.: Bergen, October 1872
SEE: Bull, ed., *Ole Bulls Breve i Uddrag,* 408 (nos. 72 and 73 as separate pieces); Linge, *Ole Bull,* 269 (as two pieces), 366 (as one piece)

NORWAY 1873

74. *Far to the West there Lies a Land (Yderst mod Vesten ligger et Land)*
DED.: to collect funds for the Leif Ericson monument
1ST PERF.: Christiania, 27 August 1873
SEE: Reidar Mjøen, "Ole Bull," in O. M. Sandvik and Gerhard Schjelderup, eds., *Norges Musikhistorie* (Christiania, 1921), 1:175.

UNITED STATES 1877

75. Variations on "We Won't go Home until Morning"
DESCRIP.: improvisation
PERF.: New York, March 1877
SEE: Linge, *Ole Bull,* 279

UNDATED

76. *Barcarolle* (Text: an unknown French poet)
COMP.: 1833–35 (tentative)
FOR: voice and piano
DESCRIP.: Italian-style melody
AUTOGRAPH: two drafts (location unknown)
ARRANG.: for voice and piano by Ola Linge from Bull's two drafts, Oslo: Edition Gamma, 1950
SEE: Linge, *Ole Bull,* 369

List of Works

B. WORKS RELATED TO BULL

B1. *La Belle Fanny, Waltz from Ole Bull* arranged for piano by A. Foreit, Boston: G. P. Reed [1845]; as "Walzer" No. 64 copied by Ole Tobias Olsen (UOslo); as "Vals," melody only, copied by Anders Moestue (UOslo) (part of a larger lost work?)

B2. *Fantasia* (potpourri style) for piano and violin with orchestra instruments suggested, unknown copyist (UOslo)

B3. "Ole Bulls Polka" published by Christian Olsen, Torpelund par Eskebjerg, Denmark: Chr. Olsen, 1926 (written down from memory three generations removed from Bull)

B4. *Ole Bull's Waltzes, as Performed at the American Institute, with Enthusiastic Applause, by Ole Bull* by Joseph Labitzky, New York: Firth & Hall [1844]

B5. *Ole Bull Violin Instruction Book,* Boston: Keith's Music Publishing House, 1845 (possibly by Ole Bull, junior)

B6. "Hornpipe" by Ole Bull, hand copy by Mat. O. Bræin (Minneapolis, 1 December 1909) (UOslo)

B7. "No. 9" by "Olle Bull?" hand copy by Hans Schjelle (UOslo)

B8. "No. 12" by Ole Bull?, hand copy by J. E. Prytz (UOslo)

B9. "Alke-Valsen" by Ole Bull?, hand copy by Th. Elnan of Tröndelag (UOslo)

B10. "Halling til Studenternes Selskab den 10de December 1848" "according to Bull's notations," hand copy by Sophonias Christian Krag (29 March 1849) (Bergen Offentlige Bibliotek)

B11. "Halling," "Springdands," "Springdands" from Bull's notations?, hand copy by Sophonias Christian Krag (Bergen Offentlige Bibliotek)

B12. Ole Bull autograph of six tunes: "Fjeldsang," "Hallingdans," "Sætervise," "Fra Gudbrandsdalen," "Klage" (see no. 66 above), "Untitled" (location unknown; as one-page facsimile in Hopp, *Eventyret,* facing p. 45)

C. WORKS WITH UNCLEAR OR INCOMPLETE REFERENCE

C1. Fantasies for violin solo (Paris, 13 January 1846) (Linge, *Ole Bull,* 160)

C2. Fantasy on Scandinavian themes (Aarvig, *Den unge Ole Bull,* 104)

C3. Two drafts for Norwegian fantasies (UOslo) (Linge, *Ole Bull,* 366)

C4. *The Hemlock* by Bull, arranged by Helgi Sigurdur Helgason, 1902 (Library of Congress, Washington D.C., lost 1989) (possibly "In the Spruce Forest," no. 67 above)

D. WORKS BY OLE BULL, JUNIOR, OR MASTER OLE BULL
(Frederick Buckley)

D1. "Tambourine Dance and Polka," Philadelphia: Walker 1849 (piano)

D2. "Poor Linda," Boston: Wade, 1850 (voice and piano)

D3. "Little Rose," Boston: Wade, 1850 (voice and piano)

D4. "Philadelphia Yaller Gals," Boston: Wade, 1850 (voice and piano)

D5. "Lucy Bee," Philadelphia: Ferrett, 1850 (voice and piano)

D6. "Juney at the Gate" (voice and piano) Philadelphia: Smith, 1850; also Boston:

Oliver Ditson, 1850; arr. for piano by W. P. Cunnington, Philadelphia: Lee & Walker, 1850
D7. "Awake my Love for Me," Boston: Reed, 1850 (voice and piano)
All but "Awake my Love for Me" are for the New Orleans Serenaders.

E. PERFORMABLE WORKS

Complete information on these pieces and their sources is to be found in the List of Works above. In general, copies of the nineteenth-century editions are available in larger libraries. Only three works have been published in modern editions, and, of these, no. 8 is incomplete, no. 39 is simplified, and no. 76 consists of two conflated drafts. Certain other works exist only as original autographs or as hand copies. Because much is not fully written out in these primary sources, the works in question would need significant reconstruction to be made playable.

ORIGINAL WORKS (without arrangement by others)

For violin and orchestra: A Mother's Prayer, Opus 1: *Adagio Religioso;* see no. 15. *Bravura Variations,* Opus 3; see no. 8. *Concerto in E minor* (reconstruction necessary, especially for mt. 3); see no. 29. *Greetings from Afar* (extensive reconstruction necessary); see no. 33. *Nocturne,* Opus 2; see no. 36. *Siciliano and Tarantella* (slightly altered by Ola Linge); see no. 39. *Visit to the Sæter* (hand copy); see no. 53.

For violin and piano: A Mother's Prayer or Opus 1: *Adagio Religioso* (differs from violin/orchestra version); see no. 15. *Bravura Variations,* Opus 3; see no. 8. *Concerto in E minor,* movement 2 only; see no. 29. "In Moments of Solitude" (autograph); see no. 66. *Nocturne,* Opus 2; see no. 36. *Polacca Guerriera;* see no. 19. *Siciliano and Tarantella* (slightly simplified by Ola Linge); see no. 39. *Visit to the Sæter;* see no. 53.

For violin with piano and organ: Greetings from Afar (extensive reconstruction necessary); see no. 33.

For chorus, orchestra, and soloists: Music for *The Mountain Cottage* by Henrik Wergeland (autograph); see no. 56. "Away, Over the Ocean" (unison female chorus and orchestra); see no. 56a. "Stop Now, Mayor" (female unison chorus, strings, oboe); see no. 56b. "Sigrid's Song" (Text: "Here, Where in Everything") (female solo voice, orchestra); see no. 56c. "Huldre Song" (Text: "Go in Now") (female solo voice, orchestra); see no. 56d.

For men's chorus and orchestra: The Power of Art (Text: "Lægger du dit øre") (autograph); see no. 58.

Miscellaneous: Norwegian Mountain Melodies: "Halling from Hallingdal" (piano), "Old Tougeslaat from Silgjord" (voice and langeleik), "Tougdands: Haugtusslaaten"

List of Works

(piano), "Springar from Thelemarken" (piano), "Folksong from Orkedalen 'Ifjol gjætt' e gjeitinn'" [sic] (voice and piano), "Vosserulla" (piano); see no. 59.

ARRANGEMENTS BY OTHERS

For many of Bull's pieces there are partial or complete arrangements by others. See the List of Works. Some of the better-known examples are: *Barcarolle* arranged for voice and piano by Ola Linge (see no. 76); "In Moments of Solitude" arranged for string orchestra (also violin and piano) as *La mélancolie* by Johan Halvorsen (see no. 66); "In the Spruce Forest" arranged for men's chorus by Johan Behrens (the original voice/piano version does not exist) (see no. 67); "Sæter Girl's Sunday" (Text added: "På solen jeg ser") arranged in many versions (see no. 53a); "Sigrid's Song" (Text: "Here, Where in Everything") arranged for men's chorus by Johan Behrens as "The Abandoned One" ("Den forladte") (see no. 56c).

F. RECORDINGS

RECORDINGS

Bull, Ole. *En Jubileumskonsert,* Arve Tellefsen, violin, Harmonien with conductor Karsten Andersen. *Bravura Variations,* "Adagio" from the *Concerto in E Minor, A Mother's Prayer, Polacca Guerriera, Nocturne, Visit to the Sæter, In Moments of Solitude* (*La mélancolie*). Norsk Kulturråds Klassikerserie, Polygram Records, 1980 (NKF 30041 Stereo) (CD NKFCD 5008–2).

Individual works appear (especially "Sæter Girl's Sunday") on various recordings.

TAPE

Bull, Ole. *Melodiminner fra Lysøen: A Melodic Memorial,* Arve Tellefsen, violin, Kaare Ørnung, piano. *In Moments of Solitude* (*La mélancolie*), "Adagio" from the *Concerto in E Minor, Visit to the Sæter, Barcarolle, A Mother's Prayer,* section from *Polacca Guerriera.* NCB Stereo, Norsk Plateproduksjon (NKK3).

TELEVISION

I Ole Bulls Spor (*In Ole Bull's Footsteps*), directed by Inger Bjørnstad. Arve Tellefsen, violin. Five television programs for Norsk Rikskringkasting–Children's Division (Norwegian Broadcasting). See Arve Tellefsen, "Ole Bull og verden," in *Programbladet* issued by Norsk Rikskringkasting, no. 51/52, 1982.

Appendix A: The Bull Name

Various people found it advantageous to capitalize on Bull's name. During Bull's first American tour a "Little Ole Bull" was the chief attraction of a minstrel group called the Congo Melodists, and an "Ole Bull, junior," identified only as Master Howard, performed with Barnum's Museum.[1] In 1844 a blackface ballet dancer called "Oiley Bull" appeared in a comedy called "Tom and Jerry in America" by John Brougham.[2]

Another entertainer, Frederick Buckley, a violinist in the minstrel troupe called the New Orleans Operatic Serenaders, used the stage name "Ole Bull junior" or "Master Ole Bull." He seems to have done imitations of Bull, and he also composed music under this pseudonym. His colleagues in the group did imitations of Jenny Lind, Giulia Grisi, and other operatic stars, using the pseudonyms Signor Boni and Signor Bonjoni.[3]

A Norwegian country fiddler, Anders Sørensen, known for a popular waltz (Sørensens Vals), traveled about the countryside in the 1890s, claiming to be "a pupil of Ole Bull," though at most he had spent a couple of hours with Bull.[4]

1. George C. D. Odell, *Annals of the New York Stage* (New York, 1928 and 1931), 4:73, 5:227.
2. Pat Ryan, Trondheim, personal communication.
3. Odell, *Annals,* 5:490. See chap. 21.
4. Dag Gundersen, Oslo, personal communication.

Appendix B: Memorabilia

Numerous personal recollections about Bull are found in newspapers and periodicals of the time. We have included many in the text and bibliography. Olav K. Lundeberg wrote a charming story about his grandmother, who as a maid in a hotel in Holden, Minnesota, in the 1860s sang the "Värmland Song" for Ole Bull.[1]

In 1879 porcelain busts of Bull were advertised for sale at six kroner by Carl Warmuth in Christiania.[2] When Bull played in the Old South Meeting House in Boston in January, 1880, the occasion was memorialized with an inscribed tablet there.[3] Ole Bull's champagne glass and a gilded table setting, gifts from the Czar of Russia, were donated to the Bergen Museum of History in 1983 by a grandson of John Lund, Bull's associate in the Norwegian Theater.[4]

Bull's Guarnerius from 1744 became the subject of a brochure by Henry Werro, a violin maker in Bern, Switzerland.[5] Bull's Gasparo da Salò went to the Kunstindustri Museum, Bergen, in 1902, donated by Sara Bull.[6] A Stradivarius from 1687 that Bull bought in Hungary and then sold to English collectors in 1861 is now housed at the Smithsonian Institution, Washington, D.C.[7]

In 1951 a woman of Norwegian and Swedish descent, Ida Corliss, opened a restaurant in Rockport, Massachusetts. Inspired by a news story about the Oleana colony, she called her restaurant "Oleana by-the-Sea."[8] In Mantonville, Minnesota, friends brought in table mats from a restaurant called Hubbell House displaying an autograph of Ole Bull. In 1974 a Universalist pastor in California, Harmon Gehr,

1. Olav K. Lundeberg, "Grandmother Sang for Ole Bull," *Lutheran Herald* (1 December 1936): 1147–69.
2. Program 1879.
3. Report by Øyvind Gulliksen.
4. *Bergens Tidende* (4 April 1983).
5. Henry Werro, *"Ole Bull": Joseph Guarnerius del Gesú 1744 IHS* (Berne, 1971).
6. Sara C. Bull, *The Gaspar da Salo — Benvenuto Cellini Violin,* Disposition of to Vestlandske Kunstindustri Museum, Bergen, 1902.
7. The Ole Bull violin belongs to the Herbert Axelrod string quartet of instruments. All four instruments are made by Stradivarius. Thanks to Gary Sturm, Smithsonian Institution, and Edwin M. Good, Stanford University. See also Henry W. Hill, Arthur F. Hill and Alfred E. Hill, *Antonio Stradivari: His Life and Work* (1902; reprint, New York, 1963), 80.
8. She has kindly supplied us with clippings and brochures.

317

traveled about giving a talk on the "Saga of Ole Bull," while demonstrating with an imitation of Bull's playing.[9] In 1979 a journalist from the Eau Claire, Wisconsin, *Leader-Telegram* wrote a story about a local violinist playing an "Ole Bull violin."[10]

9. Warren Winfield, "'Ole Bull' Reborn in Herman Gehr," *UU World* (15 October 1974).
10. Bill Kelly, 15 December 1979. Thanks to Clarence Kilde.

Appendix C: Pictures and Statues

Bull was a welcome subject for painters, sculptors, and photographers. He was painted in Italy by the Norwegian painter Fearnley and the Italian Gambardella in the early 1830s. He was sketched in St. Petersburg and in Hamburg. A youthful picture made from a drawing by E. T. Parris in 1836 in London appears as the frontispiece of a poem in his honor by Cécile Gay in 1881.[1] He was lithographed by Biow in 1838. A drawing with a particularly soulful expression was made of him by Krehuber in Vienna in 1839. After he bought his Gasparo da Salò violin in 1840, his picture was painted with it by Elisabeth Baumann (Jerichau) (1819–81). This painting is one of Bull's best youthful portraits.[2]

A Byronic lithograph of Bull from 1841 signed by Ramberg, is from Schuberth of Hamburg and Leipzig. In 1843 a rather strange drawing was made of the thirty-three-year-old Bull by F. O. Darley, either in Boston or New York. It has been repeatedly reissued as "the young Ole Bull." A picture of Bull and Vieuxtemps, presumably in New York, is extant. In 1850 Bull was painted by Fritz Jensen, his helper with the Norwegian Theater. There is an undated photograph from Minneapolis, presumably from 1856.

There are photos of Bull with his family at Valestrand from the 1860s and from the wreathing ceremony in San Francisco in 1870. A gray- or white-haired Bull is seen in a photo by E. Milster in Berlin in 1876. There are several photos from the 1870s, including an especially dramatic one supposedly taken in Steinway Hall in April, 1877. In the 1870s James Stuart made drawings of Bull holding his bow and violin in various poses. In 1880 Bogardus in New York took a photo that shows his aging very markedly. A copy of this portrait from 1880 is in the Wayside Inn, dedicated to Horsford's daughter Cornelia.

Paintings of Bull are said to hang in the Bologna Philharmonic Society and in Boston's Unitarian Church. There is one in the Norwegian-American Museum "Vesterheim" in Decorah, Iowa. Probably they can also be found elsewhere.

An interesting drawing from 1912 by the Swedish artist Anders Zorn (1860–

---

1. Cécile Gay, *Ole Bull, violiniste norvégien* (Paris, 1881).

2. Reproduced in Finn Benestad and Dag Schjelderup-Ebbe, *Edvard Grieg: The Man and the Artist,* trans. William H. Halverson and Leland B. Sateren (Lincoln, Nebr., 1988), 5, and in Mentz Schulerud, *Norsk Kunstnerliv* (Oslo, 1960), 144.

1920) titled "Vallkullans söndag" clearly represents Bull's popular song "Sæter Girl's Sunday." It is reported that Zorn asked his model to keep singing Bull's song in order to produce the right mood of melancholy![3]

The first statue of Ole Bull was erected by Norwegian-Americans, sculpted by Jakob Fjelde, born 1859 in Ålesund, Norway. The statue stands in Minneapolis, in Loring Park, where it was dedicated on 17 May 1897. The speaker of the day was attorney J. W. Arctander, while the music was by Bull's son Alexander, who played "Sæter Girl's Sunday." Arctander said, among other things, that Norwegian-Americans erected this statue on account of Ole Bull's having taken up his residence in America. Bull "admired our institutions, he was proud of its free government, and he felt at home among a free people."[4]

The second statue was commissioned in Bergen already in 1881, but the committee did nothing after collecting funds for twenty years. A statue was finally ordered from Stephan Sinding (1846–1922) and dedicated on 17 May 1901. It has a singularly attractive position on a street in the center of Bergen, with Bull playing above a waterfall and a *nøkk,* the water sprite of Norwegian folklore, standing below.

A third statue was sculpted by Ambrosia Tønnesen (1859–1948), a woman who did not win the competition of 1901, but who persisted and succeeded in getting her statue placed in the foyer of the new theater erected in Bergen in 1909. She appears to have been Norway's first woman sculptor. Born in Ålesund, she taught in Bergen and then went abroad for artistic instruction, living in Paris until 1910. Her Ole Bull, writes Arnljot Strømme-Svendsen, "is a handsome work in her sensitive naturalistic style. Ole Bull welcomes with a smile all guests to the theater he founded."[5]

3. Called to our attention by Eric Kula, of Lexington, Mass.
4. John W. Arctander, "Ole Bull," *Skandinaven* (26 May 1887). Thanks to Orm Øverland.
5. Arnljot Strømme-Svendsen, "Ole Bull statuene og deres skapelse," *Bergens Tidende* (30 September 1980).

Appendix D: Musical Dedications

Bull was honored with many musical compositions. The popular Viennese violinist and dance composer Joseph Lanner (1801–43) dedicated *Norwegische Arabesken für das Pianoforte* (*Norwegian Arabesques for the Piano*), Opus 145 (1839) to Ole Bull. Andreas Munch added a text to the melody of *Polacca Guerriera* to make a song for chorus in honor of Bull on 10 January 1842.[1] Rudolf Hasert (1826–77) wrote a piece called *Ved Mindets Bæger: Sang til Ole Bull* (*At the Beaker of Memory: Song to Ole Bull*), and Otto Winter-Hjelm wrote a festival march *Til Ole Bull 872–1872* (*To Ole Bull 872–1872*) for Norway's thousand year's celebration on 18 July 1872.[2] Johan Svendsen's *Norsk rapsodi nr. 2* (*Norwegian Rhapsody no. 2*) composed in 1876 is dedicated to Bull. Johannes Haarklou's early piece, *Adagio Religioso* of 1878, was also dedicated to Bull, and his song for six-voice chorus (Work 32, no. 7) "In Memoriam," used the Welhaven poem that honored Bull.[3]

Friedrich August Reissiger wrote a *Sørgemarsch over Ole Bull* (*Funeral March over Ole Bull*) that was published in 1880 by Warmuth as part of a collection titled *Ole Bull's Favorit-Compositioner,* and Henry Strauss wrote a *Grand Funeral March in Memory of Ole Bull* published in Boston by L. E. Whipple. In 1901 Grieg composed music to the above-mentioned Welhaven poem: "To Ole Bull: How Sweet to be Embraced by the Peace of Evening." This music was first performed at the dedication of the Ole Bull statue in Bergen, 17 May 1901.[4] Because of its compositional date (1901), it cannot have been the music played at Bull's funeral, based on the same text. Will George Butler's *Visions of Oleona* was written for the "pilgrimage" to Oleana in 1920.[5]

1. Henrik Winter-Hjelm, "Træk af Ole Bulls Liv," *Morgenbladet* (1852).
2. Copies of all of these are in the University of Oslo Library.
3. "In Memoriam" was printed in 1892; Finn Benestad, *Johannes Haarklou: Mannen og verket* (Oslo, 1961), 110.
4. Grieg, No. CW159 in Finn Benestad and Dag Schjelderup-Ebbe, *Edvard Grieg: The Man and the Artist,* trans. William H. Halverson and Leland B. Sateren (Lincoln, Nebr., 1988), 427.
5. Copy in Potter County Historical Society, Coudersport, Penn.

Appendix E: Posthumous Studies

BIOGRAPHICAL STUDIES

After Bull's death in 1880, the first complete biographical survey of his life was written by author and journalist Jonas Lie.[1] Lie's deeply felt characterization of his friend appeared as an introduction to Bull's correspondence, chiefly with his wife Félicie and son Alexander (who furnished the letters). Lie began with the idea that must have been thought by every Bull biographer: "How can one give a true and sober portrayal of a man about whom there has been fantasizing and the making of fairytales for fifty years in most of two continents?" He summed up Bull's contribution: "Bull was the greatest living representative of the so-called romantic era of the virtuoso, when the inspired violin took the lead and the individual genius was permitted to electrify the audience, while the orchestra was reduced to playing a supportive, fulfilling role."[2] Bull's correspondence with Félicie was almost entirely in French, but was here translated into Norwegian. While these letters read well and are informative, one is troubled by the unavailability of the French originals.

In 1882 a volume by Bull's widow Sara followed, entitled *Ole Bull: A Memoir.* With this was included "Violin Notes" by Bull and "The Anatomy of the Violinist" by Dr. Alpheus Benning Crosby, with James Stuart's drawings of six hand positions on the violin by Bull. (See p. 215.) It concludes with a section of "Poems and Personal Tributes." In a copy preserved in the Boston Public Library, a one-time owner has pasted a large number of American reviews of Bull's concerts. Sara Bull's book was generally well received, though one reviewer objected to what he called "making out Bull as a saint." While the book reveals great effort on her part, it can hardly be called an objective account.

The same was true of Oddmund Vik's Norwegian biography of 1890. Vik, himself a writer from Bergen, declared in his postscript that his goal was not to "propose new judgments about Ole Bull as a violinist," but to "set forth his deeds at home and from that base to trace his journeys abroad."[3] Vik's bibliography in-

---

1. Jonas Lie, "Ole Bull, hans Karakteristik og Liv," in Alexander Bull, ed., *Ole Bulls Breve i Uddrag. Med en karakteristik og biografisk Skitse af Jonas Lie* (Copenhagen, 1881), 1–154.
2. Lie, "Ole Bull," 1.
3. Oddmund Vik, *Ole Bull* (Bergen, 1890), 535.

cluded Lie's and Sara Bull's biographies as well as most of the notices of Bull's life that had reached Norway by this time. For two generations, Vik's biography remained the chief Norwegian source for Ole Bull's life. The fact that it was written in a somewhat labored New Norwegian did not make it particularly accessible.

The first twentieth-century biography was by Christian A. Aarvig, a Danish writer and violin teacher in Copenhagen. It was entitled *Den unge Ole Bull: En Violinspillers Ungdomskampe* (*Young Ole Bull: The Youthful Conflicts of a Violinist*). Aarvig dealt primarily with Bull's youth and his rise to fame, but his book was also a valuable analysis of Bull's qualities as a musician. He saw Bull's significance as transcending the field of the violin: "The story of Bull, the fairytale that became a reality, gave his nation self-confidence, courage, and strength to aspire to the summit, to contribute the best. . . . Bull was the bringer of light, a spark that fired his nation's consciousness and roused its slumbering powers to action."[4]

In 1943 a new American biography appeared, written by Mortimer Smith. Smith was (then) married to Sylvea Shapleigh Bull, an adopted daughter of Olea Bull Vaughan, Bull's daughter by Sara. Sylvea had inherited the island of Lysøen from Olea, and Smith was therefore a frequent visitor to Norway in her company. His biography was well written and gave a lively, at times even humorous, account of Bull's life. In his preface he (quite justly) accused the previous biographies of being "extended eulogies." He had the advantage of having access to the "voluminous papers" left by Sara Bull, "only a small portion of which she used in her book."[5] Even so, Ola Linge found that Smith "was often in error in his evaluation of Bull both as a person and as an artist, both because he was not aware of a great many facts, because he knew no Norwegian, and because he had no musical expertise."[6]

The next Bull biography (1945) by Zinken Hopp, a Norwegian writer of children's stories, took a different approach. It was called *Eventyret om Ole Bull* (*The Fairytale about Ole Bull*).[7] Linge characterized it as "a cocktail of the three preceding biographies [Lie's, Sara Bull's, and Vik's] with rather much spice added." While he granted her lively style, he noted that some of Hopp's stories "tell more about the author's interests than about the real Ole Bull."[8]

We come at length to Ola Linge's biography, *Ole Bull: Livshistoria, Mannen, Kunstnaren* (*Ole Bull: Life Story, The Man, The Artist*) (Oslo, 1953). As any reader of the footnotes in the present volume will see, we have depended extensively on the facts presented in his book. Linge (1885–1973) was born and died in Valldal, a West Norwegian community some distance to the north of Bergen. He studied French at the University of Oslo and then went to Paris, where he operated a music store for about twenty years. During this time he collected information about Ole Bull, piecing together what he could find in the European (and American) press. His Bull archive is now in the University of Oslo Library. He did some composing on his own and played various instruments, even proposing an improved system

4. (Copenhagen, 1934), 108.
5. Mortimer Smith, *The Life of Ole Bull* (Princeton, N.J.), vii.
6. Ola Linge, *Ole Bull: Livshistoria, Mannen, Kunstnaren* (Oslo, 1953), 12.
7. (Bergen, 1945).
8. Linge, *Ole Bull,* 11–12.

of musical notation.[9] One's only regret is that his Bull biography is too detailed for easy reading and that it lacks necessary bibliographical references.

Additional biographical materials on Bull are to be found in two volumes published in Bergen in 1901 and 1910. The first volume was edited by John Lund, chairman of the committee for the raising of an Ole Bull statue in Bergen: *Festskrift ved Ole Bull statuens afsløring 17/5 1901 (Festival Volume at the Unveiling of the Ole Bull Statue May 17, 1901)* (Bergen, 1901). The second volume was issued in the centennial of Bull's birth. It contains letters from Bull to his family in Norway: *Ole Bull 1810–1910: Et Mindeskrift (Ole Bull 1810–1910: A Memorial Volume)* (Bergen, 1910).

More recent studies of Bull are found in Mentz Schulerud's *Norsk Kunstnerliv* (Oslo, 1960), especially pages 99–113, 144–152, and 164–168. Schulerud emphasized the humorous aspects of Bull's relationship to fellow artists. A more coherent account is Carl O. Gram Gjesdal's "Ole Bull" in *Norske Klassikere,* edited by Peter Anker, K. Bækkelund, and E. Straume (Oslo, 1985). Gjesdal cites extensively from Bull's letters and tells anew the story of his concert tours.

STUDIES OF SPECIFIC TOPICS

The earliest research on any specific aspect of Bull's career was a series of articles on his Oleana venture by Torstein Jahr, a Norwegian librarian employed in the Library of Congress in Washington.[10] Jahr provided a detailed history of the settlement and its fate, but he accepted the idea that Bull had been swindled, which later research has disproved. Otherwise his study is of major importance.

An article on "Ole Bull and his Wisconsin Contacts" appeared in the *Wisconsin Magazine of History* in 1924 (vol. 7, pp. 417–44). It was written by Albert O. Barton, a highly conscientious historian and a journalist who also assisted Rasmus B. Anderson in writing Anderson's autobiography.

John van Schaick, Jr., wrote a series of articles in 1939 on "The Characters in the *Tales of a Wayside Inn*" which appeared in *The Christian Leader.* Two of them were devoted to Ole Bull as "The Musician." It seems that there was actually a group of friends who met at the Inn from time to time, though Bull was not one of them. However, "the writings of Mr. Longfellow have created an imperishable tradition. In the larger sense Ole Bull often has visited the Inn. . . ."[11]

Arne Bjørndal (1882–1963) was a specialist in Norwegian folk music who repeatedly published studies of Ole Bull's relation to the music of Norwegian fiddlers. Articles of his appeared from 1922 to 1966. His most important study was *Ole Bull og norsk folkemusikk* (Bergen, 1940). He probably exaggerated Bull's dependence on the country fiddlers.

A charming contribution was an article by Francis Bull, professor of Norwegian Literature at Oslo University, "Ole Bull og Norge," which appeared in 1940.[12]

---

9. *Sunnmørsposten* (13 October 1973).

10. Torstein Jahr, "Oleana—Et blad af Ole Bulls og den norske indvandrings historie, *Symra* (1910), 6:2–37, 129–62, 195–216.

11. *The Christian Leader* 11 (6 May 1939): 422.

12. *Samtiden* 51 (1940): 449–68.

Appendix E

Francis Bull was himself a member of the Bull clan, but he was also a scholar and a gifted lecturer on all aspects of Norwegian literature. He cast light on Bull's special fascination with Norwegian nationality, the patriotic side of his being. It is significant that his article was published in the same year that Norway was invaded by Hitler.

Schak Bull (1858–1956) was a Bergen architect who gave an informal talk on Ole Bull at a four-hundredth reunion of the Bull family on 28 August 1950. His talk offered personal recollections of his famous uncle, who not only played enchantingly, but "was in his nature the most charming person I have ever known."[13] He recalled some Bull episodes, for instance Bull's correction of Schak's boyish stance with the violin. He retold some of Bull's anecdotes. There are minor lapses in his account; for example, he attributed liaisons to Bull for which there is no other evidence.

Another anniversary was celebrated in Pennsylvania in the hundredth year after Oleana (1952), and for it Mary E. Welfling wrote an excellent account of the colony, including its later history. Only three families remained after Bull left, the German doctor Edward Joerg, Henry Andresen, who became a storekeeper, and the Olson family. Welfling included two poems of welcome to the Ole Bull settlers (see chap. 12).[14] She also described the 1920 "pilgrimage" to the site.

In 1954 Eric Danell, a Swedish critic, took up the conflict of the 1840s between Bull and Pratté.[15] Danell quoted passages from Pratté, whose critique of Bull he judged to be largely based on professional jealousy, pointing out that Pratté was one of the best harpists of the day. Danell also cited the opinions of Jonas Lie and Wergeland. Pratté was lodged in Wergeland's home, so that Wergeland too got involved in the conflict. Danell explains that the whole problem was resolved when Pratté issued a new review in 1843, in which he completely revised his judgment of Bull from one of condemnation to one of admiration.

In 1960 author and radio critic Mentz Schulerud (b. 1915) published a brochure in memory of Bull's 150th anniversary. Schulerud's piece does not bring out anything new, but it is an entertaining account of Bull's career from a modern point of view. When Bull was driven home by the February Revolution in 1848 he hoped to make a revolution in Norway, or, as Schulerud says, "at least put an end to his country's Sleeping Beauty existence."[16] Schulerud wove in episodes of Bull's life in his book *Norsk Kunstnerliv,* which appeared in the same year.[17]

In 1975 a commission (*arbeidsgruppe*) appointed in 1973 brought in a proposal (*Innstilling*) on the future use, administration, and financing of Lysøen, which Sylvea Bull (now Curtis) had donated to the Society for Preservation of Ancient Monuments in 1973. This was a joint report by Norwegian administrative authorities,

13. Schak Bull, *Kåseri: Holdt ved den trønderske slekt Bulls 400-års jubileum, 28. august 1950* (Oslo, 1950), 3.

14. Mary E. Welfling, *The Ole Bull Colony in Potter County 1852: One Hundredth anniversary observed July 31–August 1, 1952* (Coudersport, Penn., 1952), 18.

15. Eric Danell, *Ole Bull och Pratté: Några Kritiska randanmärkningar* (Stockholm, 1954).

16. Mentz Schulerud, *Ole Bull: Et minneskrift til 150-årsjubileet for hans fødsel 5. februar 1960* (Oslo, 1960), 21.

17. (Oslo, 1960). See especially pp. 100, 104, 107, 109, 144, 149, 165, 167.

including the local communes, for an appropriate use of the island and its preservation as a memorial to Ole Bull. The *Innstilling om Lysøens framtidige bruk* . . . includes a description of the island, Bull's relation to it, its future use and administration, and its financing. In effect the Norwegian state took over responsibility for the island, admitting a moderate number of visitors and arranging concerts in Ole Bull's villa. A stone memorial to Mrs. Curtis was erected on the grounds of the island. In this way Bull's frequently expressed wish that Lysøen should become a national Norwegian memorial was fulfilled.

The year 1980, a century after his death, was an obvious occasion for remembering Bull. The Bergen Public Library (Bergen Offentlige Bibliotek) mounted an exhibit. The Bergen Theater (Den Nationale Scene) put on a festive program. The 17th of May Committee published a brochure. On November 11 the musical society Harmonien presented a Bull program.[18]

In Oslo the person who made the most of this occasion was Ladislav Reznicek, a Czech scholar and collector and a relatively recent emigré to Norway. He edited a pamphlet dedicated to Ole Bull.[19] It contained pictures of Bull and his violins, poems about Bull, quotations from the literature about Bull, and samples of his music. He also edited a small selection from Bull's letters to his mother, *Min kjære Moder. En kjærlighets erklæring* (*My Dear Mother: A Declaration of Love*) (Bergen, 1980). The selections by Bull were "placed in a dramatic connection" by the editor.

In 1982 Anders Buraas, a Norwegian journalist, published a volume on well-known emigrants from Norway: *De reiste ut* (*They Went Abroad*) (Oslo, 1982). One chapter dealt with Ole Bull (pp. 200–26), and its main emphasis was on the Oleana colony. Buraas corrected previous errors about the colony, including ruling out the idea that Bull was swindled.

Finally, we list a dissertation by Inez Bull, a "grand-niece" of Bull's. She is a music teacher and singer in New Jersey and has a small Bull museum at Carter Camp (formerly called New Bergen), Pennsylvania. Her dissertation entitled *Ole Bull's Activities in the United States between 1843 and 1880: A Biography* was submitted in 1982 to the School of Education at New York University. The dissertation shows inadequate mastery of the Norwegian sources and inaccurate work.

LEXICA

Bull is naturally mentioned in many biographical dictionaries. We shall consider only four significant entries.

O. M. Sandvik wrote a biographical sketch in 1925 for *Norsk Biografisk Leksikon*. This was a fairly complete presentation of Bull's restless life. Sandvik somewhat freely characterized his "artistic career as a self-taught man." He noted that Bull learned much from Italian singing, "handling the violin so that it reproduced the sound he sought." The criticism Bull got from Fink, says Sandvik, was due to the fact that the men of another school, that is, the Germans, had found a spokesman. "If one expects an interpreter in the concert hall and gets instead

---

18. Information from the Music Division of the Bergen Offentlige Bibliotek.

19. Ladislav Reznicek, ed., *Tilegnet Ole Bull 1980. 1810. 1880* (Oslo, 1980).

an improviser, one will be disappointed."[20] Sandvik exaggerated the number of Oleana settlers to seven hundred (instead of three hundred) and erroneously stated that Bull became an American citizen.

Reidar Mjøen wrote the article on Bull for *Norges Musikhistorie* in 1921. He observed that Bull had his greatest triumphs in "the great, 'primitive,' musically spontaneous and unspoiled America, where a certain Italian taste has always been predominant in the art of the solo." He found Bull's early meeting with Spohr significant, for "Spohr was the creator of the German school in violin technique," who "entertained nothing but contempt for any folkish or national element in music." Spohr and Bull were opposites, Mjøen said, and Bull ended in "the school of Paganini with its freedom and fire, its virtuoso coloring." Bull's originality was due to "the beautiful, warm, intense and intimate relation of the artist to the peculiar character of his people and his country."[21]

In 1980 the musicologist John Bergsagel wrote the article "Ole Bull" in *The New Grove Dictionary of Music and Musicians* (ed. Stanley Sadie [London, 1980], vol. 3). This concentrated biography is excellent, containing in brief compass an extensive listing of works and an adequate bibliography. His account is a thumbnail sketch of Bull's life and works, suggesting about the latter that "they probably deserve more serious attention than they have received" (p. 447). (The name "Lundholm" is misspelled on page 445.)

Carl O. Gram Gjesdal, a Bergen editor, who had written essential parts of *Innstilling* (1975), was given the task of writing the article on "Ole Bull" in the work *Norske Klassikere (Norwegian Classics).*[22] This is an emotionally marked survey of Bull's life, emphasizing the musical heritage he left behind—not just the two popular folk songs "In Moments of Solitude" and "Sæter Girl's Sunday." From childhood Bull stood "in the field of tension between European salon music and the ancient Norwegian folktunes" (p. 69). Gjesdal describes "the gathering of myths that would spice the Ole Bull legend" (p. 70) and points out that "his actual repertoire was hardly large, but it would be greatly enriched through his art of improvisation" (p. 79).

20. Sandvik, "Ole Bull," in *Norsk Biografisk Leksikon* (Oslo, 1925), 2:407, 411, 413.
21. Reidar Mjøen, "Ole Bull," in O. M. Sandvik and Gerhard Schjelderup, eds., *Norges Musikhistorie* (Christiania, 1921), 1:172–84.
22. Ed. Peter Anker, K. Bækkelund, and E. Straume (Oslo, 1985), 66–81.

Bibliography

Aarvig, Christian A. *Den unge Ole Bull: En Violinspillers Ungdomskampe.* Copenhagen, 1934.

Abbott, Eleanor Hallowell. *Being Little in Cambridge, When Everyone Else was Big.* New York, 1936.

Abell, Arthur M. "Ole Bull." In "Famous Violinists of the Past, VII," *Musical Courier* 57.10 (1908): 5–6. New York.

Amerika, Ole Bull og det nye Norge. Bergen, 1852.

Andersen, Hans Christian. "En Episode af Ole Bulls Liv. Fortalt efter Kunstnerens egen muntlige Meddelelser (1839)." In *Samlede Skrifter,* 6:125–28. 2d ed. Copenhagen, 1877. Reprinted in *Vestlandske Tidende* 25 (24 September 1839) and in Stavanger, 1945.

Andersen, Hans Christian. "Pen og Blækhus." In *Samlede Eventyr og Historier,* 2:11–12. Copenhagen, 1975.

Anderson, Rasmus B., assisted by Albert O. Barton. *Life Story.* Madison, Wisconsin, 1915.

Anker, Øyvind. "Et ukjent Manuskript av Ole Bull." *Norsk Musikkliv* 15 (1948): 16–17.

Anker, Øyvind. "Ole Bull som økonomisk kannestøper." Four letters from Ole Bull to Bjørnstjerne Bjørnson. Clipping, n.d. [1937?].

Arctander, John W. "Ole Bull." *Skandinaven* (26 May 1887). Chicago.

Asbjørnsen, Peter Christen. *Hjemmet og Vandringen.* Christiania, 1847.

Aubert, Elise. *Fra Krinoline-Tiden.* Christiania, 1921.

Barth, C. H. "Har 'Sæterjentens Søndag' vært 17-mai marsj?" *Morgenavisen* (16 May 1950), no page.

Barton, Albert O. "Ole Bull and his Wisconsin Contacts." *Wisconsin Magazine of History* 7 (1924): 417–44.

Benestad, Finn. *Johannes Haarklou: Mannen og verket.* Oslo, 1961.

Benestad, Finn, and Dag Schjelderup-Ebbe. *Edvard Grieg: The Man and the Artist.* Trans. by William H. Halverson and Leland B. Sateren. Lincoln, Nebr., 1988. Also published as *Edvard Grieg: mennesket og kunstneren.* Oslo, 1980.

Berg, Adolph, and Olav Mosby. *Musikselskabet Harmonien 1755–1945.* Vol. 1. Bergen, 1945.

Berge, Rikard. *Myllarguten.* Oslo, 1908. New ed., O. Fjalestad, 1972.

Bibliography

Bergsagel, John. "Ole Bull." In Stanley Sadie, ed., *The New Grove Dictionary of Music and Musicians,* 3:445–48. London, 1980.

Beyer, Harald. *Norsk Kulturhistorie.* Vol. 4. Oslo, 1940.

Beyer, Harald. *Norsk Litteraturhistorie.* Oslo, 1963.

B[iow], H[ermann]. *Ole Bull: Eine biographische Skizze.* Hamburg, 1838.

Bjørndal, Arne. *Norsk Folkemusikk.* Bergen, 1952.

Bjørndal, Arne. "Ole Bull og folkemusikken." In Torleiv Hannaas, ed., *Norsk Årbok,* 1922:11–17. Bergen. Also in *Bergen Turlag Aarbok,* 1955:98–109.

Bjørndal, Arne. *Ole Bull og norsk folkemusikk.* Bergen, 1940.

Bjørndal, Arne. "Ole Bull og Valestrand." Reprint from *Frå Fjon til Fjosa.* Stord, 1950.

Bjørndal, Arne, and Brynjulf Alver. *– Og fela ho lét. Norsk spelemannstradisjon.* Oslo, 1966.

Bjørnson, Bjørn. *Mit Livs Historier: Fra barndommens dage.* Christiania, 1922.

Bjørnson, Bjørnstjerne. *Brev.* Ed. Halvdan Koht. Vol. 1. Christiania, 1912.

Blanc, T[harald H.] *Christiania Theaters historie 1827–1877.* Christiania, 1899.

Blanc, T[harald H.]. *Norges første nationale scene.* Christiania, 1884.

Blanche, Aug. *Minnesbilder.* Stockholm, 1872.

Blegen, Theodore C. *Land of Their Choice.* Minneapolis, 1955. Letters from Oleana colonists.

Blegen, Theodore C. *Norwegian Migration to America 1825–1860.* Northfield, Minn., 1931.

Blegen, Theodore C., and Martin B. Ruud, eds. *Norwegian Emigrant Songs and Ballads.* Minneapolis, 1936.

Blytt, Peter. *Minder fra den første norske scene i Bergen.* Bergen, 1907.

Bowen, Eli. *The Pictorial Sketch-book of Pennsylvania.* 2d ed. Philadelphia, 1853.

Brækstad, H. L. *Ole Bull, Biografisk Skitse.* Bergen, 1885.

Broadhouse, John. *How to Make a Violin. The Violin: Its Construction. Practically Treated. . . . Violin Notes by Ole Bull.* Rev. ed. London, [1910?].

Bull, Alexander, ed. *Ole Bulls Breve i Uddrag. Med en karakteristik og biografisk Skitse af Jonas Lie.* Copenhagen, 1881.

Bull, Francis. "Ole Bull og Norge." *Samtiden* 51 (1940): 449–68. Oslo.

Bull, Inez. *Ole Bull's Activities in the United States between 1843 and 1880: A Biography.* Dissertation, submitted to New York University, School of Education, Smithtown, N.Y., 1982.

Bull, Jens. *Den trønderske slekt Bull.* Oslo, 1937.

Bull, Marie. *Minder fra Bergens første nationale scene.* Bergen, 1905.

Bull, Ole. *Min kjære Moder. En kjærlighets erklæring.* Ed. Ladislav Reznicek. Bergen, 1980.

Bull, Ole. *Ole Bull 1810–1910: Et Mindeskrift.* Bergen, 1910.

Bull, Sara C. *The Gaspar da Salo – Benvenuto Cellini Violin.* Disposition of to Vestlandske Kunstindustri Museum, Bergen, 1902.

Bull, Sara C. *Ole Bull: A Memoir.* With Ole Bull's "Violin Notes" and Dr. A. B. Crosby's "The Anatomy of the Violinist." Boston and New York, 1882.

Bull, Schak. *Kåseri: Holdt ved den trønderske slekt Bulls 400-års jubileum, 28. august 1950.* Oslo, 1950.

Buraas, Anders. *De reiste ut.* Oslo, 1982.

Bibliography

Cai, Camilla. "Italian Opera through the Eyes of a Norwegian: Ole Bull's Virtuoso Violin Works." *The Vioexchange* 6.2 and 3 (1992): 23–28. With edition of *Bravura Variations* for violin and piano.

Child, Lydia Maria. *Letters from New York.* 2d Series. New York, 1846.

Collection of Memorabilia, Wayside Inn, Sudbury, Mass.

Collection of Programs, University Library, Oslo.

Compte-Rendu de divers Concerts donnés par M. OLE-BULL. Paris, 1848. Twelve concerts from 1846 to 1848. Broadsheet. University Library, Oslo.

Cooke, George Willis. "Ole Bull's First Appearances in America." *Music* 11 (November 1896–April 1897): 296–309.

Crosby, Alpheus Benning. "The Anatomy of the Violinist, Mr. Ole Bull: His Pose and Method of Holding the Violin." Appendix to Sara Bull's *Ole Bull: A Memoir*, 329–46. Boston and New York, 1882.

Danell, Eric. *Ole Bull och Pratté: Några kritiska randanmärkningar.* Stockholm, 1954.

Debut des Herrn Ole Bull auf dem King's Theatre. Paris. n.d. Twelve reviews from English press, May–June 1836. Broadsheet in German. Trans. in French as *Début de M. Ole Bull, au Théatre du Roi.*

Dietrichson, Lorentz. *Svundne Tider. I Bergen og Christiania i 40- og 50- aarene.* 2d ed. Christiania, 1913.

Doremus, Dr. R. Ogden. "Edwin Booth and Ole Bull." *The Critic* 48.3 (March 1906): 234–44. New Rochelle, New York.

Draxten, Nina. *Kristofer Janson in America.* Northfield, Minn., 1976.

Dunker, C. C. H. B. *Ole Bulls Process med Bergens Politi.* Copenhagen, 1851.

Dwight, [John Sullivan]. "Ole Bull and his Colony." *Dwight's Journal of Music* 3 (28 May 1853): 60–61. Boston.

Ebeling, Adolf. *Bilder aus Kairo.* Stuttgart, 1878.

Eldal, Jens Christian. "'Bulla-huset'—Nordens eldste sveitserhus?" *Husbukken: Medlemsblad for fortidsminneforeningen* 3 (1990): 10–13.

[Elling, Catharinus]. "Ole Bull." In Gerhard Gran, ed., *Nordmænd i det nittende aarhundrede,* 454–93. Oslo, 1902.

Filler, Louis. "Lydia Maria Child." In E. T. Jones *et al., Notable American Women 1607–1950.* Vol. 1:330–33. Cambridge, Mass., 1971.

Finck, Henry T. "Masters of the Violin." In *The Mentor,* 4th ser., no. 5. New York, 1916.

Fink, G. W., ed. *Leipziger Allgemeine Musikalische Zeitung* 41.11 (March 1839): 216–17 and 41.12 (March 1839): 237–39. Leipzig. Editorial on Bull.

FitzLyon, April. *Maria Malibran.* Bloomington, Ind., 1988.

Gaukstad, Øystein. "Fortegnelse over Ole Bulls komposisjoner." Typescript, University of Oslo Library.

Gay, Cécile. *Ole Bull, violiniste norvégien.* Paris, 1881.

Gjesdal, Carl O. Gram. "Fra Ole Bull til Sigbjørn Bernhoft Osa." In Ingjald Bolstad, Arnfinn Kyte, and Jostein Mæland, eds., *Norske tonar. Heidersskrift til Sigbjørn Osa på 75-årsdagen,* 52–61. Oslo, 1985.

Gjesdal, Carl O. Gram. *Lysøen: Variasjoner over et vestnorsk tema.* Bergen, 1972.

Gjesdal, Carl O. Gram. "Ole Bull." In Peter Anker, K. Bækkelund, and E. Straume, eds., *Norske Klassikere,* 66–81. Oslo, 1985.

Gjesdal, Carl O. Gram. "Ole Bull bibliografi." In *Innstilling om Lysøens framtidige bruk.* . . . Bergen, 1975.

Goetz, Wolfgang. "Johan Storm Bull (1787–1838) and Johann Bartholomaeus Trommsdorff (1770–1837)." In *Norges Apothekerforenings Tidsskrift* 97.9 (13 May 1989): 256–59.

Goldschmidt, Meïr. "Thorgeir Audunsen, Violinspilleren paa Haukelidfjeldet." In *Nord og Syd,* 345–61. Copenhagen, 1851. Also in Meïr Goldschmidt, *Blandede Skrifter* 4:287–303.

Goldschmidt, Meïr. "A Norwegian Musician." *Cornhill Magazine* 6 (23 April 1862): 514–27. Translated in *Morgenbladet* 276 and 277 (1862).

Grinde, Nils. *Norsk Musikk Historie.* Oslo, 1971. Also published as *A History of Norwegian Music.* Trans. and ed. by William H. Halverson and Leland B. Sateren. Lincoln, Nebr., 1991.

Grønvold, Aimar. "Med Ole Bulls Billede." In *Norske Musikere,* 122–33. Christiania, 1883.

Haarklou, Johannes. "The Life of Ole Bull. From the Danish of Johannes Haarklow [*sic*]." *Music* 21.1 (December 1901): 29–52. Also in Norwegian, in *Folkevennen* 48.1 (1900): 1–37.

Hanslick, Eduard. "Ole Bull" (1858). In *Vienna's Golden Years of Music 1850–1900,* 65–67. Trans. and ed. Henry Pleasants. 1950. Reprint. Freeport, N.Y., 1969.

Haugen, Einar. "Ole Bull and the Isles of Shoals." *The Norseman* 3 (1991): 42–43.

Haugen, Eva Lund, and Einar Haugen, ed. and trans. *Land of the Free: Bjørnstjerne Bjørnson's America Letters, 1880–1881.* Northfield, Minn., 1978.

Haugen, Eva Lund, and Ingrid Semmingsen. "Peder Anderson of Bergen and Lowell: Artist and Ambassador of Culture." In Brita Seyersted, ed., *Americana Norvegica.* 4:1–29. Oslo, 1973.

Hilen, Andrew. *Longfellow and Scandinavia: A Study of the Poet's Relationship with the Northern Languages and Literature.* New Haven, Conn., 1947.

Hill, W. Henry, Arthur F. Hill and Alfred E. Hill. *Antonio Stradivari: His Life and Work.* 1902. Reprint. New York, 1963.

Holberg, Ludvig. *The Weathercock,* in *Four Plays by Holberg.* Trans. Henry Alexander. Princeton, N.J., 1946.

Hopp, Zinken. *Eventyret om Ole Bull.* Bergen, 1945.

Horton, John. *Grieg.* London, 1974.

Hustvedt, Lloyd. *Rasmus Bjørn Anderson: Pioneer Scholar.* Northfield, Minn., 1966.

Innstilling om Lysøens framtidige bruk. . . . Bergen, 1975. Joint report by Norwegian administrative authorities on future use, administration and financing of Lysøen.

Jacobs, Stanley S. "The Violinist who Thrilled Your Great-Grandmother." *Etude* 65.3 (1947): 140 ff.

Jahr, Torstein. "Oleana—Et blad af Ole Bulls og den norske indvandrings historie." *Symra* 6 (1910): 2–37, 129–62, 195–216. Decorah, Iowa.

Janson, Kristofer. *Den bergtekne.* Hamar, 1876. Also in Dano-Norwegian as *Den Bjærgtagne,* La Crosse, Wis., 1880; and in English as *The Spellbound Fiddler,* trans. Auber Forestier (Aubertine Woodward Moore) with an introduction by R. B. Anderson. Chicago, 1880.

Jordan, Sverre. "Et 50-aars minde." *Bergens Tidende.* Clipping, 1930.

Kelly, Bill. "Famed violin virtuoso, Ole Bull of Norway, has ties to Eau Claire." *Eau Claire Leader-Telegram*, 15 December 1979.

Kerr, J., ed. *Dictionary of Australian Artists*. Sydney, 1984.

Kolderup, Carl Fred. "Sætergjentens Søndag." In *Bergen Turlag Aarbok*, 73–78. Bergen, 1954.

Laighton, Oscar. *Ninety Years at the Isles of Shoals*. Boston, 1930.

Lange, Kristian, and Arne Østvedt. *Norwegian Music: A Brief Survey*. London, 1958.

Lapidus, Leif. "Ole Bull" and "Torgeir Augundson, Myllarguten." In *Av berømte menns saga*, 9–26, 45–55. Drammen, 1944.

Lawrence, Vera Brodsky. *Strong on Music: The New York Music Scene in the Days of George Templeton Strong, 1836–1875*. Vol. 1, *Resonances: 1836–1850*. New York and Oxford, 1988.

Lie, Jonas. "Ole Bull, hans Karakteristik og Liv." In Alexander Bull, ed., *Ole Bulls Breve i Uddrag. Med en karakteristik og biografisk Skitse af Jonas Lie*, 1–154. Copenhagen, 1881.

Linge, Ola. *Ole Bull: Livshistoria, Mannen, Kunstnaren*. Oslo, 1953.

Linge, Ola. "Når skrev Ole Bull melodien som blev 'Sæterjentens Søndag'?" *Aftenposten*, 10 November 1934, no page.

Linge, Ola. "Ole Bull's Lysøy bør verta norsk nasjonaleigedom." *Bergens Tidende*. 25 September 1954.

Lloyd, Thomas W., and Charles T. Logue, with a preface by Henry W. Shoemaker. *Ole Bull in Pennsylvania . . . the Pilgrimage . . . July 29, 1920*. Altoona, Penn., 1921.

Longfellow, Henry Wadsworth. *The Skeleton in Armour*. Boston, 1877.

Longfellow, Henry Wadsworth. *Tales of a Wayside Inn*. Boston, 1863.

[Lund, John]. *Festskrift ved Ole Bull statuens afsløring 17/5 1901*. Bergen, 1901.

Lundeberg, Olav K. "Grandmother Sang for Ole Bull." *Lutheran Herald* 5 (1 December 1936): 1147–69.

Lütgendorff, Freiherr von, Willibald Leo. *Die Geigen- und Lautenmacher vom Mittelalter bis zur Gegenwart*. 6th ed. Frankfurt am Main, 1922. Reprint, Nendeln, Liechtenstein, 1968. Vol. 2.

Meyer, Michael. *Ibsen, A Biography*. Garden City, New York, 1971.

Midbøe, Hans. *Dikteren og det Primitive*. Oslo, 1964.

Mjøen, Reidar. "Ole Bull." In O. M. Sandvik and Gerhard Schjelderup, eds. *Norges Musikhistorie*, 1:172–84. Christiania, 1921.

Monrad-Johansen, David. *Edvard Grieg*. Oslo, 1934.

Moore, Aubertine Woodward (Auber Forestier). "The Real Ole Bull: Personal Reminiscences." *Etude* 30.4 (1912): 251–52.

Moore, John W. "Ole Bull." *Western Musical World* 5 (May 1868): 5. Cleveland, Ohio.

Morand, F. *Notice sur Ole Bull*. Boulogne, 1835.

Mucchi, Antonio Maria. "L'Ole Bull." In *Gasparo da Salo: La vita e l'opera 1540–1609*, 185–93. Milan, 1940.

Nelke, D. I., ed. *Representative Men in the United States: Wisconsin Volume*. Chicago, 1895. (The Columbian Biographical Dictionary).

Nørlyng, Ole. "Les Souvenirs de la Norvège: Om Komponisten Herman Severin

Bibliography

Løvenskiolds norske Klaverværker opus 3, 1831," *Studia musicologica* 8 (1982): 149–78.

Nørregaard-Nielsen, H. E., ed. *Kongens København.* Copenhagen, 1985.

"Norwegians in America." *New York Weekly Times,* 29 September–2 October 1852.

Nygaard, Knut. *Henrik Anker Bjerregaard: Dikteren og hans tid.* Oslo, 1966.

Odell, George C. D. *Annals of the New York Stage.* Vols. 4–11. New York, 1928–39.

"Ole Bull." Programs and reviews of concerts in Havana, 1844. University Library, Oslo.

"Ole Bull." *Vert-Vert, Revue du Monde Parisien* 8.39 (8 February 1840): 1.

"Ole Bulls Koloni i Nordamerika." *Lillehammer Tilskuer* 12 (17 December 1852): 101. Reprinted from *Bergens Stiftstidende;* in turn from a New York paper.

Pratté, Anton Edvard. *Upartisk dom over Violinspilleren Hr. Ole Bulls i Christiania den 10de December givne koncert.* Christiania, 1843.

Rasmussen, Janet. "The Byronic Lover in Nineteenth-Century Scandinavian Fiction." Pacific Northwest Council on Foreign Languages, *Proceedings* 29.1 (21–22 April 1978): 119–22.

Reznicek, Ladislav, ed. *Tilegnet Ole Bull 1980. 1810. 1880.* Oslo, 1980.

Rosén, Joh. Magnus. *Ogsaa et omdømme om Ole Bulls kunstnerværd.* Copenhagen, 1838.

Rudjord, Kåre. *Oddernes bygdebok* 1:182–85, 2:320–21. Kristiansand, 1968.

Rutledge, Lyman V. *The Isles of Shoals in Lore and Legend.* Barre, Mass., 1965.

Sand, George. *Malgrétout.* Paris, 1870.

Sandvik, O. M. "Ole Bull." In *Norsk Biografisk Leksikon* 2:407–17. Oslo, 1925.

Schaick, John van, Jr. "The Characters in the *Tales of a Wayside Inn.*" *The Christian Leader* 10 (29 April 1939): 394–96 and 11 (6 May 1939): 420–22.

Schelderup, W. Collection of clippings. Bergen Offentlige Bibliotek.

Schulerud, Mentz. *Norsk Kunstnerliv.* Oslo, 1960.

Schulerud, Mentz. *Ole Bull: Et minneskrift til 150-årsjubileet for hans fødsel 5. februar 1960.* Oslo, 1960.

Schumann, Robert. Haushaltbücher. Ed. Gerd Neuhaus. Leipzig, 1982.

Schumann, Robert. *Jugendbriefe.* From the original by Clara Schumann. 2d ed. Leipzig, 1886.

Simister, Frances P. "The Ole Bull Place in West Lebanon." *Down East Enterprise* 17 (1970): 127.

Smith, Mortimer. *The Life of Ole Bull.* Princeton, N.J., 1943. Also in Norwegian, trans. Sverre Hagerup Bull. Oslo, 1948.

Spohr, Louis. *Selbstbiographie.* Vol. 2. Cassel and Göttingen, 1861.

Strømme-Svendsen, Arnljot. "Ole Bull statuene og deres skapelse." *Bergens Tidende* (30 September 1980).

Skedsmo, Tone. "Knud Geelmuyden Bull." In Stephan Tschudi-Madsen, ed. *Norsk Kunstner Leksikon,* 1:354–55. Oslo, 1982.

Stubseid, Gunnar. "Ole Bull Akademiet: Ein spelemannsdraum vert røyndom." In Ingjald Bolstad, A. Kyte, and J. Mæland, eds., *Norske tonar. Heidersskrift til Sigbjørn Osa på 75-årsdagen,* 130–36. Oslo, 1985.

Sundler, Eva. "Ole Bull och den nationalromantiska villan." In Brita Linde, ed., *Studier i konstvetenskap tillägnade,* 167–80. Stockholm, 1985.

Tellefsen, Arve. "Ole Bull og verden." In *Programbladet,* issued by Norsk Riks-kringkasting (Norwegian Broadcasting), no. 51/52, 1982.

Thomas, Theodore. *A Musical Autobiography.* Ed. George P. Upton. New York, 1964.

Tørnblom, Folke H. *Grieg.* Stockholm, 1945.

Trojan, Jan. "Das Brünner Konzertleben in der Zeit der Nationalen Wiedergeburt." *Sborník prací filosofické fakulty brněnské university* 8 (1973): 161–83.

Tschudi-Madsen, Stephan. "Det var ikke Ole Bull som tegnet Villa Lysø." *Bergens Tidende,* n.d. Clipping, Bergen Offentlige Bibliotek.

Vik, Oddmund. *Ole Bull.* Bergen, 1890.

Vinje, Aasmund Olavsson. *Skrifter i Utval.* Christiania, 1883. ("Olaf Bull reiser til Heidemork," *Dølen* [10 October 1858]; "Myllarguten og Olaf Bull," *Dølen* [14 November 1858]; "Ogso eit Vitnemaal," *Dølen* [25 December 1859]; "Nokot um Felespil," *Dølen* [3 May 1860]).

Welfling, Mary E. *The Ole Bull Colony in Potter County 1852: One hundredth anniversary observed July 31–August 1, 1952.* Coudersport, Penn., 1952.

Welhaven, J. S. C. *Samlede Digterverker.* Vols. 2 and 3. Christiania and Copen-hagen, 1907.

Wergeland, Henrik. "Ole Bull: Efter opgivelser af ham selv biografisk skildret." In D. A. Seip, ed., *Samlede Skrifter,* 4.5:182–233. Oslo, 1927.

Werro, Henry. *"Ole Bull": Joseph Guarnerius del Gesú 1744 IHS.* Berne, 1971.

Whittier, John Greenleaf. *Letters.* Ed. John B. Pickard. 3 vols. Cambridge, Mass., 1975.

Wilkinson, Norman. "Ole Bull's New Norway." Historical Pennsylvania Leaflet, No. 14, 1953. Rev. 1962 and 1988 by Robert Currin *et al.*

Williams, Adrian. *Portrait of Liszt.* Oxford, 1990.

Wilson, James Grant. *Thackeray in the United States.* Vol. 1. New York, 1904.

Winfield, Warren. "'Ole Bull' Reborn in Herman Gehr." *UU World* (15 October 1974).

Winter-Hjelm, Henrik. "Træk af Ole Bulls Liv," *Morgenbladet* (1852). Christiania. Reprinted in *Lillehammer Tilskuer,* nos. 46–89 (8 June–5 November 1852).

Wolf, Lucie. *Livserindringer.* Christiania, 1897.

Index

Index

Index

Nordraak, Rikard, 152, 155, 275; and Bull, xxvi, 143–45
"Norges Farvel til Ole Bull" ("Norway's Farewell to Ole Bull") (Wergeland), 56–57
Norges Musikhistorie, 328
Norges Musikkhøgskole, 285
"Norge til Amerika ved Ole Bulls Didreise" ("Norway to America on Ole Bull's Departure") (Wergeland), 76–77
Norse Mythology (Anderson), 176
Norsk Biografisk Leksikon, 327
Norske Klassikere, 328
Norske Nationaldragter (Norwegian National Costumes) (Tønsberg), 123, 207, 307
Norske Selskab, Det. *See* Norwegian Society, The
Norsk Folke-blad (journal), 162
"Norsk Frihedsmarsch" ("Norwegian Freedom March"), 264
Norsk Tidskrift for Videnskab og Litteratur (journal), 278
North American Review, 175
"North Fjord, The" ("Nordfjorden") (folk tune), 205
Norway: history of, xxv–xxvi, 3, 99; Bull leaves, 19; Bull's visits to, 56, 101–14, 135, 150–53, 162, 165–66; Bull buys property in, 100; Thorps' visit to Bull in, 169; Bull leaves, with Thorps, 170–71; Bull returns to, to die, 197. *See also* Andøen; Bergen; Bull, Ole Bornemann: nationalism of; Christiania; Lysøen; Valestrand
"Norway's Farewell to Ole Bull" ("Norges Farvel til Ole Bull") (Wergeland), 56–57
"Norway to America on Ole Bull's Departure" ("Norge til Amerika ved Ole Bulls Didreise") (Wergeland), 76–77
Norwegian Academy of Music (Oslo), xxvi, 170, 150–53, 274, 285, 290
Norwegian-American(s): Bull as, xvii, xxiv; pattern of travel of, 171–72; fondness of, for "Sæter Girl's Sunday," 268. *See also* Norwegian immigrants
Norwegian-American Museum (Decorah, IA), 319
Norwegian colony in America. *See* Oleana, Oleona (PA)
Norwegian Constitution, 3
Norwegian Folkmelodies (Grieg), 223
"Norwegian Freedom March" ("Norsk Frihedsmarsch"), 264

Norwegian immigrants, 78, 161, 172; to Oleana, 115–30. *See also* Norwegian-American(s)
Norwegian Mountain Melodies. See Norwegian National Costumes
Norwegian Music Academy (Oslo). *See* Norwegian Academy of Music (Oslo)
"Norwegian Musician, A" (Goldschmidt), 149–50, 279
Norwegian National Costumes (Norske Nationaldragter) (Tønsberg), 123, 207, 307, 312–13
Norwegian National Theatre (Bergen), xxvi, 170, 198, 274, 290; Bull's involvement with, 102–14, 137–41. *See also* Bergen Theatre
Norwegian parliament. *See* Storting (Norwegian Parliament)
Norwegian's Lament for Home (Bull), 68. *See Mountains of Norway, The*
Norwegian Society, The, 143
Norwegian style of music, 259–68
"Norwegian Theatre in Bergen," 107
Notice sur Old Bull (pamphlet) (Morand), 38–39
"No. 9" (Bull?), 311
"No. 12" (Bull?), 311
Nya Dagligt Allehanda (newspaper), 181
Nynorsk. *See* New Norwegian (language)

Oehlenschläger, Adam, 58, 272
"Oiley Bull," 315
Olaf Trygvason (King), 154
Old Norwegian (language), 3. *See also* New Norwegian (language)
Old South Meeting House (Boston), 317
Old South Preservation Fund, 197
Oleana, Oleona (PA): Bull's colony at, xviii, xxiv, xxvi, 115–30, 128–29, 174, 274, 290; myths about, 150; reports about, 162, 325, 326, 327, 328
"Oleana by-the-Sea" (Rockport, MA), 317
"Ole Bull, junior," 257–58, 311–12, 315
Ole Bull: Livshistoria, Mannen, Kunstnaren (Linge), 293
Ole Bull Akademiet (Voss, Norway), 285
Ole Bulls Polka, 255, 257, 311
Ole Bull State Park (PA), 285
Ole Bull Stradivarius, 280–81
Ole Bull's Waltzes (Labitzky), 257, 311
Ole Bull Violin Instruction Book, 257, 311
Olsen, Christian, 257

349